BESTSELLING BOOK SERIES

Australi

Cricket For Dummies®

Typical Field for an Opening Bowler

This diagram shows a field usually set for quality right-arm fast bowlers, such as Australia's Glenn McGrath and Brett Lee, when they're opening the bowling to a right-handed batsman in a Test match. Note the importance of the following fielding positions:

- Slips and gully: In place to take a catch if the ball hits the outside edge of the striker's bat.
- Point, cover and mid on: Stationed to try to prevent any runs being scored from shots hit to these areas.
- Short leg: To take a catch if the bowler delivers a bouncer, a ball that lands about halfway down the pitch and is aimed at a batsman's head or upper body. To avoid being hit, the batsman may fend the ball away with the bat, which could present a catch.
- Deep fine leg, also known as long leg: To stop the ball crossing the boundary for four runs, and to catch the batsman if they attempt to hit the bouncer with a hook shot (a horizontal swing of the bat).

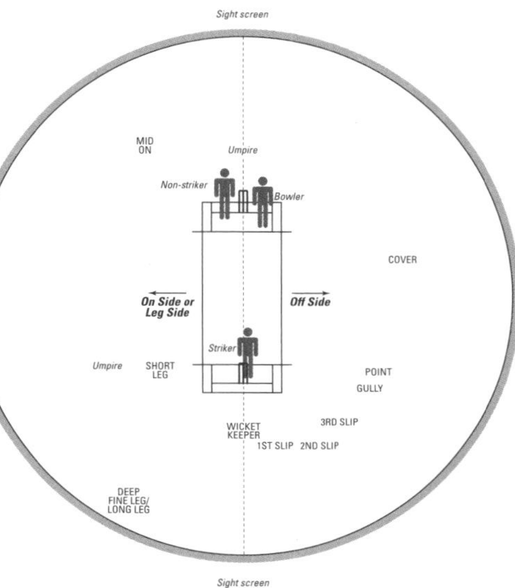

The Major Cricket Nations

These ten nations are known as the Test playing countries and together make up the International Cricket Council, the game's governing body. However Bangladesh, given full Test status in 2000, is widely regarded as below standard for a major cricket nation. The Zimbabwe team is in decline and was suspended from Test cricket in 2004 and 2006.

- Australia
- Bangladesh
- England
- India
- New Zealand
- Pakistan
- South Africa
- Sri Lanka
- West Indies
- Zimbabwe

Associate Cricket Countries

The countries below the Test match nations are called the associate countries. Associate cricket countries number 32 and are of varying standard. The best six associates will contest the World Cup in the West Indies during 2007, along with the major cricketing countries. These associate countries are:

- Bermuda
- Canada
- Ireland
- Kenya
- The Netherlands
- Scotland

For Dummies®: Bestselling Book Series for Beginners

Australian Edition
Cricket For Dummies®

International Game Formats

Cricket has a variety of the game for everyone. Following are simple clues to these three popular formats to tell which game is what:

Test match:

- Players wear white clothes.
- A red ball is used.
- The match is played during the day.
- A match lasts up to five days.
- The playing day lasts at least seven hours.

One-day match:

- Players wear coloured clothes.
- A white ball is used.
- A match is usually played under lights.
- Most matches start early afternoon.
- The playing day lasts about eight hours.

Twenty20 match:

- Players wear coloured clothes.
- A white ball is used.
- A match is usually played under lights.
- Most matches are played in the evening.
- Play lasts just three hours.

LBW Law

Cricket has 42 laws. The most contentious and complicated law is the leg before wicket (LBW) law. A player can be dismissed LBW when the bowler delivers the ball and the batsman is struck on the pads (leg guards) by the ball.

The umpire standing behind the stumps at the bowler's end can give a batsman out in certain circumstances if the umpire believes the ball would have hit the stumps and bowled the batsman.

Here are the three points of Law 36 (leg before wicket). Judge the law for yourself!

1. **Out LBW: The striker is out LBW in the circumstances set out here.**
   - The bowler delivers a ball, not being a no ball.
   - The ball, if it is not intercepted full pitch, pitches in line between wicket and wicket or on the off side of the striker's wicket;
   - The ball not having previously touched his bat, the striker intercepts the ball, either full pitch or after pitching, with any part of his person;
   - The point of impact, even if above the level of the bails, either (i) is between wicket and wicket, or (ii) between wicket and wicket or outside the line of the off stump, if the striker has made no genuine attempt to play the ball with his bat, and
   - But for the interception, the ball would have hit the wicket.
2. **Interception of the ball:**
   - In assessing points (c), (d) and (e) in Step 1, only the first interception is to be considered;
   - In assessing point (e) in Step 1, it is to be assumed that the path of the ball before interception would have continued after interception, irrespective of whether the ball might have pitched subsequently or not.
3. **Off side of wicket:**
   - The off side of the striker's wicket shall be determined by the striker's stance at the moment the ball comes into play for that delivery.

Australian Edition

Cricket FOR DUMMIES®

Australian Edition

by Malcolm Conn and Julian Knight

Wiley Publishing Australia Pty Ltd

Cricket For Dummies®

Australian edition published by
Wiley Publishing Australia Pty Ltd
42 McDougall Street
Milton, Qld 4064
www.dummies.com

Offices also in Sydney and Melbourne

National Library of Australia
Cataloguing-in-Publication data

Conn, Malcolm.
Cricket for dummies.

Australian ed.
Includes index.
ISBN-13 978 0 74031 173 1.
ISBN-10 1 74031 173 6.

1. Cricket - Sport - Popular works.
I. Conn, Malcolm. II. Knight, Julian.
Title. (Series : For dummies).

616.99449

Cover image: © Digital Vision; Getty Images/AFP/Greg Wood

Printed in Australia by
McPherson's Printing Group

10 9 8 7 6 5 4 3 2 1

About the Authors

Malcolm Conn is one of Australia's leading cricket writers. He began writing with a local newspaper in country Victoria while completing secondary school and joined *The Age* in Melbourne during 1984 to concentrate on his two great sporting passions, cricket and AFL football.

Malcolm began writing for *The Australian* in 1985 and, after brief stints with the former *Times on Sunday* and *Melbourne Sun* newspapers, he returned to the national broadsheet as chief AFL writer. In 1992, he was appointed chief cricket writer for *The Australian*, regularly touring all the major cricketing nations.

After winning several awards for his writing on Australian football, in 1999 Malcolm became the first cricket writer to win a Walkley Award (Australian journalism's highest honour) following an investigation that revealed Mark Waugh and Shane Warne had secretly taken money from illegal bookmakers.

Malcolm has become a strong voice against corruption in cricket, and has covered match-fixing hearings in Pakistan's Lahore High Court, as well as the Hansie Cronje match-fixing investigation in Cape Town, South Africa.

A regular contributor to magazines in Australia and abroad, Malcolm has also written for a number of overseas newspapers, including *The Hindu* in India and London's *Sunday Times*. He is a regular cricket expert on radio and makes guest appearances on television sports shows.

Malcolm is secretary of the Australian Cricket Media Association.

Julian Knight was born in 1972 in Chester in England. He was educated at the Chester Catholic High School and later Hull University, where he obtained a degree in History.

Since 2002, Julian has been the *BBC News* personal finance and consumer affairs reporter and has won many awards for his journalism. Previous to this, Julian worked for *Moneywise* magazine and wrote for *The Guardian,* among many other publications. He has also authored the publications, *Wills, Probate and Inheritance Tax* and *Retiring Wealthy For Dummies*. Julian has played league cricket for 20 years. He is a former captain at Blackheath Cricket Club and has played for several clubs in London and in the north-west of England.

Dedication

From Malcolm:

To my loving wife Pru, who became a cricket widow again during the holidays, weekends, early mornings and late nights that were dominated by the constant tapping of a keyboard and rapidly approaching deadlines. This book would not have been possible without your support and understanding.

To my sons, Robert and Alex, who continue to light up my life.

From Julian:

To my father for bowling endlessly at me in our back garden when I was a child, and for helping me to develop a love for the game of cricket. And to the players and members of Blackheath, Westminster Park, Hainault & Clayhall and Chester Water cricket clubs.

Authors' Acknowledgments

From Malcolm:

To Lesley Beaumont for giving me the opportunity to further my passion for cricket, Charlotte Duff for her constantly smiling emails and cheery voice and Carolyn Beaumont for her great skill, patience, care and advice.

To Adam Gilchrist, Damien Fleming and Belinda Clark for sharing your passion and expertise, with apologies to Damien for not being able to squeeze you into my top 10 players. You're still in my top 10 blokes! It has been a pleasure dealing with all of you on cricket's great journey.

I had the rare pleasure of reporting on James Sutherland when he was a Victorian fast bowler. James is now chief executive of Cricket Australia and making a significantly greater impact. James, the contribution from you and your staff to this book is greatly appreciated. Thank you to the ever-smiling Peter Young and a special mention to Steph Beltrame, who was never too busy for my constant emails and phone calls. Steph, you are part of this book.

From Julian:

I would like to thank the Wiley publishing team in the United Kingdom (UK), in particular, Jason Dunne, Alison Yates, Wejdan Ismail and Simon Bell. Thanks also go to cricket coach, Gary Palmer, for his technical review of the UK edition of *Cricket For Dummies.*

Publisher's Acknowledgments

We're proud of this book; please register your comments through our Online Registration Form located at `www.dummies.com`.

Some of the people who helped bring this book to market include the following:

Acquisitions Development and Editorial

Project Editor: Carolyn Beaumont

Review Editor: Zoë Wykes

Acquisitions Editors: Alison Yates, Lesley Beaumont, Charlotte Duff

Technical Reviewer: Damien Fleming

Editorial Manager: Gabrielle Packman

Photo Credits: Getty Images: pp. 92 and 208, Hamish Blair; p. 319, AFP/Sena Vidanagama; p. 351, Central Press; p. 383, Paul Kane • Australian Picture Library: p. 139, Popperfoto • Newspix: p. 307, News Ltd; p. 315, John Feder; p. 361, Phil Hillyard; pp. 329, 395 • Out of copyright: p. 420 • All other photos from *Australian Cricket Coach*, courtesy of Cricket Australia. © Shooting Star Productions. Photos by Norman Krueger, featuring Kelly Applebee, Aidan Blizzard, Robert Cassell, Cathryn Cheong, Belinda Clark, Cathryn Fitzpatrick, Jack McNamara, Peter Nevill.

Artwork: International Cricket Council, teachcricket.com (formerly The Albatross Partnership) and the Wiley Art Studio.

Production

Layout: Wiley Composition Services

Proofreader: Liz Goodman

Cartoons: Glenn Lumsden

Indexer: Michael Ramsden

Contents at a Glance

Table of Contents

Part IV: Planet Cricket 321

Forewords

Adam Gilchrist

My earliest memories of cricket are sitting at a country cricket ground on a Saturday afternoon watching my father's team play. I was only four or five and that's when I developed my passion for cricket. I fell in love with the game. The smell of the leather gear and bat oil and the feel of a cricket ball, which seemed so big in my hands back then, are vivid memories from those distant, happy days.

To me cricket was always a family game. Mum and dad, brothers, sisters and friends, battling it out in the backyard. Christmas was never quite the same without a cricket match. Walking along the beach and seeing those same games being played today among excited children and smiling parents, gives me great pleasure.

As I've grown up with the game and been lucky enough to represent Australia on the big stage, I've realised that some things about cricket just don't change, regardless of where you're playing. You can walk into any change room, whether it's at a bush club or at the Melbourne Cricket Ground, and you feel exactly the same way. The same diversity of characters are there, the same banter, the same jokes, and the same serious side in a tense match when a wicket falls.

I've always loved cricket because it's a team game. You share the joys and the disappointments with your mates, strengthening bonds and savouring special moments. Cricket mateship happens all over the country every weekend, every summer — in cities, towns and country districts.

This specialised Australian edition of *Cricket For Dummies* can help you begin to enhance your journey through cricket. Whether you want to find a club, improve your skills, discover the mystery of cricket's strange world and fielding positions, or simply watch the big games on television or at the ground, *Cricket For Dummies* can explain everything you want to know about cricket.

Enjoy the journey and welcome to Australian cricket's extended family. I hope cricket brings you as much joy and pleasure as it has given me over the years.

Adam Gilchrist

James Sutherland

This witty dialogue has been around for some time as a tongue-in-cheek attempt to explain the game of cricket (and please note: cricket is not just for men, but the reference here keeps this explanation a tad simpler).

> *You have two sides, one out in the field and one in. Each man who's in the side that's in goes out, and when he's out he comes in and the next man goes in until he's out. When they're all out, the side that's out comes in and the side that's been in goes out and tries to get those coming in, out. Sometimes you get men still in and not out. When a man goes out to go in, the men who are out try to get him out, and when he is out he goes in and the next man in goes out and goes in. There are two men called umpires who stay out all the time and they decide when the men who are in are out. When both sides have been in and all the men have been out, and both sides have been out twice after all the men have been in, including those who are not out, that is the end of the game.*

Those with a passion for Australia's favourite sport, cricket, can appreciate its intricacies and complexities. But for those new to the sport, I can understand your mystery about such a game! Thankfully, *Cricket For Dummies* provides a way to help explain and introduce our game to those who are interested to learn more.

Figuring out everything from where silly point is, keeping score, game formats, earning a baggy green cap and observing proper cricket etiquette is all made easier to reference and understand in *Cricket For Dummies.*

And that's a credit to its author, Malcolm Conn — one of the world's most respected cricket writers. He's done a superb job of translating a wide and comprehensive subject into digestible pieces. Well played, Malcolm!

It's fantastic for Australian cricket to have this book on the shelf, particularly at a time when one of our major priorities is to attract more people to be involved in our game — as players, coaches, spectators, volunteers, umpires, administrators ... you name it.

If you're reading this book, you're obviously keen to learn more about cricket; a game that offers a sense of history, values, tradition, camaraderie, friendship, respect and tremendous fun.

I am sure this book will answer everything you need to know and I hope it gives you a taste for more so that one day, you too will be able to rationalise that tongue-in-cheek explanation of cricket in real terms. Long Live Cricket!

James Sutherland

Introduction

Welcome to *Cricket For Dummies* Australian Edition, your vehicle for a journey through the wonderful world of cricket. With this book you can navigate your way through a game that has subtleties and joys shared by millions around the globe. Whether you're totally mystified by cricket or have spent a lifetime in the game, you can always broaden your understanding of Australia's national summer obsession.

Men and women, boys and girls, from many different walks of life and cultural backgrounds, embrace the game. From locations as exotic and diverse as Barbados, Bangalore and Brisbane, the common language of cricket is a golden thread that links such disparate people and places. This book enables you to speak that language — to understand why the simple toss of a coin can have such a huge impact on a cricket match, why fieldsmen are placed in such dangerous or distant places on a cricket field and just where 'short fine leg', 'deep extra cover' and 'wide mid on' actually stand!

This book can help the cricket beginner to discover the game quickly and easily without feeling overwhelmed or intimidated by cricket's seemingly strange traditions, customs, laws and language. Before long, you can become an expert in this fascinating and entertaining game, and your summers are never going to be the same again!

About This Book

Cricket For Dummies Australian Edition provides you with everything you need to know about the game of cricket. With the 2006–07 Ashes series between Australia and England one of the most popular series ever, this book tells you everything you need to know to sit back and enjoy cricket played at its highest level.

Whether you're male or female, old or young, a complete novice or have followed the game for decades, all the information is right here. You don't have to read the book from cover to cover to gain something of value from it.

Each chapter covers a specific cricket topic so you can easily turn to the chapter that suits your needs and take from it what you want. Whether you're looking for a basic understanding of the game, a sense of cricket traditions, what to look out for when you're watching cricket on television, how you can find the best seats at a game, or technical advice for your batting, bowling or wicketkeeping, this book has the goods for you.

If you want to become a player, you can easily navigate your way to the sections that explain the skills of the game in clear and simple detail, and you can also take advantage of the many tips from our experts. Armchair critics, avid fans, parents who want to coach their kids and those just trying to find out what all the fuss is about are all catered for in *Cricket For Dummies*.

Why You Need This Book

Cricket For Dummies Australian Edition is not a book you flip through once and put on the shelf to gather dust. This book is about to become your cricket companion. Keep it handy for constant reference. Whether you want to find a cricket club, know what to take along to the next big match, correct a flaw in your game or simply understand what on earth the TV commentators are talking about, you have the answers right here.

Like golf, cricket looks to be an easy game, until you try it! In golf, the ball just sits there, waiting to be hit by someone with a club specifically designed for the purpose. Yet most people who attempt to play golf find that simply making contact is a challenge, let alone hitting the ball straight and gaining elevation.

Cricket can be a bit the same. Cricket has a bigger ball than golf and a cricket bat is bigger than a golf club, but a cricket ball is moving, in all sorts of different ways, when you try to hit it, making the task all the more challenging. This book explains how to develop your game so you can play like an expert.

How to Use This Book

To make life easier for you, *Cricket For Dummies* Australian Edition, follows certain conventions. Everything is explained very, very clearly so that if you don't understand the game yet, you won't feel swamped by the strange language of cricket. And if you're not sure about a cricketing word or phrase, you can simply turn to the glossary for a full explanation.

Don't feel restricted on how you use this book. If you simply want to know the fielding positions, turn to Chapter 2. Flick through the book and have a look at the diagrams and pictures for that part of the game that most interests you. Do this and you'll get a quick and easy understanding of the basics.

This book is constructed as though it were a set of building blocks, expanding your knowledge and understanding of the game. So if you turn straight to ... say, the batting chapters, you can find references to other chapters that explain aspects of the game relevant to batting, such as fielding positions, bowling and training.

How This Book Is Organised

This book is organised in five distinctly different parts, which cover different aspects of the game. For those who have no background in cricket, the best tip is to start at the beginning so you can find out just what everyone is doing out in the middle, why the batsmen dress so strangely and why some of the games appear to be played at night in pyjamas.

However, if you've come to grips with the basics of cricket and want to know more, choose the part that best suits what you're looking for, whether it be a broad view of the game in Australia and overseas, whether it be training at the nets, or whether it be some of the great controversies in cricket.

Part I: Introducing the Game

If you're completely new to cricket and have no idea what goes on beyond the fence at many, many sporting grounds around the country every weekend, all summer long, then start right here. In Part I, you can discover what the point of the game is, how cricket is played, the basic laws that hold the game together, what the players wear and the different time periods they play. By the end of Part I, cricket is no longer a mystery.

Part II: Playing the Game

This is the part that can make you into a player, or the game's most knowledgeable spectator. The cricket babble that some of the game's former great players talk on television, day after day all summer, now begins to make sense. Extensive and detailed, Part II covers all the necessary skills required to become a top-class cricketer, or at least to understand what top-class cricketers are trying to do. Cricket is a game that can be watched or played at many levels as you work your way to the top.

Part III: From Backyard to the Big Time

Just how did the superstars of today end up in the Australian cricket team? Part III explains how to start off in the game, where to find a club, how children can begin playing cricket and how to coach the kids. This part outlines the journey to the top for cricketers as they work their way up cricket's pyramid — including in Australia's burgeoning indigenous cricket community — and also discusses the umpires who control the game.

Part IV: Planet Cricket

Cricket is an international game played in some unlikely places. Although the United States of America and many continental European countries have teams, these nations are 'minnows' when it comes to the big matches. Part IV introduces Australia's major opponents and examines the history of these rivalries. This part also looks at the game closer to home and tells you how to follow a match either at the ground, at home or at work. In Part IV as well, you can explore women's cricket, discovering the significant — if little known — impact that women have had on the game for well over two centuries.

Part V: The Part of Tens

More than just about any other sport, cricket is a game that builds on the great players and deeds of the past. The game's best players and matches, most controversial moments and amazing events are detailed in Part V to round out your knowledge of the cricket world.

Glossary

Cricket has a language all its own. The glossary helps you understand and learn this language and understand what so many strange words and phrases mean, so that you can follow the game with greater understanding and sound like an expert when the next cricket controversy rages.

Icons Used in this Book

Leading Australian cricketers have written tips for *Cricket For Dummies* to help you enjoy the game, and you can find other specialised reading tips and technical bits, marked by icons throughout the book. Here's how the icons look and what they mean.

Adam Gilchrist, the Australian vice-captain and occasional captain, unveils his secrets for success as one of the greatest batsmen and finest wicketkeepers ever to play the game. Look out for his advice on how to become a better player.

Damien Fleming was a fine fast bowler for Australia during the 1990s before taking up a senior coaching position at Australian cricket's finishing school, the Centre of Excellence in Brisbane. Here he passes on the same advice that's being given to Australia's next generation of stars.

Belinda Clark is widely regarded as the best female cricketer ever to represent this country. She played for Australia from 1991 to 2005, captaining the side for the last 11 years, before becoming the manager of the Centre of Excellence in Brisbane. Belinda's expert tips and analysis are in Chapter 18.

This icon highlights tips and snippets of advice that can help you, whether you want to be a better player, coach or spectator. Keep an eye out for tips.

Paragraphs containing this icon offer information that's especially useful to remember. If you come across facts and figures that are particularly important to you, circle them for future reference.

This icon pops up occasionally to warn you of the pitfalls that may trap the unwary player or spectator. Take careful notice.

This icon means that a more technical explanation is being offered. If you want a quick grasp of the basics, skip this paragraph and come back later when you want to stretch your knowledge further.

Cricket has many stage words and phrases. Most of this language is explained in simple terms along the way, but some words are so unusual or important that they beg to be singled out for special treatment.

This icon explains laws of the game of cricket to highlight exactly why something can or can't be done in a particular way.

Where to Go from Here

Now you're ready to begin your journey of discovery. Just which direction you take is entirely up to you. Have a good look at the Table of Contents to see what interests you most as a starting point.

For the beginner, the best place to start is at the beginning. But if you want to look first at great players, women's cricket or how to improve your bowling, just dive in. Wherever you go — enjoy yourself!

Part I
Introducing the Game

In this part . . .

Welcome to the wonderful world of cricket! You may dream of becoming a batsman or a bowler. You may already be one, joining the many thousands of Australians who love to pass long summer days playing the great game at their local oval. Or you may enjoy stretching out in front of the television to watch the action.

In this part, you have loads of information to help you unravel the mysteries of cricket. You can work through the basics and look at which of the cricket formats most interests you — from five-day Test matches to the exciting new Twenty20 contests.

And if you're one of the bravehearts who's prepared to pull on the pads and have a go at Australia's favourite summer sport, here you find exactly what gear you need and where you can get it.

Chapter 1

Catching On to Cricket

In This Chapter

- Talking about the game you love
- Understanding the aims of the game
- Upholding the spirit of cricket
- Cricketing women
- Starting your cricket career
- Watching cricket at your leisure
- Taking in the wide world of cricket
- Discovering the Ashes

What is it about the game of cricket that excites so many people all summer long? How can a game that appears to have most of its players standing around doing nothing most of the time, create so much hype among millions of culturally diverse people around the globe? The answer simply is: Cricket has cast its spell over them.

Cricket fans are seduced by cricket's mystery, impassioned by cricket's power and consumed by the suspense of what may come next. The more deeply cricket's mysteries are explored, the greater hold cricket seems to take on your psyche. Played well, cricket is an entertaining and exhilarating game, and no side has played cricket better than Australia during the past ten years.

If you love cricket — whether you're a fan who's happy to pass your summer holidays in front of the TV, whether you've always yearned to play the game at club level or whether you're young and dream that one day you'll represent your country — now is the time to get involved. Join your local cricket community and make a start!

Talking the Cricket Talk

Begin a conversation with a cricket lover about their sacred game and you soon find yourself subjected to a weird new language. This strange game, where 11 human beings wait patiently for their heavily clad opponent to hit a ball with a bat, has a vocabulary so vast and deep that a simple explanation of what is going on at first seems impossible.

But don't let the language of cricket deter you. The vocabulary is explained in the glossary in the Appendix. Understanding it now isn't important because you'll soak up the sayings as the game becomes more familiar to you. Just sit back and enjoy the energy and skill of the bowlers (see Chapter 7 and Chapter 8) as they send the ball down the pitch to the batsmen. Be taken by the power and grace of the batsmen (see Chapter 5 and Chapter 6) as they attempt to hit the ball into or over the fence. And appreciate the speed and desperation of the fieldsmen (see Chapter 9) whose job is to try to take a catch, or to chase and stop the ball.

Cricket offers many different facets for players and spectators. These facets come together to form a game that is unrivalled around the globe, not just because of its unique language, but because men and women must develop supreme skills to play cricket well. And yet, cricket is basic enough a game that almost anyone can have a go at playing it — whether you're 6 or 60. More than half a million Australians can't be wrong — that's how many Australians have a go at playing the game every summer. About twice that number flock to watch the Australian cricket team in action at capital cities around the country, and millions more watch cricket on television, follow it on the radio, and read about it in the newspapers and online. Cricket is a fast and ever-growing phenomenon.

Unravelling cricket's origins

Hundreds of years before Captain James Cook sailed into Botany Bay and claimed Australia as part of the British Empire in 1770, shepherds in England are believed to have been rolling stones along the ground at each other. While one rolled the stone, another attempted to hit it with his staff or *crook* (a shepherd's curved stick) before the stone rolled into a hole. If the stone ended up in the hole, then the roller of the stone would become the hitter and vice versa. Indeed, the word *cricket* comes from *cric*, the Anglo-Saxon word for a curved stick, or more particularly, a shepherd's staff or crook.

Cricket historians claim that documents can trace the game back to 13th-century English royalty and that, by the 18th century, the game had become a diverse and popular pastime, albeit unrecognisable when compared to the modern game. No wonder that a game steeped so deeply in the past has so many strange words and phrases!

Examining the playing field

One thing that cricket buffs won't be able to tell you is the size of a cricket ground. No hard and fast rules about the area of a playing field exist. This flexibility is odd for cricket because the game has 42 laws and some of them are notoriously precise. But no such precision applies when staking out a piece of ground to play cricket, as long as plenty of room exists for 11 players to spread out and *field* (take their positions to catch the ball or stop it reaching the *boundary*).

Major grounds are usually oval shaped with the pitch running longways from north to south so the setting sun doesn't get in the batsmen's eyes. Other grounds can be round and vary greatly in size from location to location and country to country. The distance from the middle of the ground to the boundary can be anything from 50 to 80 metres on major grounds. However, local club grounds can be tiny and all sorts of odd shapes, so long as a game of cricket can be played on them.

Australia's major cricket grounds — one in each state capital city — are vast compared to those in England. The two main reasons for this difference are that Australia had plenty of available real estate when the grounds were being set up — in some cases, as long as 150 years ago — and that Australia's major grounds also accommodate Australian football. Plenty of room is needed for 36 men to chase an oval football — but that's another story covered in *Aussie Rules For Dummies*. English grounds are often used only for cricket.

Despite what you may see on your television set during summer, white clothing is the norm on the field for almost all cricket matches. Certainly anyone playing below the very highest standards of the game, playing under national and state level, wears white. You don't have to dress up like a yellow canary or green parrot as the Australian team does at times. Australia does that for a special type of cricket called *one-day cricket,* almost always played under lights and with a white ball (see Chapter 3 for the various formats of the game).

Just as cricket clothes are traditionally white, a cricket ball is traditionally red. Cricket balls are about the same size as tennis balls and one fits comfortably into an adult hand, although a cricket ball is harder and heavier than a tennis ball and is encased in leather.

When players use a leather cricket ball, the batsmen and the wicketkeeper should be wearing the appropriate protective gear (for more on protecting yourself, see Chapter 4).

Explaining the pitch and stumps

Although a cricket ground has no precise measurements, very strict dimensions apply to the strip that the game is played on in the middle of the ground. This strip is called a *cricket pitch*. The cricket pitch can also be called a *wicket*, which is one of cricket's more confusing terms. Since cricket was invented by the English, the dimensions of the cricket pitch were set down in imperial measurements. In imperial measurements, the pitch is 22 yards long and 10 feet wide. The conversion of these measurements to the metric system makes for a rather clumsy 20.12 metres long and 3.05 metres wide.

Pitches are usually made of a special type of fine soil, which is watered and rolled until it feels as hard as concrete — if well constructed — and is covered with a very fine layer of grass. The idea is to have a flat, hard surface that allows a ball to bounce consistently. Turf pitches are used for all matches involving national and state teams, and also many club games of varying standards below those high levels. However, turf pitches take a lot of maintenance so many local club sides and schools have artificial pitches made of concrete that are usually covered by some sort of synthetic or carpet surface. (See Chapter 2 for more on the vagaries of cricket pitches.)

At each end of the pitch is a set of three *stumps*, which are round pieces of wood and which also have simple imperial measurements — 28 inches long and $1^1/_2$ inches wide. For anyone born in Australia after the mid 1960s, or who has come to live in Australia from one of the many countries that use the metric system, this use of imperial measurements can be confusing. When converted to metric, 28 inches is 71.1 centimetres; and $1^1/_2$ inches is 3.81 centimetres.

The three stumps are centred at each end of the pitch, side by side, with small gaps between them. The total width of the set is 9 inches, or 22.86 centimetres. On top of each set of stumps are two small, rounded pieces of wood called *bails,* which sit in grooves. Each framework of three stumps and two bails is also called a *wicket* — hence the confusion with the name of the playing surface.

Four feet, or 1.22 metres in front of each set of stumps, a white line (called a *crease*) runs across the pitch. The crease is very important for reasons that soon become clear (see Chapter 2 for more on the crease).

Don't be overwhelmed by the technicalities and jargon of cricket. You don't need to know all the right words, phrases, laws, fielding positions and measurements to appreciate and enjoy watching the skills of those playing at the highest level. Just enjoy what you see in front of you and, bit by bit, you'll become consumed by cricket's culture.

Discovering the Objectives of Cricket

Cricket can seem a complex and confronting game, but the aims or objectives of the players on the field could not be simpler. The batsmen intend to score more runs than the other team, while the bowlers and fieldsmen intend to stop the batsmen scoring runs and to have the batsmen *dismissed*.

The particulars of the game

Each cricket team has 11 players. The national and six state teams also have a player called a *12th man,* who can act as a substitute fieldsman in case one of the other players is forced to leave the field for any reason, such as illness or injury. The 12th man cannot bat or bowl. Any team can use a 12th man if they have a spare player. (See Chapter 11 for more about the 12th man.)

The coin toss

Before a game can start, the two captains of the opposing sides toss a coin to see which team bats and which team bowls. Standing together beside the pitch, the home-team captain flicks the coin in the air and the away-team captain calls either heads or tails. Usually the captain who wins the toss chooses to bat first. The theory behind this choice is that making runs first is easier than facing the psychological pressure of chasing the target by batting second. Another reason for choosing to bat first is that a turf pitch can also deteriorate as a match goes on. However, a captain sometimes has very good reasons for wanting to bowl first, too (see Chapter 11 for why a captain sometimes chooses to bowl first).

The umpires

Before any players walk onto the field to begin play, two umpires walk out. One stands behind the stumps at one end of the pitch and the other stands at *square leg,* which is one of cricket's many oddly named fielding positions (for more on fielding positions, see the diagram in Chapter 2). The square leg umpire stands about 25 metres from the pitch in line with the white crease at the opposite end to where the other umpire is standing. The umpires are the two most important people on the field and their decisions must be respected at all times (see Chapter 2 for more on the role of umpires).

The fieldsmen

After the umpires, the 11 players from the team that's fielding walk on to the ground. This is called *taking the field* (see Chapter 9 for more on fielding). Next, the two batsmen take the field while their nine team mates sit on the sidelines and watch. The fieldsmen, with the bowler and the wicketkeeper, have the job of dismissing the batsmen.

The batsmen

One batsman stands at each end of the pitch with the batsman at the opposite end to the umpire said to be *on strike.* This word doesn't mean that the batsman on strike is refusing to work, but rather that this batsman has the opportunity to 'strike' the ball delivered by the bowler (see Chapter 7 and Chapter 8 for more on bowling).

The batsmen look a bit like modern-day gladiators, dressed in all manner of protective equipment to protect them from the potential impact of the hard cricket ball. The batsmen have leg guards called *pads*, which run up their legs from the ankle to mid thigh, they wear padded gloves to protect their hands and a helmet to protect their head. Under their clothing, the batsmen wear a thigh pad on the thigh facing the bowler for extra protection, and all male cricketers wear a protector, also called a *box*, to protect their groin. (All this protective equipment is essential and is fully explained in Chapter 4.)

A cricket bat must be made of wood. A bat has a cane handle with a rubber grip. The handle is fitted into a blade of specially selected willow. The blade has a flat surface used to hit the ball and the back of the bat usually forms into a ridge running down the length of the blade. The total length of the bat can be no more than 96.5 centimetres (38 inches) and the blade can be no wider than 10.8 centimetres ($4^1/_4$ inches). (See Chapter 4 for more on cricket bats.)

The bowler

The captain of the fielding team gives a new, shiny red ball to his best fast bowler, who is at the same end as the umpire standing behind the stumps. The bowler's job is to run in and deliver the ball to the batsman. Once the bowler has bowled six deliveries, the umpire at the bowler's end calls *over.* Suddenly the umpires and fieldsmen begin wandering about. The umpire at the bowler's end usually wanders off to his right and the umpire at square leg comes and stands behind the stumps at the opposite end. These movements mean that the game has been reversed. Another bowler now bowls from the opposite end, with the fieldsmen swapping places to mirror this change. Only the batsmen stay at the same ends where they were when the umpire calls 'over'. The umpire who began at the bowler's end is now the square leg umpire. This routine is repeated every six deliveries throughout the day.

A bowler cannot bowl two consecutive overs in a match, although a bowler can bowl as many overs in a row from the same end as the captain of the fielding team chooses. Usually this is five or six overs for a fast bowler, who becomes tired quickly because of the long run-up. However, *spin* bowlers, sometimes also known as slow bowlers, use much shorter run-ups and can bowl long *spells* before being replaced by another bowler.

The bowler's main job is to dismiss the batsman — get the batsman *out.* The result of a dismissal is that the batsman has to walk back to the sidelines to be replaced by another batsman from the batting team, until ten batsmen have been dismissed. The last batsman cannot bat without a partner and is considered *not out.* Once ten batsmen have been dismissed, the team's *innings* has come to an end (individual batsmen also have innings). When the batting team is *all out,* the teams swap roles. Depending on the type of game, the teams have one innings each or two innings each. The team that scores the most runs wins, most of the time! In some two innings-a-side matches, the teams run out of time to complete the match, often because of bad weather. If no result is achieved, the match is called a *draw* (see Chapter 3 for a full explanation of the different formats of cricket).

Unlike football, cricketers don't play through heavy rain or in conditions that are too dark or wet. These conditions are considered too dangerous for play. Wet conditions make the ground slippery for bowlers and fieldsmen while bad light makes it too difficult for the batsmen to see the ball properly.

The wicketkeeper

At the opposite end to the bowler, standing behind the stumps, is the wicketkeeper from the fielding side (wearing large gloves and pads). The wicketkeeper's pads are shorter and lighter than a batsman's pads. Like the batsmen, if this player is male, he also wears a box for extra protection.

This wicketkeeper is the player who takes the ball delivered by the bowler every time the batsman decides not to hit the ball, or attempts to hit the ball but misses it. Part of the wicketkeeper's job is also to take the ball when a member of the fielding team throws it in after the batsman has struck it (see Chapter 10 for more on wicketkeeping).

The match

If you're watching the Australian team play cricket on television, you can easily tell whether each team has one or two innings. If the players are dressed in whites and using a red ball, then you're almost certainly watching a *Test* match, a traditional form of the game stretching back more than 100 years (see Chapter 17 for more about Test matches). Each team has two innings and the match is scheduled to last up to five days! If Australia is playing in coloured clothes with a white ball, then this game is a *one-day* or *limited-overs* match, with each team having just one innings (see Chapter 17 for more). Each innings is restricted to 50 overs (remembering each over is six balls) and the match is over in a day. Almost all one-day matches in Australia are played in the evening under lights.

If coloured clothes are worn, the match could also be a rare Twenty20 game, which is like a one-day match but shorter. Each team bats for just 20 overs instead of 50 overs and the whole game lasts about three hours.

A batsman can be dismissed in five common ways:

- If a batsman misses the ball delivered by the bowler, and the ball hits the stumps, the batsman is out *bowled*.
- If the ball hits the batsman's pads — leg guards — and the umpire at the opposite end believes the ball would have gone on to hit the stumps and bowl the batsman, the umpire can give the batsman out *leg before wicket* (LBW).
- If the ball is hit by the batsman to a fieldsman or the wicketkeeper, who catches the ball, and the ball has not touched the ground, the batsman is out *caught*.
- If the batsman hits the ball and is not standing behind the white crease line when the ball is thrown back by one of the members of the fielding side and hits the stumps, the batsman is *run out*.
- If the batsman is not behind the crease and misses the ball after it has been delivered by the bowler, the batsman can be out *stumped* if the wicketkeeper behind the stumps takes the ball and knocks the bails off.

See Chapter 2 for more on dismissing the batsman.

An umpire gives a batsman out by raising the index figure of their right hand and pointing it skyward.

To gain a dismissal, the fielding side must *appeal* to the umpire by asking '*How is that?*', which is usually abbreviated to an excited shout of '*Howzat*' if the fielding team believes the batsman has been dismissed.

Scoring runs

A batsman's job is to score runs. To score a run, a batsman must hit the ball then both the striker and the *non-striker,* standing at the bowler's end, must run to the opposite end of the pitch and touch their bat, foot or some part of their body behind the crease. In theory, no limit applies to the number of runs batsmen can run. In reality, however, usually only one, two (when the batsmen run up and back down the pitch) or occasionally three (when the batsmen run up, back and up the pitch again) are possible. The number of runs taken depends on how well the ball is struck and how close the ball goes to any fieldsmen trying to catch the ball, or stop it and throw it back to run the batsmen out.

If the ball is struck well, it can go past the fieldsmen all the way to the boundary, usually marked by a rope, which gives the batsman four runs without the need to run. If the ball is struck really well into the air, and it carries all the way over the boundary, the batsman is credited with six runs without the need to run between the creases. Fours and sixes are the most exciting part of cricket and the main reason why many thousands flock to see the Australian cricket team in action all around the country each summer (Chapter 5 and Chapter 6 explain how to bat like a champion).

To signal a four, the umpire at the bowler's end holds out their right arm horizontally to the side and waves it across their body, bending the elbow, before bringing it back to the straight position. A six is signalled by the umpire raising both arms straight up.

Avoiding dismissal

Not every delivery bowled is hit for runs. Achieving this result would be like having ice-cream for every meal. The smooth, sweet joy of scoring runs would soon wear off! In reality, no runs are scored from most deliveries in most cricket matches. To score runs, the batsman must first make sure that they're not dismissed. One mistake or silly shot and suddenly your *innings* can be over. Sitting on the sidelines when you're out, watching your team mates score all the runs is no fun. So, while runs are scored from *attacking* shots, most of the shots, or *strokes,* played in a cricket match are defensive shots. When playing defensive strokes, the batsman's sole objective is to *block* the ball with the bat to avoid being bowled, caught or leg before wicket. And, if the ball is not bowled at the stumps by the bowler, the batsman may simply not play a shot, lifting the bat high out of the way and letting the ball go through for the wicketkeeper to take.

A bowler cannot dismiss a batsman if the bowler delivers a *no ball.* The most common no ball is when the bowler fails to keep some part of the *front foot* in their bowling action behind the crease (for more on the front foot, see Chapter 7). A much rarer and controversial type of no ball happens when the bowler is deemed by the umpire to be *throwing* the ball. A bowler cannot bend their elbow and then straighten it as they deliver the ball. This action is deemed a *throw.* With very rare and controversial exceptions, a bowler's arm must be straight as it rotates over to deliver the ball. The only common way a batsman can be dismissed from a no ball is to be run out. A one-run penalty is automatically given to the batting side for a no ball, and a no ball does not count as a legitimate delivery. The bowler must bowl it again. The umpire at the bowler's end calls 'no ball' and holds their right arm out horizontally to signal a no ball (see more on umpire's signals in Chapter 2).

A real stigma is attached to bowlers who are deemed to throw the ball when delivering it to the batsman. Throwing is widely considered to be cheating by gaining an unfair advantage. Umpires in international and state matches no longer decide if a bowler may be delivering the ball illegally by throwing. Instead the umpires talk to the match referee, usually a former player, after the match and make a report to the cricket authorities if they have concerns about the way a bowler delivers the ball. This report prompts a complex procedure to determine if the bowler is delivering the ball illegally. This development in the game has become a very touchy subject at the highest levels of cricket.

If a bowler delivers the ball too far away from the batsman and the umpire deems the batsman cannot reach it, the umpire signals a *wide.* The umpire does this by raising both arms horizontally to the side at the same time. A one-run penalty is given to the batting side. This ball is not considered a legitimate delivery and the bowler must deliver it again. The only common forms of dismissal from a wide are run out and stumped, but a batsman is considered a bit of a dill if they're dismissed by a wide.

Wides and no balls are called *extras* or *sundries*. These runs are credited to the batting side although they're not scored by the batsmen hitting the ball and running. Other extras are *leg byes*, when runs are scored after the ball hits the batsman's body or protective gear instead of the bat and the batsman runs or the ball goes to the boundary; and *byes*, when both the batsman and wicketkeeper miss the ball and runs are scored.

Bowling batsmen over

Just to add to the intrigue of cricket, different types of bowlers have different ways of attempting to dismiss the batsman. Very broadly, bowlers are divided into two categories — fast bowlers and slow bowlers — although some fast bowlers are not particularly fast (see Chapter 7 and Chapter 8 for everything you want to know about bowling).

Very fast bowlers try to intimidate batsmen, launching the ball at great pace at a batsman, who may make a mistake because they're concerned about being hit and hurt, or simply don't have time to react quickly enough because the ball is moving so quickly.

Fast bowlers sometimes aim the ball at the batsmen. This delivery is called a *bouncer* or *bumper* and the ball bounces towards the head, throat or upper body. These bowlers are usually not bloody-thirsty but they do want the batsman to believe they are after blood, so that the batsman becomes tentative and can be more easily dismissed. Few more electrifying sights exist in cricket than watching a lightning-fast bowler in full flight.

However, these born-to-rule fast bowlers are few and far between. A wonderfully designed freak of nature, a genuinely fast bowler is like a thoroughbred racehorse. Most fast bowlers are not fast enough to intimidate or *blast out* batsmen so they must use guile. Fast bowlers try to move the ball either in towards the batsman or away from the batsman, using two different methods — *swing* and *seam* bowling.

A cricket ball has a stitched seam, about the width of a person's thumb, all the way around it and raised slightly higher than the remainder of the ball. Skilful fast bowlers attempt to use the seam on the ball as a rudder to make the ball move into or away from the batsman. Here's how:

- **Swing bowling:** A swing bowler attempts to make the ball deviate in the air before it lands on the pitch.
- **Seam bowling:** A seam bowler attempts to land the ball on the seam, which may prompt the ball to deviate off the pitch.

Swing and seam bowling are comprehensively explained in Chapter 8.

Spinning the batsman out

Slow bowling is the other type of bowling, commonly called *spin* bowling. The bowler uses a short run-up and flicks the ball with their wrist or fingers as they deliver the ball, attempting to make the ball spin — once it lands on the pitch — either into or away from the batsman. Spin bowlers also attempt to trick the batsman with *flight* by *tossing the ball up*. This means the spin bowler flicks the ball higher into the air in the hope the batsman will attempt to play an attacking shot, make a mistake and be dismissed (see Chapter 8 for all about spin bowling).

The easiest way to tell whether a fast bowler or spinner is bowling is to look at the length of the bowler's run-up and look at where the wicketkeeper is standing. If the bowler has a long run-up and the *keeper* is standing a long way behind the stumps at the opposite end, then you're watching a fast bowler. If the bowler has a short run-up and the wicketkeeper is very close to the stumps and the batsman on strike, then a spinner is almost certainly bowling.

Playing in the Right Spirit

Cricket is unique in many ways. One of the unique aspects of the game is the importance placed on not only how the game is played but also the way the game is played. At the front of every cricket law book is a preamble that defines the *spirit of cricket.* It reads:

> *Cricket is a game that owes much of its unique appeal to the fact that it should be played not only within the laws but also within the spirit of the game. Any action which is seen to abuse this spirit causes injury to the game itself. The major responsibility for ensuring the spirit of fair play rests with the captains.*

This emphasis on fair play is what prompts such outrage among the wider cricket community if one of the Australian players is seen to step out of line and misbehave.

Always remember that respecting the umpires, your team mates and your opponents is an essential part of the game.

Acknowledging Women

The highly successful and very popular Australian men's team playing cricket is what becomes wallpaper across television screens around the country every summer. But don't be fooled! Cricket is not just a men's game. Women have been playing cricket for well over 200 years.

Australia has a very strong and successful women's team. And just like the better-known Australian men's side, the women's national team is well supported by a vibrant competition among all six states. The men's and women's teams, which represent this country with such pride, are both chosen in exactly the same way: The best players in the state competition are picked to form the national side.

Below state level, more than 10,000 women are playing the game in all manner of grade and club competitions. Again, don't even for one minute believe that cricket is just a men's game! Women have made a big impact on the sport through the ages and girls and women of all ages have never found it easier to begin playing cricket. You can find all the details for women who want to play cricket in Chapter 18.

Beginning to Play Cricket

Cricket Australia, the organisation that runs the game in this country, is pouring ever-greater resources into developing the sport around the country. Better and more coordinated programs help young people start playing the game. Specially modified cricket games have been developed for primary school-aged boys and girls, who play together and are given exactly the same opportunities. The emphasis in these games is on fun and constant activity, with no children hanging around waiting to bat. Children are either batting, bowling or fielding and the game is played with specially designed plastic equipment that's safe for youngsters and requires no protective gear.

But children aren't the only Australians wanting to take up cricket. Cricket clubs around the country welcome new junior and senior players. Whether you or your children are looking to play the game, or to find a club in a new area, the Cricket Australia Web site has a specially designed section to help locate the clubs nearest you. Chapter 13 explains all the different types of cricket available to junior and senior players and how to find exactly what suits you.

Looking beyond the Boundary

Although more than half a million Australians satisfy their passion for cricket by playing every weekend in summer, millions more gain just as much joy by watching the best players in action either on television or at grounds around the country.

The cricket season in Australia runs from late September or early October through to the end of March and in the middle of the season — from November to February — the Australian players strut their stuff for the nation's entertainment. Two teams from overseas come to Australia each summer to compete against the Australians in Test and one-day matches, which are played in front of big crowds in each capital city.

Telling the difference between Test and one-day cricket is easy. Test cricket is a traditional form of the game, which lasts up to five days. Players dress in white and use a red ball. One-day cricket is played in coloured clothes with a white ball, usually under lights, and lasts just one day. Not surprisingly, one-day cricket is sometimes referred to as *pyjama cricket*.

Such has been the success of the Australian team over the past decade and the rise of its greatest rival, England, that the 2006–07 season attracted unprecedented interest, with cricket grounds in almost every capital city selling out well in advance. Whether you want to watch the cricket at the ground in your capital city or on television, follow it on the radio or read about it in the newspapers or online, Chapter 20 can tell you exactly how to access your daily cricket fix.

Discovering Australia's Opponents

Tracing cricket's development around the globe isn't difficult. Simply search out an old map of the world and look at all the countries coloured pink that once made up the British Empire, and now make up the Commonwealth of Nations. Chances are that cricket is still played to a greater or lesser extent in every one of those countries.

However, the game has developed to a high standard of play in only a handful of those countries. Just ten nations make up cricket's elite — Australia, England, India, Pakistan, South Africa, the West Indies, Sri Lanka, New Zealand, Zimbabwe and Bangladesh. These countries have special status as Test playing countries and combine together as the International Cricket Council to run cricket around the world. However, many cricket followers do not consider teams from Zimbabwe and Bangladesh up to Test standard. The political upheavals in Zimbabwe have had a seriously negative impact on cricket in that country; as for Bangladesh, many observers believe its promotion to Test status was premature.

To find out more about the international teams that compete with Australia, either in this country or overseas, and for a look at some of the great grounds they play on, turn to Chapter 16.

Rising from the Ashes

No sport reveres its history quite like cricket does, and nowhere is this highlighted more than in the battle for the Ashes between the game's two founding Test countries, Australia and England. The first Test had been played at the Melbourne Cricket Ground in 1877 and a few years later, when Australia scored its first win on English soil, the legend of cricket's most famous trophy, the Ashes, was born with an English newspaper publishing a mock obituary to English cricket (for the details, see Chapter 17).

When England next played in Australia, a tiny urn only a dozen centimetres high and containing some ashes was presented as a joke to the captain of the victorious England team, which had beaten Australia in Sydney. Well over a century later, that tiny urn has become Australia's greatest sporting symbol. Remarkably, because of the urn's fragile state, the Ashes has since been to Australia only twice, in 1988 and for the 2006–07 season, despite Australia 'winning' the Ashes regularly by beating England in Test series, which usually contain five Test matches. (For all about the Ashes, and other great cricket rivalries around the world, turn to Chapter 16 and Chapter 17.)

Despite preconceived ideas that cricket and its history are old, crusty and dull, nothing could be further from the truth. Cricket's rich past is full of colourful characters, great players, exciting matches, amazing moments and great controversies, all of which are explained in Part V of this book.

Cricket's history is enriched and enhanced almost every day as more players compete in more matches around the world. Every time you watch cricket on television, or spend a day at one of Australia's famous cricket grounds, you're watching history unfold. You can even create some of your own history by pulling on some whites and having a go.

Chapter 2

Getting to Grips with the Basics

In This Chapter

- Meeting the players
- Looking over the field
- Appreciating the cricket umpire
- Figuring out the scoring system
- Dismissing the enemy
- Breaking the play

If you want the low-down on how cricket works — from the scoring system and the pitch to the role of the players and where they stand in the field — then this chapter is for you.

Introducing the Players

Put simply, cricket is a game where two teams of 11 players square off against each other.

Every player gets the chance to bat and, in theory, everyone can be called on by the team captain to bowl. But players tend to specialise, either as batsmen, bowlers or wicketkeepers. Here's what each type of player is meant to do:

- **Batsmen:** Players who are adept at defending their stumps from being hit by the cricket ball and who are adept at hitting the ball with their bat to score runs become the leading batsmen. However, everyone in the team gets the chance to bat. (See Chapter 5 and Chapter 6 for the low-down on batting.)
- **Bowlers:** Players whose job is to deliver the ball in the direction of the stumps with the purpose of dismissing the batsmen are the bowlers. The team captain decides which players get to bowl. (See Chapter 7 and Chapter 8 for the ins and outs of bowling.)

- **Wicketkeepers:** Keepers stand behind the batsman's stumps when the bowler delivers the ball. Clad in a pair of giant gloves, the wicketkeeper's main jobs are to catch the ball delivered by the bowler, if it passes the batsman and the stumps, and to gather the ball when thrown by fielders. Each team has only one wicketkeeper. (See Chapter 10 for more on wicketkeeping.)
- **Fielders:** Everyone in a team gets to field. Fielders are there to support the bowlers in their quest to dismiss the batsmen. Fielders do this by taking catches and making run outs. (See the section, 'Dismissing the Batsmen,' later in this chapter for more on these modes of dismissal.) Fielders also have to chase, gather and return the ball to the bowler or wicketkeeper after the batsman has hit the ball with the bat. (See Chapter 9 for information on mastering the art of fielding.)

Some players are good at multitasking. They can bat and bowl or bat and wicketkeep to a decent standard. In cricket speak these players are called *all-rounders* and, no, that's not because they have enjoyed too many sumptuous cricket teas and developed a bit of girth. Because they can perform two important roles in the team, *all-rounders* are very valuable cricketers. Most players only specialise in one role, although everyone is expected to practice and develop all their skills. (See Chapter 12 for more on training.)

A cricket match isn't simply a case of two teams of 11 players; you need the help of others to make it all happen. These cricket helpers include:

- **Umpires:** Umpires are the people who apply the laws of the game to match situations. Umpires decide whether batsmen are dismissed and signal to the scorers. Someone has to umpire or the game does not take place. The umpires' role is key to the game of cricket (see the section, 'Umpiring: The Men in White Coats', later in this chapter).
- **Scorers:** Scorers sit on the sidelines, keeping a log of all the runs scored by the batsmen as well as the wickets taken by the bowlers (see the section, 'Understanding the Scoring System', later in this chapter for more on scoring).

In local club cricket, sometimes persuading someone to give up their Saturday or Sunday to act as umpire or scorer can be difficult. Therefore, teams tend to improvise, with players waiting for their turn to bat or players who have already been dismissed taking on the jobs of umpiring or scoring.

Taking In the Field

Unlike most sports, the exact size or shape of a cricket field is not designated in the laws of the game, although the pitch in the middle of the field, where the bowler delivers the ball to the batsmen, is clearly defined.

Roughly speaking, most cricket fields are oval shaped but some can be more like circles or even squares. The size of the playing field can vary dramatically. Some cricket fields like the Melbourne Cricket Ground are great big expanses. Other grounds are much smaller, with the boundary merely a stone's throw away from the pitch. Cricket grounds in Australia are usually significantly bigger than those in England.

The boundary is the line marking the limit of the cricket field. In big international matches, the boundary is a rope a couple of metres in from the fence. For local club matches, the boundary could be a white line, some cones placed around the ground, the fence itself, a gutter, or even a mown strip of grass. If the batsman hits the ball over the boundary without the ball bouncing, then the batsman scores six runs. If the ball bounces on its way to crossing the boundary, then the batsman scores four runs. (See the section, 'Understanding the Scoring System', later in this chapter for more on scoring runs.)

Looking at the pitch, infield and outfield

A cricket field can be divided into three parts: the *pitch*, the *infield* and the *outfield*.

- The *pitch* is the strip where the stumps are located and the bowler delivers the ball to the batsman.
- The *infield* is the part of the playing field where the wicketkeeper stands behind the stumps and fieldsmen are stationed within about 30 metres of the bat when the ball is being delivered to the batsman.
- The *outfield* is everything else from the infield to the boundary rope. When the batsman hits the ball into the outfield, then they usually attempt a run.

Like the game itself, the origins of many cricket terms are shrouded in mystery. For some reason, a cricket pitch is also referred to as a *wicket* (for more on pitches and wickets, refer to Chapter 1). For clarity and simplicity, this book refers to the playing strip in the centre of the ground, which has three stumps at each end and is surrounded by a playing field, as the pitch. (See Figure 2-1 for a diagram of the entire playing field.)

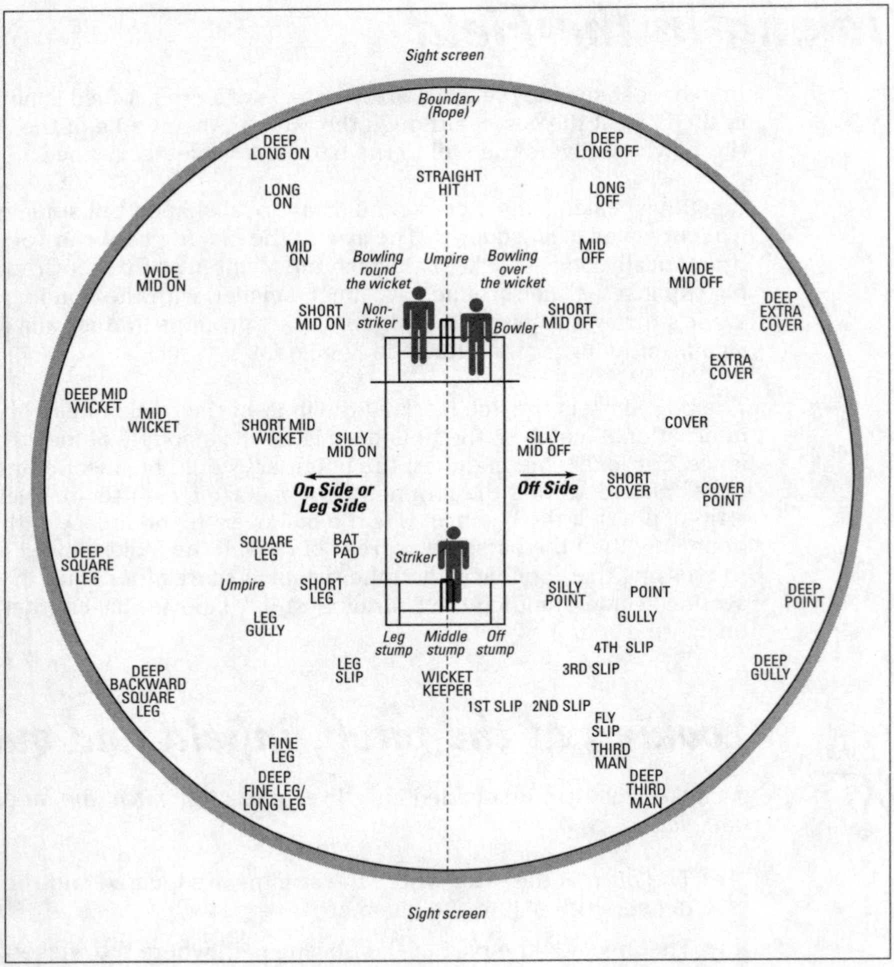

Sight screen
Boundary (Rope)
DEEP LONG ON
DEEP LONG OFF
STRAIGHT HIT
LONG ON
LONG OFF
MID ON
MID OFF
WIDE MID ON
Bowling round the wicket
Umpire
Bowling over the wicket
WIDE MID OFF
SHORT MID ON
Non-striker
Bowler
SHORT MID OFF
DEEP EXTRA COVER
EXTRA COVER
DEEP MID WICKET
MID WICKET
SHORT MID WICKET
SILLY MID ON
SILLY MID OFF
COVER
On Side or Leg Side
Off Side
SHORT COVER
COVER POINT
SQUARE LEG
BAT PAD
Striker
DEEP SQUARE LEG
Umpire
SHORT LEG
SILLY POINT
POINT
DEEP POINT
LEG GULLY
GULLY
Leg stump
Middle stump
Off stump
4TH SLIP
3RD SLIP
DEEP GULLY
DEEP BACKWARD SQUARE LEG
LEG SLIP
WICKET KEEPER
1ST SLIP
2ND SLIP
FLY SLIP
THIRD MAN
FINE LEG
DEEP THIRD MAN
DEEP FINE LEG/ LONG LEG
Sight screen

Figure 2-1: Cricket's many fielding positions for a right-handed batsman facing a right-arm bowler.

In one-day matches, the edge of the infield is often marked by a white circle about 30 metres from the pitch. The captain of the fielding team is supposed to keep nine fielders, including the bowler and the wicketkeeper, within this circle for the first ten overs of the innings, at least. No such markings exist for Test matches (see Chapter 3 for more on the different types of cricket matches).

Understanding the importance of the pitch

The *pitch* is in the centre of the playing field and is where most of the action takes place. The pitch is where the ball is delivered by the bowler to the batsman who then tries to defend the stumps from being hit by the ball, or where the batsman executes an aggressive scoring shot. (See Chapter 5 and Chapter 6 for the ins and outs of batting.)

Compared to the size of the playing field, the pitch is relatively small (refer to Chapter 1 for the dimensions of a pitch).

Every time you turn the television on and see a cricket match taking place, the game is being played on a *turf* pitch. This type of pitch is a traditional pitch used in all higher standards of cricket, including advanced levels of club cricket. Turf pitches are made of a special type of soil, which is usually black and sets rock hard once it is watered and rolled.

A good *turf pitch,* which means a pitch that is good to bat on, is hard and has a thin covering of thatched grass, which has been cut very low and rolled into the pitch with a heavy roller while still damp. The grass is meant to turn a straw colour and help hold the pitch together. The grass dries out further during the course of a match. The pitch should be perfectly flat and not start to crack unduly or break-up as a match goes on.

A turf pitch can be poor and difficult to bat on for one or more of the following reasons. The pitch:

- Has been rolled unevenly
- Has too much green grass on it
- Is too moist
- Doesn't have enough grass so has cracked and broken up, becoming uneven.

In Australia, much of the local club cricket, which takes place in the parks and community recreation reserves, is played on *artificial pitches.* These pitches are made of concrete that is covered by some sort of hardy surface. A variety of different surfaces are available, including variations of what looks like green outdoor carpet and others that are synthetic rubber. The idea is to try to emulate a turf pitch. The first artificial pitches were known as *matting,* which was basically matted rope often just stretched out over hard ground, which may not have been all that even. These early artificial pitches could be difficult to bat on.

Turf pitches need a lot of maintenance. Turf must be mowed, carefully watered and rolled for hours, making the pitch hard and flat enough to play on. If the pitch is too wet, particularly early in the season during spring in Australia's southern states, then making a good pitch is impossible. Likewise, a pitch that gets wet can become unplayable. Hence, artificial pitches are a lot more practical for local cricketers, particularly if rain is about.

The condition of a turf pitch — how much grass, bumps or cracks it has — has a huge impact on the outcome of the game. These conditions relate to the dynamics of a cricket ball. A cricket ball, which is about the size of a tennis ball but much heavier and harder, has a pronounced stitched seam running around its circumference. This seam acts as a ridge. When the ball hits the pitch, either it carries on straight or it deviates in towards or away from where the batsman stands. In addition, the ball can either bounce high — even above head height — or keep low.

Here are some typical scenarios for how the condition of the pitch can influence what happens to the cricket ball on bouncing:

- If the pitch is *even but grassy,* then the ball is likely to deviate towards or away from where the batsman is standing, but the bounce will be regular.
- If the pitch is *uneven but grassy,* then the ball is likely to deviate either towards or away from the batsman, who has the added headache of uneven bounce.
- If the pitch has *little grass and is even,* then it's happy days for the batsman. The ball is unlikely to deviate towards or away from where the batsman is standing and the bounce will be regular.
- If the pitch has *little grass and is uneven,* then don't expect to see much movement towards or away from the batsman. When the ball bounces, it may keep very low or fly uncomfortably high, making batting very difficult.

Batsmen hate uneven bounce because they can never be quite sure at what height the cricket ball delivered by the bowler is going to reach them.

If the turf of the cricket pitch has large cracks, then the surface is highly likely to produce uneven bounce. In addition, if a bowler lands the ball on a crack in the pitch, then the bowler can expect the ball to deviate alarmingly into or away from the batsman instead of continuing on in a straight line, causing great problems for the batsman.

Whether or not a pitch is moist can have a huge influence on the movement of the ball on bouncing. Generally, a moist pitch will lead to the ball deviating into or away from the batsman a great deal, slowing sharply on contact with the pitch. The seam of the ball tends to grip on a moist pitch and acts as a rudder, changing the direction of the ball instead of allowing the ball to continue straight on the line of its delivery from the bowler. This movement is called *seam movement* (see Chapter 7 for more on seam movement).

Bowlers, through a combination of wrist and finger movement, can cause a cricket ball to deviate in the air, or to deviate once it bounces off the pitch. Bowlers usually aim to bounce the ball on the cricket pitch within a few metres of the batsman in the hope of moving the ball into or away from the batsman. (See Chapter 7 and Chapter 8 for how to master the art of bowling.)

The head groundsman at the major cricket ground in each of Australia's state capitals is usually called a *curator.* His job is to make sure that the ground has the best possible turf pitches and outfield for the international and state matches played in that city every summer. In most cases, AFL football matches are played on the grounds during winter, causing the ground staff to have to make frantic changes at the start of the cricket season to make sure the grounds are ready for major matches. (See Chapter 19 for more on state and international matches and Chapter 16 for Australia's main cricket grounds.)

Because state cricket matches are also played at Test match venues, the groundsmen prepare several cricket pitches side-by-side for use throughout the season. The area of the cricket field encompassing all these pitches is referred to as *the square* or *pitch block.* These major grounds have covers wide enough to protect the entire square from rain.

Getting the covers

Rain is cricket's worst enemy. A turf pitch that gets wet can be dangerous for the bowlers, who may slip, and difficult for the batsmen because the ball can behave in strange ways. Every ground that has a turf pitch should have covers — a big tarpaulin that not only covers the pitch but extends far enough at both ends to cover the last part of the bowler's run-up as well.

Changing ends explained

The batsman *on strike* stands at one end of the pitch and the bowler delivers the ball from the other end to the batsman. Simple!

After the bowler has delivered six balls, the *over* is complete. At this point the fielding side *changes ends*. Put simply, the next set of six deliveries is bowled from the opposite end of the pitch to the previous set.

A different player from the fielding team then becomes the bowler and delivers the ball, again six times, until the over is complete.

The fielding team then changes ends again and the game goes on in this way until the batting side's innings is complete.

However, the two batsmen do not change ends, unless they run between the wickets to complete a single or three runs (adding one or three to the team's score).

A bowler cannot bowl two consecutive overs in the one innings, but they can, and usually do, bowl every second over. This means a bowler bowls from the same end for as long as the captain wants them to continue. That's usually until the bowler becomes tired and needs a rest. The bowler is then replaced by another bowler who most likely bowls a number of overs from the same end. This happens alternately at both ends as the game progresses.

If the batsman who is taking strike hits the ball in the air and is *caught* by a fielder, then that batsman is dismissed (see the section, 'Dismissing the Batsmen', later in the chapter). But if, while the ball is in the air, prior to being caught, the batsman runs towards the other end of the pitch, crossing with the non-striking batsman, then the non-striking batsman faces the next delivery bowled, as opposed to the new batsman who comes in. The only exception to this law is if the ball that the batsman has been caught off is the final ball of the over; in that case, the fielding team changes ends and the new batsman will be taking strike.

Taking note of the creases

Two sets of identically spaced white lines, called the *creases,* are at each end of the cricket pitch.

Three stumps stand at each end of the pitch. The bowlers try to hit the stumps and batsmen try to defend them. This happens from alternate ends as each over of six balls is delivered.

The batsman stands at one end of the pitch in front of one set of stumps and the bowler at the opposite end.

One line dissects where the stumps are located, running across the width of the pitch. This line is called the *bowling crease.* The other white line is 1.22 metres (4 feet) in front of the bowling crease. This line is called the *popping crease* for reasons lost deep in cricket's past.

The bowling and popping creases are joined on either side of the pitch by the *return creases*. These lines run at right angles to the other creases and are 1.32 metres (4 feet, 4 inches) either side of an imaginary line running down the middle of the pitch.

If a bowler fails to land his or her back foot (right foot for a right hander), wholly inside the return crease, then the umpire calls and signals *no ball* (for more on no balls, refer to Chapter 1. This delivery is illegal, meaning the bowler cannot dismiss the batsman. However, this type of illegal delivery almost never happens during a match (see Chapter 7 and Chapter 8 for more on bowling).

The popping crease in front of the stumps is by far the most important. This line is where the batsman stands and the line also dictates some types of dismissals. Also, if the bowler's front foot (left foot for a right-arm bowler) strays beyond this line while delivering the ball, then the delivery is called a no ball by the umpire. A no ball is not a legal delivery and the bowler can't dismiss the batsman.

The popping crease in front of the stumps is also the marker for the batsman to complete a run. The two batsmen, in order to complete a run, have to run between the two creases and touch their bats or some part of their body down beyond the popping crease. If they don't do this, then the run isn't complete.

The bowler's front foot (left foot for a right hander) must land with some part of the foot, whether grounded or raised, behind the popping crease. Umpires look to see where the bowler is planting his or her front foot when delivering the ball. Sometimes though, the umpires don't spot a no ball being bowled.

Bowlers don't usually deliver six balls — called an over — and give up. The captain usually asks them to deliver several overs or more from one end of the pitch in succession; this is called a *bowling spell*. The idea is that the bowler has time to get into the rhythm of delivering the ball and, hopefully, to spot and exploit weaknesses in the batsman's technique.

Leg side versus off side

Throughout this book you read about batsmen playing shots or bowlers aiming their deliveries to either the *off* or *leg side*. Put simply, this bit of cricket jargon helps players, commentators and spectators divide the cricket field into two. The division is an imaginary line that runs from one end of the ground to the other, right down the middle of the pitch through the middle stump at each end. (Refer to Figure 2-1 earlier in the chapter.)

From the bowler's position, a right-handed batsman facing the bowler stands with their legs to the right of the bat. Understandably, this is called the leg side, or *on side*, because this side is closest to the batsman's legs. The *off side* is the side furthest away from the batsman, on the other side of the bat. Just to confuse things, the on and off sides are the opposite for a left-handed batsman because they stand on the opposite side of the bat facing the bowler. So if a left hander and a right hander are batting together, and they take one run, which means they change ends, the on and off sides automatically swap with the batsmen (see Chapter 5 and Chapter 6 for more on batting).

Discovering the weird world of fielding positions

In true cricket tradition some laugh-out-loud names exist, such as *silly point, short leg* and *fine leg*. You can even have a *short fine leg* if you really want one! (Refer to Figure 2-1 earlier in this chapter for a diagram of positions on the field.)

As a general rule, the slips, gully and fieldsmen closest to the bat are catching positions, there solely to dismiss the batsmen. The fieldsmen in a ring to the side and front of the batsmen, about 25 to 30 metres from the pitch, are positioned to stop any runs, as well as take a catch if one comes their way. Those fielding on the boundary are happy to concede one run so they can stop the ball crossing the boundary and going for four runs, but these fieldsmen are also expected to take catches when the ball is hit high into the outfield.

With just nine fieldsmen available after the bowler and wicketkeeper, who are doing specialised jobs at each end of the pitch, obviously cricket has many more positions than fieldsmen.

Although fielding is comprehensively covered in Chapter 9, feel free to flip back to Figure 2-1 as a reminder of where the fieldsmen stand.

The Ashes . . .

The most famous contest in cricket, the Ashes, is named after a tiny urn which apparently contains the charred remains of a bail. This bail was said to have been burnt and put in an urn, as a kind of joke, after England beat Australia in a Test match in Sydney way back in 1883 (see Chapter 17 for more on the tradition of the Ashes contest).

Talking stumps and bails

The stumps and bails are essential pieces of cricket kit. A bit like goalposts in football. Without stumps and bails, you can't have a proper match.

A *stump* is a long straight piece of wooden rod about 70 centimetres long and about 3.5 centimetres across with a groove cut into the top. Stumps are hammered into the ground.

One set of three stumps is located at each end of the cricket pitch. On top of each set of stumps rest two bails. *Bails* are like little pieces of wooden rod that sit in the grooves at the top of the stumps and, for something so small, their role in a cricket match is surprisingly large.

In order for a batsman to be bowled, run out or stumped, one bail must be removed from the top of the stumps through contact with the ball. If the ball makes contact with the stumps but one of the bails is not dislodged, then no dismissal takes place.

Books on umpiring and the laws are very precise about the height and width of stumps. The width must be right because the umpire doesn't want the cricket ball to pass through a gap between the stumps without knocking a bail off.

A correctly erected set of stumps should be 71.1 centimetres above the pitch and 22.86 centimetres wide. Stumps and bails must be made of wood.

The stumps each have a name and, unlike many of cricket's stranger notations, these names make some sense. The *leg stump* is closest to the batsman's legs and the leg side; the *middle stump* is — you guessed it — in the middle; and the *off stump* is closest to the off side.

Umpiring: The Men in White Coats

The role of the two umpires is crucial. Without them, you can't have a game. The umpires judge the following:

- When six balls have been bowled and the over completed
- When the game should start and finish and when the players should go off the field during a rain shower
- When to ask the batsmen if they wish to continue batting, if the light is poor
- Whether a batsman has been dismissed
- Whether a batsman has completed a run
- Whether the ball hit by the batsman has crossed the boundary and thereby scored four or six runs
- Whether the bowler has bowled a legal delivery; that is, not a no ball or wide.

As you've probably worked out by now, the umpires have a lot on their plate during a match. The umpire has to make decisions all the time, often in only a split second. In short, being an umpire is not easy because umpires have to concentrate through every ball bowled.

Making the big calls

When players in the fielding team believe they have a chance of dismissing the batsman, they appeal to the umpire. Usually they shout 'How is that?' — often shortened to '*Howzat!*'

The umpire then adjudges whether or not the batsman is out.

If the umpire decides that the batsmen is out, the umpire raises their right index finger in the air, as though pointing to the sky.

TECHNICAL STUFF

Once a batsman has been given out, the batsman must leave the field immediately without making comment or being demonstrative. This lack of response revolves around the spirit of cricket and is most fundamental to the game. (Refer to Chapter 1 for more on the spirit of cricket.)

If the umpire has any doubt over whether the batsman is out, the umpire should give the benefit of this doubt to the batsman and give a not out decision.

Umpiring: Working together as a team

One umpire stands behind the stumps at the end of the pitch from where the bowler is delivering the ball. This position gives the umpire a prime view to judge *leg before wicket* (LBW) appeals (see the section, 'Dismissing the Batsmen' later in this chapter for the LBW law). The umpire can also see whether catches have been properly taken by fielders. In addition, the umpire has a bird's-eye view of the popping, or front, crease and is able to spot whether the bowler's front foot lands over the crease, leading to a no ball.

The other umpire stands at the square leg position, on an invisible line that's a continuation of the popping crease, in a line with where the batsman stands (refer to the diagram in Figure 2-1 for the square leg position).

The square leg umpire adjudges appeals from the fielding side for run outs and stumpings.

When the fielding team changes ends after the completion of an over, the umpire who was standing at square leg moves to behind the stumps at the end of the pitch from where the bowler is now about to deliver the ball. The other umpire moves out to square leg.

Respecting the umpire

The umpire's job is to interpret the laws of the game of cricket and apply them to the match situation.

Thankfully, no soccer-style histrionics are accepted in cricket. A long tradition of players accepting the umpire's decision as final exists in the game. The world's best umpires are used in Test match cricket and are chosen by the International Cricket Council (ICC), the game's governing body. The ICC draws up a panel of umpires who travel the globe standing in Test matches and one-day international games.

In international cricket, the match referee monitors players' behaviour on the field. An ex-Test player, the match referee keeps discipline and ensures that the umpire's decisions are accepted without question. Match referees have sweeping powers, able to fine and even ban players who break the laws of the game or show dissent to the umpire.

Accessing the laws of cricket

Cricket has 42 laws and some of them can be quite long and detailed. Everyone keen to play the game at a senior level should have a basic understanding of these laws, although many only apply in bizarre and obscure circumstances which you may never encounter. The laws were compiled by cricket's most famous club, the Marylebone Cricket Club (MCC) based at Lord's in London, well over 200 years ago, and have been modified regularly since. You can find the most up-to-date laws at the MCC's Web site: `www.lords.org`. Click Laws & Spirit. Alternatively, contact your state or territory cricket association for details on how to obtain a copy of the laws (see Chapter 13 for the contact details).

Recognising umpiring signals

One of the main jobs of the umpire is to let the scorer know what's going on in the match. The umpire does this through a series of signals, which are interpreted by the scorer. Some of these signals look bizarre, but get your head around the following umpiring signals and you'll better understand what's going on in the match.

Right arm outstretched — no ball

The umpire stretches out the right arm horizontally to the side, as shown in Figure 2-2, indicating that the bowler has failed to land some part of his or her front foot (left foot for a right hander) behind the front line, the popping crease. The delivery is deemed illegal.

Figure 2-2: The umpire signals a no ball.

Both arms outstretched — wide

The umpire stretches out both arms horizontally to the sides, as shown in Figure 2-3, indicating that the ball was out of reach of the batsman.

Figure 2-3: A wide is signalled.

Right leg raised and tapped by the right hand — leg bye

The umpire raises the right leg and taps it with the right hand, as shown in Figure 2-4, indicating the ball has hit some part of the batsman or their protective gear, except the batting gloves holding the bat. The batsmen are free to attempt a run if the ball has ricocheted far enough, even though the ball did not hit the bat.

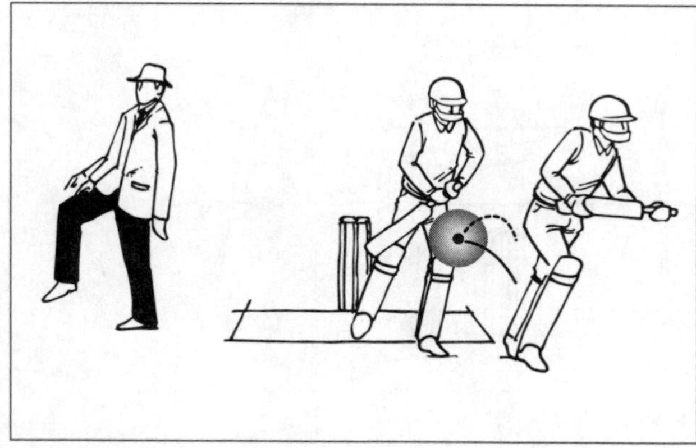

Figure 2-4: A leg bye is scored.

Right arm raised skywards — bye

The umpire raises the right arm skyward, as shown in Figure 2-5, indicating the ball has been missed by both the batsman and the wicketkeeper, and the batting team has scored one or more runs.

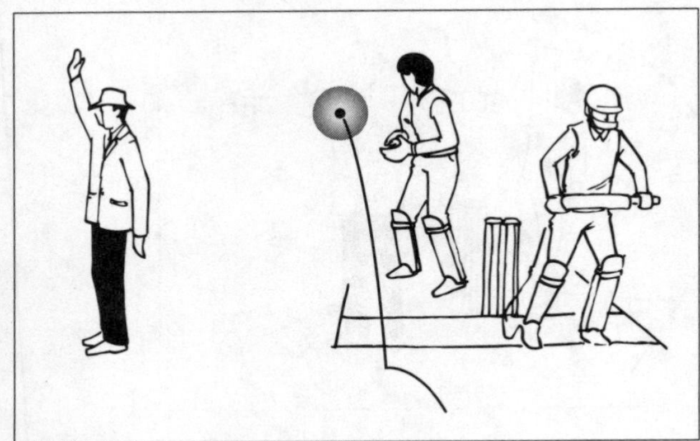

Figure 2-5: The umpire signals a bye.

Right hand and arm swept across the chest — four runs

The umpire raises the right arm horizontally to the side and sweeps the right hand and arm across the chest, as shown in Figure 2-6, indicating the batsman has hit the ball all the way to the boundary. The ball has bounced before reaching the boundary.

Figure 2-6: Four runs are scored.

Both arms held straight up high — six runs

The umpire holds both arms up high, as shown in Figure 2-7, indicating the batsman has hit the ball over the boundary without the ball bouncing.

Figure 2-7: The umpire signals six runs.

Index finger pointed to the sky — out

The umpire points the index finger to the sky, as shown in Figure 2-8, indicating the batsman has been dismissed and must leave the field immediately.

Figure 2-8: A batsman is given out.

Right arm held out horizontally then bent at the elbow with finger tips touching right shoulder — short run

The umpire holds out the right arm horizontally to the side, then bends it at the elbow with finger tips touching the shoulder, as shown in Figure 2-9, indicating one of the batsmen has failed to touch their bat down beyond the front crease (popping crease) when going for a run. The scorer is being told to take that run off the score. Failing to complete a run properly is called a *short run.*

Figure 2-9: The umpire signals a short run.

Straight arms pointing down crossed back and forth — dead ball

The umpire has straight arms pointing down and crossed back and forth, as shown in Figure 2-10, indicating the ball is no longer in play. This signal is usually given when a bowler drops the ball during their run-up to bowl.

Figure 2-10: A dead ball is signalled.

Video replays and the role of the third umpire

In international cricket matches, umpires can call on the help of video replay technology. When an umpire feels he hasn't had a good view of an incident, he can refer to the *third umpire*. The third umpire sits in a room in the grandstand in front of a TV screen. He will then review the video evidence and communicate his decision, using a walkie-talkie, to the two umpires on the field.

Referrals to the third umpire, though, are limited to the following match situations:

- The fielder has chased the ball to the boundary but the umpire is unsure whether the ball, or the fielder, while holding the ball, has made contact with the boundary. If contact was made, then the third umpire tells the two umpires on the field that four runs should be awarded.
- The fielding side claims a catch but the umpires on the field are unsure that the ball carried to the fielder without touching the ground. If the ball has carried, then the batsman is dismissed; if not, then he or she will be given not out.
- An appeal for a run out or stumping has been made to one of the umpires and they are unsure whether the batsman has placed his bat or any part of his body behind the front crease before the bails are removed by the fielding side (see the section, 'Dismissing the Batsmen', later in this chapter for more on these modes of dismissal).

When one of the umpires on the ground needs help from the video umpire, he draws an imaginary box in the air with his index fingers. Anticipation rises as the crowd watches the large video screen at the ground to see if the batsman is judged out from the replays.

Understanding the Scoring System

Generally, in cricket games, whichever team scores the most runs wins. Therefore, nailing down exactly how runs are scored is important. Mostly, batsmen score the runs, but runs can be awarded by the umpires when the bowler bowls a delivery that the umpires deem contrary to the laws of the game. In addition, the umpires are free to award penalty runs to the batting side in some unusual instances.

A batsman scores runs by using the bat to make contact with the ball. The two batsmen — the striker who hits the ball and the non-striker at the opposite end of the pitch — then run between the wickets to register runs.

In theory, the batsman can score an unlimited number of runs off a single contact of the bat with ball — called a *stroke* or *shot*. But, in reality, the fielding team will gather and throw the ball to the bowler or wicketkeeper to stop the batsman from scoring more than four runs for any one hit.

Generally, you find that batsmen run one, two, three or occasionally four runs after making contact with the ball.

If the batsman hits the ball all the way to the boundary, then the umpire awards runs and the batsmen do not need to run. If the ball bounces before crossing the boundary, four runs are awarded. If the ball clears the boundary without bouncing, then six runs are scored.

Pretty simple so far? Sadly, cricket's scoring system doesn't stay this easy for long.

The umpires may also award runs for the following scenarios (these runs are referred to as *extras*):

- **Leg bye:** When the ball strikes any part of the batsman or protective equipment, except the gloves holding the bat, without touching the bat, then the batsman is free to attempt to run a leg bye. Any runs scored are added to the batting team's total but not to that of the individual batsman. Unlike a wide or a no ball, the delivery counts and the bowler doesn't have to repeat it.
- **Bye:** If the ball is missed by the batsman, then fails to hit the stumps and is fumbled or missed altogether by the wicketkeeper, then the batsmen are entitled to run. Like a leg bye, the run is added to the batting team's total but not the individual batsman's score.
- **No ball:** Some part of the bowler's front foot (left foot for a right hander) has not landed behind the front crease (the popping crease). The umpire calls no ball and a run is automatically added to the batting team's total. In addition, the bowler cannot dismiss the batsman and the delivery doesn't count. The bowler has to deliver the ball again. On very rare and controversial occasions, the umpire can also call no ball if they believe the bowler is throwing the ball by flexing the elbow when the ball is delivered, instead of keeping the elbow straight (see Chapter 7 and Chapter 8 for more on bowling).
- **Wide:** The umpire can call wide when the bowler delivers the ball so far wide of where the batsman is standing that the batsman has no prospect of making contact. Again an extra run is added to the batting team's score and the delivery doesn't count. The bowler has to deliver the ball again.

The umpire won't allow a leg bye if, in their judgement, the batsman hasn't attempted to play a shot or avoid the delivery. Perhaps the batsman has simply let the ball hit his protective pads or body on purpose to avoid being dismissed.

Should the umpire call no ball and the batsman hit the ball to a fielder in the air to be caught, or missed it altogether and the ball hit the stumps, then the batsman is not out. Batsmen can hit a no ball delivery to score extra runs with wild abandon, as they can only be dismissed by a run out when a no ball has been bowled.

Extra runs are very common. On average you can find that around five per cent of a team's total runs are extras.

Umpires can also award penalty runs to the batting team. Penalty runs are awarded for offences committed by the fielding team. For example, should the ball hit a protective helmet or piece of clothing discarded by the fielding team, then the batting side is awarded five penalty runs. The law governing penalty runs is fiendishly complex and, fortunately, the incidence of penalty runs being awarded are few and far between. In fact, you could play cricket for decades and never see a penalty run awarded.

Keeping count: The role of the scorer

The scorer's job is to keep his or her eyes peeled for the number of times batsmen run between the wickets to register runs, and to watch for signals from the umpire (see the section, 'Umpiring: The Men in White Coats', earlier in the chapter for more on the signals given by umpires).

The scorer sits with a score book and keeps a tally of the following:

- The total runs scored by each team when it bats
- The runs scored by individual batsmen
- The extra runs awarded by the umpires
- The number of balls delivered by each bowler, whether any runs were scored off a delivery, how many runs were scored, and whether runs scored were extras
- The mode of dismissal of each individual batsman; who was the bowler and catcher or, in the case of a run out, who was the fielder throwing the ball at the stumps
- The team score when each batsman was dismissed
- The number of overs bowled by the fielding team
- The number of overs bowled by individual players and how many runs have been scored during the overs.

As you can probably guess, this amount of scoring is an awful lot for one person to get their head around. But the key to scoring is to have a routine; after each delivery is bowled, the scorer makes a note of what has just happened. Score books are printed allowing all this information to be jotted down in double-quick time using a type of scorer's code.

Breaking the scorer's code

Here's a look at the basics of the scorer's code:

- Each over has six deliveries, therefore a mark is made relating to each delivery.
- A number indicates that runs have been scored off the delivery. For example, the number 4 indicates 4 runs scored.
- A dot mark (like a full stop •) indicates that nothing has happened off the delivery, no runs have been scored.
- The mark X indicates that a batsman has been dismissed by the bowler's delivery.
- W indicates that the delivery has been adjudged wide by the umpire, an extra run is added to the batting team's total score and the delivery has to be repeated.
- A circle around a dot or number indicates that the delivery is a no ball, an extra run is added to the batting team's total score and, what's more, the delivery has to be repeated. A number inside the circle denotes how many runs have been scored by the batsman off the no ball.
- A triangle indicates that the delivery has gone for byes. The number in the triangle denotes how many byes have been scored.
- An upside-down triangle indicates leg byes and the number in the triangle denotes how many leg byes have been scored.

The use of triangles to indicate byes and leg byes is optional. Many scorers in local cricket simply put a dot to show no runs were scored off the bowler. This system is often simpler when adding up the bowlers' figures at the end of the innings.

Scoring may vary slightly from district to district and even club to club, often depending on the type of scorebook used, so always be guided by your more experienced team mates. A scorer always sits with the scorer from the opposition side so they can constantly check to make sure everything tallies up. Often in local cricket the opposition won't have a scorer so two members of the batting team usually score. If you end up playing cricket for a local team, chances are you'll be asked to score at some stage, but don't panic. Explain that you haven't done it before and a more experienced team mate is usually happy to help. Usually everyone is expected to take a turn at scoring at some stage.

If you watch TV coverage of a cricket match or go to a big game, don't worry, you're not going to be bombarded by dots, Xs and the like. A scoreboard is on the ground to give you the low-down on the match situation. The scoreboard tells you the total number of runs scored by the batting team, the number of batsmen dismissed and the overs bowled. In addition, the scoreboard tells you how many runs have been scored by the individual batsmen, as well as the runs conceded, and batsmen dismissed by the individual bowlers. Part of the scorer's job is to keep the scoreboard up to date.

You often hear the batting team's score referred to as being *for* something. For example, Australia is 7 for 300 (written 7–300). This score means that seven of Australia's batsmen have been dismissed and the team has scored 300 runs. Just to confuse matters further, in England the runs are always put first, so the English say 300 for 7.

If the batsman fails to score any runs in the over, the over is called a *maiden*. As far as bowlers are concerned, maidens are great news; second only in the happiness-inducing stakes to dismissing a batsman. Best of all possible worlds for a bowler is a *wicket maiden*. This occurs when no runs have been scored off the over and a batsman has been dismissed. Sometimes you find two batsmen are dismissed and no runs are scored and this over is called a *double wicket maiden*; now the bowler is in fantasy land. In the score book, a maiden is indicated by the letter M under the six dots that show that no runs have been scored from the over. A wicket or double wicket maiden is indicated in the score book by WM or 2WM under the six dots.

Cricket boffins have come up with an incredibly complex scoring system for rain-affected one-day international and state cricket matches. The Duckworth/Lewis system, as this system is called, means that a result can still be possible in a match where weather interruptions ensure that not all the scheduled overs are bowled. (See Chapter 3 for the ins and outs of the Duckworth/Lewis scoring system.)

Dismissing the Batsmen

The game of cricket revolves around a tussle between batsmen and bowlers. Batsmen may hold the whip hand for a while, creaming the bowlers' deliveries to the boundary and getting the team score to rattle along. But sooner or later, the bowlers get their turn to enjoy the good life by dismissing the batsmen. Once 10 of the team's 11 batsmen have been dismissed, the innings is at an end and either the fielding team has a turn to bat (unless the fielding captain enforces a follow-on), or the game has reached its end. (See Chapter 11 for information on the follow-on.)

Batsmen can be dismissed in ten different ways. The most common are:

- **Bowled:** The bowler has managed to hit the batsman's stumps and the bails have been dislodged. High fives all round for the bowler.
- **Caught:** The batsman has hit the ball in the air to a fielder who has caught the ball before it touches the ground.
- **Leg before wicket (LBW):** The ball has struck the batsman's leg guards, called batting pads, and the umpire judges that the ball would have hit the stumps. The batsman is dismissed LBW.
- **Run out:** The fielder has managed to dislodge the bails with the ball before the batsman has completed a run. In other words, the batsman is still running between the wickets and hasn't yet managed to get the bat down beyond the line of the popping crease (the front crease) when the bails are taken off the stumps using the ball.
- **Stumped:** The batsman has strayed out of the crease in an attempt to play a shot and the bails have been removed by the wicketkeeper with ball in hand.

For a run out or stumping the ball doesn't have to hit the stumps for the batsman to be out. If the wicketkeeper or a fieldsman takes the ball they can remove the bails with the hand, or in the wicketkeeper's case, gloves, as long as the hand or glove is holding the ball. In most cases wicketkeepers and fieldsmen try to gather the ball in two hands to be sure of taking it and then whip off the bails with the hands together cupped around the ball.

When the bowler catches a ball hit by the batsman in the air, the bowler is said to have dismissed the batsman *caught and bowled*.

If the batsman's bat — or gloves holding the bat — makes contact with the ball and then ricochets off the leg guards (pads) to be caught by a fielder, then the batsman is dismissed *caught bat and pad*. Spin bowlers are particularly adept at getting batsmen caught bat and pad (see Chapter 8 for more).

Some cricket matches involve sides having to complete two innings each, others just one. (See Chapter 3 for more on the different formats of cricket matches.)

Unusual dismissals

Almost all batsmen are dismissed by being either bowled, caught, LBW, run out or stumped. But every so often, a batsman is dismissed for one of the following five unusual transgressions:

- **Handled the ball:** The batsman, trying to stop the ball hitting the stumps, instinctively hits the ball with a hand not gripping the bat handle.
- **Hit the ball twice:** The batsman has a brain freeze and decides to hit the ball not just once but twice with the bat. This situation is different from a batsman stopping the ball rolling onto their stumps if they've attempted to play a shot and things have gone wrong.
- **Hit wicket:** The batsman hits their own stumps, dislodging the bails with the bat, body or protective equipment. Why would a batsman do such a silly thing? Well, it would be an accident, usually caused by the batsman knocking the stumps while moving their feet to get into position to play a shot, or by over-overbalancing.
- **Obstructing the field:** The batsman uses the bat or the body to stop a catch being taken, or to stop a fieldsman from attempting or completing a run out.
- **Timed out:** When a batsman has been dismissed, a new batsman is expected to take their place within three minutes. If the new batsman fails to turn up in the allotted time, the batsman can be timed out — one of the rarest of all modes of dismissal.

A batsman is allowed to *retire*. This doesn't mean that the batsman suddenly ends up spending an inordinate amount of time in the garden. Retiring simply means that the batsman has had enough for that innings and may want to rest or give another team member a chance to bat. A batsman who retires is deemed to be dismissed and is not allowed to return to bat again in that innings. However, a batsman who *retires hurt*, for example, one who was struck by the ball or who pulled a muscle, is allowed to return to bat at a later stage of the innings.

A batsman can't be given out by the umpire unless the fielding side has appealed to the umpire. However, when a player has been bowled or a catch is clearly taken, the batsman walks off towards the pavilion, without waiting for the umpire's decision.

Comprehending the LBW law

The leg before wicket (LBW) law is a little like those governing offside in soccer, or what constitutes a maul in rugby union; most people involved in the game claim to know it inside out but few actually do.

Put simply, a batsman is dismissed LBW when the ball hits the leg guards — batting pads — and the umpire judges that the ball would otherwise have hit the stumps.

Simple, eh! But several provisos exist, including:

- If the ball has bounced — also referred to as pitched — outside of the batsman's leg stump, the batsman cannot be out LBW under any circumstances.
- Where the ball has bounced outside the batsman's off stump and has moved in towards the batsman's stumps off the pitch but is not in line with the stumps, and the batsman has attempted to play a shot, the batsman can't be dismissed LBW.
- If the ball hits the batsman's bat before striking the leg guards (pads), then, again, the batsman can't be out.

Judging whether a batsman is dismissed LBW is one of the most difficult calls an umpire has to make. Umpires are mere humans and can make mistakes. Some fielding teams make life hard for the umpire by appealing nearly every time the ball strikes the batsman's pads.

Figuring Out a Scoreboard

Cricket scoreboards have a wealth of information but can look terribly confusing. Scoreboards appear in newspapers or online. The size of the scoreboard and the amount of information contained often depends on how important the match is.

Test matches, in particular, often have a board with screeds of numbers, bringing back dark memories of difficult days at the back of the maths class.

Once you've learnt how to read a cricket scoreboard, you can tell much about the state of a match without even having to read the adjoining match report.

The scoreboard in Figure 2-11 represents the final of the 2002–03 World Cup, cricket's major one-day tournament, when Australia triumphed over India in South Africa to win by 125 runs.

See if you can figure out how this scoreboard works. Don't worry if it looks too much like logarithms; you can read the full explanation in the sections following the scoreboard.

Australia v India 2002–03 World Cup Final

at Johannesburg (Wanderers) 23/3/2003 Australia won by 125 runs

Australia		Runs	Mins	BF	4s	6s
AC Gilchrist+	c Sehwag b Harbhajan	57	66	48	8	1
ML Hayden	c Dravid b Harbhajan	37	93	54	5	
RT Ponting*	not out	140	138	121	4	8
DR Martyn	not out	88	112	84	7	1
DS Lehmann						
MG Bevan						
A Symonds						
GB Hogg						
AJ Bichel						
B Lee						
GD McGrath						
Extras	[2b, 12lb, 16w, 7nb]	37				
Total	205 min 50 overs	**359**				
Fall	1–105 (Gilchrist), 2–125 (Hayden)					

India - bowling	O	M	R	W	wd	nb
Zaheer Khan	7	0	67	0	6	2
J Srinath	10	0	87	0	2	3
A Nehra	10	0	57	0	3	
Harbhajan Singh	8	0	49	2		
V Sehwag	3	0	14	0		
SR Tendulkar	3	0	20	0	1	
D Mongia	7	0	39	0		2
Yuvraj Singh	2	0	12	0		

India		Runs	Mins	BF	4s	6s
SR Tendulkar	c and b McGrath	4	2	5	1	
V Sehwag	run out	82	107	81	10	3
SC Ganguly*	c Lehmann b Lee	24	44	25	3	1
M Kaif	Gilchrist b McGrath	0	4	3		
RS Dravid+	b Bichel	47	87	57	2	
Yuvraj Singh	c Lee b Hogg	24	48	34	1	
D Mongia	c Martyn b Symonds	12	18	11	2	
Harbhajan Singh	c McGrath b Symonds	7	12	8		
Zaheer Khan	c Lehmann b McGrath	4	20	8		
J Srinath	b Lee	1	6	4		
A Nehra	not out	8	7	4	2	
Extras	[4b, 4lb, 9w, 4nb]	21				
Total	180 min 39.2 overs	**234**				
Fall:	1–4 (Tendulkar), 2–58 (Ganguly), 3–59 (Kaif), 4–147 (Sehwag), 5–187 (Dravid), 6–208 (Yuvraj), 7–209 (Mongia), 8–223 (Harbhajan), 9–226 (Srinath), 10–234 (Zaheer)					

Australia - bowling	O	M	R	W	wd	nb
GD McGrath	8.2	0	52	3	2	
B Lee	7	1	31	2	2	4
GB Hogg	10	0	61	1		
DS Lehmann	2	0	18	0	4	
AJ Bichel	10	0	57	1	1	
A Symonds	2	0	7	2		

Captains: RT Ponting (Aus), SC Ganguly (Ind)
Toss: India
Umpires: SA Bucknor, DR Shepherd

Figure 2-11: The scoreboard for the 2002–03 World Cup Final.

Reading the scoreboard

Following all the preliminary details about which teams were playing where and when, and the result, you read a scoreboard from left to right. You see the:

- Batsman's name
- Mode of dismissal (including the catcher's name if caught)
- Bowler who dismissed the batsman
- Runs scored by each batsman
- Minutes each batsman batted
- Balls faced by the batsman
- Fours and sixes hit by the batsman.

Looking at abbreviations

Cricket scoreboards rely on abbreviations to minimise the clutter of information on the board. Once you become familiar with these abbreviations, you can easily read a scoreboard, keeping up with the changes at a glance. The following abbreviations can keep you on top of the scoring system (refer to Figure 2-11):

- **c:** The most common form of dismissal is to be *caught*, listed as 'c' on the scoreboard. For example, on the scoreboard, Adam Gilchrist was caught by the Indian fieldsman, Sehwag, from a delivery bowled by Harbhajan for 57 runs.
- **c and b:** If a bowler takes a catch from the delivery they have just bowled, the dismissal is known as *caught and bowled*, listed as 'c and b'.
- **b:** A batsman who is bowled is listed as 'b' followed by the name of the bowler who dismissed him or her.
- **lbw:** A batsman dismissed leg before wicket is 'lbw', followed by the name of the bowler who claimed the dismissal.
- **st:** A batsman who is stumped is listed as 'st' before the name of the wicketkeeper who performed the stumping, followed by 'b' for the bowler's name.
- **hit wkt:** A batsman who stands on their stumps attempting to play a shot is out hit wicket — 'hit wkt' on the scoreboard.
- **run out:** A batsman is 'run out'. The bowler is not credited with the wicket so no bowler's name is listed beside it.
- **not out:** The batsman has not been dismissed.

Sometimes not all the batsmen have a chance to bat in an innings, particularly in a one-day match when batting time is limited, as is obviously the case with Australia in the scoreboard shown in Figure 2-11.

Under the batsmen, the extras are listed. These are runs not scored by the batsmen and are detailed earlier in this chapter (refer to the section, 'Understanding the Scoring System'). Extras are also known as sundries and are written on the scoreboard as:

- **b:** for byes
- **lb:** leg byes
- **w:** wides
- **nb:** no balls.

Under the extras, the team's total batting time is written in minutes as 'min' and the number of overs the team faced is written as 'ov'.

And finally you come to the total. The total is worked out by adding up all the batsmen's scores, the first column of numbers on the scoreboard, and the extras. If the team is not dismissed, then the number of wickets to fall is listed before the total. In Australia's case, the total score was 2 for 359, often written as 2–359.

An asterisk (*) next to a player's name in the batting line-up denotes the team captain and a plus (+) denotes the wicketkeeper.

'Fall' explains what the team score was at the time each batsman was dismissed and who the batsman was.

The bowling figures follow, listing each bowler in the order they first bowled during the match. The opening bowlers, who share the new ball, are the first two bowlers listed. On the scoreboard shown in Figure 2-11 from left to right are the following abbreviations:

- **o:** The number of overs delivered by each bowler. Occasionally a bowler's overs will be written with what appears to be a decimal point, although it is not. For example, Glenn McGrath bowled 8.2 overs. This means he bowled eight completed overs plus two balls of his ninth over. The presence of the decimal point usually signals that a bowler dismissed the last batsman before being able to complete their over. Occasionally a bowler will suffer an injury and will be unable to complete their over, which will be finished by another bowler.
- **m:** The number of maiden overs. A maiden over has no runs scored off it.

- **r:** The number of runs scored off all the deliveries sent down by the bowler.
- **w:** The number of wickets taken. This is the column that makes a bowler's eyes light up! The more wickets the better for the bowler and the fielding team.
- **wd:** Total wides delivered by the bowler.
- **nb:** The number of no balls.

Each wide and no ball is penalised one run and the runs are added into the total runs scored off the bowler.

Last on the scoreboard are the names of the opposing captains, the team which won the toss and the two umpires who officiated in the match on the ground.

For two-innings games, such as Test and first-class matches, the scoreboard is doubled, listing each team's batting and bowling in both innings. In less high-profile matches, sometimes a lack of space on the scoreboard means you see only the runs scored by the batsmen. Minutes, balls faced, fours and sixes are left off.

Many, many books totalling millions of words have been written about cricket. In the end, cricket is a game of numbers!

Looking at Breaks in Play

Cricket is a long game. Even Twenty20 matches, the shortest format of the game, take more than three hours from start to finish (see Chapter 3 for more).

No surprise, therefore, that cricket is littered with breaks in play. Some of these breaks, for example, drinks, lunch, tea and changeovers between innings, are agreed between the sides before the match, or set down in competition rules; others are called at the umpire's behest, due to poor light or rain.

Dividing up the playing time

The number and length of prearranged breaks in play tend to vary between the match format and the competition rules. For example, in a Test match, breaks of 40 minutes for lunch break and 20 minutes for tea are always taken. However, most one-day competitions have just one long break between the changeover in innings, when teams get to eat and drink. Twenty20 has a short break between innings.

A Test match is supposed to have three two-hour sessions of play each day; also in the middle of each session, a drinks break of about five minutes is usually held. A trolley or cart runs drinks out to all the players and the umpires on the field. On very hot days, two drinks breaks may be called during each session. (See Chapter 3 for more about Test matches.)

Going off the field for bad light or rain

Umpires tend to take players off the field when it rains. In big matches the groundsmen can cover the pitch to protect it from moisture in an attempt to protect bowlers from injury. Once the weather is better, the players return and the game recommences.

A bit more controversially, umpires can also take the players off the field when they believe poor light could constitute a hazard to the batsmen. A cricket ball is a very hard object — particularly dangerous when propelled by bowlers such as Australia's Brett Lee at up to 150 kph.

Some cricket spectators argue that umpires have used their powers to take players off the field far too often. In other words, umpires are too willing to take the players off the field. Umpires now use light meters in Test matches to get a more accurate idea of the conditions.

When assessing light conditions, the two umpires on the pitch consult and, if they deem that the light is potentially dangerous, they offer the batsmen the chance to leave the pitch. The batsmen then have the choice of whether to leave. If they do troop back to the pavilion, the batsmen are said to have *accepted the light*.

More often than not, batsmen accept the umpires' offer to leave the field because of bad light and head for the comforts of the dressing room. However, when only limited time is left in the game and the batting team is on top in the match, the batsmen may decide to continue.

Chapter 3

Three Hours to Five Days: The Many Formats of Cricket

In This Chapter

- Examining one- and two-innings formats
- Introducing Test match cricket
- Looking at first-class matches
- Moving right along with one-day cricket
- Deciphering the Duckworth/Lewis scoring system
- Having fun with Twenty20

Cricket matches can last for days or just a few hours. They can be highly charged occasions with batsmen playing big shots or more genteel affairs where, to the untrained eye, not much seems to be happening. The viewing and playing experience alters with each format of the game.

Think about it: Football is essentially the same whether played for a few minutes or to the end, while golf is all about . . . well . . . getting a ball into a little round hole. In cricket, though, the format of the match has a huge influence on everything from team tactics to the scoring system adopted to decide the winner.

This chapter looks at the different formats of cricket, from Test cricket through to the crash, bang and wallop of one-day cricket, and the super sprint of the new Twenty20 game. Ultimately all of cricket's formats offer the spectator and player something unique.

Test matches are the longest cricket format, lasting anything up to five days. One-day cricket is just that — one day long — while at the other end of the scale, Twenty20 — 20 overs a side — games finish the quickest, lasting around three hours.

Looking At an Innings

Cricket matches are divided into innings. Each of the two sides has at least one innings, no matter what the format.

An innings works by the batting side sending in its first two batsmen — numbers 1 and 2 in the batting order. These two bat and bat until one of them is dismissed by the fielding team.

Being dismissed may sound like being freed from class in your school days but, in cricket, being dismissed refers to the batsman being *out*. This means that the batsman's innings has been brought to an end by the fielding side and the batsman must leave the field. (Refer to Chapter 2 for more on modes of dismissal in cricket.)

Now the dismissed batsman's place is taken by another player. This player is said to be batting at number 3 in the *batting order.*

When one of these two batsmen — the batsman remaining from the start of the innings or the number 3 batsman — is dismissed, then that batsman's place is taken by another player, batting at number 4 in the batting order and so on until the 11th batsman emerges from the pavilion.

When 10 of the 11 batsmen have been dismissed — a batsman cannot bat without a partner — the batting side is *all out*. In other words, the batting team's innings is over.

Once the batting side is all out, the team that was batting swaps places with the fielding side, which then sends their number 1 and 2 in to bat.

So, the fielding side becomes the batting side, and the batting side now becomes the fielding side. The new batting side now goes through its innings until 10 of the 11 batsmen have been dismissed or until a result has been achieved.

In very simple terms, the winner of the game is the team that manages to score the most runs in its innings.

The team players who are the most skilled at batting usually occupy high numbers in the batting order, while those less able to score runs and defend their stumps bat lower in the batting order. (See Chapter 5 and Chapter 6 for more on batting skills.)

Who gets to bat first is decided by whichever of the team captains wins the toss of a coin before the start of the match. (See Chapter 11 for the importance of the toss.)

Every weekend during the summer, hundreds of thousands of men and women, young and old, turn out for their local club teams. Matches are usually one- or two-day matches. Either both teams bat on the same day or matches are played across one day on each of two weekends, with one team batting on the first weekend and the other batting on the second.

Throwing the second innings into the mix

The most traditional forms of cricket, such as Test and first-class matches, involve teams having not one but two innings each. That format can also apply even at club level if both teams are dismissed quickly and time is available for a second innings.

The result is that after the two sides bat once, the teams have to come out and bat again.

Two innings are considered to be a truer test of each team's abilities. Sometimes, an inferior team can get lucky and score more runs than a better side, yet this is less likely to happen if teams have to bat twice.

When the game is over, the total runs scored in both innings are added together to decide which team wins.

For example, during the first innings, team A scores 250 runs and team B scores 200. Now in a single-innings match, team A would be the winner by 50 runs. However, this is a two-innings match and this gives team B the chance to fight back. In the second innings, team A scores 130 runs, giving A a total aggregate score of 380; 130 plus 250 from their first innings. Team B, therefore, needs to score 181 runs to beat A's aggregate and win the match. Team B reaches 181 runs but six of B's batsman have been dismissed. This means B wins by 4 wickets because four batsmen of the 10 who could be dismissed by team A were not dismissed.

As soon as one side passes the total amount of runs scored by the opposition, regardless of whether teams are playing a game that consists of one or two innings each, the match is over. The match is over even though the winning team has plenty of batsmen who have not been dismissed. These batsmen do not get the chance to bat, and this applies to all forms of cricket.

Sometimes after the completion of both teams' first innings, the team that has just batted has scored far fewer runs than the fielding side managed when it was batting. For example, team A scored 600 runs while team B managed just 200 runs. When a big enough gap exists, the fielding side is allowed to tell the batting side to bat again. This is called *enforcing the follow-on* (see Chapter 11 for more on enforcing the follow-on).

Taking extra time to complete two innings

The fact that some matches involve teams having two innings means that more time is needed to establish a winner.

Finishing a match of two innings each in a single day is nigh on impossible. The batsmen are too skilled to be dismissed by the bowlers in such a short time frame.

Therefore matches of two innings each are usually spread over four or five days.

Whether the match is scheduled to run for four or five days depends on whether it is contested by players representing their countries or states.

Contests between two teams of 11 players representing their countries are the most important cricket matches and are, therefore, given the most time to reach a finish. The reason is that players who represent their countries are meant to be the *crème de la crème* of cricket. The players' skill levels are so high that the two innings take longer to complete. These matches of two innings a side between international teams are called *Test matches* and they last a maximum of five days.

Matches of two innings a side between state sides are scheduled to last four days, slightly less time than for a Test match because the skill level of the players is a little lower.

Scheduled five-day Test matches and four-day state matches are classified as *first-class matches*.

However, just because a match is scheduled to last four or five days, the match doesn't necessarily last that long. Often one team dominates the other, or other factors, for example, the ground or weather conditions, favour bowling over batting, and a result is reached prematurely (refer to Chapter 2 for more on the conditions).

Conversely, having four or five days to finish a match doesn't always mean that one side will triumph over the other.

Bad weather can take time out of the match, or the players on both sides can bat well, and the time allotted to reach a result is used up without either side being able to force a result. If this situation happens, then the match is a *draw*.

A draw in cricket is unlike a draw in football or any other sport. A *draw* simply means there wasn't enough time for a result. In a funny kind of way, a draw is the purest form of a sporting result because neither team was good enough to beat the other. However, a draw *can* get rather boring in the end if the match goes on for days with no prospect of either side winning. In other sports, a draw, which is when the scores are level at the end of the game, say 1–1 in soccer, is what cricket refers to as a *tie*. A tie occurs rarely and is very different to a draw. In nearly 130 years of Test cricket, only two Test matches have ever been tied.

Captains can move along a match with two innings a side to get a result; for example, the batting side can *declare* its innings at any time. By declaring, the captain of the batting side is saying to the opposition, 'We have scored enough runs, our innings is now over and it's your turn to bat'. The idea of a declaration is to leave enough time in the match to achieve a result. (See Chapter 11 for the ins and out of declaring an innings and some instances of how this tactic can occasionally go horribly wrong.)

Cricket aficionados can become very excited about drawn matches, particularly when one of the teams comes close to defeat but somehow manages to last the distance and draw the match. However, most people new to the game of cricket find it very odd indeed that two teams can lock horns for four or five days and yet no clear winner may emerge.

First-class status only applies to games played between teams of men — very sexist in this instance. Playing first-class cricket is a big deal because this format is meant to be close to the pinnacle of the sport, second only to playing in a Test match (women do play Test matches).

Test matches are also first-class matches but generally of a significantly higher standard, making Test matches elite first-class games.

Whatever the format, when a side triumphs, the victory is recorded in one of two ways. If the team winning the match does so while batting, the victory margin is said to be the number of wickets they have spare (ten batsmen minus the number dismissed). For example, when team A scores 200 and team B scores 201 with only one of its batsmen dismissed, the margin of victory is nine wickets. On the other hand, if the team winning the match bats first, then the victory margin is said to be the total number of runs that side has to spare. For example, team A scores 200 runs and team B scores 150 — team A is said to have won by 50 runs.

Introducing Test Cricket

As far as keen cricket buffs are concerned, Test matches are what watching cricket is about.

Test matches see two national teams slug it out over five days. The results of these Test matches are flashed around the world and great individual performances are recorded and pored over by cricket fans and cricket historians.

Test matches started way back in 1877 and, since then, more than 1,800 Tests have been played (see Chapter 16 for more on the tradition of Test cricket).

Test matches are great set-piece occasions. Much care is taken over the condition of the pitch used in a Test match (refer to Chapter 2 for more). Ideally, a Test match should last into its fifth day.

Test matches can be long drawn-out affairs and very hard on the players' bodies. Nevertheless, unlike other major team sports, such as the various football codes, players can't be substituted for performing poorly or because they're simply tired. However, if a player is injured during the match, then a substitute can be used to field, but not to bat or bowl. This substitute is called the 12th man.

Four results are possible in Test and first-class cricket matches — win, lose, draw or tie.

Ten nations have joined the elite Test playing 'club' over a long span of time. For example, the first two nations to play Test matches were England and Australia in 1877. Bangladesh became the tenth nation to start competing in Test matches in 2000 (see Chapter 16 and Chapter 17 for Test cricket's major competitions and rivalries).

Test matches haven't always been allotted five days. In the 19th century, most Tests played in England were only scheduled for three or four days. Later, time was stretched to the other extreme, with *timeless Tests* being played. These winner-take-all Tests were meant to be played to a finish, regardless of the number of days. The longest timeless Test ever played was between England and South Africa in 1939. The match went on and on and on for 10 days before it had to be called off because the England team would have missed its boat journey home! Since World War II, the norm for Test matches has been five days.

Taking it carefully: Test and first-class tactics

Matches with two innings a side can sometimes be quite slow-paced affairs, although modern Test and first-class matches are played at a much faster pace than they were a few decades ago. This mostly has to do with the attitude of the batsmen.

Generally, when a batsman starts to bat, their approach is cautious. The batsman is focused on not being dismissed. This means the batsman plays defensive shots — or even no shots at all to some deliveries. The reason for this is survival — the batsman allows time to get used to how the ball is bouncing off the pitch and what tactics the bowler is using. This process is called *playing yourself in* or *getting your eye in* and is examined extensively in Chapter 6.

Naturally a batsman doesn't stay on the defensive forever. As confidence grows, the batsman starts to play more aggressive run-scoring shots. But because a Test or first-class match lasts four or five days, batsmen can afford to take their time before going on the attack.

All this means that the rate of run scoring in first-class and Test matches traditionally has been very slow, although the current Australian Test team has scored consistently faster than any other in history.

Scoring gone mad

Scoring rates have increased so dramatically in recent years that in March 2006, Australia became the first team to score 400 in a one-day international. The world champions made 4–434 (only four batsmen were dismissed) in their allotted 50 overs (300 legal deliveries). Quite remarkably, South Africa became the second team to achieve this amazing feat just three hours later, scoring 9–438 (nine batsmen dismissed) from 49.5 overs (299 legal deliveries — just one delivery was left to be bowled in the match). South Africa won in astonishing fashion by one wicket. The teams made a combined total of 872 runs, smashing the previous record of 693 for the most runs scored in a one-day match, set by India and Pakistan two years earlier. Now that's entertainment!

A full day's play in a Test once saw about 250 runs scored. Now that score could be closer to 350, such has been the change in attitude of batsmen in Test cricket.

In one-day matches, however, you can see scores of 500 or even 600 runs in a day, with Australia's one-day team now frequently reaching 300 or more runs in a one-day innings of 50 overs. This scoring rate equals a run a ball.

Looking behind the big shots

Slower scoring in Test matches doesn't necessarily spell boredom. The crowd enjoys the tussle of batsman versus bowler. Watching a batsman work really hard to prevent dismissal against a top-quality bowler can be very absorbing and, then later in the day — when the batsman has their *eye in* — watching the batsman start to get on top and play aggressive shots can be exciting.

Test and first-class matches have more frequent breaks than in a one-day game. The players come off for lunch and tea breaks during four- or five-day games, while a one-day match has just a single break in play between innings. (Refer to Chapter 2 for more on breaks in play.)

In one-day cricket, the pace of run scoring is generally faster than in a Test or first-class match.

To ensure that spectators get value for money, cricket's authorities have laid down strict guidelines governing the minimum number of overs that must be bowled in a day's play. In Test matches, fielding sides are expected to bowl at least 90 overs a day, while in the state first-class matches, known as the Pura Cup, the minimum is 96 overs. In Test matches, play can be extended by half an hour to ensure the 90 overs are bowled and fielding teams are fined for slow over rates. In the Pura Cup, the sanctions are even harsher for slow play, with the offending team docked a percentage of its hard-earned points from the league table for failing to bowl the required overs in the allotted time.

Teams compete in a *series* of Test matches, involving from two to five separate Test matches. The team that wins the most Tests is said to have won the Test series. Over a six-year period, all ten Test playing nations play each other in series home and away, earning points for series won or drawn. The team with the highest points tally is crowned world champions. (See Chapter 17 for more on the Test world championship.)

First-class cricket, which in Australia is mostly played in the Pura Cup state competition, is a proving ground for players with ambitions to play Test cricket. A player has to perform in state cricket before being selected for the national side.

Ensuring a Result: One-Day Cricket

About 40 years ago, cricket's bigwigs woke up to the fact that many people would like to attend a cricket match for just one day and be assured of a result. One-day cricket was born to try to quench this thirst for a winner in an era when Test and first-class cricket was often much duller than is the case today.

In one-day cricket, teams get just one innings each and the number of overs is limited. In international and state matches, each team has a maximum of 50 overs to bat.

This strict approach ensures that a result is reached within a day, hence these games are referred to as either one-day or limited-overs matches. A limited-overs match and a one-day cricket match are the same thing at international and state level.

Many spectators love the one-day format because unless the game is a wash-out — in other words, rain falls for most of the day — the fans get to see a result. (See Chapter 19 for more on what makes one-day cricket special from the fans' perspective.)

Although in many ways one-day cricket is the fans' favourite, Test cricket is considered the more prestigious. Cricket purists, including international players, believe that a match with two innings a side truly shows which teams are the most skilful.

One-day matches, even if played between national sides, are not given first-class status.

Gauging the difference between one-day, Test and first-class matches

One-day matches differ from the longer formats of the game — first-class and Test matches — in several key ways.

- **The number of innings differs:**
  - **One-day match:** Each side only has one innings.
  - **Test and first-class match:** Each side has two innings.
- **The number of overs a team can bat differs:**
  - **One-day match:** The match has a maximum set number of overs.
  - **Test and first-class match:** The match has to be finished in a prearranged number of days, but no maximum limit is placed on the number of overs that a team can bat.
- **The number of overs a bowler can bowl differs:**
  - **One-day match:** Each bowler can only bowl a maximum set number of overs. For example, in a match with 50 overs a side, the standard for international and state matches, an individual bowler is limited to 10 overs so at least five bowlers must be used in the innings.
  - **Test and first-class matches:** Bowlers are free to bowl as many overs as they and their captain want. The record for any Test match is a staggering 129 overs, bowled by West Indian spin bowler, Sonny Ramadhin, against England at Edgbaston, Birmingham, in 1957. Sonny would have needed a bit of a lie down after all that!
- **The placement of fieldsmen differs:**
  - **One-day match:** For a proportion of the batting side's innings, up to 20 overs in a one-day international, the fielding side is allowed only 2 of its 11 players, including the bowler and wicketkeeper, outside a 30-metre circle around the pitch in the middle of the ground.
  - **Test and first-class matches:** Captains are free to place fielders wherever they want on the field (with one exception) for as long as they want.

So, what's the exception, you ask! Read on.

Captains are forbidden from placing more than two fielders backwards of the square leg umpire on the leg side (refer to Chapter 2 for a diagram of fielding positions, and to Chapter 9 for a greater explanation of fielding). This fielding rule was introduced after the controversial bodyline tour of Australia by England in 1932–33. On this tour, the England captain asked his bowlers to bowl at the Australian batsmen's bodies with the aim of making the batsmen fend the ball to a gaggle of fielders placed backwards of the square leg umpire (see Chapter 23 for more on this controversy).

In one-day matches, umpires tend to be very strict in their interpretation of what constitutes a wide delivery, which is deemed out of a batsman's reach (refer to Chapter 2 for more on wides). Such a strict ruling gives the batsman the best chance of playing a shot to entertain the crowd. The upshot is that any delivery by the bowler that's directed down the batsman's leg side (that goes behind the batsman's legs) is in serious jeopardy of being called wide. (Refer to Chapter 2 for more about the leg side.)

Understanding the one-day trade-off

The key to winning any cricket match is to score more runs than the opposing team.

In one-day matches, the batsmen usually play more aggressively than in first-class or Test matches because they have much less time, and therefore fewer overs to bat.

However, the batting team has to balance the need to score runs with preventing batsmen being dismissed by the bowlers.

If batsmen take too many risks — play too many aggressive shots — the danger is that all the team's batsmen will be dismissed and the innings brought to a premature end. The batting team that fails to use up the full 50 overs available to it is considered to have committed one-day cricket's worst sin.

In one-day matches, if a team is dismissed before the allotted number of overs have been bowled, the innings is at an end. For example, in a match with 50 overs a side, team A scores 250 runs in 48 overs, but ten batsmen are dismissed, the innings is finished and the two overs that were scheduled to be bowled are not bowled.

What tends to happen is that if the batting team has a few batsmen dismissed early in its innings, some of the batsmen who follow tend to play a little more cautiously to ensure extra batsmen remain in reserve so the team can go for its shots near the end of the innings.

This choice can mean the final few overs of a one-day innings can be frenetic affairs with batsmen throwing all caution to the wind and going for aggressive shots, which also give bowlers a better chance of dismissing the batsmen. All very exciting for the spectators!

Day–night one-day cricket

One-day cricket is big business when matches are played between national sides. The television companies love one-day cricket for much the same reason as spectators — one-day cricket attracts TV ratings and the game's all over in a single day. No wonder that broadcasters, particularly in cricket-mad India, pay a king's ransom for the broadcast rights.

What also appeals to the broadcasters is the colour of the one-day game. For starters, teams wear coloured clothing and the ball used is white, rather than the traditional red. But what makes one-day cricket come alive, from a visual standpoint, is the use of floodlighting. Day–night games, as they're called, start in the afternoon and conclude late in the evening, normally around 10 pm. These games can be atmospheric occasions, full of razzamatazz and pizzazz.

The pinnacle of one-day cricket is the World Cup, held every four years. The 10 Test playing nations, plus up to six second-tier 'associate' member countries of the International Cricket Council (ICC), the game's governing body, take part in what has now become a two-month tournament. The World Cup is the biggest cricketing event on the calendar. (See Chapter 17 for more on the World Cup and which teams take part.)

Examining the Unexplainable Duckworth/Lewis System

Sadly, cricket is a game that is constantly at the mercy of the weather. Either through rain or bad light, playing time can be lost — which isn't too much of a problem in two-innings matches scheduled to last four or five days.

However, in one-day matches run to a very tight schedule, any breaks due to bad weather can mean that the full number of overs can't be bowled. Therefore, cricket boffins Frank Duckworth and Tony Lewis came up with a mathematical formula so a result can often be reached in a match when bad weather has significantly reduced the time available.

Before you start here's some background: The idea behind the Duckworth/Lewis method was to find an equation that determined the winning runs target for the team batting second in the match should bad weather intervene, reducing the number of overs the second team has to bat.

The method is based on how many batsmen in the batting side have yet to be dismissed and the number of balls remaining to be bowled in the innings when play is interrupted.

The match umpires and scorers are given spreadsheets, which clearly show what the team's score or target to win would be — under the Duckworth/Lewis method — at any given point should weather intervene and the number of overs be reduced.

Scorers put this information on the scoreboard in major matches so that players and spectators know what the result would be should the heavens open and the game be washed out.

The mathematics behind Duckworth/Lewis is fiendishly complex and best left to those who have some sort of mathematics obsession. If you're mathematically inclined, grab your calculator and slide rule (and turn on your computer); this is more like a maths lesson than a sporting solution! If you're a cricket fanatic, you may love this challenge. If you're not, skip the Duckworth/Lewis system and move on!

Now go to the International Cricket Council's Web site at the following link: `www.icc-cricket.com` and search for Duckworth/Lewis system. Have fun!

Everyone else and I suspect that's most of you — should simply trust the scoreboard to let you know what's going on if the heavens open at some stage during a one-day match.

The Duckworth/Lewis method isn't very popular, mainly because it's so incredibly complex. But no one, as yet, has come up with a fairer system.

You tend to find that umpires are a little less willing to take players off the ground for a light shower in one-day cricket matches compared to longer and more complex Test matches. Conditions and the influence that rain can have on those conditions have a far greater impact in Test matches. Players are usually just happy to get one-day games over and done with.

Some matches are marred by weather to the point where no result is possible. Each side must receive at least 20 overs in a one-day match at international and state level for a result to be registered, otherwise a no result is listed.

Crash, Bang, Wallop: Twenty20 Is Born

In 2003, the Twenty20 format was born, the most exciting development to happen to cricket in a generation — at least for those spectators who like the fast new game.

Whereas most traditional one-day matches consist of innings of 50 overs a side, in Twenty20 — as the name suggests — teams have just 20 overs to bat.

Going crazy: Cricket in a fun rush

The shorter format means less chance of all the batsmen in a team being dismissed. Therefore, batsmen have *carte blanche* to go for aggressive shots right from the word go.

In addition, compared to Test matches, Twenty20 games are over in a flash; the games take just over three hours from start to finish.

Twenty20 matches are very popular at state and national level. If you fancy going along to a game, you should consider booking a ticket in advance, otherwise you may not be able to get into the ground. (See Chapter 20 for full contact details for international and state cricket associations.)

The Twenty20 format is very spectator friendly with hold-ups in play kept to a minimum. For example, when a batsman is dismissed, he has to be replaced by another batsman within 90 seconds. In addition, strict penalties apply for fielding teams failing to bowl their 20 overs within 75 minutes.

In Test matches, batting sides often score an average of between three and four runs an over. In one-day matches with 50 overs, the scoring rate is a little faster, usually between four and six runs an over. But in Twenty20 games, the scoring rates can be higher still — seven, eight, nine even ten runs an over is the norm.

In one-day matches, the economy rate is often a key determinant of how well a bowler has performed. Put simply, the economy rate is how many runs the bowler has conceded, divided by the total number of overs the bowler has bowled. Therefore, a bowler who has conceded 50 runs off 10 overs has an economy rate of five. A bowler is usually said to have done well in a 50-over match if they have an economy rate below four.

In Twenty20 matches, the benchmark for what constitutes a good economy rate is higher still because batsmen are more inclined to play aggressive shots — an economy rate of less than six is considered top drawer in these games.

Going global: Twenty20 catching on

Twenty20 games started as contests between English county sides (which are like Australian state sides) in 2003, but the popularity has been such that in 2005 the first Twenty20 match took place between national teams.

The marketing men and women took about a nanosecond to work out that people loved Twenty20 matches between national teams. Games have been sold out around the globe and the number of fixtures has grown ever since.

However, the International Cricket Council (ICC) is concerned that this new phenomenon may harm the popularity of one-day cricket, so the ICC has restricted each national side playing at home to a maximum of two Twenty20 matches in any series, and three in a year.

Still, such has been the appeal of Twenty20 that the ICC has also decided on a World Cup of Twenty20 cricket, scheduled for South Africa in September 2007.

Chapter 4

Grabbing the Right Gear: Cricket Equipment

In This Chapter

- Getting together the right equipment
- Choosing and looking after a cricket bat
- Making sure you have the right protective gear
- Dressing the part

Enjoying cricket in its simplest form takes hardly any equipment at all. Grab a tennis ball or something similar, find anything comfortable to hold that can act as a bat, and you're ready to go. One batsman, one bowler, and lots of fun!

A makeshift bat and ball is what most people use to gain their first taste of cricket. Frantic sessions amid boisterous cries start and finish at the drop of a hat — or perhaps catch — in the backyard or on the beach. However, when you turn on the TV, cricket becomes a very different game.

On the TV screen, batsmen appear dressed like modern-day warriors who would not be out of place in the latest re-make of *Star Wars*. From helmets with metal grilles, which can make it impossible to see who's who, down to bulky batting gloves, often an arm guard and big pads protecting the legs, this battle dress is sophisticated armour.

And the fashion of the cricket field doesn't stop there. Even more padding and protection is hidden under the clothing, helping to ensure that cricket's hard ball doesn't leave too much of a lasting impression.

This chapter explores the gear you need to shape up in a proper cricket match, giving you a good idea of what kit you have to buy or borrow to play cricket safely, how much it costs and where you can get it.

Most equipment in cricket is designed for the batsmen. After all, he or she must defend their stumps — and their body — from a ball bowled at up to and beyond 150kph by the likes of Australian fast bowler Brett Lee.

Getting into Gear: The Essentials

Cricket equipment can be divided into two different groups — items necessary for the game to be played, and items of personal equipment essential to your performance and protection. Most of this chapter relates to personal equipment but first, check out this basic equipment that you need to get the game started:

- **Two sets of stumps and bails:** Each set consists of three stumps and two bails, which are positioned a little over 20 metres apart at each end of the pitch. Refer to Chapter 2 for more on setting up your stumps and bails.
- **Boundary markers:** A cricket ground always needs a clear boundary. Often cricketers use boundary markers, such as a rope, cones or flags, to indicate where the field of play ends. At other times, grounds may have a permanent boundary marker, such as a white line, gutter, fence or mown strip. International and state venues have a rope placed a few metres in from the fence.
- **Score book:** Each club side must have a score book. In local club cricket, members of the batting side — waiting their turn to bat or having already batted and been dismissed — take on the job of scoring. Refer to Chapter 2 for more on scoring.
- **Cricket bat:** A batsman may wear all manner of protective equipment (see the section, 'Getting the Right Protection' later in the chapter) but the batsman's central focus is always on their tool of trade — their cricket bat.
- **The ball:** A cricket ball is as essential as a bat. Unless you're playing one-day cricket for your state or country, the ball will be shiny red. A standard cricket ball is about the size of a tennis ball and usually weighs 156 grams. Slightly smaller versions are used for women's cricket, with cricket balls being slightly smaller again for juniors.

For more than two decades now, bat manufacturers have attempted to create bigger 'sweet spots' or 'middles' in a bat by changing the shape of the back to offer a greater spread of wood without harming the balance of the bat. The bat makers have also been using different manufacturing techniques (see the section, 'Defining a cricket bat' later in this chapter).

Looking back at cricket bats

The first cricketers were believed to be shepherds and the first cricket bats simply a shepherd's staff. A stone or small piece of round wood was rolled along the ground to be hit by the staff. And instead of the bowler aiming at a set of stumps, the ball was directed towards a hole in the ground. If the stone or piece of wood was missed by the staff-wielding batsman and if the 'ball' rolled into the hole, the batsman was out.

Indeed, the word *cricket* is a derivative of 'cric', meaning a shepherd's curved staff or 'crook'.

Even as cricket developed with more sophisticated balls and rules, underarm bowling was still the only legal form of delivering the ball until well into the 19th century (see Chapter 18 on how women developed overarm bowling). Hence many of the early bats were shaped like hockey sticks or clubs, with the weight at the bottom designed to hit balls rolling along the ground.

As balls began to bounce more with the introduction of overarm bowling in the 1860s, cricket bats began to straighten out and take on their modern shape.

Over time, cricket gear generally has changed a huge amount. Early drawings and paintings of cricket matches depict players whose only protection seems to be a well-starched pair of trousers and a stovepipe hat.

Stumps also evolved from that hole in the ground to become two small wooden sticks with a single stick across the top that became known as a *bail.* Today, three stumps and two bails are the bowler's target. In some Test matches and one-day internationals, TV technicians even build a miniature camera into one of the stumps — the *stumpcam* — to give TV watchers an up-close and personal view of the action.

All About Bats and Balls

Whether your main job in your cricket team is to bat, bowl or wicketkeep, you're going to need to learn to bat as well as you can. Every member of a cricket team gets to strut their stuff as a batsman and is expected to make some sort of contribution.

So is it essential that you have your own bat? Most local club sides have a team kit bag with all the gear you need to get started. If you're new to the game, you don't have to race off and spend hundreds of dollars buying all your own equipment.

However, many established players like to have their own gear for comfort and convenience. This trend applies particularly to cricket bats, which can become very personal items to be treated with tender love and care.

Although cricket bats do not become lifelong partners — most bats eventually crack or break after years of constant use — the relationship between a batsman and their bat can be very important to the success of a player. Preferences as to the weight, balance and general 'feel' of a bat can be very individual.

Inspecting a modern cricket bat

Although cricket bats may have been all manner of shapes and sizes through the centuries, very strict laws now govern a bat's dimensions. A bat can be no longer than 96.5 centimetres (38 inches) in length, 10.8 centimetres ($4^1/_4$ inches) wide and must be made solely of wood.

Bats today have a cane handle that is fitted or *spliced* into the blade, which is made of willow. The bat has a flat face to hit the ball and the back is usually shaped into a ridge running the length of the blade. The back is usually thickest about 15 centimetres (six inches) from the bottom or *toe* of the bat. This thickness is designed to give the batsman a *sweet spot* for maximum *timing* when the ball hits the *middle* of the bat.

In typical cricket fashion, the 'middle' of a cricket bat is not the mid-point between the top and bottom of the blade but lower down, where the batsman attempts to hit the ball for maximum result. No better feeling exists in cricket than hitting the ball in the 'middle' of the bat, feeling the ball fly sweetly off the blade and watching it race between the fielders to the boundary.

When a batsman is said to have *mistimed* a shot, this means that the batsman has not hit the ball with the middle of the bat. The ball has either hit too high or low on the blade or hit closer to one of the edges. A mistimed shot doesn't feel good and often doesn't look good. The ball travels relatively slowly and is often inadvertently hit in the air, presenting a catch to one of the fieldsmen. (You can read more about batting in Chapter 5 and Chapter 6.)

Pricing up a cricket bat

You can pay anything from $200 to $600 for a decent cricket bat. Like any purchase, the rule of choice applies to cricket bats: You get what you pay for. The manufacturer grades the willow; the better the willow, the more expensive the bat. However, when you're looking at the top of the range, you may find that the most expensive cricket bat is not automatically the best. Nor is the fact that a famous player uses a particular brand of bat, proof that this bat is the best. Manufacturers pay top players enormous sums of money to use their bats. Some Australian players have been known to put their sponsor manufacturer's stickers on a different brand of bat because they actually preferred the other type. A growing number of small, independent bat manufacturers offer quality bats at good prices. Finding a good bat takes patience and research.

Cricket bats are made from willow because this wood has the characteristics of being hard-wearing, relatively light, and easy to sand and carve into shape. Willow has been produced mainly in just two areas of the world — England and Kashmir. Now some small producers are growing an increasing amount of willow in Australia. Like just about all things cricket, England is the traditional home of bat manufacture and English willow was once *the* only wood that could be used to make a bat. English willow is still generally regarded as the best, but in recent years the quality of Kashmir willow cricket bats has improved and the Indian bat-making industry has grabbed a fair chunk of the international market.

Manufacturers make bats especially designed for young children and teenagers; junior bats are smaller and cheaper. Remember, cricket gear is expensive and children can quickly grow out of it. All junior club sides have the necessary equipment to play cricket although juniors need to supply their own cricket clothes.

Deciding on the right bat

If you've fallen in love with cricket — like half a million people in Australia every summer — and you want to buy your own bat, consider these important details when making your bat selection:

- **Weight of the bat:** Weight varies from approximately one kilogram to approximately one and a half kilograms, although bats are often discussed in the old imperial measurements used in England — making them just over two pounds to over three pounds. The difference may not sound like much but when you lift a light bat and then a heavy one, you really notice the difference.
- **Length of the bat handle:** Bat manufacturers can offer up to three types of handle sizes — short, normal and long. Which type you choose depends very much on your height and the size of your hands. If you're tall and have great big mitts, it follows that you may need a long handle. If you're short with smaller hands, a short-handled bat may be for you. However most people, particularly those just starting off, use a normal-length handle.

Unless you're an experienced player who has mastered a successful grip suitable to your needs, both hands need be placed comfortably together in the middle of the handle. Holding the bat too low, known as *choking* the bat, can make it difficult to play *straight bat* defensive and attacking shots — the most fundamental shots in the game, while holding a bat too high on the handle can make it difficult to control. (See Chapter 5 and Chapter 6 for all the essential details on batting.)

Do you need a full-sized bat? Full-sized bats are too big for juniors and possibly some players of short stature. Fortunately, a great range of bats are available in many different sizes. Shop around until you find one that suits you.

The lighter a bat, the more quickly you can manoeuvre it into position, particularly against fast bowling when you have little time to react. On the other hand, the heavier a bat, the more impact it may have on the cricket ball. Most hard-hitting, powerful batsmen tend to use heavy bats. However, heavy bats can be detrimental to the proper development of young players and those starting off in the game. No prizes are awarded for being the macho man with the heaviest bat, and such a bat could be the culprit if you keep getting out! If you're not sure which bat to use, consider starting with a bat weighing a little more than a kilogram (about two and a half pounds).

Cricketers describe how a bat feels in your hands as you lift it off the ground, as the *pick up*. A pick up has nothing to do with small trucks or dodgy one-liners. Generally, batsmen prefer bats to have a light pick up yet still be weighty enough to give the ball a frightful whack.

No two bats ever feel exactly the same in your hands, even if the bats have the same weight and handle length. Each piece of wood used in bat manufacture is unique.

The price of a cricket bat can vary enormously, depending on the quality of the willow and whether the bat has been mass produced. The vast majority of club cricketers buy their bats off the shelf, but these cricketers do spend time hunting around the shops for the bat that feels just right.

Some cricketers, though, go the extra mile and pay for a manufacturer to make a bat to their own specifications. This practice can be very expensive and is not necessary for the average club cricketer who plays at a local level. Sports stores offer plenty of good bats.

If you join a cricket club, you may find that a batsman will sell you one of their cricket bats. The batsman may be retiring or may have more than one bat. As long as the bat's in good condition (no cracking of the wood or splintering of the handle), you can get your hands on a good-quality bat for a reasonable price. What's more, the bat is ready for play, oiled and knocked-in (see the next section, 'Preparing the bat for play').

Even if your main job in the team is bowling or wicketkeeping, the captain still expects you to be able to bat. In fact, one great way to get in the captain's good books is by being a bowler who is a bit of a dab hand at batting. After all, the more runs your team scores, the better the chances are of your team winning cricket matches.

Preparing the bat for play

A cricket ball is a very hard object, often propelled at great speed. Consequently, bats have to go through an important process of preparation before they're ready to take on such force.

Proper bat preparation includes:

- **Oiling with linseed oil:** Linseed oil protects the wood. Generally applied over two days, four coats are sufficient initially. You need a very light oiling of the blade every month thereafter. After the first coat, leave the bat in a horizontal position to dry before the next coat of oil is applied. You can buy the bat oil when you buy the bat. Once the bat is in use, a light sand with fine sandpaper before oiling helps remove any marks on the blade.

  Do not, under any circumstances, oil the area of a cricket bat where the handle joins the blade of the bat. This area is a long, thin triangle at the top of the blade known as the *splice*, and is where the cane handle has been fitted, or spliced, into the willow blade. If oil is applied in this area, the oil could eventually lead to the weakening of the join between bat and handle. The best rule to follow is do not oil the manufacturer's logo, which almost always covers the splice on the front and back.

- **Hitting the bat with increasing force:** You have to get the wood used to the impact of a cricket ball. Therefore, a good idea is to spend several hours hitting the bat with a ball, but not with the protruding seam of the ball (see Chapter 7 for more on the seam). A specially designed mallet is also available at extra cost but is not essential. This process of hitting ball against bat is called *knocking-in* and is essential, otherwise the bat cracks or shatters when you finally put it to use in a match. To protect your valuable investment, follow the recommended stages of preparation, issued by manufacturers.

  - **Stage one:** The *knocking-in* process for a cricket bat needs to be undertaken carefully, using a special mallet or an old, quality cricket ball. The bat is repeatedly struck across and down the front of the blade, gradually increasing force over a period of time. This conditioning must be performed with patience. Particular attention is given to hardening the edges, by deflecting the mallet or ball across them, not at right angles, to minimise damage from an edged shot. The toe area of the bat needs to be struck carefully to prevent causing cracks or splits across the base of the bat if struck too hard. This stage is important and takes approximately eight to ten full hours. (This is an ultra-cautious approach, with four to six hours often sufficient, but most good bats are sold with instructions for care, which give the appropriate knocking-in time for that particular bat.)

- **Stage two:** The next step is to use the bat to prepare it for match conditions. Throw-downs in the nets (someone throwing the ball from about half-pitch distance) to practise playing *straight bat* shots (see Chapter 12 for more on batting practice) or hitting short catches with an old, quality cricket ball is advisable. However, if the seam of the ball marks the blade or small surface cracks and indentations are visible, you need to return to 'stage one' for further conditioning for another two hours. Marks or small cracks are not a sign of a faulty bat but a good indication the bat requires further attention at the knocking-in stages.

After these steps have been taken, the bat is used against older balls in the nets at training before being used against newer, harder balls in matches.

Sometimes bats are sold as *ready to use*. This means that a machine has been used to knock the bat in and that a plastic protective film has been applied to the face and edges of the bat. However, these bats still need knocking-in, although often not for as long.

A bat can be for life — not just one summer — if you maintain it properly. Before the start of each cricket season, you give the bat a light sand before applying a healthy coat of linseed oil. Over time, you discover the blade of the bat darkening, turning a similar colour to the linseed oil.

Defining a cricket bat

Administrators have become increasingly concerned in recent years about the bat's growing domination over the ball, in part because of manufacturing techniques. So much so that in 2006 the International Cricket Council (ICC), the game's governing body, banned a bat used by Australian captain Ricky Ponting and other leading players.

The law relating to bats permits a thin covering to protect it — only 1.56 millimetres. Ponting's bat manufacturer covered the entire back of the bat with a thin layer of graphite and used this for large, colourful logos that, normally, would be allowed. However, cricket authorities ruled that the graphite covering was not protective but performance enhancing and banned it.

An ICC committee made up of leading former players has been investigating bat development. Concerns include the covering of bats, such as the one banned by the ICC, and a process known as *corking*. In this process, parts of a bat are hollowed out and replaced by cork so the bat can be made thicker without being heavier. This allows more wood to be concentrated in the middle of the bat where the ball strikes it most. This combination allows batsmen to hit the ball further if their timing is good.

Cricket bats used by elite players are more powerful than they once were because manufacturers no longer press the bat so firmly. As a result, bats of the same weight are less dense than they were in the past and, therefore, thicker than they were, even a decade ago. The modern bat offers more *spring*, allowing the ball to be hit further. Bats which aren't firmly pressed don't last very long. However, the world's leading players have an endless supply from their manufacturers, so longevity isn't a concern for them.

Taking a peek at the cricket ball

The cricket ball is the key to the game. The seam that runs around its circumference can make it bounce away from or towards the batsman once the ball hits the pitch. The seam can also make the ball deviate in the air, towards or away from the batsman. (See Chapter 8 for the low-down on how to make the seam your friend.)

A cricket ball is made of cork and latex, which are bound tightly in string and covered by leather held together by stitching. The stitching is called the *seam*. A cricket ball weighs between 155.9 grams and 163 grams and the circumference measures between 22.4 centimetres and 22.9 centimetres. A woman's cricket ball is slightly smaller and lighter, weighs between 140 grams and 151 grams and measures 21 centimetres to 22.5 centimetres in circumference.

In Test and first-class cricket matches, a red cricket ball is used. In one-day limited-overs matches, at international and state level, a white cricket ball is used. The white colour means a batsman can more easily see the ball at night under lights. Almost all one-day internationals in Australia are day–night matches. In club cricket, red cricket balls are used.

Getting the Right Protection

Always wear a cap or a hat and use plenty of sunscreen, even when the sky is cloudy. Without sunscreen, you're not only risking the discomfort of becoming sunburnt, you're potentially putting your long-term health at risk. Cricketers are prime candidates for skin cancers. Broad-brimmed hats are better than caps for protection and cost as little as $8, a very sound investment. Your local club will usually supply you with a club cap, at a price.

Being hit by a cricket ball is no laughing matter. Cricket may not be as dangerous as motor sport, horse riding or football, but nevertheless some people sustain serious injuries playing cricket each year.

Fortunately, protection aplenty is available. In fact, name a part of the body and you can bet that someone has invented some form of padding to keep it nice and safe.

Starting from the top, the main types of personal protection are:

- Helmets
- Batting gloves and arm guards
- Box and thigh pads
- Batting and wicketkeeping pads
- Wicketkeeping gloves.

Each type of protection is discussed in the following sections.

Using your head: Wearing a helmet

Wearing a cricket helmet when batting or standing in the field close to the batsman — refer to Chapter 2 for a diagram of fielding positions — can be a real life saver.

Batsmen started wearing helmets back in the 1970s. At first, helmets were rudimentary affairs similar to motorcycle crash helmets. Designs have improved over time. The modern generation of helmets are lightweight and offer batsmen a good field of vision.

All batsmen need to wear a helmet no matter what grade of cricket they play. The risks are too great to ignore. If Ricky Ponting and Adam Gilchrist, the best batsmen in the world, believe wearing a helmet is a good idea, then everyone else would be wise to follow their example. Wearing helmets in junior competitions is compulsory for batsmen and wicketkeepers.

Helmets can cost up to $100 in Australia, although a number of very good brands are available in the $40 to $60 range — these helmets are perfectly adequate for club cricketers.

Most manufacturers recommend that a helmet be replaced after it receives a heavy blow because it may not be as protective as before it was damaged. International and state cricketers certainly heed that advice.

Sometimes cricket sides, when in the field, have a spare helmet ready in case a fielder is told by the captain to stand close to the batsman in the hope of taking a catch. When not in use, this helmet is usually placed directly behind where the wicketkeeper stands. If the ball hits the helmet, while it is lying in the outfield, five runs are automatically credited to the batting side's score.

Protecting your hands and arms

A batsman's fingers are vulnerable to injury if jammed against the bat handle by the cricket ball, particularly when the ball is delivered by a fast bowler. Therefore, all players, when their turn comes to bat, wear batting gloves.

The palm of a batting glove is made of leather, which ensures easy gripping of the bat handle. The outer side of the batting glove is encased in padding to cushion any blow received from the cricket ball.

For some players just wearing gloves isn't enough. They choose to strap on an armguard, which is a little like a shin pad but covers the forearm. Armguards are rarely used in club cricket but at international level, where the bowling is faster and the ball impacts harder, some batsmen wear them regularly.

Expect to pay from about $35 to more than $100 for batting gloves and around $15 for an armguard. Again, with batting gloves, you get what you pay for and a good set of gloves is important, but plenty of quality products that are suitable for club cricketers are available well below top-of-the-range prices.

Looking after your body

The one piece of protective equipment designed only for men is the protector, or *box*. Whatever jokes are made about watery eyes and high-pitched voices, being hit in the genitals by a cricket ball is no laughing matter. The box is a vital piece of equipment that must be worn by any man or boy while batting or wicketkeeping.

The box is a triangular-shaped hardened plastic bowl-like object surrounded by a rim of softer lining. The protector is best placed between two pairs of firmly fitting underpants. An attempt to wear a protector with your Blinky Bill boxer shorts or other forms of loose-fitting underwear will see it disappear down your trouser leg. Never leave the pavilion to bat without a box. Wicketkeepers also wear a box and fieldsmen stationed in close catching positions also need to wear one. This vital piece of equipment is also cheap in cricketing terms, costing about $5.

Guarding your legs from injury

Another popular form of protection used by batsmen is the *thigh pad*. This covers the area above the *pads* — the leg guards that batsmen wear — and continues up to the waist. A thigh pad is worn on one leg only, the front leg of the batsman, the leg closest to the bowler. Therefore, a right-handed batsman would wear a thigh pad on the left leg; the reverse applies to lefties. Thigh pads cost anywhere from $15 to $50 and are well worth the investment.

Every player going out to bat wears batting pads on each leg. These pads are meant to cushion the impact of the cricket ball and prevent bruising. In bygone times, batting pads were made of cane strips surrounded by padding and encased in canvas. These days, though, pads are made of ultra-modern materials, such as high-density foam and secured with Velcro straps. The idea is that modern batting pads need to be light, allowing the batsman to move freely.

Expect to pay anywhere between $60 and $200 for a pair of batting pads. Again, a price somewhere in the middle of that range will equip the club cricketer with a quality pair of pads.

Chest guards are also a protective option but are usually only used by state and international cricketers against very fast bowling.

Kitting out a wicketkeeper

Wicketkeepers also wear gloves and pads when their team is in the field, but this equipment is very different to that used for batting. Wicketkeeping gloves are thicker and bigger than batting gloves. Wicketkeeping gloves have a dual purpose; they are designed to protect the hands and also make it easier for wicketkeepers to catch the cricket ball. Expect to pay from $40 to $140 for a pair of wicketkeeping gloves.

Along with these large gloves, wicketkeepers also wear a second set of smaller cloth gloves called *inners* to help with comfort and protection. They cost around $20 to $25.

Wicketkeepers' leg guards are unlike batting pads, which go well above the knee. The pads sported by wicketkeepers reach only to around knee height. Wicketkeepers' leg guards cost from $40 to $120. See Chapter 10 for more on wicketkeeping.

Looking at Cricket Clothing

When playing in matches, cricketers traditionally wear white clothing called — you guessed it — *whites*. The idea of diving around a field in white clothing appears at first to be a bit odd. Fields are covered in grass and can sometimes be muddy and dirty so a nice bright set of cricket whites can soon look very dishevelled. Whites are worn for a reason: To help create a white background so batsmen, fieldsmen and wicketkeepers are more easily able to spot the red cricket ball. White is also cooler in summer.

Dressing to thrill

If you play cricket, you need to buy whites — trousers, shirt and sweater or jumper. A long and short-sleeved jumper is a good idea, particularly if you're a bowler and want to keep your back warm, even if the day is not all that cold. On cold days, in the southern states in particular, players often wear both jumpers, and bowlers bowl in the sleeveless pullover. Make sure your jumpers have plenty of length so your lower back is well covered. Short-sleeved sweaters cost approximately $45 to $55 and long-sleeved sweaters are closer to $65. Shopping around to see what's available at major sports stores can often turn up a bargain.

Shirts and trousers tend to be made of a cotton and polyester mix and are machine washable, which is essential considering all the diving around you do playing the game. A good stain remover and a bit of a hand scrub is recommended for stubborn grass stains. Cricket shirts generally range from $30 to $40 and trousers from $20 to $40. Again, shop around.

International and state cricketers dress in coloured clothing for one-day limited-overs matches. Refer to Chapter 3 for more on these type of matches.

Taking care of your feet

Having good footwear is crucial to batting, bowling and fielding. Wear slippery or inappropriate footwear and you can come a cropper, potentially injuring yourself. Bowlers, and particularly fast bowlers, need strong, comfortable, well-fitting boots to support the constant heavy landing of the feet every time the ball is delivered. (See Chapter 7 and Chapter 8 for more on bowling.)

The standard of the competition you are playing dictates what type of boots you require. Many local club competitions have artificial pitches with a concrete base and some type of synthetic covering. These pitches require rubber-soled shoes.

However, if you're playing on a traditional turf pitch, which is hard, rolled earth (refer to Chapter 2 for more on cricket pitches), you need thin metal spikes in your boots for extra grip. If you're mainly a batsman, then a slighter style of cricket shoe with not many spikes is fine for batting and fielding. However, if you're a bowler, particularly a fast bowler, you need all the support you can get from your footwear.

Spiked boots range in price from $60 to $160 and rubber-soled shoes from $40 to $90.

Some fast bowlers like to cut out the area of the boot directly above where the big toe of their front foot (left foot for a right hander) goes. This modification prevents the big toe banging against the end of the boot when the bowler delivers the ball. Don't go chopping away at your boot unless you really need to!

Some fast bowlers at international and state level have been so particular that they have had their boots handmade. This detail is not necessary for club cricketers.

Choosing a kit bag

Having decided on all the appropriate gear, you now need something in which to carry it around — you need a kit bag. The more equipment you have, the bigger the bag you need.

The choice of kit bags to lug all this stuff around in is huge. You can pay anything from $40 to nearly $100 for a bag. Here are some of the options:

- **A duffel bag with shoulder straps:** Duffel bags are very easy to carry but they are the smallest of all the kit bags, which means you can only transport the bare necessities. These cost about $40.
- **Standard over-the-shoulder kit bag:** These bags are bigger than duffel bags and you can transport large amounts of equipment in them. Some of these bags come with separate pockets for boots. Prices vary from $45 to $70.
- **Kit bags with wheels:** Wheeled bags are well worth the investment if you want to save your back for batting and bowling. These bags include a standard kit bag but with the added luxury of two wheels at one end, and a strong handle at the other so they can be wheeled instead of carried. Prices range from approximately $80 to $100.

Stumps and bails are supplied by the cricket club or the venue at which the game is being played.

Shopping for cricket gear

You don't have to go far to find a sports store selling cricket gear. Indeed, if you want to do your research on what's available and the prices you can expect to pay, you can check out all those details before leaving home! A Google Australia search of 'cricket equipment' brings up numerous online options for all sorts of cricket gear on sale.

However, unless you're an experienced cricketer who knows exactly what you want, right down to the size and type, you're better to always try on the gear and try out the equipment. Having your gear feel comfortable to wear and use is essential to your peace of mind if you want to be a successful cricketer.

If you can, visit a large sports store with a wide range of cricket gear, rather than a sports store that sells a bit of everything. You want plenty of choice and good advice. Don't be afraid to ask an in-store specialist for help and, if you're not satisfied, try somewhere else. Buying cricket gear is a significant investment so you want to be sure you're making the right choices.

Here are some of the major cricket equipment brands available in Australia and how to find their retail outlets:

- **Puma:** `www.pumacricket.com/retailers.jsp?country=Australia`
- **Kookaburra:** `www.kookaburra.biz/stockists_aus.php`
- **Gray-Nicolls:** `www.gray-nicolls.com.au/graynicolls/index.htm`
- **Slazenger:** `www.slazenger.com.au/contact-us/default.asp`.

Part II
Playing the Game

Glenn Lumsden

'I take it their opening bowler's pretty quick then...'

In this part . . .

Now here's the nitty-gritty of how to play cricket. In this part, you can discover the batting skills with tips from the experts, have a go at bowling and try your talents on the field for a lesson on catching out the opposition.

Wicketkeepers: Are they the forgotten heroes? Australia has produced some of the world's best and you can meet them here.

This part also looks at the special skills needed to captain a cricket side and explains how you can improve your game in leaps and bounds with regular training.

Chapter 5

Perfecting Your Batting Skills

In This Chapter

- Understanding batting
- Going into battle
- Examining the scoring shots
- Batting aggressively
- Knowing how to play straight

Batting looks so easy on television! Especially when one of Australia's batting superstars sends another of the bowler's deliveries careering over the boundary rope.

Although you may never end up on television or in front of big crowds, the thrill that comes from batting is exactly the same whether you're a national hero or merely playing down at the local park with your mates. Batting is all about understanding the basics — and then performing them well to ensure plenty of runs and plenty of fun.

Batting is akin to a battle, albeit on the comfortable surrounds of a cricket ground. Bowlers and fielders are the enemy and they share a single-minded intention — to get you out and see you gone. Your weapons in this war are your talent, determination, powers of concentration and your team mates. Use all these and you can put the bowling to the sword and pile on those precious runs.

This chapter is for all those Australians who harbour a secret dream to hit a ball like Australian captain Ricky Ponting or vice-captain Adam Gilchrist. Armed with the information you get here, you're going to be just itching to grab your bat and take on any bowler who dares to come your way.

As a bonus, in this chapter, Adam Gilchrist — Australia's brilliant wicketkeeper–batsman — offers advice to help you become the best batsman you could hope to be. Gilchrist scores runs faster than any other batsman on the planet. And he's not just a fast scorer with a bat; Gilchrist is fit too — thanks in part to some extraordinary weights sessions devised for him, as a youngster, by his father (see sidebar, 'Fore-armed is fore-Warne'd').

Look for the icon *Adam Says* as you read on, and take careful note of Adam's batting advice. You never know! One day you could be the batsman out there thrilling the crowds — Adam Gilchrist style (see Figure 5-1).

Put simply, the objective of batting is to score as many runs as possible before losing your wicket, otherwise called *being dismissed* — which sounds a bit like being dismissed from class and ordered to report to the principal's office.

Figure 5-1: Australian wicketkeeper Adam Gilchrist celebrates another century.

Batting to Win

Being a successful batsman isn't just about owning the right equipment, displaying the latest brand of bat and knowing how much zinc cream to spread on your face.

Being a successful batsman is about having all (or, at least, most) of the following:

- **Natural talent:** All the best players — those who play for their state and country — have keen hand–eye coordination. Even if you don't have an abundance of natural talent in this area — and few of us have — you can work on this. One way to practise your hand–eye coordination is to hold a cricket bat in the horizontal position and bounce a cricket ball on the blade as many times as you can. After you become good at this, rotate the bat 90 degrees and see how many times you can bounce the ball on the edge. That takes great skill!
- **Excellent judgement:** Batting is all about making split-second decisions — what shot to play (or not to play), when to run between wickets, when you should look to be defensive or take the attack to the opposition.
- **Concentration:** If you want to be a good batsman, you have to concentrate intensely on each delivery. If you don't focus, you may find yourself being dismissed.
- **Physical fitness:** You don't have to be fit to play cricket but it helps. Being fit improves your concentration, your ability to move quickly to play attacking shots and your ability to run between the stumps to boost the score.

The most crucial aspect of batting is that it takes only one mistake to end your innings with dismissal. As a batsman, you can develop a persecution complex because nearly everyone else on the field is trying to get you out. The bowler is trying to knock over your stumps or trap you *leg before wicket* (LBW), the fielders are looking to take a catch, or run you out, the wicket-keeper wants to stump you and the umpires are poised to adjudge whether you're going to take the long, lonely walk back to the pavilion.

Whistling down a coal mine

During cricket's earliest days in England — and we're talking way back to the 19th and early 20th centuries — batsmen were usually gentlemen, whereas bowlers were characterised as working class. In cricket circles, it used to be said that you could whistle down a coal mine in Yorkshire and a fast bowler would emerge (although he'd need a pretty good wash before putting on his cricket whites). On the batting side, county and national sides were chock full of batsmen with double-barrelled names and titles. Bowlers would no doubt claim that a bit of this class divide still exists in olde England today.

In this regard, batsmen often claim that bowlers have it easy; bowlers bowl a bad ball, which gets hit for four runs, and as soon as they retrieve the ball they bowl another delivery with which they have the chance to grab a wicket.

But batting does have its upside. Batsmen enjoy most of the glory and the adulation. When batsmen strut their stuff on the field of play, the eyes of the crowd, their team mates and their opponents are on them. Batsmen who execute scoring shots with particular panache are often described as the entertainers — the artists of the cricket world with their cavalier approach. However, being a batsman is nowhere near as physically tough as being a fast bowler, especially on long, hot summer days.

Preparing to Do Battle

Successful batting is as much about preparation as perspiration. Rocking up to the ground, bat in hand, relying purely on talent may find you out in no time.

Put in effort outside of playing hours and you can reap the rewards out in the middle, when the action is taking place between batsman and bowler. (See Chapter 12 for more on smart training.)

Remembering practice makes perfect

All it takes is one mistake for the batsman to find him or herself dismissed. This tightrope walker-like existence is why regular practice is crucial for a batsman. The best way to practise is in the *nets*. The *nets* are fenced-off areas, either indoors or on a specially prepared outdoor pitch, where bowlers try to hone the skills of bowling, perfecting their wicket-taking deliveries. Batsmen use the nets to practise defending their stumps from being hit, and to execute shots which, if replicated in a game situation, could yield them runs — hopefully, lots of runs! These practice areas are called *nets* simply because the practice spaces are usually fenced in by netting. (See Chapter 12 for more on nets.)

Most good coaches say that you play as you train. Working hard in the nets ensures you are improving the fundamental skills to maximise your enjoyment of the game. Although fitting training into a busy life can be difficult, trying to get to practice twice a week leading into and during the season is very important. Summer holidays are an ideal time for anyone at school to get down to their local nets and have a bat and a bowl. Don't waste your time mucking around, and don't stay so long that you start to feel stale. Batting and bowling at an improving standard in the nets is fun and gives you plenty of confidence for your next match.

Batting is all about timing, rather than power. For more than a century, most of the world's best batsmen have been small in stature. Just look at Australia's Ricky Ponting, the West Indies' Brian Lara and India's Sachin Tendulkar. They are great players, not because of brute strength, but because they move quickly into the correct position to play their strokes, and then execute them correctly.

Don't make the mistake of trying to hit the ball too hard. If you follow these instructions, you should begin to experience that wonderfully sweet exhilaration as the ball springs off the middle of your bat.

Exercising for successful batting

People sometimes scoff when told that being a batsman requires physical fitness. Think about this advice! The object of batting is to score runs and, in order to score sufficient runs to help your team win, you may have to bat for several hours, sometimes in high temperatures.

Unfit batsmen tire more easily. In turn, fatigue causes them to be more prone to making a mistake, which can lead to their dismissal.

Before the start of play, and before walking out to bat, spend a minute or two doing some stretching exercises. Stretching can stop you pulling a muscle while batting. (See Chapter 12 for more on stretching prior to play.)

Fore-armed is fore-Warne'd

(***Note:*** Wicketkeeper Adam Gilchrist has claimed 35 stumpings during his amazing Test career up to the 2006–07 Ashes series — most of them from the bowling of the game's greatest spinner, Shane Warne. But when Adam lets loose with his brutal batting, that's when his physical strength is most obvious.)

People sometimes ask me about the power in my batting. The secret comes from my father who always encouraged me to strengthen my forearms. This strengthening not only helped with power in my batting, but aided timing the ball. To strengthen my forearms, I'd get an old container, such as an oil tin or milk container, put some water in it, tie a thin rope to it and wind the rope around an old broom handle. Holding my arms out straight at shoulder height, I'd wind the handle in my hands, which lifted the container up and down. Starting with a little water in the container, I gradually added more water as I became stronger. I'm not a great fan of the gym, but this tin-and-broom exercise is a basic weights drill.

Looking at Playing Shots

Nothing is better during a day at the cricket than watching Australia's batting stars in full flight, smashing the bowling to all parts of the ground. Hitting the ball well starts with holding the bat correctly and standing properly as you wait for the bowler to deliver the ball.

Being sure of yourself: The grip

Batting is taken step by step and the first step is simply picking up the bat. Although seeming very basic, picking up the bat correctly gives you the grip you need to begin your life as a successful batsman (see Figure 5-2).

First, you have to find out whether you're a right-handed or a left-handed batsman. You hold a bat with both hands. If you're a right hander (which most players are), your left hand is your 'top' hand, the hand nearest to the top of the handle. This means that when you stand in the side-on position, which all batsmen use, your left shoulder is facing the bowler. Your right hand is your 'bottom' hand because that hand is closest to the bottom of the bat handle. The right side of your body is facing the stumps and the wicketkeeper. Left handers take the opposite position.

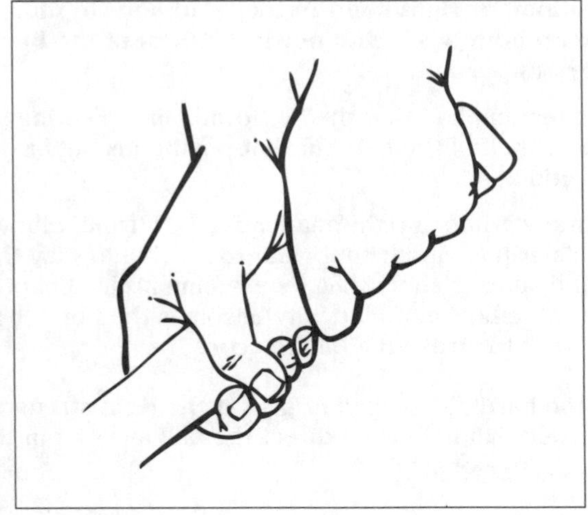

Figure 5-2: Gripping the bat correctly (the right-handed grip).

Here's how you hold the bat like the superstars:

1. **Lay the bat down in front of you on the ground or floor with the handle pointing towards you and the flat side of the bat face down.**
2. **Put your arms out in front of you and spread your thumb and index finger on each hand so that a natural 'v' forms between them.**
3. **Bend down and pick up the bat, grabbing the middle of the handle with both 'v's pointing down the back of the bat.**

   If you're a right hander, your right hand should fit comfortably into the 'v' of your left hand, and your fingers should wrap around the front of the bat handle. If you're a left hander, the opposite will apply.
4. **Stand with your feet comfortably apart, say about the width of your shoulders (around 15 centimetres or six inches is common) and bend your knees slightly so that you can gently and comfortably rest the bat behind the toes on your right foot (if you're a right hander).**

   Rest the bat behind the toes on the left foot if you're a left hander.

   This position is called your batting stance, and is examined in more detail a little later.

The natural inclination, when standing in this initially unfamiliar position, is to let your 'top' or left hand (if you're a right hander) turn anti-clockwise away from you. You must resist this!

5. **Keep your 'bottom' or right hand in the 'v' of your top hand and continue to keep both 'v's facing down the back of the bat. This position is very important.**

   Some coaches recommend that the 'v's form a line pointing fractionally towards the front half of the bat, but that position is only a very minor change of direction.

   This grip naturally points a right hander's left or 'front' elbow towards the bowler. This grip is vitally important to be able to play the majority of defensive and scoring shots that we examine in this chapter. In most cases, your 'front' elbow automatically becomes the pointer and guide to where you want to stroke the ball to score runs.

Don't grip the bat too hard! Keeping your grip at the right strength aids flexibility because your grip helps you direct the ball away from the fielders as you develop your range of strokes.

Make sure that you always hold the bat in the middle of the handle with your hands comfortably together and, as previously discussed, keep the 'v' — created by the thumb and index finger on each hand — pointing down the back of the bat. Some very experienced players may vary their grip a little by moving it up or down the handle, or by leaving a small gap between the hands. However, holding the bat too low, or *choking* the bat, as this position is known, makes playing 'straight' and driving 'properly' difficult. Likewise, holding the bat too high makes it difficult to control the strokes.

Facing up to the bowler: The stance

The batsman's stance tells you instantly whether the batsman is a left or right hander. Quite simply, a right hander faces the bowler with their legs to the right of the bat as viewed by the bowler, and vice versa for a left hander (see Figure 5-3).

The stance is all about maintaining good balance. If your stance is relaxed and comfortable, you can — in theory — easily stay in the middle and bat for hours, scoring runs. At least, that's your aim!

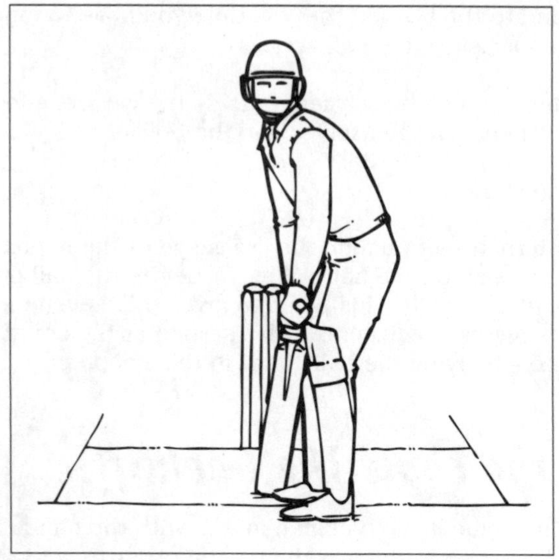

Figure 5-3: A right-hander's legs are right of the bat.

The idea is that the batsman's body and hands are in the best possible position to execute a shot, once the ball is delivered. The best batsmen like to have their weight evenly distributed in the stance. Do not lean forward or back.

Keeping the head still is also considered a key in the stance because this allows both eyes to point directly down the pitch at the bowler — allowing the optimum field of vision. Don't tilt your head! Make sure your eyes are level!

The batsman also has to consider where to stand in relation to the stumps. The umpire will help the batsman align him or herself with the line of the stumps. But the batsman has to decide how close to the stumps to stand. If a batsman stands close to the stumps, that batsman risks stepping on the stumps when attempting to play a back foot shot, such as a pull or cut.

The default position for most batsmen is to place their feet either side of the line of the crease. This position gives the batsman plenty of room to play back foot shots, if needed.

The closer you stand to the bowler, the less time you have to move into position to play a shot before the ball arrives.

Some good batsmen stand with their feet outside the crease, effectively cutting the distance between themselves and the bowler.

Why do batsmen do this?

Often, standing with their feet outside the crease gives the batsman a better chance of meeting the ball on the half volley, or before the ball pitches — called *hitting the ball on the full.* This position gives them even more opportunity to play aggressive front foot shots, such as the cover or straight drive (see the section, 'Driving the ball', later in this chapter).

Executing the shot: The backlift

The backlift is the movement the batsman makes with the hands lifting the bat and preparing to propel it towards the ball. In order to get power and timing into the shot, the batsman lifts the bat behind their back and brings it down in a pendulum motion to meet the ball when it reaches him or her.

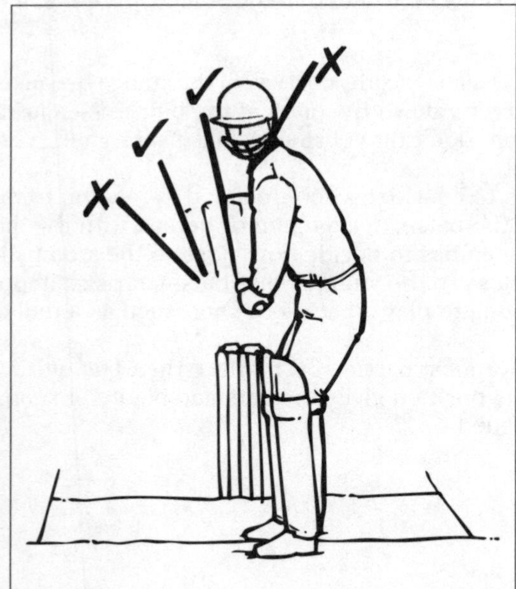

Figure 5-4: The backlift brings power and timing to a shot.

Always take the bat virtually straight back towards the wicketkeeper. At the top of the backlift, you want the end or *toe* of the bat a little above the horizontal line running through your wrists. The bat points somewhere between the keeper and second slip. If the direction the bat is pointing is any wider, say towards gully, or too far behind your body and pointing towards fine leg, bringing the bat down straight is much harder (see Figure 5-4). (Refer to Chapter 2 for the diagram of fielding positions.)

Some shots require a higher backlift than others to execute. As a general rule, the more aggressive a shot is, the higher and faster the backlift — because the batsman is trying to generate extra power. Usually, defensive shots only involve a short backlift, which has the advantage of executing the shots with great speed.

In a match or at practice, always start off with a short backlift to make the bat easier to control, particularly for defensive shots. As you spend time in the middle, building an innings and becoming more confident, the backlift may increase as you become more aggressive and the range of shots increases.

Cricketers talk about a batsman *timing a cricket ball*. This phrase doesn't mean the batsman stands on the pitch, using a stopwatch to measure how quickly the ball travels. A well-timed cricket shot is one where the bat makes contact with the ball when the bat is moving at its fastest, and the ball strikes the face of the bat around the middle. When you time a cricket shot well, the ball often races away towards the boundary at a very fast pace. All batsmen like to have good timing.

In order to score runs, or stop the ball hitting the stumps, the batsman plays a *shot*, also called a *stroke*.

You have a number of different shots available to tackle the bowling, broken into two clear types:

- **Aggressive shots:** The aim of an aggressive shot is always to score runs, but be warned, such a shot can mean risking dismissal.
- **Defensive shots:** The main aim of the defensive shot is to prevent dismissal. However, defensive shots don't always prevent dismissal. If runs are scored from a defensive shot, that's a bonus!

Building a foundation: The defensive shot

Even the greatest, most entertaining batsmen build their batting around a good defence. You must always treat the bowling with respect because one silly shot — and you're out!

A batsman's job is to make runs. The batsman must always look for scoring opportunities. However, on most occasions, particularly early in an innings, many of the strokes are defensive.

Consider playing a defensive shot when:

- A ball is headed towards your stumps. If you don't make contact with the ball, you're going to be bowled.
- You only recently started your innings — often referred to as arriving at the crease — and you're getting used to the bowlers and the extent of the bounce of the cricket ball off the pitch.

If you want to be good at batting, you must master defensive shots because defensive shots can get you out of trouble many, many times.

Defensive shots are broken down into two different types:

- Front foot defence
- Back foot defence.

Playing a front foot defensive shot

The idea of a front foot defensive shot is to get forward and smother the ball. The batsman moves their weight onto the front foot and takes a stride down the pitch towards the ball. The bat is then pushed beside the pad, with the face of the bat angled downwards towards the ground. Executed well, a front foot defensive shot stops the ball in its tracks, sending the ball from the bat into the ground directly in front of the batsman — leaving no chance of a fielder standing close to the bat taking a catch (see Figure 5-5).

Front foot defensive shots are played to deliveries landing on a good or full length, which means they *pitch* or land close to the batsman. The idea is to get the front foot (left foot to a right hander) as close to the line of the ball as possible so that the bat and front pad are together forming a wall to stop the ball from getting through to hit the stumps.

Make sure that your stride forward is comfortable so you don't overstretch or drag your back foot out of your crease, otherwise the wicketkeeper can stump you if you miss the ball. When you stretch forward, make sure your head is over the ball at the point of contact. Some coaches even suggest that you get so low over the defensive shot that you are *sniffing* the ball, but don't take this too literally. Batsmen don't get excited about the smell of a cricket ball; it's the sweet sound when it springs off the bat that matters!

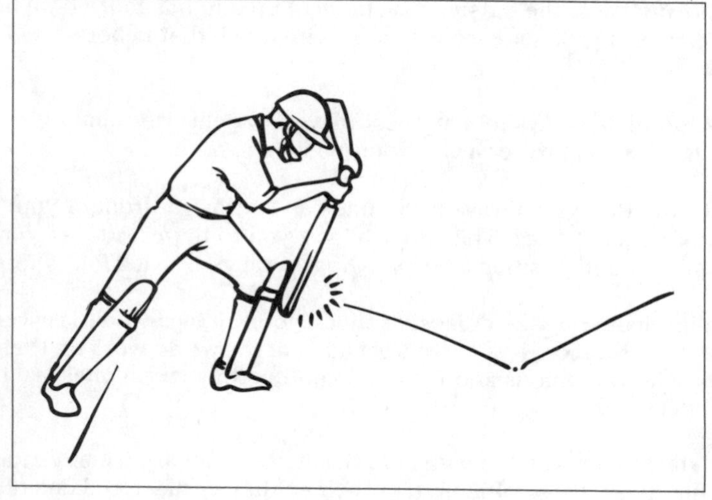

Figure 5-5: A well-executed front foot defensive shot can stop the ball being caught.

Playing a back foot defensive shot

Again, the idea is to smother the ball. However, this time, the batsman transfers his or her weight onto the back foot, moving back and across towards off stump (see Figure 5-6). Don't move too far back or you may be out *hit-wicket* by standing on your stumps (see Figure 5-6).

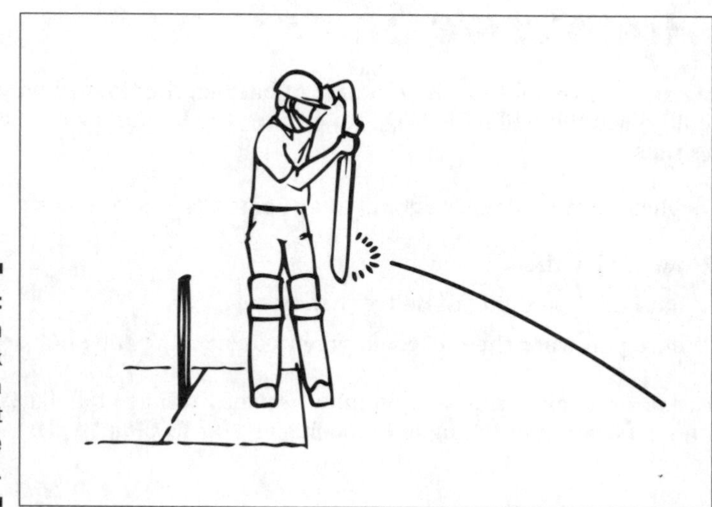

Figure 5-6: The batsman on the back foot for a back foot defensive shot.

By moving back, the batsman is standing up and has more time before the ball arrives, making it easier to cope with a ball that is bouncing high off the pitch.

Back foot defensive shots are best played to deliveries landing short of a length, which is further away from the batsman.

Make sure that you always move back and across in front of your off stump, not just straight back. This move allows you to better protect your stumps and puts you in position to play a greater range of back foot shots.

Without mastering the defensive shots, your innings won't last very long. Even the best, most aggressive, batsmen in the world work on their defensive shots. The champions know that all good batting techniques are built on a solid defence.

Kids starting to play the game of cricket seriously are usually taught how to execute defensive strokes first; only when they've mastered defensive strokes are the kids shown the ins and outs of more complex aggressive shots. You can use defensive shots whenever you decide that a scoring shot cannot be executed easily or safely.

You can score runs from defensive shots, as long as you steer the ball away from a fielder and are prepared to run between the wickets at pace. In cricketing circles, this tactic is called *taking a quick single*.

Playing Aggressive Shots

Playing aggressive shots is the fun part of batting, the time when you get to (hopefully) see the ball rocketing into or over the boundary rope as you pile on the runs.

Here's what to know if you're going to attempt aggressive shots:

- How to play them
- What length and line of delivery they suit
- Where you want the ball to go when you execute the shot properly.

In order to appreciate this section fully, you may want to familiarise yourself with the illustration outlining field placings (refer to Chapter 2).

Driving the ball

Driving is the most common scoring stroke played in cricket and is simply an extension of a defensive shot. You can play a drive off the front or back foot but most are played off the front foot when the bowler over-pitches (see Figure 5-7). Over-pitching means that the ball arrives on the full, not far off the ground, or that the ball is a half volley, which bounces just in front of you.

You can hit drives anywhere in an arc from *mid on* (on-drive) to *point* (square drive) depending on which stump the bowler aims the ball at or how far outside off stump the ball is. For example, you usually hit a ball coming in the direction of leg to middle stump with an on-drive to the onside of the bowler — just to the left of the bowler if the batsman is right-handed. A ball wide outside off stump is square driven through point, which means the ball travels at 90 degrees to the pitch through the *off side,* to the right side of the bowler if the batsman is right-handed. The principle is exactly the same as the defensive shot discussed in the section, 'Building a foundation: The defensive shot', earlier in the chapter, except that instead of angling the bat down to stop the ball, the batsman follows through with the shot.

Figure: 5-7: Top row: Left-handed batsman driving. Bottom row: Right-handed batsman driving.

Practise your driving by taking an exaggerated movement forwards. Take a big step, making sure your head is well over the ball. You rarely see a perfectly executed drive because cricket is such a reactive game. Practising this way allows you to adjust more easily to the length of the ball in a match. Continuous repetition at training programs your mind to play the shot correctly without thinking consciously about it.

Two common types of drives are cover drives and straight drives.

Cover drive

A *cover drive* is one of the most glorious shots in cricket. Here's everything you want to know about cover drives:

- **What type of delivery?** Usually played off the front foot to a full-length delivery, pitching outside the off stump. A back foot variant, which is played to short of a length bowling — when the ball pitches further away from the batsman and bounces higher — also exists.
- **How to do it?** Move the front foot to where the ball pitches and bring the bat down straight. Always keep your head over the ball because this position helps you to keep the shot 'down', which means along the ground. Back foot cover drives work on the same principle, except that the batsman's weight is on the back foot as the ball arrives. Always move back AND across when playing back.
- **In which direction does the ball travel?** Goes through — guess where? Yes, the cover region, which is located between the fielders at point and mid off. When executed well, the cover drive is widely recognised as one of the most artistic of cricket shots.

Straight drive

Few shots in cricket are more dominant than hitting the ball straight back past the bowler. Here's what you need to know about straight drives:

- **What type of delivery?** The ball is bowled at off or middle stump, usually on a full length. That is when the delivery is a full toss, a delivery that has not bounced but in this case is low to the ground, or a half volley when the ball has bounced just in front of the batsman and is yet to bounce very high. A half volley or low full toss are the easiest balls to drive.
- **How to do it?** Basically the same as a cover drive. Move the front foot (left foot for a right hander) forwards towards the ball, and bring the bat down straight. Always keep your head over the ball because this position helps you keep the shot down.
- **In which direction does the ball travel?** Straight down the ground between mid off and the bowler. You play a leg side variant in the same way, but with the ball bowled at middle to leg stump, which is then directed between the bowler and mid on.

Staying in control

Try not to over-hit the ball. The biggest mistake when the ball is over-pitched is to become so excited that your eyes light up and you want to smash it. Reduce your aggressive intent by about 20 per cent so you have more control of the shot and more chance of timing the ball. You can hit the ball just as well, and the ball travels just as fast to the boundary.

Whether driving off the front or back foot, always make contact below the eyes, which is why coaches tell you to get your head over the ball. By reaching for the ball and playing the shot too early, the batsman risks lofting a catch to one of the fieldsmen or missing the ball all together.

Playing 'Straight'

The most important aspect of batting is to play *straight,* which means that whether defending or driving, your bat is vertical and the full face of the bat meets the ball.

As a batsman, you feel a natural inclination while batting, particularly when you're first starting off in the game, to try to whack the ball with your *bottom* hand (the right hand for right handers). However, the right-hander's left hand, which is the *top* hand, is the hand that sets up the shot, with your bottom hand coming in late for extra power. Left handers: Make that the opposite way!

The best way to practise playing straight is to stand in front of a mirror as though you're about to face the bowler. But don't stand too close! Your well struck boundary may result in a shattered mirror. And check the ceiling above you in case of a dangling fan or light globe, which could become the victim of an exaggerated follow through.

In a normal batting stance, put your *bottom* hand (the right hand for a right hander) behind your back. This position leaves you able to practise all the defensive and driving strokes with your top hand.

Now push forward with your front foot (the left foot for a right hander), as you would to defend or drive, and bring the bat through. The bat is perfectly straight and is like an extension of your elbow and front shoulder. When your elbow and front shoulder line up with the bat, everything is pointing exactly where you want to hit the ball.

Using a mirror allows you to see that you're taking the bat straight back in your backlift, and then you bring it straight down again to defend or drive. You want this move to become second nature so that you instinctively make the move time after time while batting in a game — you need to play most of the deliveries you receive this way.

Every time you push forward in front of the mirror, stepping towards an imaginary delivery, assume the delivery is coming towards you with a slightly different line. Maybe begin your practice move by stepping out to a ball on leg stump, then middle stump, off stump and then little by little further outside off stump to take in the full range of drives. Always push your front foot towards the ball, real or imagined, to prevent any gap between bat and pad so the ball cannot sneak through and bowl you.

Now put your bottom hand back on the bat and do your imaginary drives again, making sure — in the mirror — that it looks the same as your one-handed strokes, with your bat, front elbow and shoulder all facing where you want the ball to go. This position means that the top hand is doing all the work and the bottom hand is not making you *play across the line* of the ball.

Playing across the line is one of the most common ways for a batsman to be bowled. Playing across the line means that the bat face is at least partly turned in and the bat is not moving in a straight line towards the ball, making contact with the ball far harder for the batsman.

The foundation of my batting came from about the ages 12 to 16. For three or four years, I did a lot of fundamental drills, and I loved doing them. I did a lot of drills with my top hand learning to play straight. My dad would lob golf balls at me because they bounced a lot more than cricket balls, and I'd practise with a bat that was cut in half, either pushing well forward or well back, with an exaggerated movement to defend. Dad and I would do that for ages. Sometimes we'd use tennis balls or cricket balls, and Dad would always tell me to finish off by whacking a few. Learning to be aggressive is important.

Mirror, mirror, on the wall, who's the battiest of us all ...

Don't feel self-conscious facing up to a mirror instead of a bowler. Even the very best players consult the looking glass from time to time, just to make sure their batting technique is correct, although video and computer technology are now taking cricket analysis many steps further, especially for international players. David Boon, a fine Australian batsman in the 1980s and early 1990s, awoke one night while on tour overseas with the Australian team to find his room mate and opening batting partner, Geoff Marsh, practising his batting — *sans* clobber — in front of a mirror. Clearly Marsh, who later became the Australian coach, was a very dedicated cricketer.

Taking wrist movements into account

Having supple wrists is a real plus for a batsman, who needs to grip the bat firmly — but not too hard. Turning the wrist on impact helps open or close the face of the bat. Once you're confident with the different strokes, you can work the ball into gaps in the field.

As you develop your shots and start to feel more comfortable in the middle, turning the wrists on impact is a great way to score runs more quickly and easily. However, like anything else, this skill improves with practice.

When you're starting off an innings, always play straight at the ball with the full face of the bat. That way you'll have the bowler wondering just how they are going to get you out.

Leg glance

The leg glance is a batsman's bread-and-butter shot (see Figure 5-8). Play the leg glance well and you can pick up lots of easy runs. Here's how you take advantage of wayward bowling.

- **What type of delivery?** The leg glance is best played to full- or good-length deliveries, pitching on or outside leg stump.
- **How to do it?** The key to the leg glance is to turn the wrists holding the bat towards the leg side when making contact with the ball. Having your head over the ball and your weight moving forward into the shot at the moment of impact is important.
- **In which direction does the ball travel?** The direction depends on how far you allow the ball to come towards you before playing the shot. If you move onto your front foot, playing the ball early, then the ball heads in the direction of square leg. Play the ball later, when it's closer to your stumps, and the ball goes behind the square leg umpire or down to fine leg.

The best players often take a heavy toll of balls delivered towards their legs, whipping them away through the leg side with a strong flick of the bottom hand as they make contact with the ball.

Be careful not to play the shot too early. Playing the shot too early can result in a *closed face*, when the bat is turned away from the ball before it arrives. Players can often be caught off the front or 'leading' edge, which is left facing the ball.

Figure 5-8: *Top row:* The front foot leg glance played by a right-handed batsman. *Bottom row:* The back foot leg glance played by a right-handed batsman.

Horizontal bat shots

Horizontal bat shots are some of the most spectacular and rewarding shots in the game of cricket, but these shots also carry a higher risk of a batsman being dismissed. Exceptions always exist, but for the most part leave horizontal bat shots until you've been batting for a while and feel comfortable in the middle.

Pull and hook shots

Pull and hook shots are a great way to take on fast bowlers who may be trying to intimidate you by bowling short balls that bounce up at the body or head (see Figure 5-9). Played well, the pull and hook shots can allow a batsman to gain the ascendancy over the bowler. Here's how the experts play pull and hook shots:

- **What type of delivery?** The ball is a short-of-a-length or bouncer-length delivery, pitching on the batsman's stumps or just outside.

- **How to do it?** A pull shot is usually played off the back foot to a rising delivery. This is a cross bat shot with the bat moving from off to leg stump, in a swatting type motion. The key is to roll the wrists over the ball on impact. This action plays the shot along the ground, minimising the chances of the ball being caught by a fielder.
- **In which direction does the ball travel?** The direction the ball takes depends on several factors, including the line along which the bowler delivers the ball, and the pace of the bowler. Pull shots played early, when the ball still has some way to go to the stumps, can end up at mid wicket or even slightly in front of mid wicket. Shots played late can end up heading towards the square leg umpire. The wider a ball is pitched outside off stump, and the faster the bowler, the straighter the ball is likely to travel towards mid wicket rather than square leg.

Figure 5-9: *Top row:* A left-handed batsman playing the pull shot. *Bottom row:* A right-handed batsman playing the hook shot.

Although pull shots are often played with the ball in line or even to the off side of a batsman, hook shots are executed by stepping inside the line of the high bouncing ball so it is on your leg side, which is why you need to go back and across when playing back, not just straight back.

Like the pull shot, when playing a hook shot you roll your wrists to keep the ball down. Fast bowlers frequently try to dismiss a batsman by bowling a bouncer in the hope that a hook shot goes sailing down the throat of the fine leg fieldsman for a catch.

If played well, hook shots head between the square leg and fine leg fielding positions.

The cut shot

A cut shot is a punishing stroke that can unsettle a bowler if played well (see Figure 5-10). Note that, as in the pull and hook shots, you roll the wrists to keep the ball on the ground away from catching fieldsmen.

Figure 5-10: Top row: A right-handed batsman playing a cut shot as viewed from the rear. Bottom row: The front view of a right-handed cut shot.

Here's how a cut shot works:

- **What type of delivery?** The cut shot is best played against a short-of-a-length delivery pitching well outside the batsman's off stump.
- **How to do it?** The batsman transfers their weight onto the back foot, moving back and across towards off stump. The bat is then brought in a chopping motion from behind the ears towards the off side. Imagine a woodchopper chopping a tree with an axe and you have the basic set-up of a cut shot. Again, rolling the wrists over the ball on contact to keep the ball down and avoid being caught is a safety-first strategy.
- **What direction does the ball take?** The ball heads either just in front or behind the fielder in the point position on the off side.

The sweep shot

The sweep is a relatively safe shot which can take a heavy toll against slow bowlers when used wisely (see Figure 5-11). Judging the line along which the bowler has delivered the ball is important. Here's more on the sweep shot:

- **What type of delivery?** A sweep shot results from a full-length delivery from a spin bowler that usually pitches on or outside the batsman's leg stump.
- **How to do it?** The batsman moves their front foot forwards to get in line with the spot where the ball is likely to pitch; at the same time the back leg bends towards the ground. This back leg movement helps transfer the weight of the batsman onto the front foot. Head over the ball, the batsman moves their bat in a sweeping motion — hence the name of the shot — from the off to leg side. Again, the batsman looks to roll their wrists over the ball at impact, therefore hitting the ball along the ground.
- **Which direction the ball does take?** Sweeps usually head behind the square leg umpire. This shot can be very productive for scoring.

Figure 5-11: The sweep shot played by a right-handed batsman.

If you play a cross bat shot such as a cut, a hook or a pull, play it with conviction. One theory says that playing cross bat shots adds a greater element of risk because you can lose a bit of control. Be very positive in the execution of these shots because anything half-hearted may get you out.

If the ball hits the batsman's pads — also called leg guards — and the umpire believes that the line of the delivery would have taken the ball on to hit the stumps, then the batsman may be given out leg before wicket (LBW) (refer to Chapter 2 for more on the LBW laws).

Avoiding short-pitched bowling

A common tactic of fast bowlers is to attack the batsman with short-pitched bowling, particularly when a batsman has just begun their innings. Although attacking short bowling with pull and hook shots can look and feel great, doing so is also high risk. Most batsmen simply try to avoid short bowling until they are settled in, and even later in their innings are choosy about which short balls to attack and which to leave. If a ball bounces above head height, the ball is probably too high to hook with control and may result in a catch to fine leg.

You need to know how to avoid short bowling for two important reasons:

- Personal safety
- Preventing dismissal.

You can avoid short bowling in three ways:

- **Stepping inside the line:** Having moved back and across in front of off stump, the ball is heading towards your back or down the leg side. Simply keep moving inside the line of the ball towards the off side (see Figure 5-12).
- **Ducking:** Having moved back and across in front of off stump, and if the ball is on a line that will take it straight at your head or front shoulder, bend at the knees and bend your body well forward so the ball passes over your back. Keep your eye on the ball in case it doesn't bounce as much as you expect. Keep your bat and gloves well down so the ball does not hit them and present a catch (see Figure 5-13).
- **Swaying:** Having moved back and across in front of off stump, the short ball is directed at or outside off stump. Push the hands and bat well down to keep them out of the way and sway the body back towards the leg side. Sometimes batsmen begin to duck a short ball but realise they are ducking into the ball, so they sway away from it (see Figure 5-14). Always keep your eyes on the ball to help you make these split-second judgements.

Figure 5-12: A right-handed batsman stepping inside the line of a short ball.

Figure 5-13: A right-handed batsman ducks under a bouncer.

Figure 5-14: Sometimes a batsman has to sway away from a short ball.

When no shot is the right shot

If anything proves how bizarre a game of cricket is, it's the fact that sometimes playing no shot and letting the ball sail harmlessly past the stumps into the gloves of the waiting keeper is the best decision to make. This 'shot' is called a *leave* and it involves the batsman raising their bat and hands above their shoulder, so as to avoid contact with the ball, and walking across in front of the stumps to protect them just in case the ball deviates back towards them.

Batsmen leave the ball when they feel that to play a scoring shot, such as a drive, holds the definite possibility of a catching chance being offered to the wicketkeeper or slip fielders. In the first few overs of a Test match, opening batsmen often leave as many deliveries as possible. Leaving the ball allows them the time to gauge the pace of the bowling and the bounce and movement of the ball off the pitch.

Strange as it sounds, cricket watchers love a good leave. This strategy shows that the batsman is being selective in the shots that they are making and a leave frustrates the bowler because the bowler has gone to all the effort of delivering the ball, only to see it harmlessly glide into the hands of the wicketkeeper. Batsmen are also keen to leave deliveries at the start of their innings, as they usually prefer to take fewer risks.

However, the leave is not always greeted with approval. In a limited-overs match, the batsmen are expected to get on with the business of scoring runs, while bowlers are trying to take wickets or deliver a ball from which no runs are scored. Therefore, if a batsman starts leaving lots of deliveries, the bowler is chuffed because the scoring rate is slowing and the fielding team will have fewer runs to make to win the match when their turn comes to bat.

What's more, sometimes the batsman can misjudge a leave. A batsman may judge that the ball is passing the stumps but, in reality, the ball actually ends up hitting the stumps or the batsman's pads in front of the stumps, therefore dismissing the batsman bowled or LBW. A batsman who leaves a delivery that subsequently hits the stumps feels particularly embarrassed.

Chapter 6

Batting: The Personal Approach

In This Chapter

- Understanding the psyche
- Finding your place in the batting order
- Starting your innings
- Making crucial judgements
- Outwitting the bowler

Most top batsmen have the basis of a great technique, but technique is not what sets them apart from the rest. Coupled with outstanding natural ability, the greatest batsmen are also usually the smartest batsmen. The champions know when and how to apply their technical skills in a whole variety of different situations.

This chapter tells you how to build your game in the same way as the world's best batsmen, by using technique to its best advantage. As well, you discover how to develop the mental side of your game, when to attack and when to defend against the bowling. You find out how to play against different types of bowling and how you build an innings so you can make impressive scores.

And watch out for those helpful 'Adam says' icons as the most entertaining player in the game helps guide you to becoming a successful batsman.

Psyching Yourself to Win

Like all great sports, cricket is as much about the psyche as the physique. Batting requires intense concentration. Once the ball leaves the bowler's hand, the batsman has a fraction of a second to decide what shot to play, if any, and to move their feet into position in line with the ball to play the right stroke.

But deciding how to play a shot isn't all a batsman's grey matter has to cope with. Batsmen have to take the following into account:

- **Ability limits:** Smart batsmen try to work out which shots suit them and which ones aren't going to be so successful. The idea is to stick to shots you can do well. Remember, only the best batsmen are good at all the shots.
- **Match situation:** Batsmen need to know if the time is right to be playing attacking or defensive strokes. If the team has lost wickets, then the batsmen may be wise to take fewer risks and aim primarily not to be dismissed.
- **Personal form:** Batsmen are expected to score runs. If a batsman doesn't score runs, they can be left out of the team for future games. If a batsman's place is under pressure, they may be less likely to take risks and play aggressive shots.
- **Playing conditions:** The batsman has to assess what's going to happen to the ball once it leaves the bowler's hand. For example, will the ball swing in the air? If so, will it swing inwards towards the stumps, or out towards the slip fielders. When the ball hits the pitch, is it likely to move off the seam? (For more on bowling, see Chapter 7 and Chapter 8.)

Having the mental side of your batting right is very important, whether you're playing for your country or your local club. Always find out about the opposition bowlers, what style they are and what they do with the ball. Think through how you're going to approach them. Have a picture in your mind of what you're going to do. If you're a nervous starter when you first go out to bat, paint a mental picture that you've already made 15 to 20 runs. You'll be more comfortable if you feel you're already off the mark and have hit a few boundaries.

Best in the business

The right mental attitude to batting is important. Before a match begins, Australian opening batsman, Matthew Hayden, spends some time at the pitch familiarising himself with the surroundings and visualising how he plans to bat. This routine seems to work because at the start of the 2006–07 season, Hayden was the most successful opening batsman of this millennium.

Have a purpose with everything you do at training. Don't just go through the motions, switch on mentally and try to replicate a match situation. If you're batting in the nets, use the first five or ten minutes, depending on the length of the session, to play every ball as if you're starting your innings. You can then finish off the session in a more attacking fashion. The worst thing you can do is go into the nets and play a big shot to every ball you receive. You might feel good but you'll be very nervous and uncertain when you come to bat in a match because you haven't practised starting your innings.

Batting in the Right Order

During a team's innings, 11 batsmen get an opportunity to strut their stuff out in the middle. This procession of players is called a *batting order.*

Teams put their best batsmen near the top of the batting order to:

- **Negate the new ball:** A cricket ball can swing in the air the most when it is new or nearly new and move off the seam once it lands on the pitch. The fast bowlers are fresh and the ball is at its hardest and most bouncy, creating quite a challenge for the early batsmen. Therefore, you need your best batsmen fronting up and using all their skills and good judgement to score runs and prevent the team losing wickets.
- **Tire the bowlers:** All going to plan, batsmen at the top of the order hope to bat for a long time and this strategy can frustrate the opposition's best bowlers because they tire.
- **Spend a longer time at the crease:** The sooner the best batsmen get to face the bowling, then the longer, potentially, they have to build a really big innings. Having your best batsmen at the bottom of the order is a waste because the risk is that they may run out of batting partners and end up *not out*.

Many of the best batsmen in the modern game, such as West Indies' Brian Lara, Australia's Ricky Ponting and India's Sachin Tendulkar, bat at number 3 or 4. The idea is that the opening batsmen, numbers 1 and 2, wear down the new ball and the bowlers. Once the openers are out, the best shot-makers in the team take full advantage of an older, softer cricket ball and fatigued bowlers.

If you're batting and all your team mates have been dismissed, you're deemed to be not out. Sadly you don't get to carry on making hay because, under the laws of the game, you need a batting partner to complete a run. However, you do have bragging rights over your team mates. You can remind them later that, unlike them, the bowlers could not get you out!

When an opening batsman — batting at either number 1 or 2 in the batting order — is not out after all their team mates are dismissed, they are said to have *carried their bat*. This achievement is a rare and exceptional feat.

No matter how good a batsman you think you are, and no matter where you think you should bat in the order, the captain is the person who decides where everyone bats. That's why working hard at training to show your captain that you can perform the basics well, and that you deserve to be one of the early batsmen, is a good start. However, nothing wins you a promotion up the batting order as much as scoring plenty of runs, particularly if you do it with a good technique.

You can divide the batting order into three categories:

- **The top of the order:** Batsmen numbers 1, 2 and 3 are the two opening batsmen and the batsman who comes out at the fall of the first wicket. These guys and girls have it hard because they take on the new ball and fresh bowlers. Fighting to stop the bowlers dismissing them can be a real battle. However, being at the top of the order can also be a great opportunity to make early runs because the fielding captain almost always has a number of his fieldsmen in close, attacking positions to take catches. That field setting leaves plenty of gaps in the field for you to hit the ball and score. Usually, the batsmen with the best defensive techniques play here.
- **Middle order:** Batsmen numbers 4, 5, 6 and 7 are good batsmen who are usually famed for their shot-making ability. All going well, these players come out once the bowlers tire and the ball is old to pile on the agony for the fielding side. However, middle order batsmen must have a sound defensive technique just in case the top order batsmen are dismissed early and they have to face the new ball and the bowlers at their freshest.
- **Lower order:** Batsmen numbers 8 through to 11 are players who are not in the team for their batting; they'll be bowlers or possibly a wicketkeeper. However, lower order batsmen — *tail-enders* — are still expected to do a job of scoring runs or at least be sound enough defensively to avoid dismissal. They often find themselves playing alongside a middle or top order batsman. In such circumstances, they are expected to stick around and give their more capable batting partner the chance to face as many deliveries as possible, by running quick singles.

A lower order batsman can still have a great impact. Brett Lee, the Australian fast bowler, is just about the best lower order batsman in the world. Batting at number 8 or 9, Lee has played some important and heroic innings in recent years, even though he's in the team as a bowler.

Tail-enders were once considered complete rabbits when it came to batting, but in the modern game, coaches emphasise the importance of bowlers and wicketkeepers practising their batting skills. Much of Australia's recent success has been built around the explosive batting of wicketkeeper Adam Gilchrist, who has often swung games and demolished tried attacks, batting largely at number 7. A wicketkeeper with good batting skills has much more chance of progressing to the higher ranks of cricket.

In Test match and first-class cricket, where each side has two innings, if it nears the close of a day's play and a top order batsman is dismissed — the batting side will sometimes promote a lower order batsman. The idea is that the team captain prefers to risk a lower order batsman being dismissed than a top order one. A lower order batsman facing the music like this is rather quaintly called a *nightwatchman.*

Starting Out in the Middle

Even at the best of times, cricket is hardly a fast game. Arriving at the wicket, prior to facing the first delivery, you have to go through some preliminaries with the umpire who is standing at the end of the pitch from where the bowler is delivering. These preliminaries may seem a bit slow but they are performed for good reasons.

Taking guard

Taking guard occurs when the umpire helps you line up your bat with the stumps. You hold your bat vertically and side on, with the edge facing the umpire (see Figure 6-1) . You then tell the umpire which stump you want your bat to be in front of. The umpire will guide you to the position you requested by instructing you to wiggle your bat towards or away from you. This position is called your *guard.*

Once you have been guided to your guard, you make a mark on the crease, usually by hitting it with the bat or scratching it with your shoe. Making a dent isn't about vandalising the pitch — it's there so you can easily return your bat to the same spot to take guard ball after ball without annoying the umpire by asking all the time to retake your guard.

Figure 6-1: Taking guard: Hold your bat vertically and side on, with the edge facing the umpire, as this left-handed batsman is doing.

You can take lots of different guards — from leg stump to off stump. But the best and easiest when you're starting off as a cricketer, is simply to ask for middle stump, or *two centres*, which means middle stump at both ends. The umpire then lines up the middle stump at his end with the middle stump at your end and tells you when your bat is directly between the two.

Listening to the umpire

When you first come out to bat, the umpire at the bowler's end offers you all sorts of useful nuggets of information, relating to the game situation and what the bowler is doing.

Expect the umpire to tell you how many balls are to go in the over. The information-fest doesn't end there. The umpire then explains:

- What hand the bowler is using to deliver the ball
- What side of the stumps, at the bowler's end, the ball will be delivered from.

A batsman can receive a delivery from the bowler from four different angles; which angle depends on the type of bowler and from which side of the stumps at the bowler's end they're bowling.

These four different angles of delivery are known as:

- **Right arm over the wicket (the most common):** Looking down the pitch towards the batsman, a right-handed player bowling *over the wicket* delivers the ball from the left-hand side of the umpire and the stumps.
- **Right arm round the wicket:** A right-handed player bowling *round the wicket* delivers the ball from the right-hand side of the umpire and the stumps.
- **Left arm over the wicket:** A left-handed player bowling *over the wicket* delivers the ball from the right-hand side of the umpire and the stumps.
- **Left arm round the wicket:** A left-handed player bowling *round the wicket* delivers the ball from the left-hand side of the umpire and the stumps.

The easiest way to understand the difference between 'over the wicket' and 'round the wicket' is to remember that *over the wicket* for a bowler, whether left or right handed, means your bowling arm is closest to the umpire and the stumps as you run in to deliver the ball. *Round the wicket* is when your bowling arm is furthest away from the umpire.

Setting the sight screens

Very few local cricket grounds have sight screens but if you happen to be playing at a ground that does, you're wise to take full advantage of it when you're batting. *Sight screens* are large panels, usually made of timber — a few metres high and wide — and painted white. Sight screens are meant to be located directly behind where the bowler releases the ball.

Having taken guard and been told what the bowler is up to by the umpire, you now check the position of the sight screen (if one exists).

When you go in to bat, you're guided by the umpire, who stands with his arm in the air, imitating whether the bowler is left or right arm and bowling over or round the wicket. Use the umpire's arm as a guide to where the sight screen will be — if the sight screen is in the right position, the umpire's raised arm will be in the middle of the sight screen.

If you're not happy with where the sight screen is placed, you can ask for it to be moved to directly behind where the bowler will release the ball — and the fielding side usually obliges by moving the sight screens for you, which is nice!

Once you've taken all that information under your belt, the time has come to face your first delivery.

Judging 'Line and Length'

When the ball leaves the bowler's hand, the batsman makes a judgement about where the ball will land on the pitch. The batsman assesses:

- The direction the ball is heading
- How near the batsman the ball is going to land.

This is a judgement made on the *line and length* of the delivery. Everything stems from this split-second judgement — what shot is going to be played and where the batsman puts their feet to get as close as possible to the ball to execute a correct scoring shot.

Looking at the line of the ball

The batsman takes guard in front of the stumps, usually in line with middle or leg stump. When the ball is delivered, the batsman assesses the line the ball is travelling down the pitch. You can break the line of the ball into three clear subgroups:

- **Ball missing the stumps on the off side:** If no shot was played by the batsman, the ball would miss the stumps and head towards where the wicketkeeper is standing.
- **Ball missing the stumps on the leg side:** If no shot was played, the ball would go behind the batsman's legs. The wicketkeeper must move to the leg side to take the ball.
- **Ball heading towards the stumps:** In all probability, if the ball was left by the batsman, it would strike the stumps and the batsman would be dismissed. Of course, the batsman doesn't want this to happen and will have to play a stroke, be it defensive or attacking.

A ball that is set on a line going down the leg side can be an excellent opportunity to score easy runs. Usually, fewer fielders are stationed on that side of the pitch to take a catch and leg side shots are often easier and safer to play.

Good batsmen can play scoring shots off deliveries regardless of whether they pitch on the stumps or not. Highly talented Australian captain Ricky Ponting is simply brilliant at playing these shots. But if you're just starting your career as a batsman, be a bit more cautious until you start to feel comfortable out in the middle.

Looking at the length of the delivery

At the same time as judging the line of the ball — whether the ball's going to hit the stumps or not if left alone — the batsman has to gauge where the ball will hit the pitch. Where a ball lands, or *pitches*, determines the length of the delivery (see Chapter 7 for more on bowling lengths).

- **A full length:** The ball pitches close to where the batsman stands in their crease. In response, generally, the batsman moves onto their front foot, pressing their weight forward. This delivery is also called a half volley and can be an easy length for the batsman to hit a scoring shot.
- **On a good length:** The ball pitches four to six metres in front of the batsman, if the delivery is from a fast bowler. With slow bowlers, a good length delivery lands about two metres in front of the batsman. A good length can be a tricky length for the batsman to judge whether to play a back or front foot shot. If in doubt, play forward! Don't be stranded standing on the crease, caught in two minds as to whether you go forward or back. The likely result is that you'll be bowled or leg before wicket (LBW).
- **Short of a length:** The ball pitches around six to eight metres in front of the batsman. The batsman is likely to play off the back foot to a ball landing short of a length.

- **A bouncer:** The ball lands around halfway down the pitch and, depending on its pace, direction and bounce, can either go safely over the batsman's head or home in towards the face.

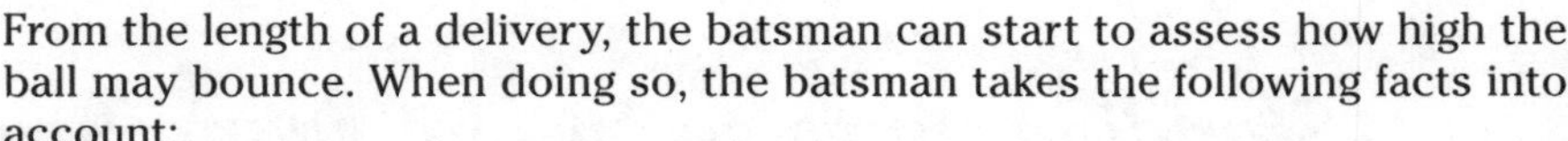

From the length of a delivery, the batsman can start to assess how high the ball may bounce. When doing so, the batsman takes the following facts into account:

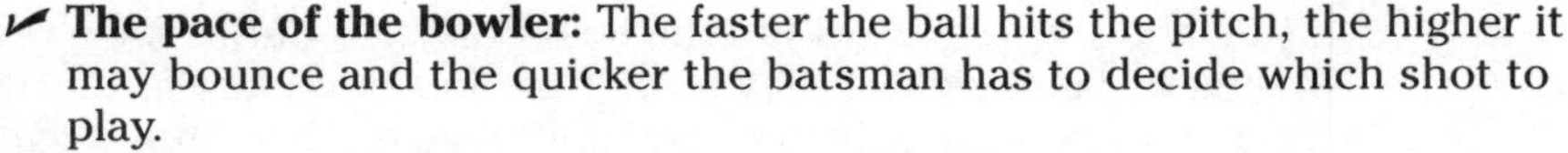

- **The pace of the bowler:** The faster the ball hits the pitch, the higher it may bounce and the quicker the batsman has to decide which shot to play.
- **The angle of trajectory:** Taller bowlers generally get a higher bounce than shorter ones.
- **How wet or dry the pitch is:** Usually, if the pitch is turf, the damper the pitch the more slowly the ball comes off the surface once it lands (refer to Chapter 2 for more on pitches). However, if you're playing on a synthetic surface, the dampness could make the ball hurry on.
- **How old the ball is:** The newer the ball, the higher it bounces and the faster it travels through the air.

Safety comes first

Avoiding being hit when facing a bouncer is the first and most important rule for a batsman to remember. Three different strategies exist to play this potentially nasty delivery (for more on avoiding short-pitched bowling, refer to Chapter 5).

- If the ball's aimed around leg stump, go back and across as you normally would to any short ball. This movement puts you in a position to hook or simply allow the ball to sail harmlessly down the leg side.
- Having gone back and across, if the ball is still coming at you, then duck, bending low at the knees and waist and keeping your bat down in case the ball hits the bat and offers a freak catch.
- If the ball is on or outside off stump, swaying back towards the leg side and letting the ball pass harmlessly by your chest or face is easier. Again, keep your bat and gloves down, well out of the way of the ball, to avoid being caught.

Generally teams give the new ball to their meanest, fastest bowlers because the new ball bounces higher and moves more quickly through the air. On the flip side, batting sides send out batsmen who are adept at playing shots off the back foot, to face the new ball. Crucially, playing shots off the back foot gives the batsman more time before the ball reaches them.

In Test and first class matches, a new ball is used every 80 overs. Generally, in club cricket, each team innings begins with a new ball.

Standing up to seam and swing bowling

Seam and swing bowlers are the heavy artillery of the game (see Chapter 8). Depending on how fast they bowl, their job is to blast batsmen out with a combination of pace, bounce and a little guile. Here are some clues as to what a batsman has to do to survive and get the scoreboard moving:

- **Be brave:** Fast bowlers try to intimidate you — often by directing their deliveries into your ribs. Get onto the back foot as quickly as you can with short pitched and bouncer bowling and decide early if you're going to play an attacking shot, such as a pull, a back foot defensive stroke, or simply leave the ball.
- **Wherever possible, use the pace of the ball to boost your run total:** You don't need to use brute strength to hit a fast delivery, merely make sure your bat makes contact with the ball and direct the ball — using a turn of the wrists at the split second of impact — wide of the fielders. You'll soon find the runs piling up.

- **Try to watch the ball as it leaves the bowler's hand:** Watching the ball gives you an idea of the direction in which it is likely to swing (see Chapter 8 for more).
- **Play the survival game:** Bowling fast is very tiring and generally pace bowlers can only bowl five or six overs in one go. What's more, the longer you last, the more you get used to the pace of the bowling and the bounce of the ball.

Playing spin bowling

Spin bowling is a mysterious art and most batting newcomers can be bamboozled by it. (See Chapter 8 for the ins and outs of spin bowling.)

Here are some pointers on playing spin bowling:

- **When playing a spin bowler off the front foot, try to keep your bat and pad close together. If you don't keep them close together, the ball could spin between them and bowl you.**
- **Advance down the wicket to where the ball pitches so you can play it on the full or just as it bounces. Advancing gives the ball no chance to spin, which prevents it turning past your bat.**

  Advancing is a good way to either attack or smother spin bowling, but make sure you have time to advance and meet the ball. If you get it wrong and miss the ball the wicketkeeper can stump you for being out of your crease.
- **The ball is tossed up, which means the spin bowler has released the ball slightly higher into the air so it arrives more slowly, giving the batsman time to advance down the pitch.**

  This advance is achieved by pushing forward as if to defend or drive, bringing the back foot quickly forward behind the front foot, then pushing forward again to defend or drive. The movement is performed in a quick skipping motion, although your body remains balanced and ready to play a shot as though you had simply pushed forward.
- **Try to hit the ball in the direction the spin is taking it.** For example, a bowler who is spinning the ball from the leg stump towards the off stump is easier to hit into the off side than the leg side. Hitting across the line of a delivery from a spinner can heighten the chances of offering a catch to a fielder.
- **Be patient and wait for the bad ball.** Spinning a ball is hard and bowlers can get it horribly wrong, dropping the ball really short or over-pitching it on occasions — this is a great opportunity to go for a boundary or even a six.

Taking Control in the Middle

When batting, you must have a plan. After all, the team is depending on you to score runs that will help win the game.

To be successful at batting, you have to build an innings — your own and the team's!

Here's how to go about building a big score that can help your team to victory and make you a hero or heroine after the game — when you get the chance to bore everyone rigid with a recounting of your legendary knock!

The basic idea of building an innings is that, except in extreme cases when only a couple of overs may be left in a run chase, or a one-day innings, you always start by occupying the crease — playing defensively to minimise the chances of getting out. Often the most difficult time in your innings is the first 15 to 20 deliveries. Once you've assessed the bowlers and how the pitch is playing, you can then begin to assess the tempo of the game and whether you need to play more expansively, bat normally or play cautiously to avoid the loss of more wickets. Most of the time, you simply play the bowling on its merits. Sometimes the scoring rate may pick up. Other times, it may be slow going.

Getting off the mark

No one likes to be dismissed without scoring. Therefore, many batsmen try to score a run off one of the first few deliveries that they face. One of the best tactics is to go for a quick run, known as a *quick single,* at the earliest opportunity. But don't get too carried away! Your batting partner and team mates in general won't be happy if you cause a run out because you're worrying too much about your first run. (For more details on dismissals, refer to Chapter 2.)

Getting your eye in

Batting is about hand–eye coordination and good footwork. But even the best players take time for their eyes to adjust to the light, as well as the pace, movement and bounce of the ball off the pitch. No matter what level of cricket you play, early in your innings you will benefit by playing low-risk defensive shots rather than expansive, aggressive ones.

Judging a run

When you play a shot, you need to let your batting partner know whether or not you want to go for a run.

You have to make a split-second decision on whether you run or not, based on the following:

- How far you have hit the ball and at what pace the ball is travelling
- How near to the ball the fielders are.

The key question you have to ask yourself is: Can my partner and I complete the run before the fielder has collected the ball and thrown it at the stumps?

Throughout, you're relying on your batting partner. Your partner has to be alert and be *backing up*. This means that your partner is walking towards you and on the verge of leaving their crease as the bowler bowls. Likewise, when your batting partner is facing the bowling and you are at the other end of the pitch — called the *non-striker's end* — then you need to be *backing up* too.

Good backing up can help you take more quick singles, which boosts the team score and annoys the bowlers.

Sliding your bat is also important when completing a quick single. As you're in your final strides towards the crease, stretch out the arm holding your bat and slide the bat along the ground so it crosses the crease well in front of you. This gains you valuable centimetres and can make the difference between being run out because a good throw by a fieldsman hits the stumps and being able to continue your innings.

A degree of etiquette is involved with calling for a run. This doesn't mean you have to politely inquire of your batting partner if they would care to run. Good run calling simply involves listening to whoever of the two batsmen — the striker and non-striker — is in the best position to judge whether a run is on.

If the ball is heading in front of square on the leg or off side, the striker is in the best position to judge whether a run is on and it's their call.

But if the ball heads behind square on the off or leg side, the non-striker is in the best position to judge because the striking batsman would have to turn around to look where the ball has gone — because in effect it has gone behind the striker.

Forward or backward of square on a cricket field is separated by an invisible line across the entire playing field. This invisible line runs through the crease of the batsman who is on strike, all the way out to the point boundary on one side and the square leg boundary on the other. (Refer to Chapter 2 for more on fielding positions.)

Don't forget to take into account the physical condition of your batting partner when calling for a run. If unfit or tired from batting for a long time, your partner's chances of completing a quick single before the fielders are able to throw down the stumps are diminished.

Three clear calls are the basis of communication with your batting partner — 'Yes' if a run is definitely available, 'Wait' if you want to see whether the ball passes a fieldsman before running, and 'No' if you don't want to run. If your partner wants a run, but you think it's too risky, call 'No' quickly and loudly, even if the call is technically their call. Likewise, if you call 'Yes' but your partner calls 'No', don't run. Basically, if either batsman calls 'No' at any stage, don't run. *Always* call quickly in case you or your partner get stranded halfway down the pitch. Getting stranded halfway down the pitch is the easiest way to be involved in a run out. Better to sacrifice what might have been a quick single than to lose your own wicket or your partner's in the confusion.

'Go' sounds like 'No' and only creates confusion. Always call 'Yes' if you want a run.

Taking more than one run

If the ball has been hit well and more than one run is obviously available, then the batsman running more in the direction the ball has been hit tells the other batsman, who is running with their back to the ball, what is going on. Calls such as 'Run hard, two in it', or 'Look for three' are an important part of the communication between you and your partner.

When you turn at the other end of the pitch to go back for a second or third run, always make sure you turn facing the direction the ball has gone. If you do not, then you are *turning blind*. Many of the former great cricketers frown on a batsman turning in this direction. For example, if you're a right hander and have hit the ball through the leg side, make sure that when you turn at the other end of the pitch your bat is in your right hand. Having your bat in your right hand gives you a clear view of how close the fielder is to the ball and whether a second or even third run is possible.

Putting your foot on the accelerator

Once you're off the mark and you get your eye in — and your confidence is up — the time has come to start playing some aggressive shots.

Judging when to take a few more risks and quicken the pace of scoring very much depends on the match situation.

Batsmen look to be aggressive earlier in their innings in one-day cricket than in Test or first-class cricket. In fact, when your team has only a few balls to make runs to win a game, you may have to bypass getting your eye in and go for your shots straight away.

Whatever the scenario, at some time in your innings you need to look to be more aggressive. After all, being aggressive is the fun part of batting.

Once you're in a positive mind-set, assess the bowling. Work out your strengths and the target areas you can hit to that are relatively risk free, such as lofting drives into the outfield if fieldsmen have not been pushed back in that area to take catches in the deep. Hitting to your target areas is possible only when bowlers give you deliveries that are suitable for the shots you want to play. The moment you start to think too aggressively and premeditate certain shots, you run a very high risk of being dismissed. If you're a bit more calculating and know what areas you're comfortable hitting the ball towards, you're better off to concentrate on those.

Reaching personal landmarks

Every time a batsman makes 50 runs, they get a polite round of applause from the crowd, their team mates and even, sometimes, the opposition. Scoring 100 runs is a big deal for a batsman. The round of applause is generally louder and the batsman traditionally waves his bat above his head to say thanks for the appreciation. Batting isn't easy and some players can go through their whole careers without once reaching 100 runs in one innings.

A batsman who scores 100 runs in a single innings is said to have scored a *century.*

Don't be a selfish batsman, concerned purely with protecting yourself from being dismissed when the team needs to make runs fast. Selfish batsmen, who won't take risks when the match situation requires risk, can get their team mates offside and spoil the fun of a good contest. Remember, the letter 'I' has no place in a cricket team.

Pairs, king pairs and cartoon ducks

Being out for a *duck* is when a player is dismissed without scoring. Being out for a *golden duck* is when a player is dismissed for a duck off the first delivery faced. When batsmen are dismissed for a duck in Test matches played in Australia, the television coverage heaps on the misery by showing a cartoon duck at the bottom of the screen as the disconsolate batsman is shown trudging back to the pavilion. Cruel, but very funny!

A batsman dismissed without scoring in both innings of the same match is said to have made a *pair*. Any batsman managing the very rare failure of being out twice in the same match without scoring, and both times off the first delivery they faced, is said to have made a *king pair*.

Cricket is a very innovative game now and some innovative shots are being introduced for the one-day game and, particularly, for the shorter Twenty20 version. Make sure you practise any new shot until you're confident you can play that shot with a relatively low risk of being dismissed. Never unveil a new shot for the first time in a game. Failing to practise a new shot first can spell disaster.

Chapter 7

Making It Big as a Bowler

In This Chapter

- Taking on the batsman
- Recognising the risks for bowlers
- Bowling different ways
- Believing in brain power

A good bowler is a bit like a magician, performing tricks to deceive the batsman. Clever bowlers can make the ball do strange and unexpected things, confusing and eventually dismissing the batsman.

This chapter examines the bowling arts: How to bowl fast, how to swing a cricket ball in the air and how to make a ball spin off the pitch.

Looking at the Objectives of Bowling

When a bowler delivers a ball, the bowler is trying to do the following:

- Dismiss the batsman, or put doubt in the batsman's mind in the hope of an imminent dismissal
- Limit the number of runs the batsman scores off each delivery.

Each over bowled consists of six deliveries. Every time the bowler runs in to bowl, a new contest begins with the batsman.

Ideally, the bowler wants to take a wicket off every delivery but, realistically, even the best in the world can't manage anything like that.

In fact, top-class batsmen are formidable foes to bowlers. The bowler has to think about what type of delivery to bowl, observe which shots the batsman is good or bad at, and vary the pace, line and length of the ball delivered to expose any weaknesses in the batsman's technique. Spin bowlers can also vary the flight — how high the ball flies in the air between being delivered and landing — and the direction in which the ball spins after landing on the pitch (see Chapter 8 for more on spin bowling).

A delivery that tests the batsman's technique is a delivery that's also difficult for the batsman to score runs off.

Australian fast bowler, Glenn McGrath, is the best at achieving the twin objectives of dismissing the batsman and stopping the batsman scoring runs. Over the past decade or more, McGrath has claimed more than 500 wickets in Test matches while conceding very few runs. He's achieved this feat not with electric pace or devastating swing bowling but through consistently bowling balls on a line and length that expose weaknesses in batsmen's techniques. The great man is near the end of his international career now and when he does eventually hang up his boots, batsmen around the globe are going to heave a sigh of relief.

Because a new cricket ball bounces higher and moves more quickly through the air, captains usually choose their best fast bowlers to *open the bowling* — bowl first.

In Test and first-class cricket, the bowling side is allowed to take a new ball at the start of the innings and replace it with another new ball after 80 overs have been bowled. (Refer to Chapter 3 for more on Test and first-class cricket.)

Checking Out Different Bowling Types

A cricket ball has a seam that runs around its circumference. This seam, about the width of your thumb and slightly raised, has a huge impact on how the ball moves through the air and bounces off the pitch. The position bowlers use to hold their fingers along the ball's seam can make the ball bounce towards or away from the batsman. Likewise, the bowler can make the ball swing in the air — away or towards the batsman — merely by pointing the seam in a particular direction. Spin bowlers rotate the wrist or fingers of the hand holding the ball as they deliver it, with the aim of getting the ball to rotate in the air so that the ball has a better chance of spinning away or towards the batsman when it bounces off the pitch.

In short, through a combination of finger, hand and wrist movements, bowlers can, on a good day, make the ball do the strangest of things. In cricketing circles, this skill is called *making the ball talk*.

Bowling can be divided into:

- Fast bowling, which includes swing and seam bowling
- Slow bowling, which is spin bowling.

A cricket ball is made of cork and latex, which are bound tightly by string and covered by leather. This leather is held together by stitching. This stitching is called the seam. A standard cricket ball should weigh between 155.9 grams and 163 grams while the circumference should measure between 22.4 centimetres and 22.9 centimetres. For women, a cricket ball is slightly smaller, weighing between 140 and 151 grams and measuring 21 to 22.5 centimetres around the circumference.

Normally, people find a type of bowling that suits them and they stick to it. But rare exceptions do exist. Some multiskilled players are able to vary between fast and slow bowling. Top-class fast bowlers can vary between relying on swing in the air and movement off the seam.

The great West Indian, Garfield Sobers, was the most multiskilled cricketer of all time. He could bowl seam, swing and spin — each to an incredibly high standard. Add to this the fact that Sobers was a fantastic, hard-hitting left-handed batsman and you can see why he features in the Ten Greatest Cricketers (see Chapter 21).

Understanding the goal of fast and slow bowlers

Whether you're a fast or slow bowler, you're striving for the same thing when delivering the cricket ball. All bowlers hope to move the ball in the air or off the pitch, either into or away from the batsman, in order to trick them into making a mistake that leads to a dismissal.

Fast bowlers, also known as *pace bowlers*, get the ball to swing in the air before it pitches or they get it to move off the pitch once it lands. Sometimes, the same delivery swings in the air, then the ball can move or *seam* off the pitch, making life doubly difficult for the batsman.

Fast bowling can be broken into three sub-groups, beginning with out-and-out fast bowlers who deliver the ball at express pace. The fastest bowlers bowl so quickly that they attempt to intimidate the batsmen with their pace. They use the fear factor, that the batsman may be hit and hurt by the ball. A team that has one or more of these fast bowlers has a decided advantage. *Fast-medium* bowlers are still quite lively but rely more on moving the ball in the air and off the pitch. *Medium pacers*, however, are steady rather than fast. Medium pacers must be very accurate and develop good variations to move the ball in the air and off the pitch in the hope of dismissing batsmen.

Like all great sportsmen, exceptionally fast bowlers are born and not made. You either have the natural ability to bowl really quickly or you don't. However, all the basic principles of fast, fast-medium and medium pace bowling are the same.

Although having one or two really potent fast bowlers is a great advantage for a team, the West Indies dominated the 1980s with a production line of fearsome pacemen, often picking four in the one side. The West Indies, at this time, made the life of batsmen around the world a constant misery.

How fast and slow bowlers try to achieve the aim of moving the ball off the pitch differs markedly.

Bowlers who specialise in moving the ball off the seam — a *seam bowler* or *seamer* — try to get the ball to move off the pitch by holding the seam of the cricket ball in different positions with their fingers, depending on whether they want the ball to move into or away from the batsman. This movement can be further encouraged with a flick of the wrist. The same basic principles apply for swing bowling. (For more on swing and seam bowling, see Chapter 8.)

Spinners deliver the ball very differently to fast bowlers. Indeed, bowling too fast is detrimental to being a good spin bowler. Spinners get their wrists and fingers into strange and wonderful positions with the aim of making the ball spin to varying degrees when it bounces off the pitch. Slow spinners try to get the ball to achieve exaggerated movement off the pitch in an attempt to bamboozle the batsman.

Generally, fast bowlers like a new ball and the spinners an older one. The only exception to this is when the older ball is *reverse swinging*, in which case fast bowlers, who are capable of swinging the ball, can't wait to get a hold of it. (For more on reverse swinging, see Chapter 8.)

Getting to grips with bowling basics

The act of bowling or delivering the ball to the batsman can be broken down into three elements. Get these three elements right and you can take a big stride towards becoming a champion bowler and a batsman's worst nightmare!

- Running up to the bowling crease to deliver the ball, unsurprisingly called the *run-up*
- Propelling the ball out of the hand, called the bowler's *action*
- Coming to a halt after delivering the ball, called the bowler's *follow through*

Starting off

Many youngsters, when they first begin to play cricket, want to emulate the heroes they see on television. Trying to be like the exciting Australian fast bowler, Brett Lee, the youngster charges in from a long way back and lets the ball go as fast as possible. Being like Brett Lee is a great goal to have but these youngsters need to gain the basic skills of bowling before they can blast batsmen out.

If you have never bowled before and are wondering how to start, stand with a bit of space around you. If you're inside, make sure no fan or light fitting is dangling from the ceiling, lest your bowling claims an unexpected victim when you bring your arm over.

If you're not sure whether you're a left- or right-arm bowler, decide which arm you would naturally use to throw a ball. That is your bowling arm. Stand comfortably and, if you're a right hander, turn your head 90 degrees and look along your left shoulder. Everything is the opposite if you're a left hander. You're now facing the 'batsman', even though your particular batsman may look more like a wall or fence.

Bring both hands comfortably up to your chest with your elbows loosely by your sides and put your left hand on your right hand. Imagine you're holding the ball in your right hand. Now raise your left arm up straight and slightly towards the batsman. At the same time, step forward with your left foot (your front foot) — this movement is called the *delivery stride* — and bring your right arm down beside you.

Check your position! An imaginary straight line should now run down your raised left arm and through your right arm as it begins to rotate. Keep this straight line as your right arm comes over and your left arm tucks in beside your body. You're now at the point of release. Your weight has transferred onto your left (or front) foot. Check your position! A straight line now runs vertically from your right hand as you release the ball all the way through your body and left leg. Your left (or front) foot should be facing the batsman.

As the ball is released your right (or back) foot comes through with the momentum and lands in front of you. This movement is the beginning of your follow through. Once you start bowling an imaginary ball comfortably, then the time has come to develop into a real bowler who may one day end up, like your heroes, on television.

Always keep your bowling arm straight as you bring it over to bowl. If you bend your arm, then straighten it again as you deliver the ball; this action is called throwing, or *chucking,* and is illegal. If either of the umpires is not satisfied with your action, the umpire may call 'No ball' (refer to Chapter 2). A no ball means you're penalised a run, cannot dismiss the batsman, and are forced to bowl the ball again properly. Being labelled a 'chucker' is unpleasant. Bowlers with suspect actions continue to create one of the biggest ongoing controversies in world cricket.

The run-up

Put simply, a run-up occurs when the bowler runs up to the crease before delivering the ball to the batsman. The run-up is sometimes called the bowler's *approach to the wicket*.

The idea is to pick up enough momentum to be able to propel the ball towards the batsman at the speed the bowler would like the ball to travel. Fast bowlers need to run faster and further in their run-up than spin bowlers. The very fastest bowlers can run-up at top speed for 20 or 30 metres in order to build up the momentum they require. This exertion of energy means that they tire more quickly than spin bowlers, who usually run-up only a few metres. Spin bowlers rely on the ball spinning off the pitch to bamboozle batsmen rather than the raw pace of the delivery.

Many aspiring young fast bowlers make the fatal mistake of believing that the further and faster they run, the faster they can bowl. This is not the case! While a long run-up may look impressive, the most important function of a run-up for a fast bowler is to make sure they not only have momentum, but are well balanced when delivering the ball. Don't run any further than is necessary to achieve this result. Running up further than necessary is a waste of energy and makes you less effective as the day progresses because you're going to tire more quickly.

A fast bowler's run-up should begin slowly and be smooth and comfortable. Avoid over-striding as this action can leave you unbalanced at the point of delivery, reducing your pace and accuracy.

Damien Fleming, a fine swing bowler who played for Australia from 1994 to 2001 (see Figure 7-1), has tips in this chapter to help you better your bowling. Damien later became a senior coach with the Centre of Excellence in Brisbane. Look for the 'Damien says' icons throughout this chapter (and read Damien on fielding in Chapter 9).

Aim to have a gradual build-up starting with small to larger steps as you run in to deliver the ball. Run as if you're a 400-metre runner until leaping into your bowling action. Be efficient with your run-up.

The momentum created by the run-up is crucial to delivering the ball. All bowlers try to get the ball to leave their hand with their front foot dissecting the line of the front crease (sometimes called the *popping crease*; refer to Chapter 2 for more). This means that the ball has the least possible distance to travel to the batsman.

Figure 7-1: Damien Fleming, playing one-day cricket for Australia, in perfect position to deliver the ball as he leaps into his delivery stride.

Get the run-up wrong and the following can happen:

- If the ball is delivered from way back behind the bowling crease, the ball has further to travel to the batsman, giving the batsman extra time to decide which shot they want to play, and extra time to execute the shot properly.
- If the front foot oversteps the crease and is spotted by the umpire, a no ball call is made. The umpire sticks out their right arm and shouts 'no ball' while the ball is in flight. Automatically, a run is added to the batting team's total. Runs scored by the batsman off a no ball count, but the bowler can't dismiss the batsman. To cap it all off, the ball has to be re-bowled. (Refer to Chapter 2 for more on the no ball rule.) Bowlers hate no balling and captains can be particularly upset by them in tight one-day matches.

The length of the run-up has to feel natural and repeatable time after time. Rhythm is a bowler's most important friend as the bowler runs up and delivers the ball. A smooth, repeatable run-up takes loads of practice in the nets (see Chapter 12 for more on net practice).

The best way to work out a run-up is to stand next to the stumps at the bowler's end facing away from the batsman on strike (refer to Chapter 5) and run away from the pitch using the same run-up that you would use to bowl the ball. Go through your bowling action (see following section, 'The bowler's action' for more) and put a mark where your front foot (left foot for a right-arm bowler) lands as you deliver an imaginary ball. This is the basis of your run-up.

After you achieve a comfortable run-up at practice sessions, pace out your run-up from the bowling crease, which runs across the pitch either side of the stumps (refer to Chapter 2). Now, walk back to where you want to start and remember the number of paces.

Before bowling in a match, pace out your run-up with the same number of strides and make a mark on the ground with your shoe so you start from the same place every time. If you're really lucky, the umpire will have a white marker to put down as well so you can more easily see where to start. Have a practice run-up. If your practice run-up doesn't feel right, pace out your run-up again to be sure. See Chapter 12 for more on practising the bowler's run-up.

The bowler's action

Changing from your run-up into your bowling action involves slowing a little in the last couple of strides to be balanced going into the delivery stride. The bowler then jumps a little and brings their body side-on to the batsman to deliver the ball.

The direction of your back foot (the right foot for a right-arm bowler) on landing dictates what sort of an action you need to develop. With our imaginary bowling practice (see section, 'Starting off', at the beginning of this section), the back foot was parallel to the bowling crease (refer to Chapter 2 for more on the bowling crease) and at 90 degrees to the direction of the pitch.

However, when bowlers jump into their bowling action after their run-up, their back foot could naturally land anywhere in a 90 degree arc pointing from straight across the pitch to straight down the pitch. Although the direction the back foot faces may vary from bowler to bowler, a bowler with a natural, comfortable action should find their back foot landing in much the same position and facing in the same direction time after time.

The direction of your back foot decides whether you bowl with an *open* or *closed* action. This situation particularly applies to fast bowlers. If your back foot naturally lands at 90 degrees to the direction of the pitch (the way your back foot was placed during our imaginary bowling session), then you're bowling with a *closed action*. This position means your chest is closed to the batsman and facing the leg side. You need to get your body directly side-on to the batsman and look over your left shoulder — if you're a right armer. You look past the outside of your left arm, which is raised high and slightly towards the batsman creating a window to look through.

However, if your back foot is pointing down the pitch towards the batsman, then you bowl with an *open action*; this means your chest faces towards the batsman. An open action is also referred to as a *front-on action*. Instead of getting side-on and looking over your left shoulder — if you're a right armer — you look past the inside of your left arm.

The type of action you use also determines where your front foot lands as you deliver the ball. If your back foot is pointing across the pitch, creating a side-on action, then the foot lands almost directly in front of the back foot. But if you have an open action, with your back foot pointed straight down the pitch, then your front foot should land a little to the left (if you're a right armer) as shown in Figure 7-2. Note the back (right) foot pointing down the pitch on landing and the bowler looking inside their left arm, not over their left shoulder as they would with a closed action. Part of the front foot (left foot) is behind the popping crease, preventing a no ball.

Figure 7-2: A right-arm fast bowler delivering the ball with an open, or front-on, action.

In reality, most fast bowlers now use partially closed actions because their back foot lands on an angle in the 90-degree arc between pointing straight across the pitch and pointing straight down the pitch. Very few fast bowlers have natural actions which take them side-on enough to look over their left shoulder and past the inside of their left arm. Almost all faster bowlers will naturally be looking past the inside of their left arm.

The reason for these slight variations, particularly in a fast bowler, is to ensure that a bowler's feet, hips and shoulders all line up. Experts have found that this position is by far the safest way for a bowler to avoid injury (see Figure 7-3).

Figure 7-3: Keeping the feet, hips and shoulders aligned.

Fast bowlers tackle the bad-back syndrome

Dennis Lillee and Glenn McGrath have been Australia's two greatest fast bowlers, yet they bowl with very different actions. Lillee, with his powerful, athletic run-up, classical action, aggression and courage, was the hero of a generation. Every aspiring fast bowler growing up in the 1970s and early 1980s wanted to be Dennis Lillee. Yet even Lillee broke down with a serious back injury and was forced to remodel his action. Unfortunately, in the days before medical science caught up with cricket, many coaches instructed their fast bowlers to get classically side-on like Lillee, even though their back foot may have been facing down the pitch. This gave many young fast bowlers mixed actions and left them particularly susceptible to injury. A generation later, Glenn McGrath, the most successful fast bowler of all time because of a high action that creates uncomfortable bounce and miserly accuracy, bowls with his back foot pointing down the pitch. He has a more open action than Lillee but has still achieved deadly results.

Recent research by Cricket Australia has found that bowlers, particularly fast bowlers, who deliver the ball with what is known as a *mixed action*, face a far greater risk of suffering serious back injuries. This situation usually means that a bowler, who has their back foot facing straight down the pitch, tries to bowl with a closed, or side-on action when they should be bowling with an open or front-on action. This creates unnecessary twisting and stress in the bowler's back.

Fast bowling is very taxing on the body. Injuries can occur for various reasons. Mixed actions put tremendous strain through the body, particularly the back region. Cricket Australia studies have found that if your hips and shoulders are more than 30 degrees out of line when delivering the ball, your chances of injuries increase dramatically. This position is called *counter rotation* and takes place in the delivery stride as weight is transferred from the back foot to the front foot. For example, a bowler's back foot may land with hips and shoulders front-on. However, when the front foot lands, the hips may stay front-on but the shoulders rotate to side-on putting strain on the lower back. If you're a fast bowler, up to 10 times your body weight goes through your body each ball you bowl. If imbalances occur, these imbalances create even more pressure on your body.

Balance is just as important as brawn in a good bowling action. When you watch a game of cricket you can see that all the great bowlers have their heads upright and their eyes level, looking at where they want the ball to land on the pitch.

The follow through

Once you go through the bowling action and release the ball, you won't be able to come to a dead stop. The momentum you build up to propel the ball at the pace and direction you want, is still going to carry you along. These extra strides you take are called the *follow through*.

Having a strong follow through is important for all bowlers, with all their momentum aimed at the batsman. This strong follow through ensures that fast bowlers generate the most pace and spinners impart as much spin on the ball as possible. Only when a bowler has followed through towards the batsman do they then start moving off the pitch and slowing down. Fast bowlers with a proper follow through can finish up halfway down the pitch.

Once you release the ball, your follow through has no impact on how fast the ball will go. However, if your follow through is stopping short, say after just a couple of steps, or you veer too quickly sideways either way, that means something has gone wrong in your run-up or action. One problem could be that you're not getting enough momentum. Generally, if you can get your run-up and action right, your follow through should be straight and powerful.

Don't run straight down the pitch in your follow through. If you're playing on turf, then you run into what is known as the *danger* area. This area is where bowlers, particularly spin bowlers, delivering alternative overs from the other end, are attempting to land the ball. The idea is to stop fast bowlers, in particular, roughing up this important area with their spiked boots (refer to Chapter 4 for details on the right equipment) and making the pitch difficult to bat on. So, once you deliver the ball running towards the batsman, start heading towards the side of the pitch (refer to Chapter 2 for more on pitches).

The danger area is listed as an area contained in a imaginary box, with an imaginary line 1.22 metres (or four feet) in front of the popping or front crease (for more on the popping crease, refer to Chapter 2), and parallel to it, and within two imaginary and parallel lines drawn down the pitch 30.48 centimetres (or one foot) either side of the middle stump. If bowlers persist in going into this area, the umpire starts to officially warn the bowler and his captain. Three official warnings and the bowler is banned from bowling for the remainder of the innings.

Looking after Promising Fast Bowlers

Because fast bowling is so taxing on the body, this aspect of the game has a much higher injury rate than any other cricket discipline. Cricket Australia studies have found that somewhere between 14 and 16 per cent of fast bowlers of all ages, about one in six or seven, are injured at any given time. Young fast bowlers, who have developing bodies, are particularly vulnerable.

Cricket Australia has released the following detailed guidelines to protect teenage fast bowlers from over bowling at training or in a match:

- **Under 14:** 5 overs maximum each spell; 10 overs maximum for the day
- **Under 15:** 5 overs maximum each spell; 12 overs maximum for the day
- **Under 16:** 6 overs maximum each spell; 14 overs maximum for the day
- **Under 17:** 6 overs maximum each spell; 16 overs maximum for the day
- **Under 18:** 7 overs maximum each spell; 18 overs maximum for the day
- **Under 19:** 8 overs maximum each spell; 20 overs maximum for the day.

Cricket Australia recommends that the guidelines shown in Table 7-1 be adopted for junior cricketers' training schedules:

Table 7-1 Guidelines for Junior Cricketers' Training

	U/14	*U/15*	*U/16*	*U/17*	*U/18*	*U/19*
Sessions per week*	2	2	2	3	3	3
Balls per session	30	30	36	36	42	48

** Note: Substitute at least one practice session for each additional match played in the week. These are maximum guidelines only. Juniors usually train only once a week unless training with a senior side, or with special representative teams.*

Focusing on the bowling workload

Current Cricket Australia research suggests that the total number of deliveries bowled in a week is closely linked to the potential for injury.

At first-class level (where the average age of players is 27 years), this research shows that total weekly workloads of more than 170 balls results in an almost 50 per cent increase in the risk of injury. This rate of injury is a potential area for concern in younger age groups when growth, development and physical maturity factors are taken into account.

Despite these guidelines (refer to Table 7-1), injury can still occur. If symptoms develop, particularly in the lower back, bowlers are advised to seek early medical assessment of the problem.

Cricket Australia developed the training guidelines for junior bowlers with weekly club and school cricket in mind. The recommendations aren't necessarily appropriate for junior cricket carnivals, which may have children playing multiple days of cricket consecutively.

In competitions over consecutive days, with one-day match formats, fast and medium pace bowlers need to bowl in a maximum of three consecutive matches before having at least one day resting from bowling.

In competitions over consecutive days, with two-day match formats, fast and medium pace bowlers should bowl in a maximum of two consecutive matches (that is, over four days consecutively) before having at least one day resting from bowling.

Coaches, administrators and parents need to be aware of the training workloads and any other competition-playing commitments of juniors in the two to three days leading up to and immediately after any competitions or junior carnivals.

These recommendations have been developed with the junior cricket player's best interest in mind. Cricket Australia hopes that coaches and team managers can understand this and help to provide the safest possible environment for junior players.

Examining the line and length of the delivery

When you're a bowler releasing the ball, you need to have a good idea of where you would like the ball to land. You aim for the part of the pitch that's going to give you the best chance of dismissing the batsman. The direction of the delivery — the line — and how close the ball bounces in front of the batsman — the length — are crucial to what happens next: Whether the batsman scores runs off the delivery or whether the batsman fails to score, or is dismissed.

You can break down the length of a delivery into four categories:

- **A full length:** The ball pitches close to where the batsman stands in their crease. Generally, batsmen move onto the front foot, pressing their weight forwards to hit full-length deliveries. This delivery is also called a *half volley* and can be an easy length for the batsman to hit a scoring shot.
- **On a good length:** The ball pitches four to six metres in front of the batsman — if delivered by a fast bowler. With spin bowlers, a good length delivery lands about two metres in front of the batsman. This distance is often a tricky length for the batsman, who may be unsure whether to play a back foot or front foot shot.

- **Short of a length:** The ball pitches six to eight metres in front of the batsman — if delivered by a fast bowler. The batsman is likely to play off the back foot to a ball landing short of a length. If the ball is bowled at a fast pace, bounces sharply and is directed at the batsman's ribs, the delivery can lead to the batsman fending a catch to any fielders close on the leg side. On the flipside, a ball landing short of a length, and which is only a slow pace and doesn't bounce high, can easily be hit for runs.
- **A bouncer:** Delivered by a fast bowler, the ball lands around halfway down the pitch and, depending on its pace, direction and bounce, can either go safely over the batsman's head or home in towards the face. The bouncer is meant to cause discomfort, unsettling the batsman. If a scoring shot is attempted, it is the hook shot, which can be a high-risk shot. (Refer to Chapter 5 for more on the hook shot.) Strict limits have been placed on the bouncer, with only one allowed per over in one-day cricket and two per over in other matches.

When a bowler delivers the ball to a batsman, the line of the ball can be broken into three basic areas:

- **At the stumps:** If the batsman misses, then the ball hits the stumps and dismisses the batsman. However, if the length of the delivery is short of a good length, the ball may bounce too high to hit the stumps.
- **The leg side:** The ball is heading towards or outside the batsman's legs, missing leg stump. This option is to be avoided. This option allows the batsman easy runs and lessens the chances of the batsman being dismissed.
- **The off side:** The ball is heading down the off side towards the wicketkeeper and slip fielders. Down the off side is the most common line for bowlers to take (see the sidebar, 'Making use of the corridor of uncertainty').

A delivery which is directed at the batsman's toes in the hope that the ball goes under the bat and hits the stumps is called a *yorker.*

Directing the ball too far away from the wicket may cause the umpire to deem that the batsman had no chance of striking the ball. If this occurs, the umpire may award a wide, which gives the batting side an extra run and the bowler has to re-bowl the delivery. On artificial pitches, any delivery that lands off the pitch is deemed either a wide or a no ball, depending on the laws the local competition has in place. (Refer to Chapter 2 for more on wides and pitches.)

Making use of the corridor of uncertainty

The 'corridor of uncertainty' may sound a bit like something from the TV series, *Dr Who*. It's nothing of the kind!

A ball bowled by a fast bowler on a good length, and directed up to a third of a metre (about one foot) outside off stump, is said to be 'in the corridor'. The batsman receiving this ball faces a quandary. The batsman may not be sure whether to play a shot or to leave the ball. Playing a shot is high risk because the slip fielders and wicketkeeper are lined up behind, waiting for the ball to hit the edge of the bat and give them the chance of a catch. Meanwhile, simply leaving the ball brings dangers if the ball moves in the air or deviates off the seam when it hits the pitch. The ball could move back to hit the stumps. No wonder most faster bowlers aim for the corridor of uncertainty.

The most common mode of dismissal in cricket is to be caught behind the wicket on the off side by the wicketkeeper or slip fielders.

Intimidation is an important weapon for a genuinely fast bowler. However, intimidation is best not overused. Bowling at a batsman's head or body can be unsettling for a batsman, who may put his own wellbeing ahead of getting out and hit a simple catch to a close fielder.

Short bowling at a batsman must be part of a greater plan. Batsmen play back to short bowling, particularly if afraid of being hit. Once a batsman is playing back consistently, a fast bowler may pitch the ball up at the stumps. If the batsman continues to play back, the batsman has a greater chance of being bowled or LBW.

Although watching a batsman jumping around as they attempt to avoid being hit by short bowling may be fun for a bowler, this practice can also be tiring and unproductive. Most wickets are claimed through catches taken by the wicketkeeper and slips off balls that are pitched up. (Refer to Chapter 2 for more on field placings.)

Fast-medium and even medium pace bowlers should attempt to develop a bouncer to stop the batsman simply pushing forward all the time, believing the ball will always be pitched up. But unless you're really quick, use a bouncer sparingly because the bouncer can lose its shock factor and batsmen can start smashing the ball to the boundary. If a fast bowler persists in bowling short at a batsman, the umpire can warn the bowler for intimidatory bowling and, after three warnings, ban the bowler from bowling for the remainder of the innings.

Choosing between over or round the wicket

Before delivering the first ball, bowlers have to tell the umpire:

- Which hand they will be releasing the ball from
- Which side of the wicket they will be delivering the ball from.

A right-handed bowler bowling *over the wicket* delivers the ball from the umpire's left-hand side. A right-handed bowler bowling *round the wicket* delivers the ball from the umpire's right-hand side. For left-handed bowlers, what constitutes over or round the wicket is reversed.

Put simply, whether you're left or right handed, over the wicket your bowling arm is closest to the umpire, and round the wicket your bowling arm is on the opposite side of your body to the umpire.

The side of the wicket that the bowler delivers the ball from has a major influence on the direction the ball heads once released. For example, if a right-handed bowler delivers the ball from round the wicket to a right-handed batsman, the ball angles from the batsman's leg side to off side, unless the bowler gets the ball to swing against this natural angle (see Chapter 8 for more on swing bowling).

Most right-handed seam and swing bowlers choose to bowl over the wicket to right-handed batsmen because this angle offers more ways to get the batsmen out.

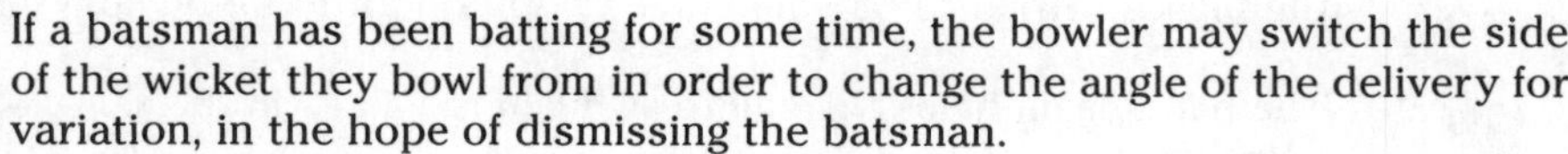

If a batsman has been batting for some time, the bowler may switch the side of the wicket they bowl from in order to change the angle of the delivery for variation, in the hope of dismissing the batsman.

If you're bowling and success is not happening for you in a game, don't be afraid to go round the wicket to change the angles for batsmen and upset their rhythm and timing. Remember, bowlers are the proactive players in cricket, and batsmen can only react to what bowlers have sent down. Use this to your advantage!

The umpire tells the batsman which hand the bowler is going to release the ball from and whether the bowler is going to deliver from round or over the wicket. The umpire tells the non-striking batsman to take up a position on the opposite side to where the bowler is delivering (for example, if the bowler delivers from the right of the umpire, the non-striker stands on the left) so as not to impede the bowler while delivering the ball.

Understanding the importance of the ball's seam

A cricket ball has a pronounced stitched seam, about the width of a thumb, running around its circumference.

The seam of a cricket ball isn't a fashion accessory. The seam has a profound effect on how the ball behaves after it has left the bowler's hand, heading towards the batsman.

The seam can alter the direction of travel of a cricket ball. A bowler, by positioning their fingers in different positions along the seam of the ball at release, can induce the ball to move in a particular direction in the air and off the pitch. Positioning the fingers along one part of the seam can send the ball away from the batsman and towards the slip fielders. In contrast, locating the fingers along a different part of the seam can, in theory, send the ball in the opposite direction towards the batsman.

How far a cricket ball deviates in the air and off the pitch depends not only on the skills of the bowler but also on the conditions. Cricket balls tend to swing more when the weather is humid and the ball moves off the seam more on turf pitches that have a bit of green grass on them and are a little damp. (Refer to Chapter 2 for more on pitches.)

If the turf pitch is hard and dry and grassless, the ball may not deviate much off the seam. In such circumstances, spin bowlers can be the ones who pose the biggest threat to batsmen (see Chapter 8 for more on spin bowling).

The ball's seam helps the ball to swing in the air — in the same way a rudder helps direct a boat.

Bowling with the Brain

Bowling isn't just about brawn — it's also about brains. All bowlers try to judge what type of delivery best gives them a chance of taking a wicket. But, sometimes, a match situation develops that requires something other than an all-out attack by the bowler. In such circumstances, the bowler has to think carefully for the benefit of the team. A good captain talks to their bowlers, outlining whereabouts on the pitch they want the bowlers to bowl. Sometimes the captain asks a bowler to direct their deliveries in a direction that leaves less opportunity to take wickets but has a wider tactical significance. Likewise, the captain may set fields and ask the bowler to bowl in a way that can concede more runs but offers a greater chance of gaining wickets.

Remembering to bowl to the field

The captain sets the field and expects the bowler to direct deliveries to make the most of the field set. For example, when the ball is new, the captain is likely to have lots of slip fielders in place in the hope that the bowler directs the deliveries around off stump, giving the best possible chance of finding the edge of the batsman's bat and a catch being taken.

Bowlers who fail to follow their captain's instruction on where to bowl often find themselves taken out of the attack. The captain decides who does and doesn't bowl (see Chapter 11 for more on the importance of the captain). Few moments in cricket are more exciting than watching a fast bowler charging in to bowl. A great anticipation of what will happen next builds with every stride. This excitement is heightened by the fact that the batsman must react quickly to avoid being hit or dismissed, or to put themselves in a position to score runs. But even the finest bowlers won't be successful if they simply run in and let fly. Brett Lee is a wonderful fast bowler for Australia who has now taken over 200 Test wickets, but he spent 18 months out of the side. That was because he failed to embrace two of a bowler's greatest friends — patience and clear thinking.

A good strike rate of balls per wicket is 55 to 60 balls — about nine or ten overs — for each wicket. A few great fast bowlers, such as Waqar Younis and Malcolm Marshall, have fantastic strike rates around 45 balls per wicket. So even the great bowlers take a lot of balls to get a wicket. Patience and working to a plan are keys. If a bowler is striving to get a wicket every ball, they are going to become pretty frustrated. On the other hand, if you haven't got a wicket for 100 balls, hang in there because it's only a matter of time until a wicket comes your way. Stay in the present and aim to bowl the best ball you can each ball. Don't worry about what has happened or what might happen. A game of cricket can change very quickly!

Winning with patience

A bowler cannot take a wicket every ball and if a bowler continues to attack, allowing a free flow of runs, the result can end up being very costly to the team. A bowler must assess the strengths and weaknesses of each new batsman quickly and have a plan. In club cricket much of the time, a bowler may simply be bowling at, or just outside off stump, with most of the fieldsmen on the off side to try to frustrate the batsman by restricting the scoring. In assessing a batsman, bowlers need to ask themselves questions, such as: Does the batsman play short bowling badly? Does the batsman play with a gap between bat and pad so that an inswinger, off break or googly could sneak through and bowl them? (See Chapter 8 for more on these deliveries.) Do they fail to get their front foot close enough to the ball when playing forward, offering the chance of a catch in front of the wicket? Consult your captain if you think a batsman needs attacking in a particular way, or if you think the field needs changing because of the way the batsman is playing.

Thinking clearly

Bowlers need clear thinking when assessing the conditions and the match situation. An opening bowler with a new ball often tries to pitch the ball up on a full length to give it a better chance of swinging. Likewise, a turf pitch, which is damp or has plenty of grass on it, can aid movement off the seam, also tempting the bowler to pitch the ball up to take advantage of the movement. However, if the ball is not swinging, the conditions are good for batting and the batsmen are *set* — they have been batting for a while and look comfortable — the bowler, who then pitches the ball right up consistently, can simply give away easy runs. Instead, bowling a good length, or even short of a length — also known as *back of a length* — is better to try to restrict the scoring and frustrate the batsmen. Again, discuss the conditions and the match situation with your captain.

Being fit for the task

If a bowler is going to make a significant impact over the course of a match, the bowler needs to develop a reasonable level of fitness. This rule particularly applies to fast bowlers. A fast bowler is not much good to their team or captain if they rush in for their opening spell with the new ball, but then become too tired or sore to bowl extra spells later in the day. Bowling at the end of a day can be very important. If the bowlers tire and cannot maintain line and length — and pace in the case of faster bowlers — the batting side can cash in big time. Bowlers who aren't fit are also more vulnerable to injury and may miss matches completely if unable to bowl properly. Fitness is developed by a combination of general exercise and bowling in the nets. (See Chapter 12 for more on training and fitness.)

Modern-day fast bowlers are more conscious of the need to develop peak physical fitness for the job. Strength and conditioning training, core stability and maximising flexibility are all important. Running techniques and recovery sessions are helping modern fast bowlers stay on the park.

Warming up

These days, people who play sport are advised to stretch and prepare properly, and never has this advice been more applicable than to cricket for bowlers, particularly fast bowlers. Before a match, bowlers are wise to have a few gentle run-throughs to warm up, then bowl some gentle deliveries off a couple of paces in the nets, or to a team mate on the outfield. The bowlers then have a good stretch, ensuring that calves, hamstrings, groin and back are all loosened before doing some more serious pre-match bowling. On the other hand, as a bowler, you have to be careful not to expend too much energy before a match. You're going to need a lot of energy for a big day in the field.

Educating Kevin: Shane shows Pietersen who's the boss

Tactically, Shane Warne is master of having a plan for each batsman he bowls to, always subtly changing his line and length and the amount of spin he imparts on the ball. Changing the angle of the delivery — whether his feet land close to or wide of the stumps at the bowler's end — is a big factor with Warne as well. For example, in the fifth Test at Edgbaston in the 2005 Ashes series, Warne was bowling on a pitch that wasn't spinning a great deal in the first innings. Bowling to Kevin Pietersen, who likes to hit to the leg side, Warne bowled a few overs very close to the stumps, pitching just outside off stump, tempting Pietersen to hit against the line to the leg side. Then Warne bowled a ball from wide of the crease, angling into middle stump, which Pietersen saw as an opportunity and tried to smash it through the leg side. The ball pitched on leg stump, spun away from the batsman, and hit off stump, which was Warne's plan all along.

Chapter 8

Bowling: Holding the Ball

In This Chapter

- Bowling fast, swing and seam
- Feeling the seam
- Swinging along
- Spinning out the batsmen

Being a successful bowler requires two broad and fundamental skills: having a strong, comfortable and repetitive action, and having the knowledge and ability to hold the ball properly. Having learnt how to develop your action in the previous chapter, you will now discover how to create magic with the ball.

Whether you're a fast bowler or a spinner, there are many different deliveries you can serve up to batsmen to confuse them in the hope of claiming their wicket. Read on to find out how you can create your own mystery with the ball.

Becoming a Seam Bowler

Often the first lesson a young bowler is taught is to bowl the ball *seam up*. Bowling seam up is probably the simplest type of delivery to bowl, yet this action can still cause considerable problems for the batsman.

With seam up, the ball is held between the middle and index finger of the bowler's hand with the seam pointing straight down the pitch. The fingers just touch each side of the seam. The thumb holds the seam under the ball and the third finger is tucked in comfortably resting below the ball.

The ball is released with a flick of the wrist straight down the pitch. This action rotates the ball backwards as it leaves the hand, adding a little extra zip and helping the seam cut through the air and grip on the pitch when it lands. If the ball lands properly, hopefully the seam then acts a bit like a ridge, sending the ball away or towards the batsman.

If the ball jags away from the batsman towards the slip fielders, this delivery is called a *leg cutter* (nothing to do with orthopaedic surgery!). If the ball jags from the slip fielders towards the body of the batsman, this delivery is called an *off cutter*.

Despite your best efforts, the ball may not move to the leg or off side but instead just carry straight on.

Bowling a leg cutter

To bowl a leg cutter, the middle finger is placed along the seam (see Figure 8-1), the index finger a couple of centimetres to the left for a right-handed bowler (remember, in a standard seam up position, these two fingers are located equidistant either side of the seam). The ball is cradled by the thumb and third finger. On release of the ball, the bowler tweaks their wrist to the off side, the left side for a right hander, and pulls the middle finger down the seam. This action rotates the seam backwards, the bowler hoping for extra grip and movement when the ball lands on the pitch.

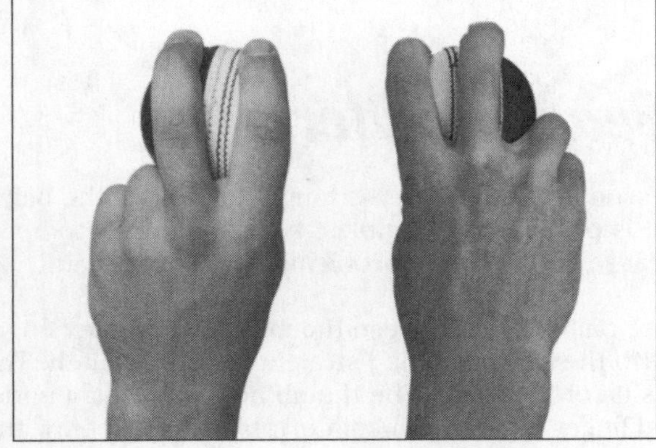

Figure 8-1: How left- and right-handed bowlers should hold a leg cutter.

If a right-arm bowler is bowling to a right-handed batsman (or left armer to left hander), the bowler's aim is to move the ball away from the batsman so the ball hits the outside edge of his bat, the edge furthest away from the batsman, and is caught by the wicketkeeper or slips. (Refer to Chapter 2 for the diagram of the fielding positions.)

Bowling an off cutter

To bowl an off cutter, the index finger is placed along the seam with the middle finger a couple of centimetres to the right for a right-handed bowler (see Figure 8-2). The thumb is also underneath the ball cradling it with the third finger again tucked in.

As the ball is released, the index and middle fingers move down the leg side of the ball (the right side to a right hander), with the index finger dragging along the seam, rotating it backwards.

If a right-arm bowler is bowling to a right-handed batsman (or left armer to left hander), the bowler's aim is to move the ball into the batsman. The bowler's hope is that the ball goes between the batsman's bat and front pad to bowl out the batsman, or to hit the pad, offering the chance of an LBW dismissal.

A bowler who relies primarily on their deliveries to move off the seam to attack the batsman is called a *seamer.*

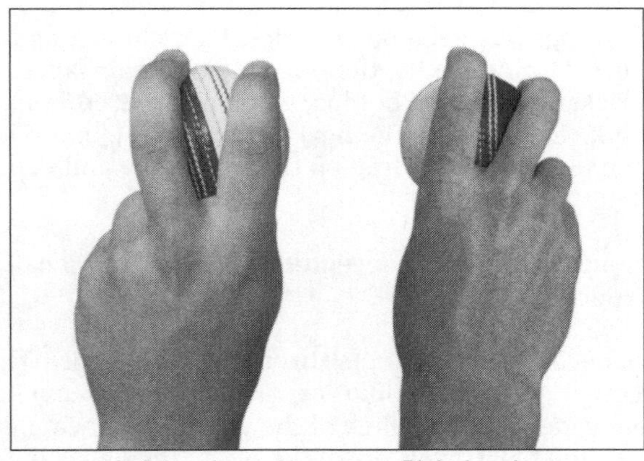

Figure 8-2: Preparing to bowl an off cutter.

Seam and swing bowlers sometimes bowl what is called a *slower ball*. The run-up and delivery action is exactly the same for a slower ball as a normal-paced delivery. However, the bowler spreads their fingers, gripping the ball further apart, and the bowler doesn't flick the wrist on release. This action has the effect of dramatically slowing down the ball in the air. The idea of a slower ball is to deceive the batsman into trying to play a shot as though the ball was bowled at full speed. The result could be a mistimed shot and a greater chance of the batsman being dismissed.

Swinging Your Way to Success

Ever since England triumphed over the Australians in the 2005 Ashes Test series, swing bowling has once again become the talk of the cricketing world. The English bowlers' ability to swing the ball in the air, seemingly at will, was widely recognised as the force that helped them put one over the great Australian batsmen.

But what is the mysterious art of swing bowling? Put simply, swing bowling means bowling deliveries that deviate — sometimes dramatically — in the air. The batsman can watch a ball leaving a bowler's hand and work out which line the ball is taking, only for the ball to suddenly swing in a different direction, catching the batsman off-guard.

Putting swing under the microscope

The reason a ball swings has been one of cricket's great talking points for more than a century. More recently, the reason a ball swings has attracted the attention of cricketing science boffins, who have placed cricket balls in wind tunnels as though they were the next generation of jumbo jets. These aerodynamics have examined the drag on the ball to try and explain exactly why it deviates.

This section sets out the generally accepted theory of why a ball swings, although some experts may disagree.

A new ball swings because the ball cuts through the air easily. The ball swings in the direction the seam is pointing, as long as the seam has a perfect backward rotation, generated by a flick of the wrist. If the seam is wobbling all over the place as the ball travels down the pitch, the ball is highly unlikely to swing.

As the ball slowly wears by hitting the pitch, hitting the bat and occasionally crashing into the fence beyond the boundary, the bowler polishes the least worn of the two sides to keep one side shiny. This is the reason fast bowlers often end up with red marks on their trousers.

The idea of this preparation of the ball is that the shiny side can cut through the air more quickly than the rough side. Remember two simple facts about what is regarded as orthodox swing bowling and you're well on the way to fooling the batsman:

- Point the seam in the direction you want the ball to swing
- Position the shiny side of the ball on the opposite side to the direction in which you want the ball to swing.

Bowling an inswinger

The *inswinger* moves in the air from the off side of a batsman to the leg side.

Here's how you bowl an inswinger: The fingers are placed on the seam, which is in a vertical position but angled slightly towards the batsman's leg side (to the right when bowling to a right-handed batsman). The thumb cradles the ball underneath the seam. The polished side of the ball is pointing towards the off side (see Figure 8-3).

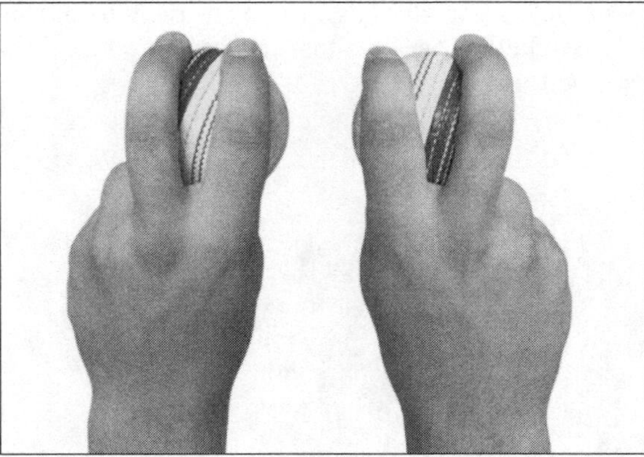

Left hand Right hand

Figure 8-3: For an inswinger, the seam of the ball points towards the batsman's leg side.

An inswinger is delivered with a very high arm action. The arm is just about touching the bowler's ear and the wrist can also be pointed slightly towards the batsman.

As with the off cutter in seam bowling, if a right-arm bowler is bowling to a right-handed batsman (or left armer to a left hander), the bowler's aim is to move the ball into the batsman. The bowler's hope is that the ball goes between the batsman's bat and front pad and bowls the batsman, or hits the pad, offering the chance of an LBW dismissal.

Bowling an outswinger

The *outswinger* moves from the leg side of a batsman to the off side — in the direction of the wicketkeeper and slip fielders.

Here's how you bowl an outswinger: The seam of the ball is to be angled towards the slips. The polished side of the ball is on the batsman's leg side, presuming a right-handed batsman (see Figure 8-4).

An outswinger is delivered with a slightly round arm action. This means the bowling arm, as it rotates, is to be slightly towards the leg side for a right-arm bowler bowling to a right-handed batsman.

If a right-arm bowler is bowling to a right-handed batsman (or left armer to left hander), the bowler's aim is to move the ball away from the batsman so it hits the outside edge of his bat, the edge furthest away from the batsman, and is caught by the wicketkeeper or slips. (Refer to Chapter 2 for the diagram of fielding positions.)

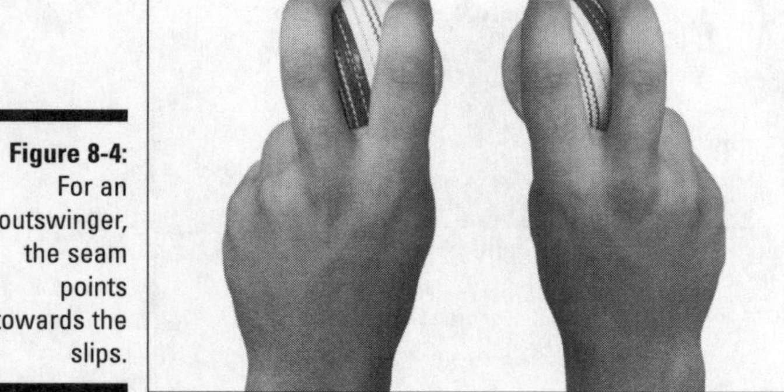

Figure 8-4: For an outswinger, the seam points towards the slips.

A swinging ball needs a stable seam

Swing is not necessarily a natural skill. If you looked at the actions of some of England's quick bowlers in the 2005 Ashes Test series — Steve Harmison, Andrew Flintoff and Simon Jones — and compared those actions to the actions of the same bowlers a few years earlier, you'd see that those bowlers have lately taught themselves to be more consistent with their wrists and fingers behind the ball at release. This action gives these bowlers a better chance of getting a stable seam, which is angled either way, to maximise the chances of the ball swinging.

Swing bowling is very difficult to master. Some bowlers, no matter how hard they try, are never able to master swing bowling, or some bowlers can manage swing bowling one day and not the next. Always practise your bowling variations at training first, so that you are confident with each variation before trying them out in a match situation.

Weather conditions seem to have an effect on cricket ball swing. When the sky is cloudy overhead and the weather is a little muggy, the ball usually swings more than on a day when the sky is cloudless and the air is cold. No one quite knows the reason why the ball reacts this way, not even the weather bureau knows! What's more, white-coloured cricket balls — used in one-day internationals — swing more than traditional red-coloured balls. Again, the reason is a mystery.

Teams go out of their way to shine one side of the cricket ball more than the other to help aid the swinging process. Some players have gone a bit too far in the past and have altered the condition of the ball by applying potions, such as petroleum jelly to polish the ball. This behaviour is called *tampering with the ball* and is against the laws of the game.

Bowling reverse swing

Reverse swing is one of the strangest phenomena in sport. Sometimes, once a ball becomes old — say after 40 overs of use — and one side is badly scuffed, the ball can start to behave unconventionally.

Different bowlers hold the seam in different positions for reverse swing, so experiment and see what works for you. Damien Fleming holds the seam straight for reverse swing while another former Australian player, Geoff Lawson, pointed it in the direction he wanted to swing the ball. However, former Pakistani great, Waqar Younis, held the seam like an outswinger for his reverse swing inswinger and bowled it with a round-arm action. Waqar was one of reverse swing's deadliest exponents.

Damien the bowler plays batsman to one of the great swing bowlers

Wasim Akram was the most skilled fast bowler I played against. He was near express pace, swung the ball both ways with new and old balls, had a good, quick bouncer, deceptive slower balls and an excellent yorker. He once bowled me in a Test in Rawalpindi in Pakistan when he released the ball from round the wicket, wide of the crease, angled the ball into me, then swung it viciously late to york me and hit my off stump. Such a fine delivery was wasted on me!

Reverse swing can create havoc for batsmen because the ball behaves in line with orthodox swing one minute, and starts reversing the next minute.

Once again, not all experts agree on why this phenomenon happens, but one theory suggests the rough side of the ball breaks up the air around the ball and actually creates less air pressure than the smooth side, allowing the rough side of the ball to travel through the air more quickly.

As mentioned earlier, England's 2005 Ashes Test series triumph was in large part due to two of England's bowlers, Simon Jones and Andrew 'Freddie' Flintoff, being able to reverse swing the cricket ball. Before these English heroes helped lead England to victory, the great Pakistani quick bowlers, Waqar Younis and Wasim Akram, were the kings of reverse swing.

Sarfraz leaves Australia spellbound

Sarfraz Nawaz, the Pakistan fast bowler from the 1970s and early 1980s, is generally regarded as the original master of reverse swing bowling. Reverse swing bowling was a skill mastered out of necessity on his Pakistani home pitches, which struggle to allow traditional swing with their flat, low, abrasive surfaces. Sarfraz once took nine wickets in an innings against Australia, including an amazing spell of seven wickets for one run!

No one has drawn an easy route map for bowlers to find the 'hidden treasure' of skills that make up reverse swing bowling. But one fact is certain: Whether reverse swing occurs — or doesn't — in a match depends on the condition of the ball.

The further the ball is pitched up on a full length, the more chance the ball has to swing (refer to Chapter 7 for more on the line and length of a delivery). Swing bowlers often have to be brave as well as clever because pitching the ball up can also make scoring runs easier for the batsmen.

Bowling is not an exact science. As hard as you try, sometimes the ball just won't move off the *straight* (will only travel in a straight line). Whether the day's conditions don't suit, whether your action's developed a technical glitch, or whether the cricketing gods simply are conspiring against you, all your attempts to swing and seam the ball are being met with deliveries that are gun-barrel straight. In this case, the only weapon you have left at your disposal is accuracy. Keep building the pressure by making it tough for the batsman to score — and the batsman may just get themself out in frustration.

Terrifying 'Thommo'

Perhaps the fastest, most dangerous and most unusual fast bowler ever seen was Australia's Jeff (Thommo) Thomson. Not particularly tall but powerful and athletic, Thomson had an amazing action, which has never really been successfully repeated at international level. While most bowlers gather their hands in front of their chest and raise one to the sky as they rotate the other to deliver the ball, Thomson flung his in opposite directions. This action meant that while his left arm was pointing skyward, his right arm was drawn right back like a javelin thrower's arm preparing to launch the javelin.

At his frightening peak in the mid 1970s, Thomson would draw his right arm so far back behind him in his delivery stride that his hand would be less than a third of a metre (approximately one foot) from the ground, while his front foot (left foot) was raised almost at head height.

This position created enormous power as Thommo banged his front foot down and flung his right arm over to catapult the ball at a ferocious pace.

Enhance your physical skills

To help build success, bowlers can develop numerous physical skills — express pace, steep bounce, swing and seam, great accuracy, subtle changes of pace both faster and slower — just to name a few. Very rarely do bowlers have all the skills. However, to be an international bowler, you must have a few. Among the Australians, fast bowler, Glenn McGrath, has good pace, great bounce and accuracy with good changes of pace. Brett Lee has express pace and good swing with the new and old ball. Jason Gillespie has pace, steep bounce and excellent accuracy. Fast bowling is the art of mixing these physical skills with strong mental and tactical skills.

Telling speedsters from slow coaches

In typically quirky fashion, cricket followers have come up with a way to categorise who is a really quick bowler and who isn't. In Test cricket, working out the pace of a delivery is easy because TV broadcasters use a radar gun — similar to radar guns that police officers use to book speeding cars — to measure how fast the ball is travelling from the bowler to the batsman. This guide includes the ultimate bowling sub-categories to show who bowls at what speed at their peak — in kilometres per hour (kph) and miles per hour (mph).

- **Fast bowler:** Delivers consistently above 140kph (approximately 90mph).
  Example: Brett Lee.
- **Fast-medium bowler:** Delivers 130–140kph (approximately 80–90mph).
  Example: Glenn McGrath.
- **Medium fast bowler:** Delivers 120–130kph (approximately 75–80mph).
  Example: Nathan Bracken.
- **Medium pace bowler:** Delivers 110–120kph (approximately 70–75mph).
  Example: Andrew Symonds.
- **Medium slow bowler:** Delivers 100–110kph (approximately 60–70mph).
  Example: Mike Hussey.
- **Slow-medium bowler:** Delivers 80–100kph (approximately 50–60mph).
  Example: Cameron White.
- **Slow bowler:** Delivers below 80kph (50mph).
  Example: Shane Warne.

In reality, only top-class professional cricketers are able to bowl a cricket ball at fast or even fast-medium pace. The fastest bowlers playing in club cricket fall into the medium fast bowling bracket.

The pace at which a ball is delivered can make a huge difference. The quicker the ball, the less time the batsman has to react. Sometimes you hear that a batsman has been *beaten for pace.* This phrase means that the batsman didn't react quickly enough to execute a shot.

Taking It to the Batsmen: Spin Bowling

The aim of spin bowling is to bowl the cricket ball with rapid rotation so that when the ball bounces off the wicket it will change direction — or spin — either towards or away from the batsman.

Spin bowlers use wrist or finger motion to cause the ball to rotate, depending on which way the bowler wants the ball to 'turn'.

Deviation — or spin — off the pitch can make it hard for the batsman to hit the ball properly. The batsman may misjudge the direction and extent of the ball spin, which could lead to the batsman missing the ball altogether and being bowled, dismissed LBW or stumped by the wicketkeeper. Alternatively, the batsman may not hit the ball properly, giving the chance of a catch to the wicketkeeper, bowler or fieldsmen.

Cricket lovers really enjoy watching a good spinner in action, trying to outsmart the batsman. The spin bowler doesn't rely on pace to get wickets, but on guile. Spinners also have shorter run-ups than faster bowlers because spinners bowl more slowly, so they get through their overs more quickly. Shorter run-ups mean spectators don't have to wait long for each delivery to be bowled, increasing the action out in the middle.

Spin bowlers prefer to bowl with an old, worn cricket ball. The older a ball, the easier it is for a spinner to grip, and the rougher a ball, the more chance it has of gripping on the pitch and spinning. In longer matches, such as Test and first class, spin bowlers tend to be more effective in the later stages of the game because the turf pitch deteriorates. The pitch is increasingly marked by the spikes of the fast bowlers' boots as the game goes on. As well, the pitch dries out and then may crack and crumble, providing more purchase for the spinning ball. (Refer to Chapter 2 for more on pitches.)

Here are some of the ways that spin bowlers can trap batsmen in their wicket-taking webs:

- **Flight:** The higher the ball loops in the air on leaving the bowler's hand, the longer the ball takes to come down. A delivery that's in flight for a long time can trick the batsman into playing the shot too soon. On the flipside, a ball that's the same pace on leaving the bowler's hand but is headed on a lower trajectory can arrive at the batsman quite quickly, possibly hurrying the batsman to play a shot.
- **Spin off the pitch:** Spin is the number-one weapon in the spin bowler's armoury. (See the next section, 'Understanding the types of spin bowler'.)
- **Variation of pace:** The ability to bowl faster or slower is not just the preserve of seam bowlers. Spinners can vary the speed too! With just a little effort, most good spinners can bowl a ball much faster or slower than normal, hoping to catch the batsman unaware, leading to a mistake.

A cricket ball bowled by a spinner can also deviate in the air. This deviation is called *drift*. When combined with spin off the wicket, flight and changes of pace, drift can make it very hard for batsmen to judge where the ball is headed and what shot is best to play.

Spin bowlers use a mix of varying pace, flight and spin off the pitch to trap batsmen. Good bowlers can produce all three several times an over, always keeping the batsmen wondering what type of delivery is coming next — looping, quick or slow?

A delivery bowled by a spinner is far slower than one from a fast bowler. Sometimes you hear spin bowlers referred to as *slow bowlers*.

Understanding the types of spin bowler

A cricket ball can be made to rotate — spin — through use of the wrist or fingers. Logically, therefore, it follows that spin bowlers can be divided into two categories.

- Players using *wrist spin* to rotate the ball — the right hander is called a *leg spin bowler*. The left hander, quite oddly, is called a *Chinaman bowler* or, simply, a *left-arm wrist spinner*.
- Players using *finger spin* to rotate the ball — the right hander is called an *off spin bowler*. The left hander is called a *left-arm orthodox*.

Each type of bowler — wrist and finger spinners — have their own set of special deliveries. The execution of these special deliveries depends on one of the following:

- In the case of leg spin and left-arm wrist spin bowlers, the position of the bowling hand at delivery.
- In the case of off spin and left-arm orthodox bowlers, the position of the fingers in relation to the seam of the cricket ball at delivery.

Wrist spinners have far more special deliveries than finger spinners, making wrist spinners the worst type of nightmare for many batsmen. But finger spin bowlers can still vary their pace and flight, as well as use drift in the air to take batsmen by surprise. Finger spinners are also usually more accurate than wrist spinners because wrist spin is more difficult to bowl.

Focusing on wrist spin bowling

Wrist spinners have lots of special deliveries to choose from. But wrist spin bowling is incredibly tricky to master. You may be able to bowl one or two of the special deliveries once in a while but, to be considered top class, you have to be able to bowl the different types of wrist spin deliveries consistently.

Leg break

The most common delivery bowled by a right-arm wrist spinner is a leg break, made famous by Australia's Shane Warne (see Figure 8-5).

Left-hand front

Right-hand front

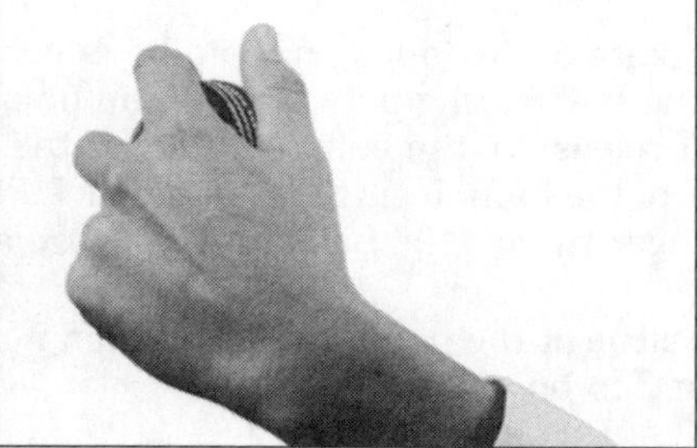

Left-hand rear

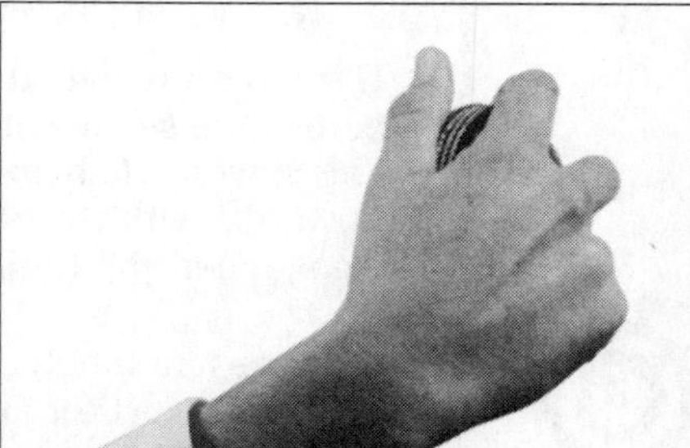

Right-hand rear

Figure 8-5: Holding a leg break with fingers across the seam.

Here's how a leg break works:

- **What happens:** The ball will *break* — spin — from the batsman's legs towards the slip fielder. This action is often considered the easiest ball for the wrist spinner to execute and, as a result, is the one bowled most often.
- **How to do it:** The top joints of the index and middle fingers are held across the seam of the ball, which is resting on the thumb and the third finger, which is bent. On release, the third finger tweaks the ball in an anti-clockwise direction and the wrist rotates to finish facing downwards towards the floor.

A well-spun leg break can drift in towards the batsman's legs and drop in the air before spinning away, further confusing the batsman.

The aim of a leg break is to have the batsman caught by the wicketkeeper or slip by the ball hitting the outside edge of the bat. Alternatively the batsman may be caught by one of the other fieldsmen by mistiming a shot. (Refer to Chapter 5 and Chapter 6 for more on batting.)

Wrong 'un or googly

The wrong 'un, short for 'wrong one', or googly is a surprise weapon for wrist spinners (see Figure 8-6).

Here's how a wrong 'un (googly) works:

- **What happens:** From the batsman's perspective, the wrist movement involved in a googly looks almost identical to a leg spinner. However, the ball, once delivered, behaves in the opposite way to a leg break and turns towards the batsman — from off side to leg side — rather than away. A wrong 'un is one of the hardest types of deliveries to master.
- **How to do it:** The top joints of the index and middle fingers are placed across the seam, with the ball resting between the thumb and the third finger, which is bent. At release of the ball, the palm of the hand opens upwards, with the back of the hand facing the batsman. Like a standard leg spinner, the third finger tweaks the ball anti-clockwise at release.

Dropping the left shoulder a little at the point of delivery can make it easier to get the wrist further around to bowl the wrong 'un.

The bowler's aim is to surprise the batsman and either bowl them or trap them LBW. Use this delivery sparingly so the wrong 'un (googly) maintains the element of surprise.

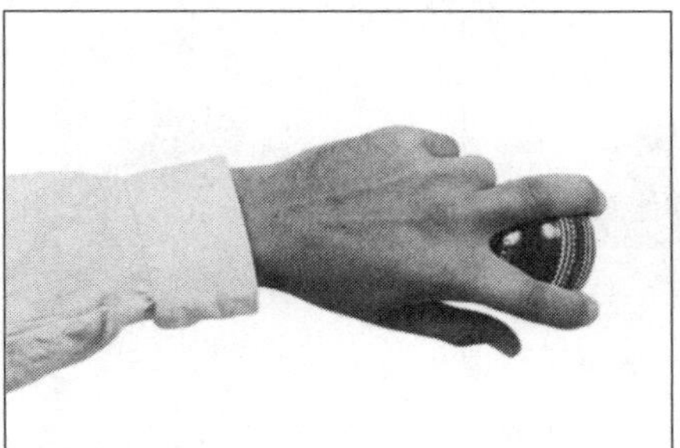

Left-hand front

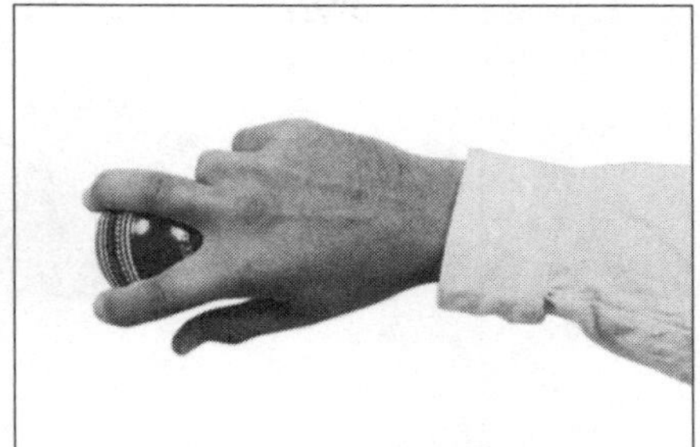

Right-hand front

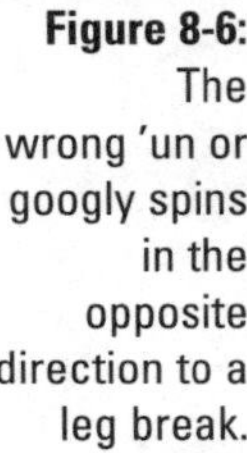

Figure 8-6: The wrong 'un or googly spins in the opposite direction to a leg break.

Left-hand rear

Right-hand rear

Top spinner

The top spinner is another variation a wrist spinner can use to confuse the batsman (see Figure 8-7).

Here's how a top spinner works:

- **What happens:** The ball can drop quickly in the air on its way to the batsman and once it bounces off the pitch, the ball heads straight on instead of spinning into or away from the batsman. A top spinner tends to bounce higher than a googly, increasing the chances of the ball striking high up on the bat or hitting the gloves and offering the chance of a catch to the fielders.
- **How to do it:** The top joints of the index and middle fingers are held across the seam of the cricket ball. The ball rests between the thumb and third finger of the hand, which is bent.

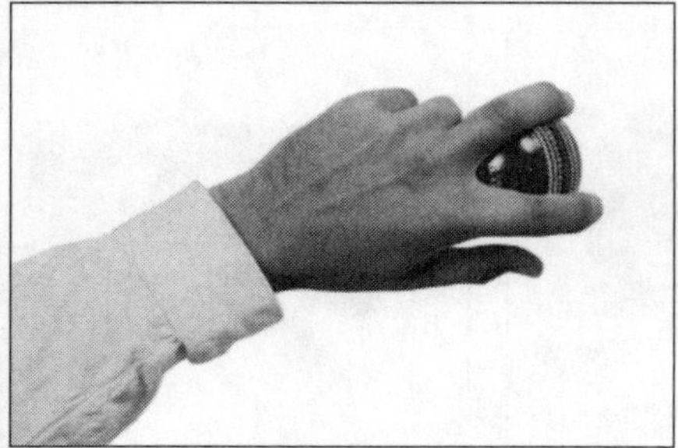

Left-hand rear

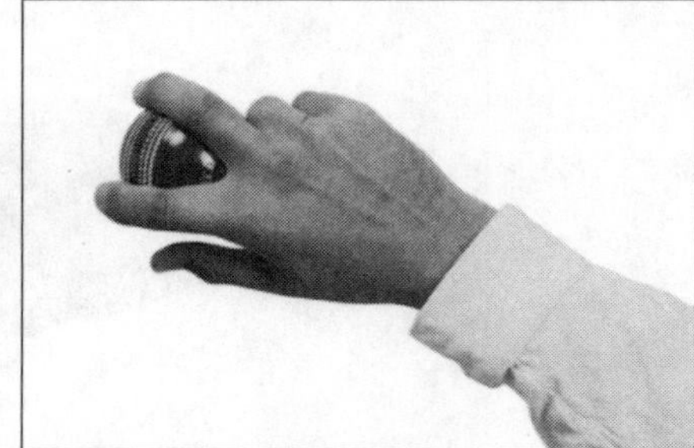

Right-hand rear

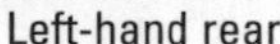

Left-hand front

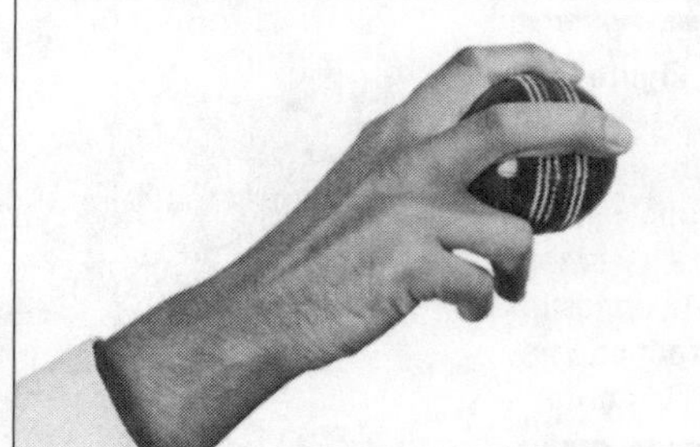

Right-hand front

Figure 8-7: Unlike the leg break or googly, the top spinner bounces straight towards the batsman.

The ball is delivered with the back of the hand facing the sky at release. The ball is delivered out of the side of the hand in contrast to a googly where the wrist is 180 degrees relative to the floor. Again, the third finger tweaks the ball in an anti-clockwise direction at release.

A top spinner can drop quite significantly after being released. This drop, like that of a leg break, is called a leg spinner's *loop*.

The aim is to fool the batsman as the ball drops, making the batsman hit a catch to one of the fieldsmen.

Flipper

The most difficult delivery in a wrist spinner's armoury is the flipper but it can achieve deadly results if developed with plenty of practice (see Figure 8-8).

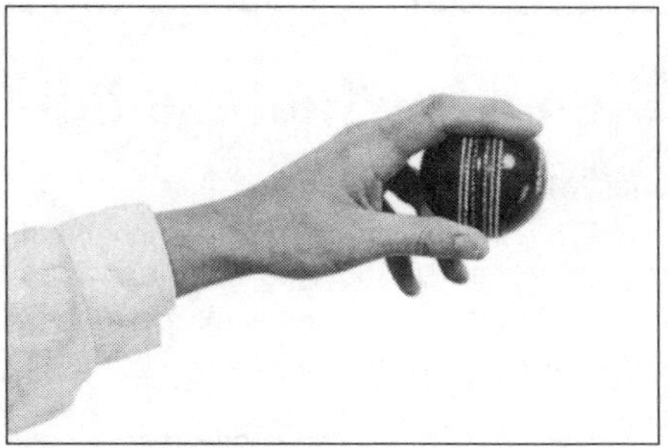

Left-hand front

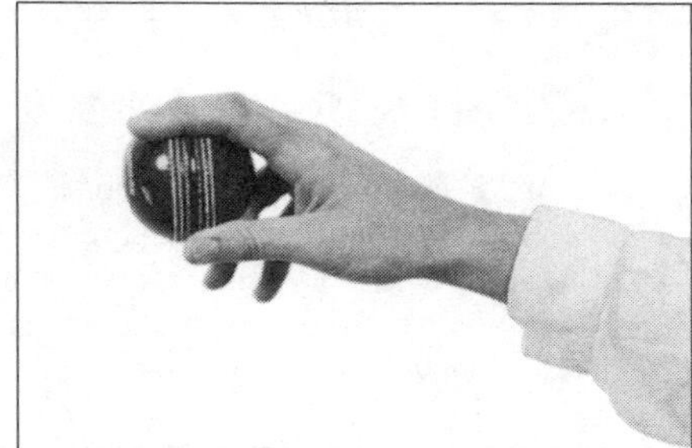

Right-hand front

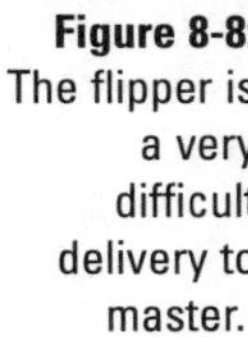

Figure 8-8: The flipper is a very difficult delivery to master.

Left-hand rear

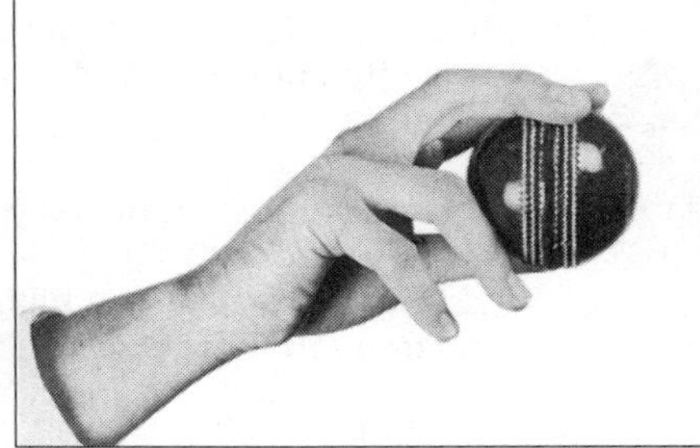

Right-hand rear

Here's how a flipper works:

- **What happens:** On pitching, this type of delivery keeps low and skids quickly towards the batsman. If directed at the stumps, a flipper can be a deadly weapon as it often takes batsmen by surprise. The ball is held in the hand like a normal leg spinner but doesn't actually spin as much or even, sometimes, at all.
- **How to do it:** The ball, like a standard leg spinner, is held with the index and middle fingers across the seam of the ball. The ball rests between the thumb and third finger of the hand, which is bent. On release, though, the thumb tweaks the ball in a clockwise direction. In effect, the bowler is clicking their fingers when releasing the ball; this motion is used to negate the natural spinning effects of the wrist spin action. If executed well, the clicking motion and the position of the wrist at release should cancel one another out. The ball should hurry on to the batsman.

Shane shows how a flipper can fool the batsman

The world's greatest leg spin bowler, Shane Warne, is also Test cricket's highest wicket taker. Warne's two greatest assets are his amazing accuracy and his ability to spin the ball sharply at times. However, he has also claimed many of his wickets with well placed flippers. Batsmen often play back to attack only to find the ball has hurried on, bowling them or trapping them leg before wicket. Heading into the 2006–07 Ashes series, Warne had 685 Test wickets.

The flipper should only be tried by more mature cricketers once the basics of wrist spin have been mastered. A bowler needs a strong hand and wrist to bowl this delivery, which can put a lot of strain on the bowling arm and shoulder.

Generally, club-standard wrist spinners can get by for their whole careers having only perfected one or two types of delivery. Bowlers who have ambitions to play at a higher level need to have more variety because the batsmen they face will be better than most.

Looking at finger spin bowling

Finger spinning is far and away the most popular variety of spin bowling. Most club, first-class and Test teams will have a finger spinner in their ranks. The popularity of finger spinning is understandable because it is easier to bowl than wrist spin. However, the best finger spinners are able to bring all sorts of other weapons to bear, such as varying flight, pace and drift in the air.

Off break

The easiest type of delivery for a spinner to bowl is an off break (see Figure 8-9).

Here's how an off break works:

- **What happens:** The ball turns from the off side to the leg on pitching, assuming the batsman is right handed.
- **How to do it:** The top joints of the index and middle fingers are spread wide across the seam of the ball and the ball rests on the third finger of

> the hand. The wrist turns clockwise on release, a bit like turning a door handle, and the index finger is dragged across the seam of the ball, making it rotate. In cricket lingo, this dragging of the index finger across the ball is called giving the ball a *rip*. The more revolutions the bowler is able to put on the ball through the dragging of the index finger, the better the chance the bowler has of getting the ball to deviate a considerable distance from the off to leg side, again assuming a right-handed batsman is facing.

The aim is to turn the ball between bat and pad, bowling the batsman.

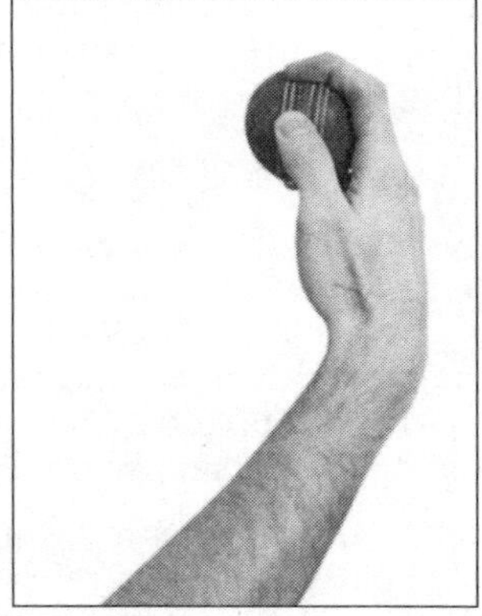
Right-hand rear

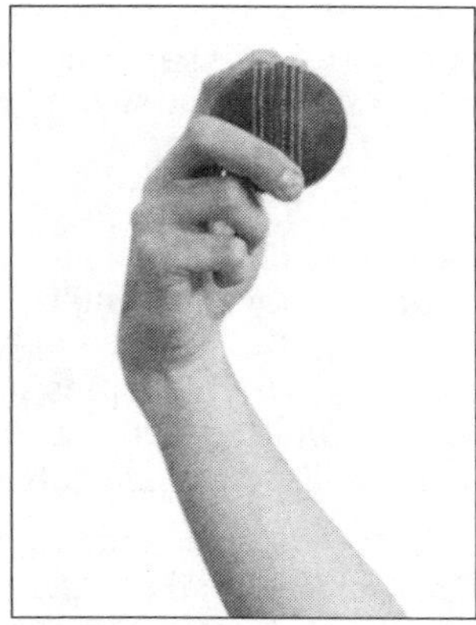
Right-hand front

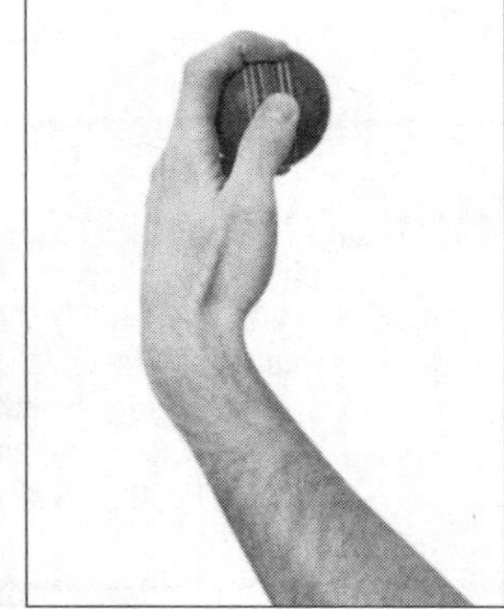
Left-hand rear

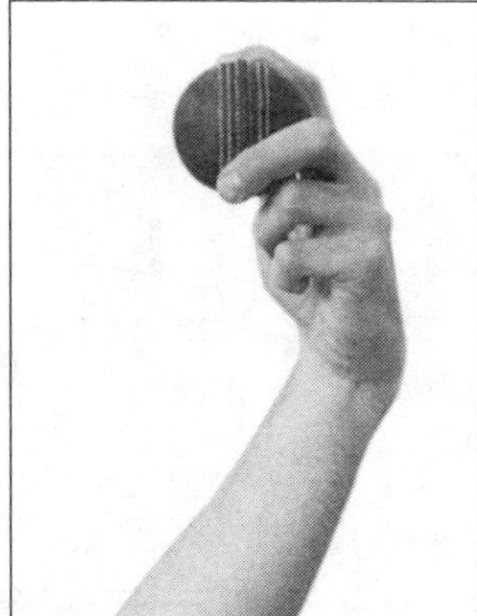
Left-hand front

Figure 8-9: An off break is bowled with a flick of the index finger.

Arm ball

The idea of an arm ball is to surprise the batsman, who will be looking for the off break turning back into them if they are a right hander.

- **What happens:** The ball drifts away from the right-handed batsman in the hope that it will hit the outside edge of the bat, producing a catch for the wicketkeeper or slip.
- **How to do it:** The bowler's action should look no different to a standard off spinner. However, the bowler places their index finger along the seam of the ball rather than across it. Instead of ripping the index finger across the top of the ball like an off break, the finger runs down the seam, making the delivery more like a little outswinger that drifts towards slip (see the section, 'Bowling an outswinger', earlier in the chapter for more on outswing bowling).

Doosra

The doosra is a rare and tricky delivery which most off spinners find difficult to bowl without illegally throwing the ball.

- **What happens:** The ball spins in the opposite direction to an off break — from leg to off for a right hander — in the hope that, like the arm ball, the delivery will produce a catch for the wicketkeeper or slip.
- **How to do it:** A doosra is an off break delivery released from the back of the hand rather than the front. The ball is held and released in the same manner as an off break except the wrist is turned right around facing the batsman. The doosra delivery tends to bounce a little higher than an off break. Very few bowlers around the world have mastered the art of the doosra.

Saqlain names cricket's difficult doosra

The doosra was named by Pakistani off spinner Saqlain Mushtaq, who perfected the delivery during the late 1990s. *Doosra* means 'the other one' in the Urdu language. While Saqlain was a master at the doosra, very few off spinners can manage this delivery without illegally throwing the ball. Indeed, off spinners must be careful because the natural action of flicking the ball with the index finger can result in a throw. (Refer to Chapter 7 for more about bowlers chucking.)

Left-arm orthodox bowlers are, in effect, just off spin bowlers who deliver the ball from their left hand. But the fact that the ball is delivered from the left hand means that the ball turns away rather than towards a right-handed batsman. Left-arm orthodox bowlers often bowl from round the wicket rather than over with the aim of getting the ball to drift towards the bat in the air, only for the ball to move away towards the slips on bouncing.

Not every ball bowled by a finger spin bowler will be an off break. Bowlers try to mix up deliveries — such as bowling the odd arm ball in a bid to surprise the batsman who is expecting an off break delivery.

With very rare exceptions, bowlers become good at one particular aspect of this sometimes difficult but rewarding craft. If you're just starting out as a bowler, experiment at practice. See what you're good at and most enjoy. You may, for example, be able to bowl accurately for long periods and become a steady medium pacer, learning to move the ball in the air and off the pitch. You may have a strong wrist that allows you to bowl sharp-turning wrist spin, the patience to work on being an off-spinner or that rare ability to bowl really quickly and unsettle batsmen.

Whatever you decide, develop a *stock ball*, a delivery that you can bowl over and over again with great accuracy and control. This is a leg break for the wrist spinner, an off break for the off spinner and, depending on your action, may be an outswinger for the fast bowler and an off cutter for the medium pacer. Having lots of tricks is useless if you can't bowl them accurately. The result is that the batsmen get easy runs and your captain takes you out of the attack.

Learn to bowl one delivery well and then add occasional variations to surprise the batsman in the hope of dismissing them. Use your special deliveries sparingly or they can lose the element of surprise. Always develop these deliveries at training before using them in a game.

Chapter 9

Fielding Made Easy

In This Chapter

- Gauging the importance of good fielding
- Looking at the role of fielding positions
- Developing fielding skills
- Getting ready to field
- Playing the field
- Thinking on your feet

Not that long ago plenty of cricketers — even some professionals — didn't take fielding seriously. These cricketers saw having to stand around in the field picking up a cricket ball, throwing it to the wicketkeeper and taking the odd catch, as nothing more than a distraction from the serious business of batting and bowling.

Those days are long gone. Today, cricketers playing at all levels of the game — from Test match down to club standard — take fielding far more seriously. Why? Because better fielding saves runs, puts extra pressure on batsmen and offers more chance of victory.

This chapter examines the fielding positions in detail and looks at how you can be a success at cricket's third major discipline. (Refer to Chapter 2 for a diagram of the major fielding positions.)

The general standard of fielding has increased dramatically in the past 20 years, mainly because in one-day cricket, where finishes are often close, saving runs has become so much more important. Players are fitter and more professional than ever and take their fielding duties far more seriously. If you're competing for a place in a team either as a batsman or a bowler, and the captain or selectors who choose the side are unsure who to pick, then the better fielder almost always gets the job.

Why Fielding Is So Important

Great feats of batting and bowling usually hog the headlines, but good fielding can make a crucial contribution to a team's success. Fielding is no easy job, especially when the temperature is hitting the highs of summer and no sea breeze is blowing to cool the day.

Concentration on the field can present a challenge to the fittest player, but concentration is a necessary ingredient when the ball is coming your way — or close enough for you to run and catch or stop it.

Being good at fielding

Being good at fielding means doing the following:

- **Taking catches:** One of the main jobs of a fielder is to take catches. A catching chance is given when the batsman hits the ball in the air within reach of the fielder. If the catch is taken without the ball hitting the ground, then the batsman is dismissed — unless the bowler has delivered a no ball (refer to Chapter 2 for more).
- **Stopping runs:** The batsmen want to score runs. The bowlers try to prevent the batsmen from scoring runs. But to prevent runs, the bowlers need the help of the nine fielders and the wicketkeeper. Fielders try to stop the ball in the outfield and throw it to the wicketkeeper — or bowler — standing by the stumps, before the two batsmen run from opposite ends along the pitch to register a run.

When a fielder fails to take a catching chance, the batsman is said to have been *dropped*.

One of the most famous sayings in cricket is that 'catches win matches'. Quite often, the team that drops the fewest catches in a match is triumphant. Bowlers work very hard to get batsmen to make a mistake by hitting the ball in the air rather than along the ground. When this happens, bowlers expect these catching chances to be taken by a fieldsman.

And speaking of fieldsmen, Damien Fleming, who has served as one of this country's top cricket coaches, has more tips in this chapter, this time on fielding. Look for the 'Damien says' icons — and here's one now!

Cricketers spend more time fielding than performing any other skill. Not being a liability in the field is very important.

Understanding fielding positions

A team always has nine fieldsmen, excluding the bowler and the wicketkeeper (see Chapter 10 for more about wicketkeepers). However, the playing field is a very large open space, which means that relatively few fielders have to cover a great area.

Over the years, captains have developed what are called *fielding positions*. Refer to Chapter 2 for a diagram of the fielding positions, which are the particular locations where the fieldsmen stand. The idea of fielding is to:

- Be in the best position to take catches
- Be in the best position to stop scoring shots.

Note that some fielding positions try to do both.

Batsmen have a range of shots they can play. (Refer to Chapter 5 for more on scoring shots.)

Shots from the batsmen don't always go where intended. Sometimes the ball hits the edge rather than the centre — or middle — of the bat and can send the ball in an unintended direction. The fielder then has a catching opportunity because balls hitting the edge of the bat tend to travel in the air.

The great variety of fielding positions significantly outnumber the nine fielders (refer to Chapter 2). The captain moves fielders to positions where they believe the batsman may hit the ball.

Captains can be as inventive as they like, sometimes asking a fielder to stand in an unusual fielding position. The captain may spot something in the batsman's technique that indicates that the ball is likely to go to a particular part of the field. (See Chapter 11 for more on tactics.)

Assessing Standard Fielding Positions

Despite the large number of different fielding positions, most captains stick to a few tried and tested ones, which fit into two distinct groups:

- Close catching positions
- Run-saving positions.

Close catching positions

If the ball hits the edge of the batsman's bat, or the batsman fails to execute a shot properly, the ball is likely to carry in the air and may present a catch for one of the close fielders to snaffle.

Close catching positions include:

- **Slip and gully fielders:** Fielders located to the right side of the wicketkeeper for a right-handed batsman and left side for a left-handed batsman are *slip and gully fielders.* The fielders form an arc. The idea is to snaffle any edges resulting from the batsman playing deliveries directed on or just outside the line of off stump. As a guide, if the wicketkeeper stretches out their right arm sideways, and the slips stretch out their arms, the extended fingers just touch the keeper or slip fielder alongside. First slip then takes a couple of paces back. All remaining slips stay in the same arc as the keeper.

  How close slip fielders stand in relation to the batsman depends on the pace of the bowler. The faster the bowler, the more carry the delivery has and the further away the wicketkeeper and slip and gully fielders stand.

  When a fielding team is on the attack, especially at the start of an innings when the best fast bowler is bowling and the cricket ball is new, you tend to find captains deploying more players in the slips because the likelihood of a batsman edging the ball in that direction is quite high. Interestingly, in one-day matches, where saving runs is at least as important as dismissing the batsman, fewer slips — and sometimes no slips — are deployed. (Refer to Chapter 3 for more on one-day cricket.)

- **Bat-pad fielders:** Bat-pad fielders are located close to where the batsman stands on the crease. Some of the fielding positions have laugh-out-loud names such as *silly mid off, silly mid on* and *short leg,* or even *short backward point*. But disregard the comedy names, these fielders mean business. The chief objective of these fielders is to take catches that result from the batsman playing a false shot. Sometimes what happens is that the batsman gets their calculation of the direction and bounce of the ball wrong and the ball strikes the bat, then hits the pad or glove and loops in the air. This is the time for the bat-pad fielders to do their work, particularly when slow spinners are bowling.

- **Short leg fielder:** Fast bowlers often have a short leg fieldsman in the hope that, when the ball bounces at a batsman's head or ribs, the batsman fends a catch while trying to protect themselves. Reacting with lightning speed, the close infielders fling themselves about to take a catch. Usually, bat-pad fielders stand no more than three or four metres from the batsman. (Refer to the fielding positions diagram in Chapter 2 for where precisely in the field these players stand, and Chapter 7 and Chapter 8 for more on bowling.)

When the ball strikes the batsman's gloves, pads or any part of their kit or anatomy after hitting the bat, and is then caught by a fielder before it bounces, a catch is made and the batsman is dismissed. If the ball strikes the glove, while the glove is holding the bat, and flies to a fielder and is then caught without bouncing, that too leads to a dismissal. However, if the ball hits the batsman's pads or any part of his anatomy, without making contact with the bat at any stage, then a catch is not awarded by the umpire.

A number of bat-pad fielders can be deployed when spin bowlers are bowling to the batsmen. On the flip side, captains tend to deploy a number of fielders to stand in the slips and gully arc when faster bowlers are attacking the batsmen.

The closer the fielder is to the batsman, the more likely the fielder is to be primarily concentrating on taking a catch. But the closer the fielder, the less time they have to react to the ball hit by the batsman.

Most close fielders concentrate on watching the bat as the ball is being delivered. Close fielders simply don't have time to turn and watch the ball, then see where the ball is going once the batsman has played it. In the slips, first slip is on such a narrow angle that the fielder can watch the ball being delivered, but everyone else in the slips and gully region focuses on the outside edge of the bat in case the ball hits it and flies towards them.

Players fielding in close in front of the batsman are not allowed to make substantial movements as the bowler runs in to deliver the ball. Movement by these fielders is considered unfair to the batsman and could distract the batsman who is concentrating on playing the delivery.

David Boon: Making short leg his own

David Boon, a great Australian batsman from the mid 1980s to the mid 1990s, made the short leg position his own. Boon was renowned for his courage and good reflexes as well as his catching ability. By keeping his body as low as possible, he gave himself the best chance of catching a low inside edge onto the batsman's pads. Being so close to the batsman, short leg fieldsmen need plenty of protection, such as helmet, box and shin pads. For more on protective equipment, refer to Chapter 4.

Run-saving fielding positions

Put simply, fielders in these positions are on the field to stop the ball once hit by the batsman. Fielders in run-saving positions usually stand around 20–25 metres from the batsman to stop them from taking any runs. This positioning gives the fieldsman some time to move to their left or right and dive, if necessary, to stop the ball if it comes in their direction. Being quick to the ball can deter the batsmen from attempting a run.

Although most fieldsmen are usually deployed in catching positions, or to try to stop a batsman from scoring any runs, some are stationed on the boundary. This positioning means the captain is happy to give up one run to stop a shot going to the boundary for four. This positioning is called *fielding in the deep.* The most common deep-fielding positions are fine leg — also known as long leg — to a fast bowler and deep backward square leg to a spinner. However, if a batsman starts to attack, a captain will put more fieldsmen in the deep, particularly for spinners. Not only are the fieldsmen set to stop fours, but they need to take catches if a batsman tries to hit the ball over the boundary for six. Deep fieldsmen are much more common in one-day cricket.

The location of run-saving fielding positions has a lot to do with angles. Captains try to gauge how the batsman is going to play and set a field that makes runs difficult to score and also leads to their dismissal. All batsmen have different strengths and weaknesses. The captain and bowler have to judge these skills and, in consultation, set the appropriate field. The captain *always* has the final say.

Generally, cricketers with good overarm throws field in the outfield; those with good soft hands for catching, field in the slips. Players with good agility and who can release the ball quickly field *in the ring* about 20–25 metres from the batsman on strike.

A captain may expect you to field in the following standard run-saving positions:

- **Cover:** *Cover* is the part of the field that is located on the off side between point and mid off. When you hear about someone being lightning in the covers, the commentator isn't referring to something being flash. The description means that the player is quick to run down the ball, gather it and accurately throw the ball at the stumps or wicketkeeper.

  Cover fielding positions extend in a wedge from in front of point, taking in cover point, cover, extra cover and short extra cover. Cover fielders are positioned to stop most of the drives played by the batsmen (for more on these drives, refer to Chapter 5).

- **Straight fielders:** *Straight fielders* are located immediately to the left and right of the bowler, called mid off and mid on. These fielders stand about 30 metres from the batsman and their role is to field off- and on-drive shots.

  Most fielding teams have a mid off and mid on. When their captain tells these fielders to stand in the deep in the same line, relative to the batsman, these positions are called *long on* and *long off.*

- **Mid wicket fielder:** *Mid wicket fielders* are on the batsman's leg side — sometimes called on side — between the mid on fielding position and the square leg umpire.

  Fielding positions include mid wicket, short and deep mid wicket. Generally, short mid wicket is an attacking position around 10–15 metres from the batsman, mid wicket is located about 25–30 metres away, while deep mid wicket fielders stand close to the boundary.

- **Square leg fielders:** *Square leg fielders* are located on the batsman's leg side near the square leg umpire. A forward square leg fieldsman is said to be in front of square, which means the fieldsman is to the left of the square leg umpire (for a right-handed batsman). The opposite is true for a left hander.

  Likewise, fielders at backward square leg are to the right of the square leg umpire for a right-handed batsman. Standard square leg positions are 25–30 metres from the batsman while deep square leg positions are on the boundary and short square leg, or short leg, is only a few metres from the batsman waiting for a catch.

  Fine leg positions are in a line not far around from the wicketkeeper's left to a right-handed batsman. Deep fine leg is usually used for fast bowlers while fine leg saving one run is more common with spinners. Short fine leg is also know as leg slip and is a catching position.

Fielders in run-saving positions are also expected to take catching opportunities when they have the chance.

When the bowler is running in to deliver the ball, fieldsmen who are not in close catching positions, such as the slips or short leg, begin moving towards the batsman facing the bowler. Being on the move helps you react quickly if the ball is played by the batsman in your direction. Cricketers call this movement *walking in* and all good cricket teams do it in the field.

To add variety and gain new skills use some of your training time to keep practising all three areas of fielding — close catching, fielding in the ring about 20–25 metres from the batsman on strike, and patrolling the outfield. Most of the great fieldsmen are multiple-positional players. Ricky Ponting and Andrew Symonds can catch in the slips, save runs in the ring and hit the stumps for run outs. As well, these two have strong, flat throws, which are at a premium in the outfield.

Looking at Unusual Fielding Positions

The standard fielding positions discussed so far in this chapter — close catching and run-saving positions — are just the main ones used. However, from time to time, captains look to mix up the strategies a little, moving fielders to unusual fielding positions to pose new dilemmas for the batsmen.

Fielding at leg slip and third man

Some of the more unusual positions are:

- **Leg slip:** The leg slip fielder is just like a standard slip fielder except they stand on the leg side of the pitch. This position is primarily for catching and is usually deployed when the bowler is spinning or swinging the ball in to the batsman. The idea is that the batsman may hit the ball in the air to this position while attempting the leg glance shot. Refer to Chapter 5 for more on batting.
- **Third man:** Roughly speaking, the third man stands on the same line as the fourth slip fielder but right back near the boundary. The fielder is there to stop the ball if it is edged by the batsman or directed by the batsman opening the face of the bat on contact with the ball. Check out Chapter 5 for more on the effect of opening the face. Third man is a run-saving position, which is particularly popular in one-day cricket.

Taking fielding restrictions into account

One-day matches played by international and state teams are usually subject to fielding restrictions. These restrictions mean that the captain of the fielding side has to keep the majority of his fielders in a circle — marked out by a white line, for 15 or 20 overs (depending on the competition rules) of the batting side's innings. This circle is usually 30 metres from the stumps. The idea of fielding restrictions is to allow more space in the outfield for the opening batsmen to hit early boundaries. This makes the game more exciting for the spectators. While the fielding restrictions are in place, the batsmen tend to play attacking shots because they know that if they hit the ball past the fielders in the 30-metre fielding circle, the ball is likely to go all the way to the boundary. If no fielding restrictions existed, captains may be more negative, placing fielders in mainly run-saving positions. (See Chapter 11 for more on tactics used in one-day cricket.)

Understanding silly, short and deep fielding positions

If a fielder is asked to move from a standard run-saving position much closer to the batsman but on the same line, the new fielding position is normally prefixed with the words *silly* or *short*. For example, mid off moves a few metres closer to the batsman to become short mid off. Closer still and the position is silly mid off.

On the other hand, if the fielder is asked to keep the same line but go further away from the batsman to near the boundary the new fielding position is prefixed with the words deep or long. For example, mid off moves out to the boundary — but on the same line — the fielder is standing at deep mid off or long off. (Check out the fielding diagram in Chapter 2 to see how this method of labelling applies to the vast majority of fielding positions.)

Preparing Properly for Fielding

Fielding can be very physically demanding. In Test cricket, teams can spend days in the field — often in high temperatures. Even in club cricket, teams can spend a day toiling away in the field.

Like all aspects of cricket, being physically fit helps. To keep yourself supple and flexible is important, so that you can run hard or dive athletically to stop the ball, to save runs or to take a catch.

Here's some advice for cricketers who want to excel at fielding:

- **Warm up properly:** Warm up and stretch before play to prevent injury. (See Chapter 12 on training for more on stretching exercises.)
- **Practise catching:** Catching is one of your key jobs as a fielder but a cricket ball is hard and can deviate in the air. You need to get used to catching a ball hit to you at speed. Practising can be as easy as getting a team mate to throw some balls in the air for you to catch or to hit them to you with a bat.
- **Practise stopping the ball then throwing it:** Basically, the more efficient and accurate you are at stopping and throwing the ball, the more likely you are to minimise the number of runs scored by the batsmen, and the greater the chances of executing a run out.

The basic fielding techniques, such as catching and throwing the ball, are explained in the section, 'Getting Out on the Grass' later in this chapter. (For specific practice drills to sharpen your fielding skills, see Chapter 12.)

Fielding can involve sudden sharp bursts of intense physical activity followed by relative inactivity. This pattern of activity is almost made to cause muscle tears and hamstring pulls. Hence the need to stretch intermittently. Playing a cricket match with a pulled or torn muscle is no laughing matter. (For more on fitness training, pre-play warm-ups and fielding drills, see Chapter 12.)

You may have no chance of stopping a ball going over the boundary rope but you are still expected to run and recover the ball.

Because of the structure of a cricket match — one side bats while the other fields — you're bound to spend a long time in the field. Work on your fielding at practice. Treat fielding seriously and become involved in the game with each ball delivered, even if the ball doesn't come to you. The more involved you are in the game, the more you will enjoy it.

One of the main objectives of a fielder is to achieve a run out. A run out occurs when the stumps are thrown down with the batsman out of their crease, while attempting a run. A run out leads to the batsman's dismissal. (Refer to Chapter 2 for more on modes of dismissal.)

Getting Out on the Grass

So you want to be a great fielder? You want to help turn the match in your team's favour through your athleticism and alertness? Great! But in order to be a top-class fielder, the skills you need to master include:

- Catching the ball
- Gathering the ball
- Throwing the ball.

Taking the perfect catch

Taking a catch is the fielder's time to shine. But a cricket ball is not soft like a tennis ball. A cricket ball is very hard and, when propelled by the force of the batsman's bat, a cricket ball can be difficult to hold onto.

When trying to take a catch, you need to bear the following in mind:

- **Watching the ball carefully:** If you don't watch the ball, you won't catch it. Once you sight the ball in the air, tracking it with your eyes all the way into your hands is essential.
- **Making sure the ball is yours:** If the ball flies high into the air off the batsman's bat, chances are that more than one fielder may run for it. The fielder who believes they are closest to where the ball is likely to land, has the responsibility of shouting 'Mine!'. This call tells team mates to stay away and lets the fielder concentrate on catching the ball. Alternatively, if you believe a team mate is in a better position, you call out that fielder's name loudly and early so they have plenty of time to go for the ball before it lands.
- **Keeping your balance:** While watching the ball, run to where you think it will land and try to be as relaxed and balanced as you can. This isn't always possible if the ball is moving quickly or has been hit some distance from you.
- **Trying to get two hands to the ball:** You know the phrase, 'Two heads are better than one'? Well, in cricket, two hands are better than one! If you have time before the ball arrives, try to cup your hands to receive the ball. Closing your hands around the ball is then easier (see Figure 9-1).

Figure 9-1: Watch the ball coming towards you and, if possible, cup your hands.

Australia and England have many differences. Different versions of the English language are just one of the ways in which Australia differs from what used to be called the 'mother country'. In cricket, a major difference lies in the way Australian and English fielders catch a cricket ball when the ball is hit high into the air. See Figure 9-2, and see the sidebar, 'Australia versus England: How best to catch a cricket ball'.

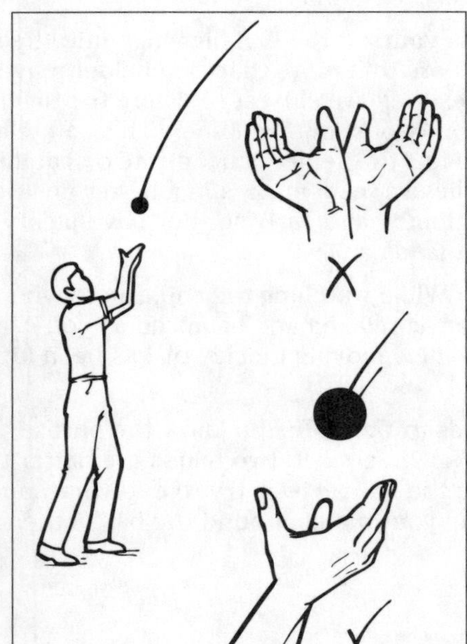
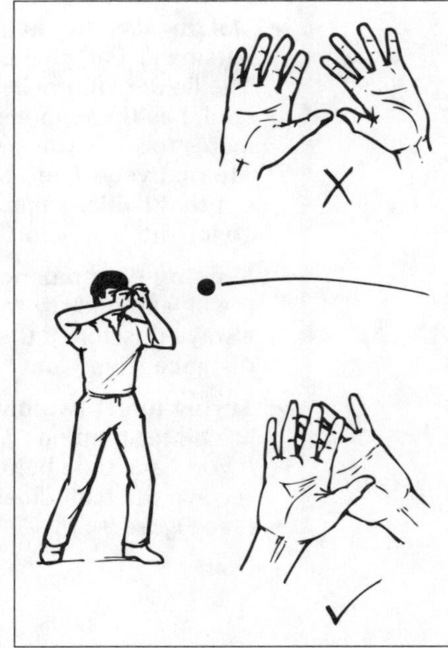

Figure 9-2: *Left:* How the English catch a high ball. *Right:* How Australians catch a ball differently.

Fielders who stand close to the batsman — say in the slips or a bat-pad position — have less time to move and *set* themselves to take a catch. Therefore, as the bowler delivers, the fielders crouch forward and cup their hands together. The idea is to be *set* for a catch when the ball is delivered. If you want to be a good close catcher, then you *set* yourself in a comfortable, well balanced position with your feet about shoulder width apart, the knees slightly bent and hands cupped out in front of your knees as you crouch slightly forward (see Figure 9-3).

When a catch that isn't obviously out is taken, the fielding side shouts to the umpire 'How is that?' Or 'Howzat!' This call is an appeal, asking the umpire to decide if the batsman is out. If no one appeals to the umpire, then the umpire cannot give the batsman out. This happens most often when the ball may have just touched the outside edge of the batsman's bat on the way through to the wicketkeeper, or in a bat-pad catch to a close fielder.

When taking a catch, if the ball arrives below the height of your chest, have your hands cupped with your fingers pointing to the ground. If the ball is headed at the height of your chest, or above, then reverse your hands, with the fingers directed at the sky. Sometimes you may need to bend your knees a little to comfortably take the catch if the ball is coming at your chest and your fingers are pointing up. (Refer to Figure 9-1.)

A catch is always best taken with *soft hands*. This phrase means that the cupped hands *give* and wrap around the ball as the fielder catches it. If a fielder attempts a catch with stiff or rigid hands and fingers, the catch is more likely to lead to injury when the hard cricket ball hits the hands. Quite apart from injury, the fielder is more likely to drop the catch because the hands won't close comfortably around the ball. If the ball makes a slapping sound against the hands as you catch it, relax a bit more. The catch is going to be easier and a lot less painful. Catches taken well create no sound — apart from that of your cheering team mates!

Figure 9-3: Close catching fielders crouch forward and cup their hands together.

Australia versus England: How best to catch a cricket ball

When the ball is hit high in the air, the English method is for the fieldsman to take the dropping ball with the hands cupped just in front of the chest and the elbows tucked in loosely near the side of the body. As the ball is caught, the hands draw towards the centre of the body to cushion the impact of the ball.

Australian cricketers go about catching the high ball differently. The Australians prefer to take the dropping ball above head height with the stretched-out fingers and thumb of one hand resting slightly across the other for extra support; the elbows pointing outwards. As the ball is taken, the hands are withdrawn a little towards the forehead, wrapping around the ball.

One of the key differences between the two methods is that the Australian method ensures the head is still and the eyes don't move. With the English method, as the ball drops past the face down towards the hands, the fielder will look down, following the line of the ball. The Australian method offers a greater chance of having a second chance to catch the ball if it comes out of the hands.

Collecting the ball

A cricket ball is not only hard, it can also deviate in different directions when bouncing in the outfield. Therefore, gathering a cricket ball isn't always as simple as it may appear.

The two main reasons for this are:

- The ball is 'sliced' by the batsman, who may have mistimed a shot. This causes the ball to spin off the bat, so when the ball lands it spins away from the fieldsman running to gather the bouncing ball.
- The ball may hit a bump or a rough area on the field.

When the ball is hit into the outfield, you must keep the following in mind:

- **Watching the ball:** Just as though you were taking a catch, you keep your eyes peeled on the ball right up until you pick it up with your hands. Watching the ball is important because it can suddenly change direction — left or right and bounce high or keep low.

  Most mistakes in the outfield are made due to the fielder not keeping their eyes on the ball.
- **Judging the speed of the ball:** When the batsman hits the ball, the ball speeds into the outfield. You then have to make a spilt-second decision as to the direction the ball is headed and where you run to intercept it.

Try not to run *around* the ball when it is hit into outfield, and therefore avoid running in a big arc. Once the ball is hit, aim to cut off the ball from the boundary in the straightest, most direct line, thus saving time and hopefully runs.

- **Deciding how to field the ball:** In most cases, how you field the ball depends on how hard the ball is hit and whether the ball is coming straight at you or to the side.

The two main types of fielding are:

- **Attacking fielding:** Attacking the ball is the most common way of fielding if you're not in a close catching position. If the ball is hit more or less straight towards you, move quickly towards it without overbalancing. As you approach the ball, turn your body about 45 degrees to the left if you throw right-handed (the opposite for left handers), bend at the knees, bring your body forward and gather the ball, getting both hands behind it in a cupping motion. Your head is positioned over the ball when you gather it (see Figure 9-4).
- **Defensive fielding:** Sometimes the ball is coming too quickly to attack. To ensure you can stop the ball properly, lower your left knee and left leg if you're right-handed (reverse for a left-handed fielder) onto the turf in the line the ball is travelling. In this case, your body is behind the ball, so even if it bounces awkwardly, the ball is far less likely to get past you. Put your hands together — fingers pointed towards the turf — with the head forward, allowing you to watch the ball into your hands (see Figure 9-5).

If you fail to collect a ball properly and it goes past you, the batsmen may take another run. This is called a *misfield.* A misfield causes you embarrassment, and annoys your captain and team mates.

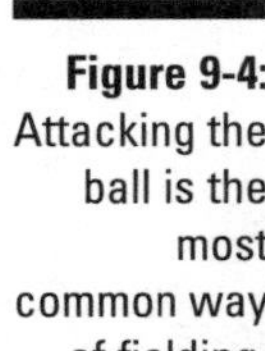

Figure 9-4: Attacking the ball is the most common way of fielding.

Figure 9-5: Defensive fielders ensure their body is behind the ball.

Throwing the ball

The *throw* is the action you use to propel the ball from the outfield back to the wicketkeeper or at the stumps. Throws come in two types:

- Underarm
- Overarm.

The underarm throw tends to be quite accurate and quick to execute but you won't be able to generate much power. The best choice is to use the underarm throw only when you're close to the stumps and a run-out chance presents itself. Fielders use an underarm throw when running in to gather a softly hit shot that has not travelled far from the pitch.

Getting the underarm throw right

With underarm throwing, timing is very important because you're usually looking to execute a run out. Here's how to do it (see Figure 9-6):

- Move quickly towards the ball, leaning forward as you get close.
- Bend forward (facing the stumps you want to throw the ball at), and, with the fingers of your throwing hand facing down, pick the ball up as you come alongside it.
- Draw the arm back in a straight line beside your body.
- Cock the wrist slightly to add power to the throw.
- Bring the arm down straight.
- Release the ball at the stumps when the throwing arm is vertical.

Figure 9-6: Throwing underarm with the aim of executing a run out.

If you hit the stumps before the batsman reaches their crease, you have executed a run out — high fives all round!

Getting the overarm throw right

The overarm throw gives you far more distance. Mastering this throw is essential if you're to be a useful fielder in the team.

The following description of overarm throwing presumes you're a right-handed thrower (see Figure 9-7). If you're a leftie, just reverse the positioning.

For attacking fielding, the fielder's body is already turned at about 45 degrees when gathering the ball. (For more on attacking fielding, see the section, 'Collecting the ball' earlier in this chapter.)

With the top joint of the index and middle fingers across the seam of the ball, the thumb holding it underneath, and the forefinger tucked in beside the ball, bring your body more side-on as the throwing arm is drawn back comfortably with the ball above head height and your left arm pointing in the direction of the target. The target can be the wicketkeeper, the bowler or a fielder standing over the stumps or the stumps themselves if no one is near them.

Now, in the same way that your body weight is transferred from the back foot to the front foot (left foot for a right hander) while bowling (refer to Chapter 7), bring the body forward as the arm comes through quickly, so that all your momentum helps propel the ball. Again like bowling, flick your wrist on release to add extra power to the throw.

Figure 9-7: The fielder throwing the ball overarm.

The momentum carries your throwing arm from the right side, across your torso and your back foot (right foot) comes through and lands in front of you. This movement is called the *follow through.* The movement ends with your head looking at the target over the throwing shoulder.

Knowing how to throw correctly to minimise the chance of injury to your elbow and shoulder is important. The elbow of your throwing arm is *always* higher than your shoulder and your throwing hand is further away from your body than your elbow on release.

Ponting throws on the run

Australian captain Ricky Ponting is widely regarded as one of the very best fieldsmen in the world. His ability to move quickly, then gather and release the ball in an instant, often hitting the stumps with his throw, makes him deadly in one-day cricket when batsmen are attempting to take quick runs. Ponting is so good he can often pick up the ball one-handed and throw without breaking stride as he is running. That takes plenty of practice to perfect!

The details of overarm throwing seem to be long and convoluted. However, experienced players can execute a throw in a matter of seconds. Practise your throwing so that it becomes second nature.

Most fielders aim to throw at the end of the pitch where the wicketkeeper stands. The fielders choose this direction because the wicketkeeper has great big gloves to collect the ball in. However, sometimes the smartest play is to aim at the stumps at the bowler's end if the batsman running to that end is struggling to reach the crease. Throwing at this end may give you a better chance of a run out. Once you collect the ball, glance to see whether you are best aiming towards the wicketkeeper or the bowler. Always aim just above the stumps — if the wicketkeeper or bowler is there to take the ball — so that they can gather your throw easily and knock the bails off the top of the stumps in the hope of a run out. (Refer to Chapter 2 for more details on bails, stumps and run outs.)

If you don't direct your throw properly, and the wicketkeeper, bowler or other fielders standing close to the stumps are unable to gather the ball, the batsman may decide to run again. This throw is called an *overthrow* and your team mates are not going to be pleased if your throw leads to the batting team taking extra runs.

A fielder's job is not finished if the ball is not hit to them. If the ball is alive and a chance of a run-out exists, the fielders close to the stumps need to run to the stumps and try to gather the ball for a run out. Others need to back up the throw by getting in line with it about 20 to 30 metres from the stumps in case those trying to gather the ball at the stumps miss it or the throw is not accurate. This support is called *backing up* and prevents the batsmen taking any extra runs (overthrows).

Thinking in the Field

Always have a quick look at your captain between deliveries or before the beginning of each new over in case the captain wants you to move positions in the field. Sometimes, the captain may move you only a metre or two forward or back, left or right. Other times, you may be required in close, on the boundary or in a completely different position. A day-dreaming fieldsman, who holds up the game because they do not respond to their captain's instructions, causes frustration for everyone involved, be they batsmen, bowlers or other fielders.

Make sure you understand what your role is in the field. If you're there to stop the batsmen scoring any runs, then don't stand too deep, allowing the batsman a quick run, or so close that the ball is easily hit past you. Sometimes, the captain can be seen holding up an index finger to the fielder, making it clear that the fielder's job is to *save one*. That is, the fielder is to prevent the batsmen taking any runs. Likewise, if you're on the boundary to stop a four or take a boundary catch, don't creep too far in so that the ball flies over your head, or so that you cannot get to a well struck shot that's hit either side of you. Running in is always easier than trying to back pedal.

Unless you're in a close catching position, you move in with the bowler every time the bowler runs in to deliver the ball. Your moving in puts extra pressure on the batsman and gives you the momentum to charge in and gather the ball should the batsman push it just a short distance in front of them. Likewise, a fielder on the boundary is always ready to run in and gather the ball if it is hit slowly towards them. Your running in, hopefully, only allows the batsmen time for one run. Captains become annoyed if their outfielders allow more than a single because the fielder has not run hard enough to attack the ball.

Chapter 10

Wicketkeeping: Taking the Gloves

In This Chapter

- Taking command behind the stumps
- Mastering the gloves
- Training to win

If the captain is the brains of a cricket team, then the wicketkeeper is the team's heartbeat. The skill, attitude and tenacity of a wicketkeeper can have a profound impact on the way the team performs in the field.

If you have boundless energy, unlimited enthusiasm, razor-sharp concentration and cat-like reflexes, then wicketkeeping is the position for you.

The *keeper,* as the wicketkeeper is often called, is always the focus of the fielding side, whether taking balls delivered by the bowler or gathering throws from the fielders.

Lively, upbeat, and always encouraging, the keeper can lift a team when spirits may be flagging in the field when the batting side is doing well. This attitude of enthusiasm and encouragement can be infectious.

So if you want to take a hyperactive journey through cricket, come for a ride through this chapter and discover how to be the team's fielding focal point.

Australia's wicketkeeper, Adam Gilchrist, is one of the finest in the world and is fast closing in on the all-time record for dismissals. Look for the 'Adam says' icons in this chapter for tips on wicketkeeping from one of the best in the business.

As a kid, I enjoyed every aspect of cricket — batting, bowling, keeping, catching. I really became attracted to wicketkeeping at age seven or eight when I saw a set of keeping gloves in a shop one day. As a result of that, I began to focus a bit more on wicketkeeping and since that time I have just loved the constant involvement. The keeper is involved in every delivery. That was what interested me the most and maintains my love of that part of the game.

Standing Behind the Stumps

The wicketkeeper is the most important fielder in the side. All teams have a player who specialises in wicketkeeping. The keeper stands behind the batsman's stumps and is kitted out with pads, a protector and a great big pair of padded gloves for taking the ball after it's been delivered by the bowler or thrown in by one of the fieldsmen. (Refer to Chapter 4 and the section 'Kitting out a wicketkeeper' for more on wicketkeeping gear. Having the right equipment is very important.)

The big gloves are not the only factor that make being a wicketkeeper different to any other fieldsman. When the team is fielding, the keeper is always in the game. Here's why:

- If the batsman misses or leaves the ball and it doesn't hit the stumps, the wicketkeeper has to stop it from flying through to the boundary for easy runs to the opposition.
- If the ball hits the edge of the batsman's bat, the ball often goes through to the wicketkeeper, who is expected to take the catch.
- Fielders often throw the ball to the wicketkeeper. The keeper's job is to take these throws.
- If a batsman doesn't make it back into the crease while attempting one or more runs, the keeper can use the ball to dislodge the bails off the top of the stumps to execute a run out. Refer to Chapter 2 for more on dismissals and an explanation of the batting crease.
- In the only dismissal that's unique to a wicketkeeper, the keeper can also stump the batsman. This can happen when the batsman leaves the crease in their attempt to play the ball, but misses. If the keeper is quick enough to gather the ball and dislodge the bails off the top of the stumps before the batsman gets their bat or at least one of their feet back behind the crease, the batsman is out stumped.

Wicketkeeper Healy premieres as a stump-mike star

Turn on the television to watch any international cricket match and you cannot help but notice the wicketkeeper. Always in the action and always on the move, the keeper is the one who is also most often heard yelling encouragement over the effects microphone near the stumps.

Australia's brilliant keeper, Ian Healy, who holds the world record for the most number of dismissals by a wicketkeeper in Test cricket, made the stump microphone famous during the 1990s.

While keeping to the great Australian spinner, Shane Warne, Healy's dry, nasal tones could be heard calling 'Bowled Shane' for ball after ball, hour after hour, during a day's play.

Claiming run outs and stumpings

The mode of dismissal, removing the bails from the top of the stumps when a batsman is out of their crease, is the same for run outs and stumpings. However, a significant difference exists between the two. With run outs, the batsman is attempting a run. But with stumpings, the batsman has advanced out of their crease in a failed attempt to play a shot. Either way, if you achieve a run out or a stumping, you're going to be very popular with your team mates!

The ball does not actually need to hit the stumps to achieve a run out or a stumping. As long as the ball is held in the gloves of the keeper (or hands of the fielder in the case of a fielder attempting a run out), then the removal of the bails is regarded as legal and the batsman is out if out of their crease. If the ball is held in only one hand, or glove, then the hand or glove holding the ball can be used to hit the stumps and remove the bails. If the bails do not come off, the batsman cannot be dismissed.

As far as fielding goes, the keeper is *numero uno*. The wicketkeeper can have a huge influence on the success of the fielding team. If the keeper consistently does well at taking catches, collecting throws from the fieldsmen, executing run outs and stumping batsmen, the keeper becomes a hero of the team.

If the batsman misses or leaves the ball, and the keeper subsequently fails to collect it, the batsman may run between the wickets. Any runs scored this way are called *byes*. If the ball runs all the way to the boundary, four byes are scored. Keepers hate giving away byes.

In reality, the skills of wicketkeeping are not skills you can pick up overnight. In order to get to the top of the tree, you have to start young and practise hard and, even then, you need the key requirements of talent, big-match temperament and quicksilver reflexes.

Caring only about the next ball is what's important. Whether you've taken a blinding catch or dropped an easy one makes no difference to what is coming next. What's happened has happened and you can't dwell on it. The only guarantee that comes with thinking about something that has already happened is that you're probably going to make a slip-up in the near future if your mind is elsewhere. Mistakes are going to happen and the better keepers are those who deal with them and move on quickly.

Finding your stance

For someone who has not experienced the joys of playing cricket, the game of cricket can seem very strange. Batsmen and bowlers get themselves into what seem quite unnatural positions to play strokes or deliver the ball. Wicketkeeping can appear the same way.

Jack Blackham: First of the modern wicketkeepers

Australia's first great wicketkeeper was Jack Blackham, a pioneer of the game, who played the first of all Tests, against England in 1877, to begin a remarkable 17-year career. He was the first of the 'modern' wicketkeepers, rejecting the *long stop* — the fielder who stood on the boundary behind the keeper to gather any misses — common in colonial and English county cricket at the time.

Blackham also broke tradition by standing up to the stumps to take the ball, even to quick bowling, although not always to Australia's first great fast bowler, Fred Spofforth. Remarkably, Spofforth refused to play in the very first Test because he wanted Billy Murdoch as his keeper. Murdoch, was selected for the second Test as a fine batsman and went on to captain Australia but Spofforth soon changed his opinion of Blackham as the number one gloveman.

As a keeper, Blackham was neat and quick with his glove work, a stumper who could whip the bails off in a flash. A bank clerk, Blackham grew a suitably black beard as a young man of 23 and kept it all his life. He made eight tours of England as Australia's wicketkeeper and was aged over 40 when he retired. Possessing a nervous disposition, he was not well regarded as captaincy material. However, he did captain Australia eight times, mainly through seniority. His reputation was not advanced by his performance in his last Test, when England won after being forced to follow-on.

But with practice, batting, bowling and keeping all come relatively naturally and comfortably. As with all sports, balance is one of the keys to success. Wicketkeeping is no different.

Facing the bowler, a keeper stands with the feet about shoulder width apart and has their body weight evenly distributed on the balls of their feet as they crouch down (see Figure 10-1).

Figure 10-1: Wicketkeeper crouches down for slow bowlers (left and right) and fast bowler (centre).

The knees then automatically spread in a crouching position, allowing the arms to fit comfortably between the legs so the fingers of the keeping gloves rest lightly on the ground below the keeper's chin. The gloves are held together with the fingers and thumbs spread wide apart, presenting the largest possible target for the ball as it is delivered by the bowler.

The wicketkeeper always crouches in a low position. Raising the body and hands to take a higher ball is much easier than going down to try to take a low delivery. Many keepers make the fundamental mistake of coming up too early instead of remaining in their crouched position.

Gloving the Ball

If *staying down* is one golden rule of keeping, then never pointing the fingers at the ball is another. Apart from giving you less chance of taking the ball properly, pointing your fingers this way greatly enhances the possibility of suffering an injured finger should the ball hit the end of a finger.

The fingers of the gloves are always pointing to the ground if the ball is coming at you below chest height; pointing to the sky if the ball is chest height or above; pointing to the right if the ball is coming to your right side and to the left if the ball is coming to your left side.

Keep the gloves together and out in front of the body but don't reach for the ball. Let the ball come to you so it settles comfortably into the cup you have created with the gloves and let your arms give with the direction and momentum of the ball so the gloves automatically close around it.

When I began wicketkeeping, the focus was on taking the ball with soft hands. I did a lot of drills with a tennis ball to focus on cushioning the ball to try to develop a soft feel and an ability to catch in a soft manner when you're giving with the ball a lot. You're going pretty well if you can develop that as a basis from which to work.

Sometimes, keeping the gloves together is simply not possible, but diving to take the ball, as spectacular as it may look on television, is a last resort for the wicketkeeper. Diving greatly increases the chances of missing the ball, possibly costing your team a catch or valuable runs, or both. The best keepers can cover a lot of ground behind the stumps with good footwork. For more about footwork, see the section, 'Being the best' later in the chapter.

Standing up . . . standing back

If you play as a wicketkeeper, you want to give yourself the best chance of dismissing the batsman while minimising the risk of giving away byes.

The quicker the bowler is delivering the ball, the more time you need to react to it. Distance equals reaction time, so it follows that for quicker-paced bowling you stand further back from the batsman than for slower-paced bowling.

In Test matches, wicketkeepers often stand 20 metres or more behind the stumps. Stand any closer and they may not be fast enough to collect the ball or it may bounce over the keeper's head. This position is called *standing back*.

But against spin bowlers, the keeper stands very close to the batsman's stumps so that the keeper's gloves can easily reach the stumps. Why so close? Well, the ball is delivered at a far slower pace and, if the ball hits the edge of the batsman's bat, it won't travel very far. In addition, being so close means you have a greater chance of stumping the batsman. This position is called *standing up*.

Standing back

Most keepers take up their stance on an invisible line just outside the batsman's off stump (see Figure 10-2). Standing just outside off stump offers you two advantages:

- **Your view is not obscured by the batsman:** Most batsmen will stand around their middle or leg stump when the bowler delivers.
- **You can easily marshal the slip fielders:** Captains may be in charge of the team as a whole but wicketkeepers normally tell the slip fielders exactly where they want them to stand.

Figure 10-2: A keeper positioning himself just outside the batsman's off stump.

Standing back, the keeper is able to take the ball comfortably at about waist height from a fast bowler's good length delivery (refer to Chapter 7 for more on bowling lengths). The keeper stands far enough back to take the ball just as it's beginning to drop (see Figure 10-3). If the ball is still rising when it gets to the keeper, stand further back. However, if the ball is coming at knee or ankle height, the keeper needs to move forward.

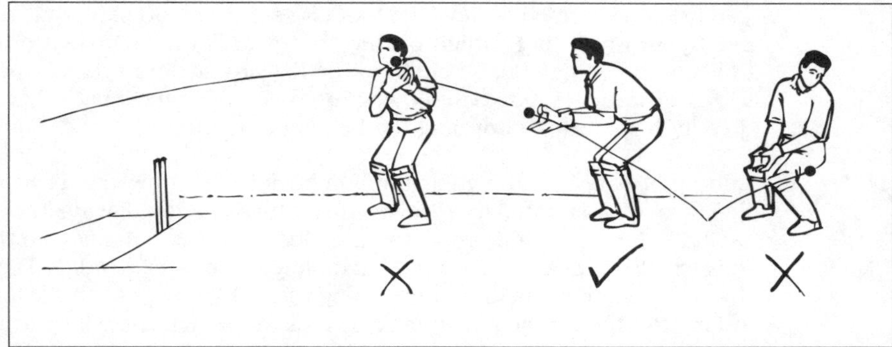

Figure 10-3: The keeper takes the ball comfortably at about waist height.

The keeper is a vital barometer to the slips, who form an arc next to the keeper waiting for the batsman to make a mistake by edging the ball to them. If the keeper stands too far back, the ball is unlikely to carry to the slips. If the keeper is too close, the slips may not have time to react to a ball travelling quickly at them. (Refer to Chapter 2 for a diagram on where the slips stand and Chapter 9 for more about slips fielding.)

When catching a ball, the natural position is to take it in front of you. Ideally, wicketkeepers standing back don't do this. Instead, keepers standing back always take the ball to the side of their body next to what is known as their *inside hip* — the hip closest to the line of the stumps (see Figure 10-4).

Figure 10-4: Standing back, always take the ball next to your inside hip.

This position allows greater give with a freer swing of the arms when taking a ball from a fast bowler. This position also means that the keeper is a little further across to the off side and is able to cover greater ground for an outside edge, the most common form of dismissal in cricket.

Should the ball be heading down the leg side, the keeper avoids diving unless absolutely necessary. Instead, the keeper almost skips across behind the stumps to the ball, eyes steady and gloves ready. To make this movement, you bring your outside foot, the foot closest to the off side, quickly across to meet your other foot, which pushes off towards the leg side. Do this several times until you can take the ball to the leg side of your body. If the ball is too wide down the leg side and moving too quickly to take it with this move, then dive in desperation. Stopping the ball is paramount.

Good footwork is vital when standing back to fast bowlers. Try to leave diving as an absolute last resort. The culture of keeping says that you take the ball on your inside hip — the hip closest to the batsman, so that moving towards the slips is easier if the batsman gets an outside edge. Try to work to that rule. Some keepers end up taking the ball in front of them and then jerking the ball to the left to make it look as though they've taken it on the side. Don't kid yourself! Always work on getting the basics right.

Once the keeper has found the correct position when standing back, the keeper and slips then spread their arms (or arm in the case of the keeper and last of the slips) until the slips are standing with their outstretched fingers just touching. First slip then takes a pace or so back, allowing the keeper room to move on the rare occasions they may need to dive for a low catch which would not carry to slip.

Any ball that flies off the edge of the batsman's bat and is heading between the keeper and first slip is regarded as the keeper's catch and the keeper must attempt to take it. Ideally, first slip never dives towards the keeper to take a catch. If the ball flies between the two of them, the keeper has failed to do his or her job properly. This outcome is much worse than the keeper dropping a difficult catch. Not everyone can catch everything all the time and no one ever means to drop a catch, in the same way batsmen don't mean to get out and bowlers don't mean to bowl poorly. This outcome means a 'Bad luck' pat on the back from the closest fielder and more work at training!

Standing up

Standing up is the toughest part of wicketkeeping (see Figure 10-5). Standing up requires great practice and skill because so little reaction time is available once the ball bounces off the pitch. Usually the keeper is standing up to a spinner who is trying to fool the batsman by flighting the ball in the air and spinning it off the pitch. With the keeper little more than a metre behind the batsman, the keeper could also be fooled by these subtle and clever variations.

Figure 10-5: Standing up to the stumps for a spinner is the toughest part of wicket-keeping.

Wicketkeepers are wise to keep to their team's spinners at training so they learn all the spin bowlers' tricks. Practising like this gives the bowler and the keeper a greater confidence in each other (refer to Chapter 8 for more on spin bowling).

As discussed earlier, keepers need to stay crouched down behind the stumps as long as possible. Only when the ball has pitched, or bounced, does the keeper begin to come up, straightening the legs slightly until the gloves are level with the ball as the ball is about to be taken. If a keeper comes up too early, then balls that stay low, including edges that could result in a catch, could scoot past the keeper. Few situations are more embarrassing for a keeper than to have the ball fly between their legs.

If the ball is heading down the leg side, stay low but push the left leg (if you're keeping to a right hander) across until the leg is well outside leg stump. Then bring the right leg into line with leg stump. Always attempt to keep the body behind the ball when taking it. When the keeper ensures that their right leg is in line with leg stump (for a right hander), that leg gives them a guide to where the stumps are in case the keeper is attempting a leg side stumping. (see Figure 10-6). The reverse is necessary when a ball goes down the leg side while keeping to a left-handed batsman.

The best keepers don't need to look at the stumps to complete a stumping. Good keepers know where the stumps are simply from the positioning of their feet and they can whip the bails off in a flash once they have gathered the ball. Like everything else with wicketkeeping, this skill takes lots of practice.

Figure 10-6: Good footwork gives you a better chance of taking the ball cleanly down the leg side.

When standing up to the spinners, try to stay as low as possible. This position is very difficult to achieve. The body has a natural tendency to come out of a crouch, particularly to a fuller delivery. Get your head in line with the ball rather than reaching one side or the other to take it. Good footwork ensures you can get in line with the ball and gives you a better chance of taking the ball cleanly. Ian Healy taught me this prior to my first Test when keeping to Shane Warne. Shane would often bowl wide down the leg side, attempting to spin the ball across the batsman with big turning leg breaks. As a wicketkeeper, you have to be decisive and committed with your footwork to ensure you are in the right position to take the ball.

A wicketkeeper is not allowed to take the ball in front of the stumps unless it has hit the batsman or the bat. So keepers attempting to make a stumping must wait for the ball to come to them. The best move is for keepers standing up to have their gloves resting just to the off side and behind the batsman's off stump. Refer to Chapter 2 for more on the off and leg side.

The keeper can dive forward to try to take a catch — if the ball has lobbed in the air after hitting the bat. Or the keeper can try to grab the ball to attempt a run out or stumping if the ball has hit the batsman.

Taking throws from the outfield

Not only does a wicketkeeper need to be fit and flexible to crouch every time the bowler delivers the ball, keepers are also expected to run up to the stumps to take the ball from a fielder's throw every time the batsman plays the ball. A wicketkeeper standing back to a fast bowler can regularly run 20 metres, sometimes at full pace, to the stumps to take the ball.

As a wicketkeeper, you always need to call to the fielders, encouraging them to stop or chase the ball, and let them know if a possible run-out chance exists so they can throw the ball back in as hard and quickly as possible.

Always make sure you're behind the stumps in a direct line with the fielder. This way, if a run-out chance is imminent, the throw may be good enough to hit the stumps without the keeper needing to take the ball first. Alternatively, taking the bails off when you're facing the stumps once the ball has been gathered is a lot easier than trying to turn around after taking the ball.

Bending over towards the stumps, with the knees slightly bent, makes gathering the ball easier if the ball is quite low when it reaches you. Again, coming up to gather a bouncing ball is easier than trying to reach down at the last minute if the ball is scooting along the ground.

When you're wicketkeeping, always try to collect and catch the ball with both hands together. This method offers a much greater chance of taking the ball cleanly.

If the ball is being thrown in to the wicketkeeper, but a run out at the bowler's end is more likely, the keeper flicks off the glove on their throwing hand. Once the keeper has taken the ball, they throw the ball at the stumps at the bowler's end. Be sure you have a chance of dismissing the batsman because if the ball misses the stumps, the batsmen may go for extra runs, which are known as *overthrows*.

As a wicketkeeper, you have long days in the field so, just like batting, you need to 'switch off' between balls. Short periods of intense concentration begin from the time a bowler is preparing to move in from the top of their mark to the time the ball is *dead* — out of play. I've learnt, more than ever in the latter stages of my career, to tell myself to 'switch on' once the bowler prepares to move in and bowl.

Adam Gilchrist is renowned throughout the cricket world for his explosive batting but he is also a top-class wicketkeeper who has the chance of becoming the most successful gloveman in the history of the game (see figure 10-7).

Figure 10-7: Adam Gilchrist: On track to beat Ian Healy's dismissals record.

Records are made to be beaten

Australia has a wonderful tradition of producing exceptional wicketkeepers. From the very earliest days of Jack Blackham (see sidebar, 'Jack Blackham: First of the modern wicketkeepers'), some revered names have stood behind the stumps. In 130 years of Test cricket, Australia has had only 28 wicketkeepers, an average of one almost every five years, and just seven, including Blackham, have managed 30 Tests or more. This great wicketkeeping dynasty extends through famous bodyline keeper, Bert Oldfield (see Chapter 23 for more on bodyline), and the first tied Test gloveman, Wally Grout (see Chapter 22 for more on the first tied Test). Oldfield claimed a remarkable 52 stumpings among his 130 dismissals keeping to great leg spinners, Bill O'Reilly and Clarrie Grimmett (see Chapter 19 for more on Grimmett).

Perhaps the greatest of all keepers have played in the modern era. In the 1970s and early 1980s, Rod Marsh set a world record for the most number of dismissals — catches and stumpings — by a keeper, adding up to 355. Ian Healy beat Marsh's record in the 1990s, and Healy continues to hold the record of 395. Adam Gilchrist could one day beat Healy's record. Heading into the 2006–07 season, Gilchrist was sitting equal with Marsh on 355 dismissals.

Working at Keeping

Keepers are expected to crouch down waiting for every ball bowled while their team is fielding. In a Test match, when 90 overs are expected in a day, the keeper can crouch 540 times over six hours of play, and sometimes a team can be in the field for two days and even part of three days.

Coupled with running up to the stumps to take the ball every time a batsman hits it, or the fielder throws it in, a wicketkeeper not only needs great skill but a good level of fitness.

My focus as a young wicketkeeper was to become stronger in the legs for the obvious reason that you're squatting up and down so much, and you're coming out of the squat position to run or sprint to the stumps.

Gathering the right gear

Cricket gear doesn't have to be over-the-top expensive. Buying gear that is efficient and protective is the best guide. Here's a list of the gear you need.

- **Gloves:** Although the most obvious part of a keeper's kit is the large and often colourful pair of gloves, keepers actually wear two sets of gloves.
  - The first pair is called the *inners* — soft, white cloth gloves to aid padding and comfort and to help absorb the inevitable sweat that gathers.
  - The main set of gloves (over the inners) must be supple and in good condition so they can wrap easily around the ball as it's taken. Hard gloves are like hard hands when attempting to take a catch. The ball is more likely to bounce off them than soft gloves, which give as the catch is taken.
- **Pads:** As light as possible, pads are used to protect the knees and shins. For many years, wicketkeepers simply used batsmen's pads, but these pads proved too big and bulky, restricting the agility of the keeper. Modern keeping pads are significantly shorter and much lighter than their batting equivalent, allowing for greater freedom of movement.
- **Protector:** Men and boys always need to wear a protector, or box, to ensure the genitals are safe from being accidentally hit by the ball. The easiest way to wear a box is to slip it between two firmly fitting pairs of underpants to hold it in place (refer to Chapter 4).

- **Helmets:** A good idea when keeping up to the stumps, helmets are compulsory for keepers playing juniors in the younger age groups. Even the finest keepers, such as Australia's Adam Gilchrist, often wear a helmet when keeping to spinners.
- **Clothing:** Clothing that's non-restrictive is best so the keeper can move quickly and easily, and a long-sleeved shirt is a good idea. Not only do long sleeves offer greater sun protection, they also help to protect the arms and elbows from abrasions if the keeper is forced to dive around, particularly on rough grounds and hard pitches.

For advice on how to find the right gear and how much money it costs, refer to Chapter 4.

Being the best

Given wicketkeepers are involved with every delivery of the fielding side's innings, fitness obviously plays a vital part in their ability to successfully contribute right to the end of a long day in the field.

Because keepers are continually crouching to take deliveries and then running up to the stumps to take throws from fielders, the keeper can easily practise these actions at training by continually crouching and then running 20 metres before walking back to the starting position.

However, too much of that can become boring and keepers can't afford to ignore the other vital areas at training, such as glove work and foot work.

As a keeper, you're better to try to combine much of your fitness work with some vigorous training routines so you can practice all the match-day facets of wicketkeeping together.

A solid base of fitness is essential for a wicketkeeper and you can get a lot of that fitness from your wicketkeeping drills at training. Your practice may range from keeping to spin bowlers in the nets to having someone throw the ball as though they were a spin bowler. Spending a lot of time squatting up and down in the match position produces strong conditioning for the legs and the body in general. Having someone hit catches as though you were taking the ball in a match is a great idea too. Take catches at the rate of 10 to the right so you're moving to take the ball inside your right hip, then 10 to the left so you're doing it on the other side. Practise diving to take the ball from varying angles and heights. If you're taking every ball, you're probably not being tested enough. Put yourself under pressure. Have the catches hit a little wider on each side. Make sure you're moving constantly, not just going through the motions and practise basic drills, such as catching up close, having fast feet and so on.

Catching up close

To practise catching up close, the wicketkeeper can have someone throw balls at him or her, or get them to hit the balls with a bat. Using a bat is more realistic and less demanding on the body than throwing.

If you're helping a keeper to practise, begin by hitting the ball at the keeper over a short distance and not too hard. Start to vary the height from waist level down and from side to side to make the keeper move quickly. Always wait until the keeper is back in their proper position before hitting the next ball. The person with the bat can begin to hit the ball from a greater distance, hitting it harder and wider to make the keeper move more quickly.

Close catching variations can also include using a tennis ball to ensure the keeper is taking the ball properly with soft hands. You can also use different coloured balls to help the keeper develop focus.

Having fast feet

This drill for fast feet is designed to increase fitness as well as to enhance wicketkeeping skills.

Two markers are placed on the ground about half a dozen metres apart (see Figure 10-8). The keeper stands in the middle and someone throws the ball to the keeper from a reasonable distance. The keeper takes the ball, underarms it back to the thrower, and moves laterally, touching one marker before moving back into the middle. The drill is repeated with the keeper moving to touch alternate markers.

Figure 10-8: The keeper moves constantly between alternate markers to take the ball.

The most important discipline in the fast feet drill is for the wicketkeeper to not simply run to the markers and back to the centre, but to use correct footwork. Correct footwork involves bringing the foot furthest away from the target marker next to the other foot before the foot closest to the target marker is then pushed sideways. This movement is achieved almost in a skipping motion but the keeper is moving sideways with their feet and body always facing forwards.

Diving for the spectacular save

The central function of the wicketkeeper is to catch the ball. However, catching the ball isn't always possible in a comfortable and well balanced way. Although diving for the ball is to be avoided if good footwork can ensure a safer and more comfortable gather, sometimes trying to take a catch or stopping the ball going for byes is essential.

In this diving drill, place two markers five metres apart (see Figure 10-9). The keeper stands in the middle and someone tries to throw the ball low and wide either side of the keeper to get it past them inside the markers. The keeper dives to take the ball one-handed. Always make sure the keeper is back in the correct position before throwing the ball again.

Figure 10-9: The wicketkeeper practises diving to catch the ball.

Taking the ball one-handed in keeping gloves is not quite the same as catching a ball in the bare hand. While the hand easily wraps around the ball, keeping gloves do not. Try to take the ball more in the base of the glove's fingers, so the fingers can be wrapped around the ball.

When diving, attempt to keep the elbow straight. Diving with a bent elbow can mean that a successful take can be ruined when the elbow hits the ground and the ball is jarred free.

Stumping for keeps

The best way to practise stumping is to simulate a match situation (see Figure 10-10). Stand up to the stumps in the correct, crouched stance with someone in the normal batting position with a bat or stump (they do not need protective equipment). Have another person stand about halfway down the pitch and throw the ball at the same pace and on the same length as a spinner would normally bowl (refer to Chapter 8 for more on spin bowling).

Figure 10-10: Create a match situation to practise stumping.

The thrower varies the line of each throw from outside off stump to down the leg side, but not directly at the stumps. The imitation batsman should play at the ball normally but deliberately miss, allowing the keeper to take the ball and then practise quickly stumping the batsman.

All wicketkeepers have their own style in the same way that all batsmen and bowlers have their own characteristics. Some keepers can look a bit untidy and may not do everything absolutely technically correctly every ball. Working hard to be technically correct with every ball is very important. In the end, what counts is not how polished you look, but whether you catch the ball!

A good, reliable wicketkeeper is essential in any successful side but the keeper is also expected to be able to make a significant contribution with the bat. Although keepers are often not expected to perform as consistently well with the bat as the specialist batsmen, their performances can't be wallowing in the tail-ender class near the bottom of the batting order.

Although batting skills in a keeper are not quite so important at local club level, any wicketkeeper who wants to progress up the ranks to higher classes of cricket must have reasonable batting skills. A keeper, therefore, needs to work as hard on their batting as their keeping.

Wicketkeeping is a tough road not only because of the physical and mental demands it imposes, but because each side has just one wicketkeeper. Although a team usually has five or six specialist batsmen, three or four faster bowlers or possibly a couple of deceptive spinners, only one keeper can fit into any side. This fact means fewer opportunities for wicketkeepers, so working hard at both keeping and batting is important to be sure of securing and maintaining a place in the team.

Adam Gilchrist: The exemplary all-rounder

The brilliant batting of Australian keeper Adam Gilchrist has changed how wicketkeepers around the world are now viewed. A fine gloveman in his own right, with an impressing 320 catches and 35 stumpings from 85 Tests leading into the 2006–07 Ashes series, Gilchrist's batting is what has set him apart from other wicketkeepers. He has not only scored more than 5,000 runs at an average of almost 50, but the speed at which he has scored them, destroying opponents when the game may have been in the balance, is extraordinary.

Gilchrist has a significantly faster scoring rate — strike rate — than any other leading batsman in Test history. See Chapter 21 for more on Gilchrist.

Some wicketkeepers may not be the best in their team and therefore miss out on the keeping position, but may still be selected for their batting skills. Adam Gilchrist played some of his early one-day matches for Australia as a batsman while Ian Healy was still the keeper.

Concentrating on success

The great Australian keeper, Ian Healy, once described wicketkeeping as like being the drummer in a band. You're rarely noticed although you're vital for the rhythm of a successful performance. For that reason, a keeper can have a faultless display and barely rate a mention in match reports. However, a keeper can also make just one mistake in a long day and that, for some reason, can become the focal point of discussion.

In this regard, wicketkeeping is similar to batting, where one mistake can have a big impact. Although one mistake can mean the end of a batsman's innings and ensure a long and fruitless stint in the pavilion until the time comes to field, wicketkeepers get the chance to redeem themselves.

Both batting and keeping require intense concentration. The trick with concentration is being able to switch off between deliveries and then regain full focus again as the bowler turns at the top of their mark to run in and bowl again. Look closely next time you're watching a Test match on television and you can see the keeper often chatting to the slips and even having a joke between deliveries.

This way the keeper doesn't need to concentrate for the full six hours of play but simply during the vital seconds when the bowler runs up and bowls. This ability to switch on and switch off means the keeper is much fresher and sharper late in the day when batting teams can often threaten to dominate the match.

The keeper not only has the job of taking the cricket ball from the bowlers or fielders, the keeper is also the team's prime motivator. An active, upbeat and lively wicketkeeper, who is continually encouraging team mates, can lift the whole side in tough situations.

The captain's second pair of eyes

No one is better placed on the fielding side to see what is happening than the wicketkeeper. The keeper has a clear view of the bowler, batsman and pitch. The keeper can see whether the ball is moving in the air or off the pitch, which bowlers are gaining the most movement and whether the batsman is having trouble with a particular bowler or a particular type of delivery. The keeper can also tell simply by the pace the ball is going into the gloves which of the faster bowlers may be tiring and could need a rest. For all these reasons and more, the wicketkeeper is constantly communicating with the captain, relaying information. An experienced keeper who has a good relationship with the captain can also help set the field. Although the keeper doesn't move players from one position to another, the keeper can fine tune the angles of the fielders in relation to the batsman because the keeper stands so close to the batsman. Adam Gilchrist often does this with the permission of the Australian captain, Ricky Ponting, particularly in one-day matches.

Chapter 11

Talking Tactics: Captaining a Cricket Team

In This Chapter

- Taking on the captain's role
- Building a strong team
- Tossing the coin
- Leading the team in the field
- Trying aggressive and defensive tactics
- Testing the batting
- Looking at one-day captaincy

Cricket is chock full of tactics. Each delivery is a game within a game. The batsman tries to score runs while the bowler and fielders try to dismiss the batsman or at least prevent the batsman scoring runs.

This chapter deciphers cricket's tactics so that you can have more fun playing and watching this most fascinating of team games.

The advice is to help prepare you for a leadership role for the day when you may be selected to captain a cricket team; when you may be the cricketer to come up with a winning plan for your team.

Understanding the Role of Captain

Few, if any, other sports allow the captain of the team to play such an important role as cricket does.

In sports such as AFL, soccer and the rugby codes, the game is so fast paced that the on-field captain has little time to breathe, never mind alter team tactics. In fact, in these quick-fire sports, captains are often reduced to the role of coin tosser and cheer leader, imploring team mates to give their best. Most of the major decisions on game day and during the week are made by the coach. But the game of cricket is fundamentally different on and off the field.

Taking in the spirit of cricket

The most important part of cricket has nothing to do with a bat or ball but relates to how the game is played. And the captain is the person who sees that the spirit of the game is always honoured. The spirit of cricket is such a fundamental foundation of the sport that the 'spirit' is written into the laws of the game. The official law book does not start with law No. 1 but with a preamble which reads:

> *Cricket is a game that owes much of its unique appeal to the fact that it should be played not only within the laws but also within the spirit of the game. Any action which is seen to abuse this spirit causes injury to the game itself. The major responsibility for ensuring the spirit of fair play rests with the captains.*

The preamble explains what is considered fair and unfair play, most of which revolves around respect for your opponents and the umpires. So seriously do cricket authorities take the strengthening and protecting of the spirit of cricket that Cricket Australia (CA) has made this attitude to the game one of the four priorities in the national governing body's formal strategic plan.

Players should read the laws of cricket as part of their cricket education when starting out in the game. A wise captain keeps a copy with his gear to check particular laws from time to time as the laws relate to match situations, equipment, playing conditions and so on.

Captains have the responsibility to ensure that their players uphold the spirit of cricket. If every player, on both teams, complies with the spirit of the game, then the game is much more enjoyable to play. (Refer to Chapter 2 for more about the spirit of the game.) For full details of both the spirit and laws of cricket, check the Marylebone Cricket Club Web site (`www.lords.org`). Click Laws & Spirit. Alternatively, contact your state or territory cricket association for details on how to obtain a copy of the laws. You can find the contact details for the associations in Chapter 13.

A good captain has plenty of self belief and this self belief instantly rubs off on the team. If the players see a captain who is a strong character, then the players feel they are being well led. A good captain communicates well, relaying to the players what is expected and how they should go about their tasks. When you become a captain — or if you've already made the grade — don't ask players to do anything they can't achieve, whether that's to do with batting and bowling, or at training. As much as possible, allow the players to play to their strengths and respect their ability to complete the tasks they've been set.

Deploying winning psychology

Cricket is as much about the state of the players as the state of play. Good captains not only need to be able to read the game unfolding in front of them, but they also need to understand how their players are reacting to the game. The power of positive thinking plays a big part in sporting success and in cricket, that positive thinking begins with the captain. Although a player can never play above their ability, self belief can allow once timid and uncertain players to blossom.

The Australian team provides two great models: Justin Langer and Matthew Hayden had hesitant and difficult beginnings to their international careers. Each was dropped from the Australian team a number of times and spent significant periods out of the side. Now each is regarded among the all-time greats of Australian cricket. Langer and Hayden rank second as the most successful opening batting combination of all time. Both claim they owe their success to the faith and confidence that their first regular captain, Steve Waugh, showed in them.

Following are tips on how captains can get the most out of their players:

- **Keep a little distance from the team:** Team captains have to make tough calls. In club cricket, those calls can be as difficult as dropping a player from the team. When captains try to be best mates and please everyone in the team, they soon find these tough decisions are harder to make and they lose respect among the playing group. By the same token, captains can't afford to be so stand-offish that they are unapproachable and isolated.
- **Build confidence when necessary:** Sports people suffer doubts and occasionally need to be told how good they are. If a player is struggling with their game, reinforce the positives before pointing out what that player may be doing wrong. On the flipside, over-confidence and complacency can lead to a team under performing. A few well chosen words from the captain can build confidence and put complacency to sleep.
- **Offer constructive criticism:** Players and the team need to have feedback on their performance, but launching into a critique of a team's performance in the dressing room after a defeat is not always a bright idea. Emotions can run high following a match. Let your feelings be known to the team in the days following the game. If a player needs to be spoken to in a stern manner, speak to the player in private. Embarrassing a player in front of the team may only make the problem worse.
- **Field close to the action:** A captain should never place themselves on the boundary unless in exceptional circumstances. Captains often field at first slip next to the wicketkeeper, where the captain can get a good view of the game. Captains who are not confident in the slips usually field at mid on or mid off so they're near the bowler and again get a good view of the game by looking more or less straight down the pitch. (Refer to Chapter 2 for a fielding diagram and Chapter 9 for more details on the fielding positions.)
- **Harness the power of team mates:** Good captains ask for tactical advice from their players, particularly those players with lots of experience. Good captains encourage players to approach them with ideas, and talk to their wicketkeeper regularly. The keeper has the best view of the game and can accurately relate how the ball may be behaving in the air and off the pitch and whether a bowler is tiring. This may lead to bowling or field changes or a completely different set of tactics. But bear in mind, ultimately it has to be the captain's call.

As soon as you find out that you're about to be named captain of your team, make sure you have a good understanding of the players in the side — what type of player and person each one is, what their best assets are and what motivates them. Then move to the opposition and do some homework on that team's players. Try to exploit their weakness with the strengths of your own players, whether you're looking at a particular bowler against a particular batsman, or a field setting that can probe a weakness.

Talking tactics

Cricket is made up of hundreds, sometimes thousands, of set pieces. Each occurs when the bowler delivers the ball to the batsman. These set pieces take a second or two to execute and then the batsmen, bowlers and fielders take thirty, forty, even fifty seconds to prepare for the next delivery. In addition, matches are stopped for drinks, lunch and tea. In short, cricket captains have an inordinate amount of time on their hands to change team tactics.

Among the crucial decisions a captain makes are the following:

- Tossing the coin with the opposition captain to decide which team bats or bowls first
- Deciding on the *batting order* of the team
- Communicating with the batsmen to let the batsmen know whether to play aggressively or defensively
- Choosing when and if to *declare* the innings
- Deciding which bowlers should be given the new ball
- Deciding when to rest bowlers
- Deciding when to tell a fresh bowler to bowl
- Letting bowlers know where, approximately, on the pitch you want them to aim the ball
- Setting and changing the position of fielders to give the best chance of dismissing the batsmen, as well as stopping the flow of runs
- Deciding when to take the second and possibly subsequent *new* balls in a longer match, for example, a Test or first-class match.

Being captain of the fielding side requires constant decision-making. From ball to ball, the position of fielders can be altered and bowlers get tired and need to be rested, in some cases every few overs. When the side is batting, however, the captain sitting in the pavilion can do little and the batsmen out in the middle playing the bowling need to decide whether to attack or defend each delivery. A captain can send occasional messages out to the batsmen, or talk to them during breaks in play, such as at the lunch and tea intervals.

Captains have decisions to make, even before a game begins. Particularly in club cricket, captains often play the key role in team selection. See the next section, 'Selecting the Right Team' for more on choosing a winning team.

On top of all this decision-making, the captains have to monitor their own performances. Captains have to be worth their place in the team. Captains have to bat, bowl or wicketkeep well enough to merit selection. The best way for a captain to lead is by example. If the captain is performing well, particularly in tough situations, then the captain can inspire team mates to greater effort and resolve.

Make sure you give direction! Try to instil a mind-set of what the team is trying to achieve and give each player clear responsibilities so they know how they're expected to contribute. Play to their strengths and give them confidence that they can do the task that has been set for them. You may have a case of a bowler who's very accurate but doesn't move the ball much. Get the bowler to bowl very defensively in one-day matches, trying to stop the runs. In longer matches, get that bowler to apply pressure by drying up the runs while bowling from one end so you can attack with different bowlers from the other end.

Selecting the Right Team

Games of cricket can almost be lost before play starts if the make-up of the side is wrong. What you're looking for, when selecting a side, is a mix of talents. In short, a mix of talents means you should have enough batsmen to score runs and bowlers capable of dismissing opposition batsmen. The ideal make-up of an 11-player cricket team is usually five or six batsmen and four or five bowlers as well as the wicketkeeper. Ideally one of the bowlers will be classified as an *all-rounder,* someone who has mastered both batting and bowling, to give the team extra batting depth.

All-rounders are worth their weight in gold. Perhaps the best in the world at the moment is England's Andrew Flintoff. Flintoff is good enough to be selected as a batsman or a bowler but occupies only one place in the team.

But selection doesn't stop there. Captains also look to blend the individual talents of the players among their bowlers and batsmen.

When it comes to the team's specialist batsmen, a captain wants two players who are adept at playing the new ball. These players are called *opening batsmen* and they tend to be good at playing defensive shots. Then the captain looks for players who are more adept at playing attacking shots but can defend if necessary. These players are called *middle order batsmen.* (Refer to the section on the batting order in Chapter 6.)

As for selecting the team's specialist bowlers, a captain usually wants a mixture of bowler styles, wanting players who specialise in seam, swing and spin bowling. This mixture gives the captain lots of options. (Refer to Chapter 7 and Chapter 8 for more on how the different bowling styles can help win cricket matches.)

The condition of the pitch — if made of turf — can have a major effect on the selection of a team's bowlers, particularly in a Test match. If the pitch has lots of grass and moisture, these conditions aid seam movement and a captain is likely to want to select pace bowlers. On the other hand, if the pitch is dry and grassless, then spin bowlers are likely to come into their own as the game progresses. (Refer to Chapter 2 for more on pitches.)

A cricket ball has a pronounced stitched seam running around its circumference. When the ball bounces off the pitch, this seam can cause the ball's direction to move towards or away from the batsman. This phenomenon is called *seam movement*.

The captain's influence on team selection tends to differ between higher and lower levels of cricket. In local club cricket, the captain can be god, getting to decide alone which players are in the side. But in major competitions, and certainly at state and national level, the team and its captain are picked by a panel of selectors. Sometimes the coach may also be a selector but this isn't the case with the Australian side. A four-man panel of relatively recent former Test players, currently chaired by former Australian opening batsman of the mid 1980s Andrew Hilditch, chooses the Australian side.

The 12th man

In state and international cricket, teams have 12 players, yet only 11 actually bat or bowl in the match. *The 12th man*, as the extra player is called, spends the match carrying drinks out to fielders, relaying messages from the captain in the dressing room to the batsmen or, if the 12th man is really lucky, getting to field as replacement for an injured team mate, or one merely dashing off for a call of nature.

Having a team of 12 rather than 11 gives the captain more tactical options in the run-up to the start of the match. The captain looks at the condition of the pitch and then decides which 11 players are to bat and bowl, and which unlucky player is to carry the drinks. The state of the pitch, if turf, often influences the decision as to which player is to be 12th man. A well grassed pitch aids seam bowling, so a spinner may be left out. A dry and grassless pitch may mean a faster bowler, often known as a *seamer*, may be left out so the captain can play one or more spinners. (Refer to Chapter 2 for more about pitches, and Chapter 8 for more about seamers.)

Usually a captain lets the player who's to be 12th man know his fate either the night before or on the morning of the match.

If you have to select a cricket team, as well as marrying up the skills of batsmen and bowlers into a winning unit, other factors need to be considered. Here are some dos and don'ts of team selection:

- **Do be honest with players that do not merit selection:** Tell your players clearly why they're not making the team on this occasion and indicate what it is in their game that they need to improve to merit reselection. They can work on their problem areas at training.
- **Do monitor individual performance:** Cricket is a game of statistics, both team and individual. While not always providing the full picture, statistics can be a good guide as to whether players merit selection. (See Chapter 20 for more on cricket statistics.)
- **Do take fielding ability into account:** If two players are roughly of the same ability as a batsman or bowler, then the deciding factor could well be fielding. In close call selections, best go for the player who is more adept at catching, collecting and throwing a cricket ball. (See Chapter 12 for more on practising your fielding skills.)
- **Don't be too hasty in your selection:** Just because a player has a few bad games it doesn't mean they are a poor cricketer. Captains should try and think long term. A player's form is temporary but class is permanent. Players often respond well to a captain who shows them loyalty and encouragement.
- **Don't select a player because that player is your friend:** All players in a team have to earn their keep.

If a captain chooses to leave out a player, it's said that the player has been *dropped*. When a player is selected to play, the player is said to have been *given the nod*.

Deciding Who Bats — at the Toss of the Coin

Half an hour before a cricket match starts, the captains of both teams walk together to the pitch. Once in the middle of the ground, the captain of the team that is playing at home tosses a coin in the air. While the coin is in flight, the captain of the team playing away from home calls either 'Heads' or 'Tails'. If the away captain calls correctly, then that captain has the choice of batting or fielding first. On the other hand, if the away skipper calls incorrectly, then the home captain gets the choice.

Whether a coin lands heads or tails is pure luck. But the choice of whether to bat or field first is a big test of a captain's acumen.

The captain's decision on whether to bat or bowl first is influenced by an assessment of the weather conditions and pitch, if the pitch is turf.

If the turf pitch or the weather look like favouring pace and swing bowling, then the captain winning the toss is more likely to field first.

Tell-tale signs of a turf pitch and weather conditions that favour fielding first include:

- **Grass on the pitch:** This situation can aid the bowlers in moving the ball off the seam.
- **Moisture in the pitch:** Again, this situation can encourage seam movement.
- **Cloudy conditions overhead:** A cloudy day can encourage the cricket ball to swing in the air, making it more difficult for the batsmen.

However, on the flipside, if the conditions look like they favour batting, then the chances are that the captain may choose to bat first. In cricketing circles, this choice is called *having a hit.*

Tell-tale signs of a batsman-friendly turf pitch and weather conditions include:

- **Dry and grassless pitch:** The ball is unlikely to deviate much off the seam but, if deterioration takes place later in the game, then spin bowlers may have some joy. (Refer to Chapter 8 for more on spin bowling.)
- **Sunny and dry overhead conditions:** The ball is less likely to swing. Making the opposition field on a hot day can fatigue the bowlers and fielders. You can be a very popular captain if you win the toss and bat with a weather forecast predicting temperatures well into the 30s.

If the pitch starts out as a paradise for batsmen, the pitch may not necessarily end the game like that. As the match progresses, dry pitches often deteriorate. The spikes used by bowlers and batsmen on the pitch can make the turf crumble. This crumbling can lead to uneven bounce, aid spin bowling and make the pitch harder to bat successfully on. Conversely, if the pitch starts off damp and green, a few days of sunshine can soon turn the pitch into a batting paradise — dry and hard!

The longer the format of the match, the more of a role pitch conditions can play. For example, during the five days of a Test match, the condition of the pitch can change enormously. But in Twenty20 games, which are over in a few hours, the game doesn't last long enough for conditions to worsen or get better. However, winning the toss is still important in Twenty20 and one-day matches. (See the section, 'Understanding one-day fielding restrictions' later in the chapter for more on the captaincy skills needed in shorter games of cricket.)

A turf pitch that has a lot of green grass growing on it is often called a *green top*. This pitch is usually a fast bowler's paradise and can be very difficult to bat on because the fresh grass greatly assists movement off the seam.

In Test and first-class matches each team has two innings, but in one-day matches each team only has one innings. The number of overs bowled to each team is limited to 50 in state and international matches. The number can be less in club cricket.

Captaining the Team in the Field

When the team is in the field, the captain is out there with the players calling the shots. Good captains have the respect of their team mates and their decisions are followed to the letter. Cricket is a complex and time-consuming game. The captain has to make the tough calls, and this fact is never more true than when the team is fielding. From the start, the captain has to make decisions.

Deciding on the new-ball bowlers

The captain has to choose which pair of bowlers are to bowl first from the two ends of the pitch. These players are called the *opening bowlers*. The ball is new so the captain usually chooses players who can deliver the ball at a fast pace but also move the ball in the air or off the seam. However, other factors enter the equation when a captain decides who should be the opening bowlers.

The captain may want bowlers who attack the batsmen from differing angles. For example, one bowler could deliver the ball with the right hand while the other delivers with the left. One bowler may deliver the ball faster than the other or make it bounce more. This is the contrast between Australia's current opening bowlers, Brett Lee and Glenn McGrath. Lee is faster and swings the ball but the wily veteran McGrath, while not as quick, has become the world's most successful fast bowler through deadly accuracy and awkward bounce from his tall, high action. Both new-ball bowlers posing different problems for the batsmen equals one very happy captain!

In Test and first-class cricket, a new ball is given to the fielding team at the start of each innings. This ball can be replaced with another new ball every 80 overs until the batting team is dismissed. However, the captain can decide whether or not to take the second and subsequent new balls when they become due. In one-day matches and usually in club cricket, the procedure is a lot simpler: A new ball is made available at the start of each innings. In club cricket, the fielding team usually supplies its own ball.

A new ball tends to swing in the air and deviate off the pitch more than an old ball. A new ball also bounces more and travels through the air faster towards the batsman. Facing fresh fast bowlers bowling with a new ball is usually the most difficult and dangerous time for batsmen.

Choosing when to change the bowlers

Bowling is physically draining, often causing fast bowlers to tire quickly. Bowlers can lose their pace, impact, and often their accuracy. Reasons for a captain to order a bowling change include:

- The batsmen may be playing the bowler well, scoring lots of runs. The captain may need a new approach to try to dismiss the batsmen, or at least to stop the flow of runs.
- The bowler needs to rest for a while before returning to the fray. The captain instructs the bowler to take a break in the field.
- The captain may see the ball starting to reverse swing and may bring on a bowler who is good at getting a ball to reverse (refer to Chapter 8 for full details on reverse swing).
- The captain wants to see if a different type of bowler — pace, seam, swing or spin — is able to dismiss the batsmen.

In one-day matches at international and state level, the number of overs an individual bowler can bowl in an innings is limited — the maximum is 10 per bowler in a 50-over match. Therefore, at some point in the innings, the fielding captain may want the bowler to stop, leaving some overs so that bowler can return later in the innings and bowl again (see the section, 'Looking at One-Day Captaincy', later in this chapter for more on one-day tactics).

When a captain is thinking about a change in the bowling, the captain tells the player he intends to bring on to bowl to warm up. The player then does some stretching exercises to help ensure that when they do bowl, they don't pull a muscle (see Chapter 12 for more on stretching).

When a captain changes the bowler, commentators often refer to a new bowler being *introduced into the attack*. Commentators can also refer to a bowler beginning a new *spell*. This spell has nothing to do with Harry Potter. A spell is what cricketers call the group of consecutive overs a bowler will bowl from the same end.

Seam and swing bowlers tire more quickly than spinners. As a rule of thumb, seam and swing bowlers show signs of tiredness after completing five or six overs, although some can breeze through eight or nine with relative ease. Spin bowling is less about physical exertion and more about guile; therefore, spin bowlers can bowl far longer. But eventually a spin bowler will tire. Generally, when a bowler tires, accuracy is lost, making it easier for the batsmen to execute scoring shots.

Some bright captains change the bowling just to unsettle the concentration of the batsmen by making them get used to someone new. Like people generally, all bowlers are different, even if some use the same basic skills. The team may have two right-arm fast bowlers specialising in outswing deliveries, but even then these bowlers deliver the ball with slightly different actions from slightly different angles and heights, and at a different pace (refer to Chapter 7 and Chapter 8 for more on bowling).

Having strong communication between the captain and the bowler is important. Always discuss your plans with the bowler and listen to what the bowler believes may be the best method of dismissing a batsman. Rarely do a captain and a bowler differ. A good captain supports the bowler's plan on most occasions, giving them extra confidence, and then making subtle changes if they're necessary. Good leadership means including other players in discussions and getting the views of your experienced players in particular. Success comes from a combined effort but remember, in the end, you're leading the team. Be decisive with whatever decisions you make.

Setting the field

The captain decides where the fielders should stand — called *setting the field*. The main fielding positions are shown in the fielding diagram in Chapter 2 and described in further detail in Chapter 9.

However, fielding positions are so important that they're worth re-capping here:

- **Close catching positions:** These fielders are placed close to where the batsman receives the ball. Their main purpose is to take a catch should the batsman hit the ball in the air, usually off the edge of the bat.
- **Run-saving positions:** These fielders are located further away from the batsman. Their job is to stop the ball and prevent the batsmen from taking a run. However, if the ball flies to them in the air off the batsman's bat, these fielders are also expected to take the catch.

Looking at Aggressive and Defensive Field Settings

Field settings are usually fairly standard at the start of an innings when a captain has his new ball bowlers on the attack trying to take cheap, early wickets. However, as the match progresses, the field placings change according to which team is dominating the match.

The team captain chooses between two main types of field settings:

- **Aggressive field setting:** The captain tells most of his fielders to stand in close catching positions.

  The main object of an aggressive field setting is to increase the chances of a catch being taken to dismiss the batsman.
- **Defensive field setting:** The captain places more of the fielders in run-saving positions.

  The main object of a defensive field setting is to stem the flow of runs scored by the batsman.

The danger of having aggressive field settings is that plenty of gaps between fielders allow batsmen to score easy runs when they hit the ball. Generally, when teams are on the attack with aggressive fields, you find that the batsmen — although at a greater risk of being dismissed — score runs at a faster rate.

Going for the jugular — using aggressive field settings

Match situations where the fielding captain goes on the attack are as follows:

- **At the start of the innings:** The bowlers are freshest at the start of an innings, and the batsmen have not adjusted to the conditions, such as the bounce of the ball. The start of the innings also means a new ball, which is more likely to fly through the air quickly and deviate before and after bouncing off the wicket.
- **When a second or subsequent new ball has just been taken:** As mentioned earlier in the chapter, in Test and first-class matches, a new ball is offered to the fielding side after every 80 overs of an innings. The arrival of a new ball marks a good time to attack.
- **When a batsman has just been dismissed and a new batsman has arrived at the wicket:** Even the best batsmen take time to be able to judge the pace of the bowling and bounce off the pitch (see Chapter 6 for more on the frailty of batsmen early in their innings).
- **When the batsman is not very good:** The batsman may be in the team for his bowling prowess and hasn't really mastered the art of batting. Such players are called *tail-enders* and are usually bowlers (see Chapter 6 for more on tail-end batsmen).

Packing the slips and crowding the bat

Attacking fields differ between each type of bowler — seam, swing and spin. A typical attacking field for a seam or swing bowler involves lots of fielders standing in the slips. Some captains deploy three, four, even five fielders to stand in the slip and gully region because the slip cordon — located to the right hand of the wicketkeeper (presuming a right-handed batsman) — is the best location for taking catches coming off the edge of the batsman's bat. The tactic of having lots of slip fielders in place is called *packing the slips.* Generally, when the condition of the pitch and the ball favours these types of bowlers, batsmen are prone to edge the ball in the air in the direction of the slip fielders.

Attacking fields set for spin bowlers, though, are entirely different. When the condition of the ball and pitch favours spinners, batsmen are prone to offer catches to fielders located in front and square of the pitch on the off and leg side. You rarely see more than one slip in place to a spin bowler but you might see a whole gaggle of fielders standing at silly mid off, silly mid on, silly point or the bizarrely named short backward square leg. In cricket speak, this is called *crowding the bat* and can create great uncertainty for the batsman who knows one miscalculation could lead to a catch being snaffled and the long, lonely walk back to the pavilion. (Refer to the fielding diagram in Chapter 2, and Chapter 9 for more on these fielding positions.)

Here's an example of an aggressive field setting for pace, seam and swing bowling:

- **Close catchers:** Wicketkeeper, first, second, third and possibly fourth slip, gully and short leg.
- **Run-saving fielders:** Point, cover, mid off or mid on and fine leg.

A new cricket ball can be referred to by cricketers as a *new cherry* because when a ball is new it is very shiny and red.

Aggressive fields are set when the fielding team feels that the condition of the ball and pitch, as well as the inexperience or lack of ability of the batsmen, gives it a better chance of claiming a dismissal, particularly if the batsmen have just begun their innings.

You'll often find in cricket that a captain who's confident and used to winning is more aggressive in their field settings, and sets aggressive fields for longer periods. In short, captains have confidence that their bowlers can dismiss the batsmen and they want fielders close to the bat to take the catching chances when they eventually come.

Treading carefully — knowing when to set defensive fields

Unfortunately, captaining a fielding team isn't all attack! Sometimes, going on the defensive and waiting for the batsman to make a mistake or the bowler to produce a great piece of bowling to claim the batsman's wicket is necessary. (Refer to Chapter 2 for more on modes of dismissal.)

Some situations that prompt a captain to go on the defensive include:

- **The ball is old and is not swinging, seaming or spinning:** If the ball is not moving off the seam, swinging in the air or spinning once bouncing off the pitch, the batsman has less chance of making a mistake.
- **The batsman is playing well:** The batsman is in form and hitting the ball well. When a good batsman has been batting for a long time, that's when the batsman is most dangerous — able to judge the bounce and pace of deliveries and execute devastating scoring shots. At this time, the captain may decide it's time for the fielding side to go on the defensive.
- **The match is a limited-overs match:** In this type of cricket, the object is as much to prevent the batting team from scoring runs as dismissing batsmen (if you can do both, all the better). Therefore, captains set more defensive fields in limited-overs cricket than in Test and first-class matches. (See the section, 'Looking at One-Day Captaincy', for more on tactics in one-day cricket.)

Here's an example of an ultra-defensive field setting used for one-day cricket, where up to five fieldsmen can be stationed on the boundary:

- **Close catching positions:** Wicketkeeper
- **Run-saving positions:** Third man, point, deep cover, extra cover, long off, long on, mid wicket, deep square leg and short fine leg.

Sometimes in Test and first-class cricket — where each side has two innings — when the batting side is set to declare its innings, the fielding side becomes ultra defensive. The captain sets a field whose sole objective is to stop runs being scored. By doing this, the fielding captain hopes to delay the batting side's declaration, giving his own side less time to survive to draw the match. (See the section, 'Looking at declaration scenarios', later in this chapter.)

Fielding teams are expected to complete their overs at a decent pace. Umpires can be strict on captains and teams that bowl their overs too slowly. In Test cricket, the captains of fielding teams that fail to complete their overs on time are often fined and can be suspended if the over rate becomes too slow. The entire fielding team can also be fined. In state cricket, the fielding team has a percentage of its valuable points deducted. The fielding side should look to complete a minimum 15 overs during each hour's play in Test cricket.

Mixing attack and defence

A lot of the time during a match, captains don't set ultra-defensive or aggressive fields. Instead, captains like to keep their options open by placing some fielders in close catching positions and others in run-saving ones.

In setting the field, the captain assesses where the batsman is likely to hit the ball and also where the ball is likely to fly if the ball hits the edge of the bat.

Here's an example of a typically mixed field to a faster bowler:

- **Close catching positions:** Wicketkeeper, two slips, gully
- **Run-saving positions:** Point, cover, mid off, mid on, square leg, fine leg.

(Refer to the diagram in Chapter 2 to see where these fielding positions are, relative to the batsman.)

A cricket field is a big expanse and there simply aren't enough fielders to cover every square metre of turf. The captain has to decide on a trade-off between having fielders who can stop runs and fielders who can take catching chances.

The captain usually has some fielders on the off side of the wicket and some on the leg side. Generally, most field settings involve more players located on the off rather than the leg side because seam and swing bowlers usually aim their deliveries at or just outside off stump. (Refer to Chapter 8 for more on this line of attack.) Occasionally, though, a captain will put more fielders on the leg side than the off, when perhaps the batsman has shown a desire to hit the ball in the air on the leg side (refer to Chapter 2 for an explanation of the off and leg side).

Handling bowlers with care

Bowlers are the team's strike weapons and captains have to handle them with care. The key to handling bowlers is a combination of the following:

- **Making sure the bowlers are well rested:** Captains take bowlers out of the attack when they become tired and put them in places in the field where they won't be expected to run around a lot after the ball. Traditionally, bowlers field on the boundary at fine leg or third man, away from the action. Fielders in more active positions, such as in the covers and at a point where the ball is hit regularly, are expected to move quickly to stop the ball and, if it passes them, to chase the ball hard.
- **Listening to the bowler's opinion:** A captain is well advised to listen to what the bowler has to say. And that doesn't mean having a chat about politics or the commodities boom! Bowlers have their views on where fielders should go and on the technical weaknesses of the batsman. A captain who doesn't listen to the bowlers and treats them in a high-handed 'Do what I say' manner is bound not to get the best from them.

A good captain, although listening to the views of the bowlers, is not bossed around by them. A captain has to be his own person. On the subject of captaincy, the adage, 'Success has many fathers but failure only one', comes to mind. And when the team fails, guess who ends up holding the baby? You guessed it: The captain. (Refer to the section 'Deploying winning psychology' earlier in this chapter for more on the captain–team relationship.)

Sometimes, a captain chooses not to take up the umpire's offer of a new ball. This decision is usually taken because the captain believes that the old ball is more likely to spin when bouncing off the pitch, or reverse swing in the air. (Refer to Chapter 8 for more on bowling techniques.)

Enforcing the follow-on

In a two innings-a-side match, if a team has performed brilliantly in the field and dismissed the opposition — in its first innings — for not many runs, then a funny thing can happen.

Provided the fielding side has already batted and scored 200 runs more than the team whose innings has just ended, the fielding captain has the right to enforce something called the *follow-on*. This means the team whose innings has just ended has to come straight back out and bat again. The second time the team bats is counted as its second innings and, if on completion, the team's aggregate run total still isn't as high as the fielding side's, then the team has *lost by an innings*!

The fielding captain chooses whether to enforce the follow-on. The following tactical factors are assessed:

- **How much time is left in the match:** The less time left in the match, the more likely the captain is to enforce the follow-on. By batting again, in an attempt to set up a victory target, the dominant captain may not be able to leave enough time to bowl the opposition out a second time.
- **How tired are the bowlers:** The captain tries to gauge the fatigue suffered by the bowlers. If the bowlers have made a huge effort to bowl out the opposition, then perhaps giving the bowlers a rest is wise. By choosing to bat again, rather than enforcing the follow-on, the captain ensures that the bowlers can be fresh for the other team's second innings.

Making a team follow-on always involves some danger. On a few occasions in the past, teams that have been made to follow-on have scored lots of runs in their second innings, taking their aggregate score way past that of the first innings score of the fielding side. Then, when the fielding team has batted, that team has been dismissed cheaply, giving the win and the glory to the team that had been made to follow-on.

The lead to enforce the follow-on in a five-day, two innings-a-side match is at least 200. The lead is 150 in a three or four-day match, 100 in a two-day match and 75 in a one-day match. Enforcing the follow-on doesn't apply to one-day matches at international and state level, where each team has only one innings.

Two follow-ons and Australia loses two Test series

Two amazing victories have been achieved by teams in the modern era after they were forced to follow-on. Unfortunately, both victories were against Australia. The first victory has become known as 'Botham's Test' and took place during the 1981 tour of England by Australia, and the second was by India against Australia in Calcutta 20 years later. The turnaround in 1981 was extraordinary. England was already trailing 1–0 after two Tests in the six-Test series, and the great all-rounder Ian Botham had just stood down as captain after failing to score in either innings of the second Test. Well on the way to another defeat in the third Test at Headingley in Yorkshire, Botham went mad, smashing 149 not out, thanks to some valuable late support from the tail-enders, to give England a slender lead. Not expecting to bat again, Australia collapsed after a solid start to be all out for 111, losing by 18 runs. England went on to comfortably win the series.

In India during 2001, Australia was beaten by an amazing batting feat. In complete command after three days, Australia was heading for a series victory in the second Test at the imposing Eden Gardens Stadium in Calcutta. Then India's V.V.S. Laxman and Rahul Dravid batted through the entire fourth day, turning a significant deficit into an imposing lead. Laxman scored a brilliant 281 and Dravid 180. India went on to win the Test and the series.

With the horrors of Calcutta in the back of his mind, Australian captain Ricky Ponting now almost never enforces the follow-on. Important practical reasons are also a major factor. Australia's leading bowlers, Shane Warne and Glenn McGrath, are now in their mid 30s. With so much international cricket crammed into a busy schedule, Ponting prefers to give his bowlers as much rest as possible. Australia's previous captain, Steve Waugh, had a different philosophy. He was always keen to make the most of the enormous psychological advantage of bowling an opponent out for not many runs by enforcing the follow-on.

Batting Tactics

A cricket captain's time is divided between marshalling the troops in the field, taking a turn at batting, and being in the pavilion watching the rest of the team bat. The tactical options open to the captain whose team is batting are fewer and farther between than those that occur in the field. After all, the batsmen facing the bowling are the two who decide whether to play aggressive or defensive shots.

Nevertheless, the captain's tactics can have a significant impact on how successfully the team bats.

When the team is in the field, the captain can make constant adjustment to tactics, such as moving a fielder or changing the bowling. When the team is batting, tactical choices tend to be more sporadic but no less important.

Drawing up the batting order

With 11 players in a team, all of whom have a chance to bat in the innings, the captain decides which players get to bat first, second, third . . . all the way down to eleven. The captain draws up a *batting order* before the team's innings begins and tells the players at which number they will bat. The players batting at numbers 1 and 2 go out first to face the bowlers. These batsmen are said to be *opening the innings*. When one of these batsmen has been dismissed, they are replaced by the batsman at number 3 in the order, and so on. This procession of players continues until only one batsman is left in the side who has not been dismissed, meaning the team is all out, or the captain declares the innings (see the section, 'Declaring the Innings', later in this chapter).

Good captains don't just decide on a batting order willy-nilly. Good captains assess the abilities of each player and assign them a place in the batting order according to those abilities. The most capable batsmen are placed at or near the top of the batting order, while the least capable go at the bottom of the batting order.

The best batsmen go in first for good reasons, including:

- **The bowlers are at their freshest and the ball newest:** The captain wants his most capable players at the top of the batting order to negate these twin dangers.
- **The captain chooses good batsmen who bat well together:** Good batsmen can build big partnerships, wearing down the bowlers and scoring lots of runs.

The best teams have a mixture of talents running through them. In the bowling department, the team has seam, swing and spin bowlers to make the most of conditions and add variety to the attack. With batting, the best teams have some batsmen who have tremendous defensive skills, and others who are best at playing attacking shots (refer to Chapter 5 for more on defensive and aggressive batting shots).

Often a captain gives the job of opening the innings to players who are the best at playing defensive shots — although these players should be capable of playing aggressive shots too.

Bending the tradition — altering the batting order

Sometimes a captain breaks with this tried-and-tested 'best goes first' tradition and re-jigs the batting order. The scenarios that can prompt a batting order change, include:

- **The team needs quick runs:** The captain may promote a player in the batting order because that batsman is particularly adept at playing aggressive shots. Perhaps the side has to score a certain number of runs to win the game with limited time or overs remaining.
- **Protecting better players:** In Test and first-class cricket, when the batting side loses a wicket near the end of a day's play, the captain sometimes promotes a player in the order. The captain would rather put the promoted batsman at risk of being dismissed than lose a more capable batsman who usually bats near the top of the batting order. A batsman promoted in this situation is called a *nightwatchman*. Usually a bowler, the nightwatchman is expected to play defensive shots with the aim of not being dismissed before the end of the day.

Conditions for the batsmen are often difficult at the end of a day's play. The light may be fading, making it more difficult to see the ball properly. What's more, batsmen are at their most vulnerable to being dismissed early in their innings. Having to bat for say 20 minutes at the end of one day and start again bright and early the next day is a difficult ask. By doing this, in effect, the batsman starts the innings twice — once late in the evening and again the next day. In the process, the batsman has to get use to the bounce of the ball off the pitch, get used to the deviation of the ball in the air and concentrate fully twice over. All these are good reasons for deciding on the nightwatchman tactic.

The end of a day's play is referred to as *stumps* or the *close of play.*

If all goes to plan, a nightwatchman is meant to avoid being dismissed before the close of play. The next day, the nightwatchman is meant to defend for the first few overs, tiring the bowlers in the process. Once the nightwatchman is dismissed, then normal service resumes with the more capable batsman who moved down a number in the batting order.

Promoting a player in the order brings risks. If you promote someone because they're good at playing aggressive shots, then chances are that player is not so hot at playing defensive shots and could easily be dismissed by the bowlers. As for the nightwatchman scenario, the risk is that the nightwatchman may be dismissed before the close of play, once again throwing the captain's tactics into turmoil.

Jason Gillespie sets high standards for the nightwatchman

Australian fast bowler Jason Gillespie set an amazing record for a nightwatchman during a Test match against Bangladesh in May 2006. Promoted to number 3 late on the first day after Australia lost a wicket close to stumps, Gillespie batted through four rain-marred days to score an amazing 201 not out. In the long history of Test cricket, only a few nightwatchmen had ever managed a century, and certainly none had reached 200 runs, a milestone that has eluded many of the game's finest batsmen.

Declaring the innings

Sometimes the team that is batting is well on top. The bowlers' deliveries are being flogged to all parts of the ground and runs are flowing freely. Happy days!

But the good times can't go on forever; a match needs to be won. In Test and first-class cricket, time is of the essence. The batting team has to finish its innings leaving enough time to dismiss the opposition batsmen and win the match.

The batting captain has the option of *declaring the innings.* Put simply, the batting captain says to the opposition captain, 'We have made enough runs, now it's your turn to go out and bat.'

Declaring an innings is a tactic used in Test and first-class matches but is not allowed in one-day matches at state and international level. In Test and first-class matches, one team has to beat the other in a specified period of time — five days in Test matches and four days in state Pura Cup first-class matches — otherwise, the match is declared a draw. (Refer to Chapter 3 for more on the different match formats.)

Sometimes you may hear about a first-class cricket match where both teams choose to *forfeit* an innings. What happens in this case is that the two captains agree to declare an innings each; thereby, in effect, reducing the match to one rather than the standard two innings. Forfeiture doesn't take place because both teams are bone idle. Instead, what has usually happened is that rain or bad light has taken time out of the game, yet both captains still want the chance to win the match.

Looking at declaration scenarios

Here are some typical scenarios that demonstrate when the captain of the batting side may decide to declare the innings:

- The batting side has made a huge first innings total but wants enough time left in the match to be able to bowl the opposition out twice.
- The batting side has built up a big lead in its second innings, or after batting second, and needs time to bowl the opposition out again.
- The captain is trying to force a result by offering the opposition a tempting total. The idea is that the opposition batsmen are tempted to play aggressive shots in order to reach the victory total, increasing the chances of being dismissed.

No hard and fast rules exist for if and when a captain should declare an innings. The captain has to make an assessment of the match situation, decide on a run target he wants to set the opposition and consider how much time is left in the match for the bowlers to dismiss the opposition team's batsmen.

Sometimes in cricket games, you see the 12th man bring the batsman out a drink or a new pair of batting gloves. Sometimes, the batsman has asked for this to happen, but often the 12th man has been sent on to the field by the captain to relay a message to the batsman. The message contains some useful tactic, such as the captain urging the batsman to attack the bowling, so that the innings can soon be declared.

In longer versions of the game, such as first-class cricket, matches usually pan out in a fairly standard fashion, depending on whether the batsmen or bowlers get on top. The state of the game dictates how attacking or defensive a captain needs to be. Big risk-taking moves may not take place until late in the game if quick runs or wickets are required in a limited amount of time. One-day cricket is more of a moving feast. Sometimes you have to take a risk and try to get a wicket to stem the flow of runs. When making decisions, taking a moment to ask yourself, 'Is there a better option?' is important.

Declarations that have gone wrong

On most occasions captains who have been in a strong position and declared have usually been able to win. However, just occasionally, those bold and confident moves have not gone to plan. While the team may have lost, at least the game was played in an exciting and attacking manner, instead of being allowed to meander to a dull and meaningless draw. Some famous examples follow:

- In 2001, at Headingley, Australia's acting skipper, Adam Gilchrist, declared his team's second innings on 3–176 after a significant amount of time had been lost through rain, leaving England 315 to score to win the match during the final day. The subtext was that Australia was already 3–0 up in the series and going for a 5–0 whitewash. Australia had been soundly beating England for the previous 15 years and most fans expected the Aussies to dismiss all the England batsmen and win the match. However, one England batsman, Mark Butcher, had a different idea. He hit his highest score in Test cricket of 173 to guide England to the victory total for the loss of only four wickets and the cricket world was stunned. Nevertheless, the hoopla around Butcher's great innings didn't stop the Aussies winning the next Test at The Oval cricket ground and taking the five-match series 4–1!
- In 1984 at Lord's, England was on the receiving end. England captain David Gower declared the team's second innings at 9–300 on the morning of the final day of a Test match against the West Indies. This result left the West Indies needing 342 to win the game. On a bright sunny day, West Indian opening batsman Gordon Greenidge went berserk, hitting boundary after boundary on the way to 214 not out. The West Indies made the victory target for the loss of only one wicket, thereby winning the match on the way to a 5–0 series whitewash of sorry England.
- In 1968 in the West Indies, another famous example occurred, again involving England. Home captain Garfield Sobers (see Chapter 21 for more on Sobers) declared his side's second innings on 2–92. This result left England 215 to win in less than four hours. The England batsmen went on the attack and reached the victory target with a few minutes of the match remaining. England had won the Test match and the series 1–0 and the great Garfield Sobers was jeered and heckled by the local supporters.

Looking at One-Day Captaincy

In one-day cricket, a team can win a match without dismissing any of the opposition's batsmen. All a team has to do is score more runs in the allotted number of overs than the opposition. This emphasis on run scoring and preventing the opposition from scoring runs is the crux to understanding one-day captaincy.

Applying one-day fielding tactics

Some of the special tactics used in one-day cricket are:

- **Employing pinch-hitters:** Some captains promote a player who's good at playing aggressive shots. This decision exploits the fact that under one-day cricket law, fielding captains must have most of their fielders within 30 metres of the batsman during the first 10 overs of the innings. (Refer to Chapter 3 for more on one-day matches.)
- **More defensive field placing:** Because the emphasis of the fielding captain is to prevent the batsman from scoring runs, the captain often deploys more defensive run-saving fields. In short, most of the players are located near the boundary, but this is all subject to the one-day fielding restrictions. (See the next section, 'Understanding one-day fielding restrictions'.)

- **Rotating the bowlers:** In one-day matches, the number of overs any single bowler can bowl in the innings is limited. For example, in a 50-over match, each bowler is limited to bowling 10 overs. The captain has to be canny, getting his best bowlers operating at the right time in the opposition innings. In cricket speak, this is called *rotating the bowlers*.
- **Bowling at the death:** Usually, the best swing or seam bowler in the team bowls some of their allotted overs at the start of innings when the ball is new and at its most likely to move in the air and off the seam. The ace bowler then returns in the final few overs of the innings when the opposition batsmen are going for their shots. The idea is that the bowler has the skill to counter the batsmen's attack by ensuring deliveries are bowled on a very full length at the stumps, making them difficult to score runs off.

The best way to prevent a batsman from scoring is to bowl *yorkers* at the stumps. A *yorker* is a ball which lands on the batting crease in the hope that it will slip under the bat and bowl the batsman. A yorker is a very difficult delivery for a batsman, intent on scoring, to swing the bat at. The ball is likely to hit the bottom of the bat, meaning the shot with have less timing and power so the ball can't travel as fast or as far after it's struck. (Refer to Chapter 7 for more on bowling lengths.)

For reasons no one quite understands, the white ball used for one-day internationals and state matches swings more than the red ball early in an innings. The white ball also scuffs more quickly, allowing the ball to reverse swing at the end of an innings. (Refer to Chapter 8 for more on swing bowling.)

Gilly averages a run for every ball bowled

Adam Gilchrist has changed the way one-day cricket is played with his ultra attacking style. A potent stroke-maker, who usually bats at number 6 or 7 in Test cricket, the powerful left hander was promoted to open the batting in one-day internationals early in his career. The results have been devastating. Gilchrist has maintained a spectacular strike rate of almost a run a ball and is among the highest run scorers for Australia in one-day cricket. Twice during the 2005–06 season, Gilchrist smashed his own record for the fastest one-day century by an Australian.

In one-day cricket, umpires tend to interpret the wide law very strictly (refer to Chapter 2 for more on this law). If the bowler delivers the ball outside the batsman's leg stump, and the batsman fails to hit the ball, then the umpire calls the ball wide. The batting side gets a run added to its total and the ball has to be re-bowled. Understandably, fielding captains expect their bowlers not to deliver the ball down the batsman's leg side in one-day cricket.

Dismissing the opposition's batsmen can have a profound effect on the result of a one-day match. Dismissing a batsman means that a new batsman comes out to bat. This player may not find it easy to play aggressive shots straight away. Therefore, the rate of run scoring slows. All in all, regularly dismissing batsmen is the best way to slow the scoring rate of the batting side.

Understanding one-day fielding restrictions

One-day fielding restrictions were introduced in order to stop fielding captains from putting all their fielders on the boundary from the start of the batting side's innings.

Put simply, these rules allow only two fieldsmen outside a 30-metre circle in the middle of the field for a specified number of overs. Two close catching fieldsmen also have to be in place. (Refer to Chapter 9 for more on field placings.)

The circle is marked by white markers or a white line on the field.

The restrictions previously applied for the first 15 overs of one-day internationals but, under a recent change of playing conditions, are now compulsory for the first 10 overs. However, the captain must now also bring the field in for another two five-over periods of their choosing. These five-over periods are called *power plays.* Power plays also restrict the captain to just two fieldsmen outside the 30-metre circle although the captain doesn't have to put in any close catchers.

Outside the first 10 overs and power plays, a captain can employ less attacking fields, but can have no more than five fieldsmen outside the circle at any one time.

Batting sides attempt to go on the attack during the first 10 overs and in power plays, looking to hit the ball over the fielders' heads to the boundary.

When attacking fielding restrictions have come to an end, the captain doesn't have to remove close catching positions or push more fieldsmen back towards the boundary. If the bowling side has taken early wickets, the captain wants to keep the pressure on the batsmen by continuing to attack and making runs difficult to score by keeping the field *up* (in the 30-metre circle) to save singles. Only when a batsman starts to look comfortable and begins to hit the ball consistently *through the field* (past the fieldsmen trying to prevent singles) should the captain start pushing the field back to save boundaries.

In a game format where the way to win is to restrict the scoring, a power play is disadvantageous to the fielding side. After all, a power play means fewer fielders are allowed to be located on the boundary to stop the ball.

Unless the batting side gets off to a flying start, fielding captains look to call the two power plays one after the other, so that the power plays are out of the way in the first 20 overs. If the batting side has an early scoring spree, the fielding captain may wait until after his team has dismissed a batsman to ask for one of the power plays. The captain tries to get the power plays out of the way as soon as reasonably possible.

Fielding restrictions apply in Twenty20 matches, but the restrictions are in place for just six overs. (Refer to Chapter 3 for more on the ins and outs of Twenty20 cricket.)

During 2005 and 2006, cricket's governing body, the International Cricket Council (ICC), began an experiment with *super subs*. Basically, the idea of a super sub is that at any point during the match, the captain would be allowed to substitute one player in his side for the man selected as 12th man. (Refer to the sidebar, 'The 12th man', earlier in this chapter.) The idea is to give captains greater tactical flexibility by allowing them to, for example, replace a bowler with a batsman or vice versa when the match situation required. However, this plan hasn't really worked because the team that won the toss usually had too much of an advantage. Consequently, leading cricket countries lobbied for the law to be scrapped.

Chapter 12

Talented Training

In This Chapter

- Understanding the importance of net practice
- Honing your batting skills in the nets
- Practising bowling
- Fielding drills explained
- Stretching to prevent injury
- Getting fit

Gary Player, the famous South African golfer, was once asked what role luck had in his success. He replied: 'You know, the more I practise, the luckier I get.'

The same principle applies to any sport, and particularly a sport with as many different and diverse aspects as cricket. The more you put into developing your game, the more you'll enjoy it.

This chapter examines basic drills you can practise to sharpen your cricketing skills and boost your fitness levels.

Honing Your Technique in the Nets

Most kids learn to love cricket by playing in the backyard, along the driveway, or maybe at the beach. Playing with your family and mates can be a great way to understand and enjoy the fun of smacking runs, claiming wickets and diving around taking spectacular catches.

But if you want to go further than just having casual fun in the sun, and you want to develop your skills to excel in cricket, then the nets are the place for you! The foundations of fine cricketing skills are laid at *net practice.* Whether you're playing in the local park or performing in front of packed stadiums around the world, net practice is where the batting and bowling skills are shaped and improved.

The nets are fenced-off areas where bowlers usually try to perfect their potentially wicket-taking deliveries, and where batsmen look to defend their stumps from being hit. The nets are where batsmen execute shots which, in a game situation, could yield valuable runs — hopefully many of them. Nets are called nets simply because the practice pitch is usually fenced in by netting or wire.

Benefiting from net practice

At practice, making mistakes in an attempt to improve your game doesn't matter. Batsmen can't be dismissed and bowlers won't concede runs, no matter how far the batsmen hit the ball.

Nets are places to get the basics right. A batsman can build their defence and learn to play *straight* before developing attack shots. (Refer to Chapter 5 and Chapter 6 for more on batting.) At the nets, a bowler can develop an action and style of bowling, learn to deliver the ball time after time, until they can bowl accurately for long periods, then add variations to trick the batsmen. (Refer to Chapter 7 and Chapter 8 for information on bowling.)

Nets give batsmen an opportunity to get used to different types of bowling such as spin, swing or fast. On the flipside, nets give bowlers an opportunity to bowl to both right-handed and left-handed batsmen.

Practising at the nets can help develop a skill called *muscle memory.* Being a batsman is about coordinating hand, eye and feet movements. Nets can help make playing shots almost second nature. Likewise, bowlers can get used to bowling the ball on a particular spot on the pitch.

Nets can be a good social occasion. You get to catch up with your mates in a relaxed and friendly atmosphere, have a chat and maybe mull over your latest match.

Nets give an opportunity for coaches and captains to see players' techniques and correct problems before those mistakes lead to poor performances in a match.

Training is vital preparation for your game whether maintaining or learning new skills and techniques. Training needs to be as close to match conditions as possible so you can go into the game with the confidence that you could have done nothing more. Practising at the nets allows all your skills to come into force in a game as if they were second nature.

Preparing for the cricket season

If you have a dream to play cricket, try to avoid rocking up to a club a week before the first game of the season. Even at local level, most clubs organise pre-season training. In juniors, training usually means turning up to practice a few weeks before the season starts, while senior clubs can begin preparing a couple of months in advance. In Australia's southern states, where the weather is more conducive to football than cricket during the winter, net sessions are usually held indoors. Get in touch with officials from the club you're looking to join by contacting the club midway through winter to find out about the pre-season program. Mid winter is also a good time to begin your fitness regime. (See the section, 'Improving your fitness', later in the chapter. As well, Chapter 13 explains how to join a club.)

Most international and even state players have a net session almost everyday during the cricket season, which runs from October to March. Club cricketers, though, have day jobs — although most would rather be playing cricket! Most local club sides have net practice after work one or two days a week. Most clubs, particularly in large towns and cities, have more than one team. Some have half a dozen, all graded on ability and performance, so your initial showings in the nets can dictate which team you end up in. Your place in the club's teams can quickly change once the season starts and your performances are matched against those of other players.

Training is a great way to catch up with your mates and have a bit of a chat and a laugh, but when you are actually training, take your practice very seriously — concentrate every time you bowl a ball, play a delivery in the nets, take a catch or gather the ball in fielding drills. The only way you can improve your game is to concentrate on your skills, whether they be batting, bowling or fielding, so you can shine in a match.

Giving your batting a net boost

It takes only one mistake for the batsman to be dismissed. This tightrope walker-like existence is the reason why practising for a batsman is crucial. The best way to practise is in the nets. Here are some tips for effective net practice:

- **Practise regularly:** Go to nets at least once a week and preferably twice a week during the season. Regular practice helps build up your technique, improves consistency, aids footwork, and makes you more confident.

- **Take it seriously:** Having sound judgement — when to play and when not to play a delivery — is one of the keys to good batting. Use nets to hone your judgement. When a ball is delivered in the nets, try to play the same shot to that delivery as you would play in a match situation. In addition, make sure you take the same guard at practice as you would in a match. (Refer to Chapter 5 for all you need to know on taking guard.)
- **Work on your weaknesses:** Use nets as an opportunity to confront head-on any problems you may have with your batting. For example, you may not be happy playing spin bowling. If that's the case, make sure you practise against spin bowling in the nets.

Working on Some Batting Basics

The nets are *the* place to get the basics right.

All batsmen need to have some simple techniques down pat if they want to succeed. (Chapter 5 and Chapter 6 offer a more detailed examination of batting.) In this section, the following techniques are examined:

- A comfortable stance while facing the bowling
- Good balance at the crease
- The ability to execute a backlift
- The skill to ensure the full face of the bat meets the ball.

Having a comfortable stance

To bat for long periods, you need to feel relaxed. Here's how you can become more at ease:

- Stand at the crease with feet shoulder-width apart.
- Stand side-on, so your left shoulder is pointed down the pitch at the bowler (reverse this if you're left handed).
- Have your bat resting comfortably behind the toes of your back foot (right foot for a right hander).
- Ensure that your eyes are level and focused on the ball as the bowler is delivering it.

- Keep your knees bent a little for a more comfortable stance. Keeping the knees bent helps to keep your eyes level by stopping your head tipping towards the off side. (Refer to Chapter 2 for an explanation of the off and on sides.)

When you're starting off as a budding cricketer, your stance is best with one foot either side of the batting (or popping) crease, which is in front of the stumps. (Refer to Chapter 2 for more on creases.)

Maintaining good balance at the crease

The key to good balance at the crease is to have your weight evenly distributed between your front and back feet and be leaning slightly on the balls of your feet. Being on the balls of your feet means you can move more quickly forward or back to play a shot. Cricket is a game of fast reactions. Being well balanced means that you can turn these reactions into a shot in the blink of an eye!

Executing a backlift

The *backlift* is the movement the batsman makes with the arms, bringing the bat back behind them as they prepare to play a shot. The bat should come straight back, ideally pointing somewhere between the wicketkeeper and second slip, not out towards the gully. (Refer to Chapter 2 for fielding positions.) This position allows you to bring the bat straight down again when defending or driving — the two most important shots in cricket. (Refer to Chapter 5 to find out why playing *straight* to minimise the chances of dismissal is vital.)

When beginning an innings, or when defending, keep the backlift *short*. Keeping the backlift short means the bat should be raised back to no higher than horizontal at about stump height. Once the innings has progressed, and you're feeling more comfortable, the backlift can be raised higher to allow more power to play shots.

Here are some other factors to bear in mind with the backlift:

- Keep the hands holding the bat close to the body during the backlift to help ensure the backlift is straight.
- Keep the head still throughout the backlift. Keeping the head still helps you retain your balance. Failing to keep your head still can mean losing your balance, which makes hitting the ball harder.

Playing straight

A great way to practise playing straight is to tie a cricket ball in a sock with a length of rope and hang it off a clothes line, or somewhere that allows the ball to dangle from above. You'll need a bit of space around you. Ensure the ball is hanging about 20–30 centimetres from the ground, a distance that emulates a full-length delivery. Stand a pace back from the ball.

Step towards the ball as if you're driving (refer to Chapter 5 for more on driving) and gently stroke through the ball. If you've hit the ball straight, it will come back straight and you'll be able to repeat the shot. Have competitions with yourself to see if you can regularly improve your personal best for the number of times you can continually stroke the ball. *Don't* hit the ball too hard or it may swing over and clobber you. And make sure you use reasonably strong rope and a well tied knot, lest the ball takes off and disappears through a window!

Working on other batting techniques

Running between the wickets is an often overlooked skill. Take some time to practise quick runs in full batting gear, which allows you to pressure the fielders when batting in a match. Always slide your bat on the ground out in front of you so it crosses the crease first. This action lessens the chances of being run out in a match.

Cricket is a game that requires good hand–eye coordination. Of course, good hand–eye coordination can be a natural talent, but it can also be developed. Consider playing other active bat (or racquet) sports, such as squash and tennis. These sports improve your hand–eye coordination as well as your fitness.

To change a technical flaw in your game, you need to know clearly what you want to achieve. Do heaps of repetition at training to make it feel natural before putting your changed technique into practice in a game. For example, if an international or state player wanted to straighten their backswing, they would first identify the flaw on video and set a plan of action to alter the backswing. In the case of club cricketers, a mirror is the best way to check your backlift. Do throw downs — someone standing in the middle of the pitch throwing ball after ball in about the same spot to practise the changed stroke — before progressing to the nets and finally a game.

Sometimes, when learning a new technique, your performances may go down. However, if you believe these changes can make you a better player, you need to persist.

Taking Giant Steps Forward with Your Bowling

Bowlers are a little more fortunate than batsmen. Just one ball can claim a batsman's scalp and finish their day out in the middle. However, if a bowler makes a mistake delivering a ball that is easy for the batsman to hit, then the bowler gets another chance at redemption with the very next ball they bowl. But this comfort zone doesn't last for long. If a bowler performs poorly, then sooner rather than later the team captain will replace the bowler with another one.

In truth, bowlers have to work at their game as hard, if not harder, than batsmen. Good bowling is all about rhythm, being able to repeat the same action of delivering the ball out of the hand towards the batsmen time and again.

Bowling laid bare

Key areas for bowlers to work on at net practice include:

- **Developing a run-up.** A good way to do this at practice is to start the run-up from the bowling crease. Head away from the pitch, starting with small steps and progressing to longer strides. When the moment feels right, leap as though you're going to deliver the ball. The point at which your front foot (left foot for a right hander) lands, is where you start your run-up in future. Now, run-up in the right direction towards the batsman. Don't forget to mark where your run-up should start by making a clear mark on the ground with your shoe.
- **Remembering to keep the head steady and eyes level from the start of the run-up to delivering the ball.** Keeping your head steady should help you direct the ball to where you want it to go. When you're a few strides from delivering the ball, direct your focus to the spot on the pitch where you want the ball to land.
- **Concentrating on keeping the arms in close to your body as you run-up to bowl.** (Refer to Chapter 7 for more on the run-up.)
- **Deciding how you're going to grip the ball.** Where you grip the ball in relation to its seam has a crucial influence on how the ball behaves once it leaves your hand — whether in the air or once it bounces off the pitch. (Refer to Chapter 8 for the different grips and their effects.)

Once you develop a *stock* ball — a delivery that you can bowl accurately over and over again — use net practice as an opportunity to build greater variety into your bowling. Experiment with different ways of gripping the ball and angles of delivery. Once you get these skills right in practice, you're ready to try them out in a match.

Bowlers don't aim at the batsman. Instead, bowlers usually try to make the ball bounce off an area of the pitch that makes it hard for the batsman to play an aggressive shot, and that heightens the chances of dismissing the batsman. (Refer to Chapter 7 for more on the areas of the wicket you should be aiming for to have the batsman in trouble.)

One great way to build bowling accuracy is to put a marker, such as a handkerchief, on the area of the pitch you're aiming at. You're not allowed to use markers in match situations, but you can use markers in net practice.

You can break down the process of delivering a cricket ball into the following:

- Running up to the pitch
- Jumping into a delivery stride
- 'Gathering' your arms in front of your body
- Rotating the arm over in the direction of the target.

The ball is released as the arm passes the ear. However, the bowler doesn't just stop in their tracks; the momentum of the bowling action means the bowler continues down the pitch. This continuation is called the *follow through*. (Refer to Chapter 7 and Chapter 8 for more on how to bowl.)

Curing the no ball curse

Bowling off your full run at training is important to develop good habits like rhythm, consistency and stamina. Bowling off your full run also helps to eliminate the curse of too many fast bowlers — *no balls.* That situation happens when the bowler puts their front foot over the front line, giving the batting team an extra run and an extra delivery. And the bowler has no chance of dismissing the batsman. (Refer to Chapter 2 for more on no balls.) Don't overdo charging in at training in case you become so tired that you start to *lose* your action through fatigue and risk injury.

Unfortunately the trend in the fast-bowling net practice culture is to bowl no balls at training and not worry about it. The attitude is that everything will be right in the game. The bowler who bowls no balls at training is flirting with danger. Reasons why bowling no balls at training is risky include:

- You're training yourself to bowl no balls in games.
- You're bowling at a different pace and length to how you'll have to bowl in a game when you're back to a full-length pitch.
- If you start bowling no balls in the game, your bowling will be affected because you don't have the confidence from training that you can keep behind the line.

Former Australian Test bowler Paul Reiffel went through stages of bowling no balls. When I asked him how he fixed this problem, Reiffel said discipline was the solution and he made sure he landed his front foot behind the line at training. This decision solved the problem in a match.

To work on aspects of your bowling, such as your action or to develop new deliveries, begin gently, shuffling in off a few paces and delivering the ball. This gentle shuffle gives you greater control of what you're trying to do, whether that's perfecting a new delivery or ensuring your feet, hips and shoulders are lining up at the point of delivery. These precautions are vitally important to avoid injury. When you feel comfortable bowling this way, go back onto your full run and try it.

Promising young fast bowlers need to be protected from too much bowling at training or in a match. Research by Cricket Australia has found that fast bowlers in their teens are susceptible to breaking down with injury, particularly with stress-related back problems if they do too much bowling at too young an age. While young bowlers need encouragement, be wary of how long they bowl, especially when they're on a winning streak and don't want to stop.

Cricket Australia has released strict guidelines for teenage bowlers and these guidelines are comprehensively detailed in Chapter 7.

Fast bowling is tough work so being reasonably fit is important. Always warm-up and stretch before practice or before a match (for more on warm-ups, see the section, 'Stretching Your Way to a Warmed-Up Game', later in the chapter).

Looking at Fielding Drills

The basics of fielding — how to catch, collect and throw the ball — are covered extensively in Chapter 9. This section examines how you can practise fielding drills or coach your juniors to help sharpen their fielding skills.

Developing a deadly throw

Try these throwing drills to be best on the field:

- **Improving your throwing arm:** Two players stand about 20 metres apart and throw the ball to each other. The players aim the ball so that it bounces a few metres in front of each other. (Refer to Chapter 9 for more on how to throw correctly.)
- **Perfecting underarm throwing:** A group of players, ideally no fewer than four, form up in the outfield about 15 metres away from a set of stumps. Behind the stumps, a player stands acting as wicketkeeper. Another player near the stumps, but not between the stumps and the players in the outfield, hits a ball with a bat into the outfield. Each player takes their turn to chase down the ball, collect it and throw it in underarm at the stumps. The wicketkeeper is there to stop the ball should the fielder miss the stumps. The wicketkeeper then throws the ball to the player holding the bat, and the ball is propelled back into the outfield for the next fielder to chase it. Do this as quickly as possible to ensure a lively training session and don't have too many people waiting to field. Breaking the drills up into small groups so that players are constantly involved is the best way.
- **Attacking fielding:** Use the same drill as for underarm throwing, except stand about 30 metres from the stumps. The player with the bat hits the ball hard along the ground and those in the outfield *attack* the ball, one at a time, by running strongly at it before gathering and throwing at the stumps. (Refer to Chapter 9 for more on attacking fielding.)

Catching to win

Catching is a vital and often underestimated skill in cricket. Practising your catching to a high standard is very important. Try these drills:

- **Catching in the deep:** Start in the same places as for the attacking fielding drill in the previous section, 'Developing a deadly throw', but instead of the player with the bat hitting the ball along the ground, the player hits it high in the air and nominates a player to catch it (again, refer to Chapter 9 for more on catching).
- **Practising slips catching:** A player with a ball stands a dozen or so metres from a player with a bat. A group of players then form an arc six to eight metres behind the player with the bat, arcing around to the right if the batsman is a right hander. The batsman holds the bat out in front of their chest and the player with the ball throws it powerfully at the bat. Changing the angle of the bat, the ball slides off the face, flying to the various players in the arc. The drill replicates slips catches in a match situation.

- **Catching in close:** A great way to sharpen the reflexes for close catches is to have four players standing just a few metres apart in a square. Give two of the players a ball each to throw to the other two players. The idea is to underarm the ball quickly, but not too hard, at a player without the ball. Mix it up by continually throwing the ball to different players in the small group. No sooner will you be rid of one ball than another one will be on its way to you. This is a great way to improve awareness and reflexes (for more on close catching, refer to Chapter 9).

Never stand around at training unless you are padded up and waiting to bat next. If you're not batting or bowling, get involved in a fielding drill. Cricketers do more fielding than anything else in a game. Fielding is a very important skill to practise and perfect.

Wicketkeeping is a very specialised skill and takes years of practice. (Refer to Chapter 10 for more on wicketkeeping.) Wicketkeepers benefit enormously from taking part in fielding drills, whether they're taking balls thrown in during outfield drills, or standing behind the player with the bat in the arc for slips practice.

One way of sharpening your wicketkeeping skills is to practise in the nets. When slow spinners are bowling to the batsman in the nets, go and keep wicket as you would in a match situation. However, don't do this against a fast bowler because practise nets are not deep enough to give you the chance to react once the ball passes the bat. In the nets, this drill could create serious injury. Ensure you're wearing all the protective gear you would wear in a match. (Refer to Chapter 4 for more on cricket equipment.)

One-dimensional players are rare these days so if you're a batsman who can't bowl, or vice versa, then you need to become a good fielder to make yourself attractive to selectors. Goal setting and good coaching is the key. Work out what area you need to improve and start improving it. Fielding can be fun and competitive and skills can be improved quite quickly.

Stretching Your Way to a Warmed-up Game

The game of cricket could almost have been designed to cause muscle tears and hamstring pulls. Think about it! Cricket involves long periods of inactivity, such as sitting in the pavilion waiting to bat, followed by sudden bursts of physical exertion, such as running at full pelt down the pitch or chasing a ball in the field.

Warming-up and then stretching your muscles is important before taking the field, whether bowling or batting if you want to avoid injury.

Warming-up exercises can take the form of moderately taxing physical activity, such as jogging for five to ten minutes.

You warm-up and stretch:

- Before play starts
- Briefly before leaving the pavilion to bat
- A few minutes before starting to bowl
- Intermittently while in the field
- At the end of a day's play.

A captain should warn you a few minutes before they expect you to bowl. The warning may come with a shout from the captain — typically, the call is to 'loosen-up' — or, alternatively, the captain may catch your eye and roll his or her arm over. Whatever method of communication used, the captain wants you to stretch because you're likely to be asked to bowl soon.

Warming-up and stretching exercises are often referred to by cricketers as *loosening-up*.

Looking at stretching exercises

Here are some basic stretches to get you flexible and fighting fit to do battle on the cricket pitch. Everyone should warm-up before a match and bowlers should adapt some of these stretches to warm-up as soon the captain asks them to prepare to bowl:

- **Calf muscles:** Take a step forward with your left leg and bend it at the knee. Keep your right leg straight behind you with the right heel planted firmly on the ground. As you bend your left knee further, you'll feel your right calf stretch. Hold for ten seconds and then reverse the procedure to stretch the opposite calf muscle. A good calf stretch before and after play and at training is done on a step. Stand with the ball of one foot on the end of the step and simply let the heel drop gently into the space below until you feel the stretch, making sure not to over balance. Hold for about ten seconds then repeat with the other leg.
- **The back:** Lie on your back. Pull both knees to your chest. Now rock backwards and forwards with your chin tucked into your chest. Repeat a few times but hold the position for no longer than 10 seconds each time. Also, lie on your back with your knees bent and together. Keep your shoulders flat on the ground. Now roll your lower body from side to side with your knees still together so that your left leg then right leg touch the ground alternately. Do this about ten times.

- **Glutes:** Sit on the ground or floor. Put the right leg straight out in front of you and put the left leg, with its knee bent, over the straight leg so your left foot is now on the outside of your right knee. Wrap your right arm around your bent left knee until the knee is in the crook of the elbow. Grab your right wrist with your left hand and pull it towards you until you feel the stretch. Hold for ten seconds and then alternate.
- **Groin:** Sit on the ground or floor with the soles of your feet together, which leaves your knees pointing outwards. Rest your elbows on the inside of your knees with your forearms running down the inside of your lower legs. Hold your ankles firmly and push your elbows outwards on your knees until you feel the groins stretch. Hold for ten seconds.
- **Shoulders and triceps:** Put one arm straight across your chest and wrap your other arm under and around it just above the elbow so that one arm is folded tightly inside the elbow crook of the other. Hold for ten seconds. Now alternate.
- **Hamstrings:** Lie on your back. Raise the left leg as straight as you can, cup your hands behind it around the knee area. All the time keep your right foot on the ground with your right knee bent. Hold this pose for ten seconds and then switch legs and repeat. Alternatively, find something solid about waist height such as the back of a bench or a low fence. This is obviously impossible while you're on the field but it's a good pre-match, post-match and lunch or tea stretch. It's also good to use at training. Make sure the support you have found is not too high in case you over-stretch and strain a muscle. Raise one leg and rest the back of the foot on the support. Keep both knees and your back straight, put your hands together behind your back, and lean forward until you feel the stretch. Be careful not to over-balance. Hold for about ten seconds and then do this again with your raised leg bent. Swap over to stretch your other leg.
- **Thighs:** Balancing on your left leg, lift your right knee straight up until you can put your right hand on the top of your right foot. Pull the foot back until the heel touches the buttocks, making sure the top of the leg is still pointing straight down and the right knee is lightly touching the left knee. Hold for ten seconds and repeat with the opposite leg. This requires good balance so be careful.

Getting stretching right

Executing stretching exercises incorrectly can be worse than not doing any stretches. Common errors that can lead to injury include hurrying through the stretch and making jerky, bouncing movements. Go through the stretch slowly until you feel the muscle stretching and then hold it for about ten seconds.

Post-match cooling-down exercises are very important. In bygone days, many cricketers' idea of a cooling-down exercise was a cold beer after the match. But the modern cool-down exercise involves stretches and even gentle jogging. These activities ensure your muscles are in better shape the next time you want to practise or do battle.

Don't perform stretches while the bowler is delivering to the batsman. Pick quiet moments to do your stretching.

Don't worry if some of your team mates think you're a bit odd doing stretches, or if they don't have the patience to do stretches themselves. If they suffer injuries for failing to prepare properly, or if they complain about being stiff and sore the day after a match because they haven't warmed-up and warmed-down, then they may re-think their decision. Stretching is particularly important for fast bowlers who must ensure they do some stretching on the field before bowling a new spell.

Improving Your Fitness

People sometimes scoff when told that playing cricket requires physical fitness. The uninitiated often wonder how playing a sport that involves little more than standing around for hours, bowling and whacking the odd ball, can possibly be considered demanding. But turn on the television and watch any game of cricket and you'll soon see why the modern cricketer is an athlete. The 'six-pack' on show is located in their abdomen and not nicely chilled in the dressing room fridge.

Being physically fit can improve your cricket game in so many ways. Being fit:

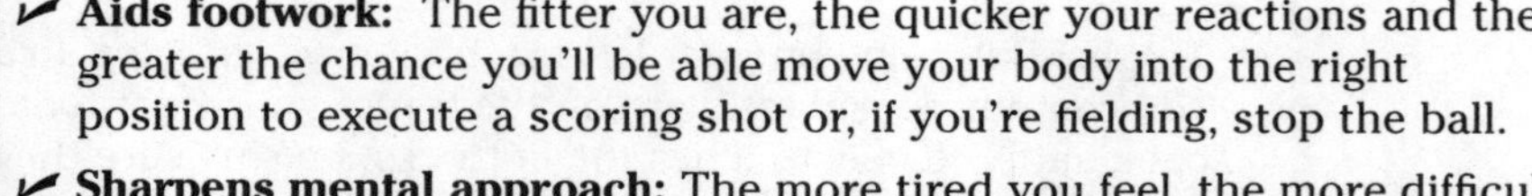

- **Aids footwork:** The fitter you are, the quicker your reactions and the greater the chance you'll be able move your body into the right position to execute a scoring shot or, if you're fielding, stop the ball.

- **Sharpens mental approach:** The more tired you feel, the more difficult concentration becomes. Above all else, cricket — whether you're batting, bowling or fielding — requires concentration. Every delivery is a match in itself and you have a chance to influence that match's course. Heard the phrase, 'Healthy body, healthy mind'? Take note!
- **Builds stamina:** While strength isn't the major factor in cricket, the stronger you are physically, the harder and further you can hit the cricket ball, and the faster you can deliver the ball if you're bowling. Most importantly, you can sustain your pace later in the day when fast bowling becomes tougher as you tire and as the conditions move more in favour of the batting team.
- **Helps prevent injury:** Cricket is a very stop–start game, which requires sudden bursts of frantic activity, whether you're bowling, charging after the ball in the field, or dashing between wickets as a batsman. The fitter and more flexible you are, the less likely injuries are to occur.

Making it through dedication

As for developing your cricketing skills, you could just trust raw talent. But unless you're exceptionally gifted, trusting raw talent is not going to get you very far. Cricket over the years has been packed with good players who became great players through dedicated practice.

For the amateur, cricket is an incredibly time-consuming game. Playing a match takes up most of a day and if you're working, that's a big chunk out of your leisure time. However, many club cricketers don't practise, which doesn't make sense. Investing so much of their free time playing the game begs the question: Why don't they invest a bit more time in honing their skills? After all, a match situation can be an unforgiving environment — even at club level.

If you're just starting to play cricket, seek advice from your coach or captain about what they believe is the appropriate level of fitness. Always consult a fitness expert, such as a gym trainer, if you're going to embark on a fitness campaign outside normal cricket practice, especially if you're young or have not exercised for a while. Whatever you do, build up the fitness training gradually over a number of weeks and don't go too hard too early. Too much exercise too fast can be counter productive and result in injury.

Getting match fit

Not many local club cricketers do much more than turn up to training once or twice a week to practise their batting, bowling and fielding. This much training may get you by if you're happy to potter around with your mates for a bit of weekend fun. However, if you want to improve your game, or look at progressing further than just a hit in the local park, then pick up the following ideas to make you fitter and stronger. As always, if you're not sure about any of the exercises, seek expert advice. If you're young or unfit, take it easy, and always warm up before exercising.

Running is a great way to become aerobically fit and it's easy. Just pull on a pair of runners and take off out the door. But before you begin clocking up the kilometres, always ensure that you have a quality set of running shoes. The very best can cost up to $250 or more, which is expensive. But if you're planning to do a fair bit of running, this price is a very sound investment to prevent short- and long-term injuries. For this reason, running on softer surfaces, such as grass, is a good idea. Finding soft surfaces is not always possible, but be aware that by avoiding concrete and asphalt surfaces you can greatly reduce the jarring through your body. As with any exercise, warm-up and stretch beforehand, then warm-down and stretch at the end.

Fast bowlers should avoid excessive running, particularly on hard surfaces. While running is an important way to develop fitness, particularly leading into a season, this form of exercise can be hard on the body. Fast bowlers put themselves under enormous strain, particularly from the pounding caused to their bodies by landing on the pitch to deliver the ball (refer to Chapter 7 for more on the delivery stride). Fast bowlers should mix up their aerobic fitness program with less stressful exercises, such as swimming, cycling or riding an exercise bike, especially when the fast bowler is undertaking a heavy match-day workload.

If you want to be the best you can be, your cricket exercise regime should focus on the following four areas:

- **Building upper body strength:** Working on your upper body helps you to develop greater control and power with your shots, helps you to bowl faster and to throw the ball at the stumps with greater venom.

  Possible exercises: Free-weight and resistance training; rowing.

- **Endurance training:** If you want to stop tiring and aid concentration, then endurance training is for you.

  Possible exercises: Long runs; cycle rides or using an exercise bike; swimming; gym step-exercises.

- **Explosive pace:** To run quickly between the wickets and chase down a cricket ball at pace, practise running at explosive pace. Bowlers benefit from explosive-pace sprints because high levels of endurance practice allow them to bowl more overs without tiring.

  Possible exercises: Short intense sprinting; spin-cycle classes.

- **Flexibility:** Exercising to improve flexibility helps you to get your body into position to play the right scoring shots, or to stop the cricket ball when fielding. These exercises can also help prevent injury. Flexibility is particularly important for bowlers, allowing them to stay *loose* during long days in the field.

  Possible exercises: Pilates; yoga; stretches.

Tiredness is one of the chief reasons why a bowler can lose crucial accuracy. In addition, unfit batsmen tire more easily. In turn, tiredness makes them more prone to error, which can lead to their dismissal.

A cricket pitch is about 20 metres in length. Therefore if you run down the pitch a hundred times when batting in a match, you cover more than two kilometres — while you're wearing padding, a helmet and carrying a bat! Similarly, a genuinely fast bowler can run up to 20 metres every time they deliver the ball. If they bowl 20 overs, which is probably the minimum during a full day in the field, that adds up to 120 deliveries, or 2.4 kilometres. The energy and effort expended in a fast bowler's delivery stride, every time they bowl, makes the distance seem even further. And this distance doesn't include chasing the ball in the field.

The faster and harder you run between the wickets, the more you can pressure the fielders into making mistakes, such as fumbling the ball, allowing greater opportunities to *steal* more quick singles.

The exercises outlined in this chapter are just a guide. If you attempt to undertake all of them, you'll be fabulously fit, but may have little time for anything else in your life. Choose the ones that best suit your goals and your lifestyle. The great bonus is that being fit not only helps your cricket, a wonderful feeling of wellbeing will descend upon you.

In recent years, personal trainers have started appearing in gyms the length and breadth of Australia. These super-fit trainers can design special training programs to build strength, aid endurance and quicken the pace at which you move. They can also help you with diet advice. A personal trainer can set you back around $50 to $70 an hour, but if you're super-keen and can afford it, this can be money well spent if you become really fit and get more out of your cricket.

Wicketkeeping is probably the most physically demanding of all fielding positions. A keeper crouches before every delivery bowled and has to be alert and fit enough to collect balls thrown by the fielders. The watchwords of fitness for keeping are *endurance* and *flexibility.* Stretching exercises are the start to gaining these qualities. (Refer to Chapter 10 for more on wicketkeeping.)

Part III

From Backyard to the Big Time

Glenn Lumsden

'Don't mind me. I'm from across the street. We're playing cricket and I have an excessively long run-up.'

In this part . . .

Playing cricket in the backyard at Mum's might seem like just a game, but for many a champion that's exactly where the skills to hit the round red ball started to develop.

This part takes you to the starting point of playing the game and then looks at the competitions that have thousands of kids around Australia playing cricket on weekends.

For those who want to become more involved, this part is where you find out about coaching kids and you can find out how to become a player, all the way from the kiddies' competition through club cricket and into the big time, where it's up, up, up.

Chapter 13

Becoming a Player

In This Chapter

- Knowing how to get started in cricket
- Helping your child to become involved
- Understanding what children can manage in their age group
- Selecting the best equipment for children

Many of Australia's most exciting cricket matches have not been played in the cavernous surrounds of this country's major cricket grounds, but in backyards, driveways and on sun-covered beaches.

This infectious fun of smashing the ball and charging off for runs, hitting the rubbish bin with a tennis ball to claim a wicket or diving backwards into the sea to take a catch is what has propelled generations of Australian children into this country's national sport.

Fun is why kids all over the country play the game — to bat and to bowl, to score runs and take wickets. Skills and drills are important as children grow into the game, but first and foremost they want to enjoy it. If a game's not fun and training's not fun, then they simply won't bother.

This chapter looks at how to begin playing cricket. Child or adult, male or female, the game of cricket has a type and a level to suit you.

Starting Off in the Game

Chances are that if you've grown up with the game of cricket you may not remember your first cricketing experience. Cricket seems to have always been a part of most Australian kids' lives. Whether your father or mother watched cricket on TV, actually played the game on a Saturday afternoon, or whether your older brothers and sisters and their friends let you field for them in the backyard at home, cricket has been a part of many childhoods in some way or other.

But for some Australians, cricket may be a complete mystery the first time they see the game, be it a Test match or a one-dayer. A quarter of Australia's population was not born in this country and many came from nations that had no knowledge of the game of cricket. Cricket is as foreign as foreign can be, if you didn't grow up with the game.

Whatever your background, anyone — boys and girls, men and women — can easily become involved. From the time children begin primary school in Australia, chances are that cricket is one of the first games offered for them to try. Modified versions of the game are designed to be suitable for youngsters. In fact, clubs all over the country cater for players of all ages and skill levels.

So if you or your children want to discover the joy experienced by more than half a million Australians every summer, and you decide to become involved as players rather than merely spectators, here's how you go about it.

Finding a club

Becoming part of Australia's cricket-playing community has never been easier. Simply go to Cricket Australia's Web site — `www.cricket.com.au` — to instantly find all the details you require.

Click 'Getting involved' and a wealth of information comes up. Click 'Club Finder' and 'Finding my nearest cricket club' appears. Fill in the basic details requested, such as your postcode, click 'search' and listings of the cricket clubs in your area become available.

For example, if you live in Mulgrave, in Melbourne's south-eastern suburbs, and type 3170, the Mulgrave postcode, a choice of ten different cricket clubs in the Mulgrave area appears.

Under the name of each cricket club, the types of teams available at that club are listed, highlighting the wide variety of cricket sides in and around just one suburb. The types of cricket teams, just in Mulgrave, include senior men's and women's teams, junior boys' and girls' sides and the modified Have-A-Go program for primary school-aged children (see the section, 'Have-A-Go: Taking the first step' in this chapter). Listed beside each club is 'Show club contact details'. Click that and a contact name appears, as well as phone numbers and an email address.

This wealth of information is available for clubs all over the country, not just in the major cities. For example, the South Gippsland country town of Wonthaggi in Victoria — population approximately 5,000 — with the postcode 3995, has ten clubs listed from the town and the surrounding area.

If you have a daughter, she can play with the local boys' junior cricket club during their primary school and even early high-school years. Cricket Australia's comprehensive junior cricket policy recommends that girls can play up to two years below their age in a boys' junior competition. For example, 13-year-old girls can play in an under-12 boys' team. For more on following and playing women's cricket, see Chapter 18.

Shopping around to find the club that feels most comfortable for you or your child is important. Talk to people from the various clubs so you're well informed with what the club has to offer your family. If you're an adult or older teenager, who has never played before, a club with a number of teams in different grades of varying standards is more likely to have a team that suits your needs.

Senior clubs often have pre-season training well in advance of the competition season, which usually begins in late September or early October, depending on which state you live in. Try these pre-season training sessions at a few different local clubs and see which you feel most suits you before making a final decision.

Likewise, if you have a primary school-aged son or daughter, you'll need a club that offers the Have-A-Go modified cricket, or something similar. Parents should find out how much emphasis a particular club puts on its junior teams. You may be better starting your child at a club designated purely for juniors.

By the mid teens, your son or daughter will probably need exposure to the lower grades of senior cricket to continue their development. Frequently, many senior clubs have a lower-grade side specifically designed as a nursery to help integrate juniors into senior cricket. These 'nursery' teams are often captained by a senior player at the club, who has played his best cricket and acts as a father figure to encourage the next generation. Often a number of juniors from the under-16's team play junior cricket on a Saturday morning and then senior cricket in the afternoon. If they move up as a group, playing in the seniors can be less intimidating than trying to fit in on their own, although most cricket clubs are very welcoming to newcomers. This transition is vital for the long-term development of the player and the survival of cricket clubs.

For anyone who does not have access to the Internet or would rather get more advice by talking to someone intimately involved with cricket, you simply get in touch with Cricket Australia or your local state or territory cricket association. All the necessary contact details are listed here:

Cricket Australia
Game Development Department
60 Jolimont Street
Jolimont Vic 3002
Phone: 03 9653 9908
Fax: 03 9653 9911
www.cricket.com.au

Australian Capital Territory (ACT)
ACT Cricket Association
Sir Donald Bradman Stand
Manuka Oval
PO Box 3379
Manuka ACT 2603
Phone: 02 6239 6002
Fax: 02 6239 7135
www.cricketact.com

New South Wales
Cricket New South Wales
Sydney Cricket Ground
Driver Avenue
Paddington NSW 2021
Phone: 02 9339 0999
Fax: 02 9360 6877
www.cricketnsw.com.au

Northern Territory
Northern Territory Cricket
PO Box 40895
Casuarina NT 0811
Phone: 08 8981 1677
Fax: 08 8981 1766
www.ntcricket.com.au

Queensland
Queensland Cricket
1 Bogan Street
Breakfast Creek Qld 4010
Phone: 07 3292 3100
Fax: 07 3262 9160
www.qldcricket.com.au

South Australia
South Australian Cricket Association
Adelaide Oval
North Adelaide SA 5006
Phone: 08 8300 3838
Fax: 08 8231 8003
www.saca.com.au

Tasmania
Tasmanian Cricket Association
Bellerive Oval
Derwent Street
Bellerive Tas 7018
Phone: 03 6282 0405
Fax: 03 6282 0428
www.tascricket.com.au

Victoria
Cricket Victoria
90 Jolimont Street
Jolimont Vic 3002
Phone: 03 9653 1100
Fax: 03 9653 1196
www.cricketvictoria.com.au

Western Australia
Western Australian Cricket Association
WACA Ground
Nelson Crescent
East Perth WA 6004
Phone: 08 9265 7222
Fax: 08 9221 1059
www.waca.com.au

Playing in the right spirit

Cricket has 42 laws but overriding them all is the *spirit* of cricket. Playing the game with dignity and respect is more important than knowing the book of laws back to front. (Refer to Chapter 1 for a definition of the spirit of cricket.)

The greatest player of all time, Sir Donald Bradman, said: 'It is the responsibility of all those who play the game to leave the game in a better state than when they first became involved.'

Cricket Australia has worked hard in recent years to promote the spirit of the game at all levels, from local clubs to the national team. A code of behaviour has been developed for players to follow.

The players' code of behaviour is as follows:

- Be a good sport.
- Control your temper. Verbal abuse of officials and sledging other players, deliberately distracting or provoking an opponent are not acceptable or permitted behaviours in cricket.
- Cooperate with your coach, team mates and opponents. Without them there would be no competition.
- Never argue with an umpire. If you disagree, have your captain, coach or manager approach the umpire during a break or after the game.
- Participate for your own enjoyment and benefit, not just to please parents and coaches.
- Play by the rules.
- Respect the rights, dignity and worth of all players, regardless of their gender, ability, cultural background or religion.
- Treat all participants in cricket as you like to be treated. Do not bully or take unfair advantage of another competitor.
- Work equally hard for yourself and your team mates. Your team's performance will benefit and so will you.

Dashing through a game

If you're too old for a frolic in the juniors, and you don't want to give up most of your Saturday to play serious cricket, then modified versions of cricket are now played in many of Australia's capital cities.

Described as social, recreational or lifestyle cricket, these games are cricket's version of touch football. Particularly suitable for women, or couples who want to experience the game in a quick and easy format together, the modified games are played on summer evenings, particularly in the states that have daylight saving.

Cricket Australia has set guidelines on how these matches should operate. If this cricket looks like the game that suits your lifestyle, then call your local state association (refer to the earlier section, 'Finding a club', for more details).

Part of the ease associated with such social or modified cricket is that you just turn up as you are — in runners and some comfortable sports clothes. Any necessary equipment is supplied. Here's what you should know:

- **Ball:** 156 gram leather ball (standard cricket ball) or modified solid core ball.
- **Batting:** 25 runs before retirement.
- **Bowling:** Minimum of one over, maximum of four overs per player.
- **Duration:** About 150 minutes.
- **Game type:** Optional — usually 20 overs a side.
- **Modifications for girls:** Mixed competitions are recommended but only using a modified ball.
- **Protective equipment:** Optional, if modified ball. If leather ball — helmets, pads, gloves for all players, and protectors for boys and men.
- **Team:** 6 to 12 players per team.
- **Training and practice:** Optional.

Getting Your Son or Daughter Involved

An enormous amount of work has been done by cricket authorities at national and state level in recent years to broaden the appeal of cricket. The bad old days of children turning up to spend long days in the field, getting the occasional bat at the bottom of the batting order and almost never getting a bowl are long gone. The idea now is constant participation for children of primary school age. Children as young as five can begin playing modified versions of the game.

Have-A-Go: Taking the first step

Organised cricket starts for many children with Cricket Australia's Have-A-Go program. This program is about being involved and having fun. Played with a plastic bat, ball and stumps to minimise any chance of injury, the program is designed for girls and boys aged between five and ten years old.

In serious senior cricket, the game is governed by a complex set of rules and almost half the time can be taken up simply waiting to bat. The modified game keeps children constantly active, whether they're batting, bowling or fielding and everyone gets a chance to do everything, regardless of age, ability or gender.

The weekly lesson plans for the Have-A-Go program have been carefully written by Cricket Australia and the program is supported by the Australian Sports Commission. Each venue has been selected for its suitability to be used for this type of program.

The program usually runs for 12 weeks in summer and children are further encouraged by giveaways such as bats, balls and hats.

All the equipment is supplied. All a child needs is the normal clothing they wear for school sport or physical education, and remember to be sun smart! A hat is always vital when playing cricket.

Parents and guardians are encouraged to become involved and enjoy the fun, whether they act as supervisors or help with the activities.

A number of local cricket clubs across the country run Have-A-Go programs. The clubs can be contacted through Club Finder on Cricket Australia's Web site (`www.cricket.com.au`) or by contacting your local state or territory cricket association.

Cricket Australia also emphasises the advantages of taking the game into schools. Have-A-Go cricket is played in an increasing number of primary schools. If cricket is not played at your child's school, talk to the school authorities about the possibility of introducing the game as part of the sports or physical education program. Cricket Australia or your local state association will be happy to help.

Cric Hit: Giving girls extra cricket

Although girls and boys all play Have-A-Go cricket together and girls can also play in boys' junior teams in proper cricket competitions, a new game called Cric Hit has been created by Cricket Australia especially for girls aged between 10 and 13 years old.

Cric Hit is an eight-week program that runs for an hour and a half, one afternoon a week, and is fully supervised by a professional Cricket Australia employed coordinator. Cric Hit is run in a safe, friendly and fun environment and caters for all abilities and skill levels, involving a range of activities that teach cricket skills and games.

Girls don't need any special equipment, just casual sports clothes. During the program, which costs $45 to join, the girls receive a welcome pack, which includes a cricket bat.

The aim of the program, which runs in 40 locations across Australia, is to introduce girls to cricket skills and activities in a structured manner with an emphasis on fun.

Contact your local state or territory cricket association (refer to the section, 'Finding a club', for more details on this new game for girls. See Chapter 18 for more on girls' and women's cricket.

Children play sport for fun. Children have a natural urge to want to be involved in constant activity. In the early primary school years, playing sport is far more important than winning and losing. If they enjoy the game, even in the most simplified, modified form, whether in the backyard, on the beach or as part of an early development program, then chances are the child will become hooked for life as a player or spectator of cricket. The technical side of the game will come as the child grows and wants to take it more seriously. Too serious too early and the child won't enjoy the game and won't continue to play it. Children who are actively encouraged to play sport learn while enjoying themselves.

Few more exciting moments occur in Australian childrens' lives than the time they turn up for their first real cricket match.

Hours of Test and one-day matches have been re-enacted against the back wall with brothers, sisters, neighbours and friends, or the child has had lots of fun with Have-A-Go cricket at school or in the early evenings — all preparation for the next big step in cricket's journey.

Already feeling special, decked out in whites just like Australian captain Ricky Ponting and ferocious fast bowler Brett Lee, this youngster is ready to carve his own piece of history.

Beginning in the Right Age Group

By the time children are in their last years of primary school, the time has come for them to begin playing in an organised under-aged cricket competition, complete with hard balls, wooden bats and, most importantly, the correct protective equipment.

Age groups can vary between local cricket teams and associations but the common practice is, particularly in cities and large towns, for local junior clubs to have a number of teams with varying ages, such as under-12, under-14 and under-16 sides. Check Cricket Australia's Web site for Club Finder, or contact your state association for more information.

Although some designated girls' junior teams exist, girls often combine with boys at the lower age groups and are allowed to play with boys two years younger than they are. For example, a 13-year-old girl can play in an under-12 boys' team.

Cricket Australia and the Australian Sports Commission have developed a comprehensive policy for under-aged cricket at all levels, designed to be compatible with the overall maturity of the child.

Called 'Well Played: Australian Cricket's Playing Policy and Guidelines', the detailed policy document offers invaluable advice and insights for parents, coaches and school teachers — for anyone involved with cricket for primary and younger secondary school children.

Anyone who wants to know more can contact Cricket Australia.

Years five to eight

At the introductory ages of five to eight, the idea is to keep the game as safe and simple as possible and keep the children constantly active so they have a great time and want to come back for more.

- **Ball:** Hollow core ball (soft).
- **Dismissals:** None. Batsmen change ends if dismissed. No LBW.
- **Game type:** Have-A-Go.
- **Modifications for girls:** None. Girls play and compete in same age groups with boys.
- **Overs and duration:** Two per batting pair. Maximum game time is 60 minutes as part of a 90-minute program.
- **Protective equipment:** None.
- **Team:** Flexible number of players.
- **Training and practice:** Fun with an emphasis on basic skills — running, jumping, hitting, throwing, and so on.

Years eight to ten

Players, aged eight to ten, concentrate on participation and fun with a slightly longer version of the game emphasising some basic skills.

- **Ball:** Hollow core ball (soft) or modified solid core ball.
- **Dismissals:** None. Batsmen change ends if dismissed. No LBW.
- **Game type:** Have-A-Go or reduced numbers, for example, six or eight players.
- **Modifications for girls:** None. Play and compete in same age groups with boys.
- **Overs and duration:** Four overs per batting pair. Maximum game time is 90 minutes.
- **Protective equipment:** Optional with soft ball. Using modified solid core ball, batsmen use helmets, pads, gloves and, for boys, protectors.
- **Team:** Ten players.
- **Training and practice:** Fun with an emphasis on basic skills — running, jumping, hitting, throwing, and so on.

Under 11 and 12

Under 11s and 12s is where the game starts to become a little more serious and structured, with the eventual introduction of a hard cricket ball and full protective equipment for the first time.

- **Ball:** Under 11, modified solid core ball or 142 gram leather (women's size) or composition (hard). Under 12, 142 gram leather or composition ball.
- **Dismissals:** Under 11, no LBW. Batsmen are dismissed if given out. Under 12, LBW introduced (only if official umpires). Batsmen are dismissed if given out.
- **Game type:** Twenty overs a side or dual pitch cricket, where the team waiting to bat fields as part of a second game taking place at the same time.
- **Modifications for girls:** None. Play and compete in the same age group as boys.
- **Overs and duration:** Maximum 20 overs per team. Maximum game time — 150 minutes.
- **Protective equipment:** Helmets, pads, gloves and, for boys, protectors.
- **Team:** 12 per team.
- **Training and practice:** Fun, with an emphasis on cricket skills development — batting, bowling and fielding with maximum participation.

Under 13

The matches at the cross-over age of under 13s — between childhood and adolescence — are longer and have more structure.

- **Ball:** 142 gram leather ball (women's size) or composition (hard).
- **Dismissals:** Batsmen are dismissed if given out.
- **Overs and duration:** Maximum 30 overs. Maximum game time — 190 minutes.
- **Game type:** One-day limited-overs cricket.
- **Modifications for girls:** Where alternatives do not exist and where participation poses no danger to any participants, girls may participate with boys two years younger.
- **Protective equipment:** Helmets, pads, gloves and, for boys, protectors.
- **Team:** Maximum of 12 per team.
- **Training and practice:** Once a week with emphasis on fun and variation of bowling, development of batting techniques and attacking fielding.

Under 14

Children in the under 14s, for the first time, are introduced to two-day cricket, played across consecutive weekends, allowing for much longer innings and greater opportunities to bowl more overs.

- **Ball:** 142 gram leather ball (women's size).
- **Dismissals:** Batsmen are dismissed if given out.
- **Game type:** A mixture of one-day and two-day cricket. Two-day cricket is played over consecutive weekends, with one team batting the first weekend and the other batting the second.
- **Modifications for girls:** Ball — 142 gram leather (women's size) or composition (hard).
- **Overs and duration:** One-day — 30 overs per team. Two day — maximum of 50 overs per team.
- **Protective equipment:** Helmets, pads, gloves and, for boys, protectors.
- **Team:** Maximum of 12 per team.
- **Training and practice:** Once a week, with emphasis on fun and variation of bowling, development of batting techniques and attacking fielding.

Where alternatives do not exist, and where participation poses no danger to any participants, girls may participate in competitions with boys two years younger.

Under 15 and above

In the under 15s and above, boys use a full-sized cricket ball for the first time and are approaching an age where those with early maturity and skills can consider also playing in the lower grades of open-age competitions.

- **Ball:** 156 gram leather ball (standard cricket ball).
- **Dismissals:** Batsmen are dismissed if given out.
- **Game type:** One-day or two-day limited-overs cricket.
- **Modifications for girls:** Ball — 142 gram leather (women's size) or composition (hard).
- **Overs and duration:** One day — maximum 30 overs. Two day — 50 overs.
- **Protective equipment:** Helmets, pads, gloves and, for boys, protectors.
- **Team:** Maximum of 12 per team.
- **Training and practice:** Fun, with emphasis on honing specific skills, team work and strategies.

Where alternatives do not exist and where participation poses no danger to any participants, girls may participate in competitions with boys who are two years younger.

Most local junior competitions end at under 16s. By that stage, players should begin to have exposure in the lower grades of senior competitions. Many local clubs, particularly those with a number of teams of varying standards, are very welcoming of juniors stepping up into senior teams. For players in an under-16 team to play juniors in the morning and seniors in the afternoons is not that unusual.

Strict guidelines are now in place for young bowlers, particularly fast bowlers, who can suffer long-term injuries if they bowl for too long while their body is still developing. This is particularly so if the player is competing in juniors and seniors on the same day. Strict guidelines exist to control how many deliveries young bowlers, particularly fast bowlers, should bowl at training. Captains and coaches of senior teams should be aware of these guidelines and the ages of the bowlers if they are still teenagers. Those guidelines are listed in Table 13-1. The guidelines are maximums only. Junior teams usually train just once a week unless the team is an elite representative squad. See Chapter 15 for more on representative cricket and refer to Chapter 7 and Chapter 8 for more on bowling.

Table 13-1 Training Guidelines

Age	*U10*	*U11*	*U12*	*U13*	*U14*	*U15*	*U16*	*U17*	*U18*	*U19*
Sessions per week	1	1	2	2	2	2	2	3	3	3
Deliveries per session	24	24	24	24	30	30	36	36	42	48

Note: One practice session should be substituted for each additional match played in the week. For example, if an under-15 bowler plays two games in the one week, they should practise only once, not twice as recommended in the preceding table.

A young fast bowler's long-term health and wellbeing is far more important than winning or losing a cricket match. Even if a game is tight and your young-gun paceman is fit and rearing to go, captains and coaches should not exceed the recommendations shown in Table 13-2. Instead, captains and coaches should better manage their bowlers to ensure the bowlers can return to the attack when most needed.

Table 13-2 Match Day Bowling Guidelines

Age (U=Under)	Overs (max. per day)	Overs (max. per spell)
U15	12	5
U16	14	6
U17	16	6
U18	18	7
U19	20	8

Setting children an example

International cricketers who gain enormous television exposure are occasionally criticised for their behaviour. Whether a batsman is disappointed because he has been given out by the umpire, or a bowler has been unlucky not to claim a batsman's wicket, sometimes the frustration boils over.

Those international players who step out of line can be fined and even suspended. Officials in charge of the game realise that these high-profile cricketers are role models and that their behaviour influences the many millions of young players around the cricketing world who look up to their heroes.

The Bradman boy hits a ball with a cricket stump to become the best batsman ever

Don Bradman is indisputably the greatest batsman of all time and is famed for his hand–eye coordination. Part of the reason given for Bradman's genius is that he spent hour upon hour in his youth hitting a golf ball against the curved brick base of a water-tank stand from a semi-enclosed verandah at the back of his now famous house in the southern New South Wales town of Bowral. The schoolboy Bradman would throw the golf ball at the stand and attempt to hit the ball with a cricket stump as it rebounded at high speed and from varying angles because of the curved surface. His goal was to prevent the golf ball hitting the laundry door behind him, which he considered the wicket. As he was in later life, when he became the world's greatest batsman, Bradman was very difficult to dismiss on that back verandah.

However, parents are the greatest role models for children. The 'ugly parent' syndrome is one of junior sport's biggest problems. To ensure that children and their parents enjoy the game played in the best possible spirit, Cricket Australia has drawn up a comprehensive code of behaviour.

The code of behaviour for parents is designed to help ensure that parents and children have the best possible experience when the child or children decide they want to take up the great game of cricket. Here's how parents are advised to behave:

- Do not force an unwilling child to participate in cricket.
- Remember, children are involved in cricket for their enjoyment, not yours.
- Encourage your child to play by the rules.
- Focus on the child's efforts and performance rather than winning or losing.
- Never ridicule or yell at a child for making a mistake or losing a game.
- Remember that children learn best by example. Appreciate good performances and skilful play by all participants.
- Support all efforts to remove verbal and physical abuse from sporting activities.
- Respect officials' decisions and teach children to do likewise.
- Show appreciation for volunteer coaches, officials and administrators. Without them, your child could not participate.
- Respect the rights, dignity and worth of every person, regardless of gender, ability, cultural background or religion.

Kitting Out a Youngster for the Game

If your son or daughter is keen to begin playing organised cricket in the juniors, be sure to put a set of whites, a broad-brimmed hat and a comfortable pair of runners on your shopping list.

Multi-coloured sports shoes are frowned on in higher levels of cricket, with players expected to wear all white, including proper cricket shoes and socks. The only coloured piece of clothing allowed is the club cap.

However, if your child is starting off at junior level, you won't have to face the extra expense of buying cricket shoes, knowing they last only one season for growing children. Runners will do the job!

Likewise, you don't need to run out and buy a whole lot of expensive cricket equipment. The junior club should be able to provide all the necessary playing and protective gear your child needs.

Protective gear must include helmets, which are compulsory for all batsmen and wicketkeepers at junior level.

All boys and men, no matter their age, must wear a protector to cover their genitals when batting or wicketkeeping, either in a match or at practice, whenever a hard ball is involved. A *protector* is a triangular, bowl-shaped piece of plastic. Be sure to wear two pairs of firm-fitting underpants and slip the protector between them to hold the protector firmly but comfortably in place. Refer to Chapter 4 for more on cricket equipment.

If your child desperately wants a bat or other cricket equipment of their own, try to persuade them to wait until they are older. Cricket equipment is expensive and children can grow out of their beloved pads, gloves or bat in one season. Bats can cost hundreds of dollars.

If you do decide to buy your child cricket equipment, make sure the equipment is comfortable and not too bulky so the child can run easily between the wickets.

Make sure the bat is not too big and heavy because if it is, your child's development as a batsman will be restricted. The child could have trouble lifting the bat and bringing it down in time to play shots correctly. Many different bat sizes, appropriate to different age groups, are on the market. If anything, having a bat a little too small is better than a bat that's a little big. The child can manoeuvre the smaller bat more easily. (Chapter 4 has more information on bats. Refer to Chapter 5 and Chapter 6 for more on batting techniques.)

Chapter 14

Coaching the Kids

In This Chapter

- Coaching for fun
- Teaching the right spirit
- Guiding the juniors
- Playing safely

So you want to become a cricket coach? You want to help create the next generation of players to take over from Ricky Ponting, Brett Lee and Shane Warne to continue Australia's long and strong tradition of domination in the world of cricket.

The lucky few who gain the opportunity to wear the baggy green cap as a Test player for Australia become national heroes. But the thousands of parents and cricket lovers around the country, who rise so early every Saturday or Sunday morning during summer, are cricket's unsung heroes.

The parents and cricket lovers who give up their weekends to be coaches of junior cricket not only create the players of the future, they also teach the fans of the future how to enjoy the wonderful game of cricket. The best way to ensure a child becomes a cricket fan for life is to get the youngster hooked on the game at an early age. Coaches of junior cricket help children understand and experience the joys of playing the game, so that when those children become adults, they continue to enjoy cricket throughout their lives.

This chapter examines the best ways to encourage youngsters to become involved in cricket, looks at what you need to become a coach and how best to pass your knowledge on to those just beginning their journey in the game. The emphasis here is about playing the game in the right spirit and enjoying it safely, ensuring cricket becomes a fulfilling experience for you and all those children under your guidance.

Making Cricket Fun

Nothing is more exciting than watching children discover something new. A child's world grows with boundless enthusiasm and excitement as new delights are uncovered.

Many budding young cricketers leap out of bed at first light, down their breakfast, pull on their cricket clothes, and wait expectantly to be taken to the local cricket ground as though the moment to start play is never going to arrive. These keen youngsters then wait all week for their next game of cricket. The weekend cannot come soon enough.

A coach's job is to enhance and encourage this excitement. A motivating coach ensures that weekend after weekend these young cricketers want to keep bounding out of bed and dashing off to play. Making sure the child's weekend game of cricket, under your watchful eye, is an enjoyable and rewarding experience is your major task. Never forget that fun is the major motivator for children to play sport.

Winning by playing

Cricket Australia recently released a major cricket policy called 'Well Played: Australian Cricket's Playing Policy and Guidelines' (refer to Chapter 13), which highlights the fact that the enjoyment of the game is paramount.

The policy points out that in various surveys, whenever youngsters are asked why they play sport, the number one reason is always the same — to have fun. Winning is on the list but it is last on the list. Children like to compete, but the fun and excitement of competing is what motivates them, not just the winning.

Junior coaches should not be measured on win–loss ratios, but rather on how many players wish to continue to play the following season. Results don't matter when children are learning the game. Participation does.

Here are some recommendations on how to create an atmosphere of fun within a team:

- Get down to the children's level and find out what they see as fun.
- Don't take yourself too seriously; get involved, don't be afraid to fail.
- Maintain a fun attitude, with lots of laughter and a sense of humour.

- Create training sessions that provide maximum activity, skill development and enjoyment. Don't have children standing around doing nothing.
- Treat all players equally.
- See the lighter side of mistakes.
- Create opportunities for all skill and ability levels.
- Be well planned and organised, and be able to supply all the necessary equipment.
- Avoid 'isolation' type punishments, such as running laps around the oval or push-ups.
- Praise in public but never criticise children in front of their peers.

Never underestimate your influence on a child. As an adult in a position of authority over the child, your influence can be profound. Making all children feel special and giving them opportunities to participate is vital. Often the children with the least confidence or ability are those who benefit most from your encouragement. These kids may never become good cricketers but the impact you're likely to have on their lives can be overwhelmingly positive. Such a result is far more important than a child's progress in the game.

Keeping the kids involved

For primary school children up to the age of about 10 years, simply being involved in constant activity is the most important element of the game. The goals you set should not involve complicated rules, entail standing around waiting to bat or mean that players miss out on a bowl because of a perception that they have less ability or experience.

The first organised experience of cricket for today's children is likely to be Cricket Australia's modified Have-A-Go form of the game. Have-A-Go can be played by 6 to12 players and takes no more than an hour and a half, so it can easily be fitted into a school sporting program or played as a twilight game after school.

Have-A-Go is played with a plastic bat, ball and stumps to reduce the risk of injury from a hard cricket ball and avoid the need for protective equipment, enabling players to easily swap from batting to bowling and fielding. Players simply wear the same sports clothing and runners they would use for sport or physical education at school.

The game is not played in teams. Children simply rotate, with fieldsmen batting and bowling as their turn arises. Importantly, children are not dismissed. The batting pair simply swaps ends if one of the batsmen is out. Each batting pair has the same amount of batting time, either two or four overs, depending on the length of the game. Each child bowls one over in turn. (Refer to Chapter 13 for more details on Have-A-Go cricket.)

Have-A-Go cricket makes sure that every child stays constantly involved in fielding and does not have to wait all that long for their turn to bat or bowl. Gone are the bad old days when a child's first taste of cricket in the juniors may have been a proper cricket match dominated by older kids so that the younger children had to field all day without getting a bat or a bowl.

Getting an opportunity to fill each role is vital at an early age, whether the children be girls or boys. Not only does this approach make cricket an enjoyable experience for children, the constant activity is physically beneficial, which is an important consideration in a society that is increasingly battling child obesity.

Becoming a coach

Starting off as a cricket coach does not simply involve turning up at the start of a cricket season at your local cricket club and offering your services. Although volunteers, usually parents, are always welcome to help with tasks such as scoring, umpiring and providing children with drinks, you need to have training if you want to be a coach. Police checks are also often required these days for volunteers who want to be involved with children's sport.

Recognised accreditation has become a basic prerequisite for aspiring coaches in Australia. Cricket Australia, together with the state and territory associations, has a range of coaching courses to suit a variety of levels. (Refer to Chapter 13 for contact details for these organisations.)

Three levels of official coaching accreditation and one non-accredited coaching course are available in Australia. Two courses are relevant to coaching junior and local club sides.

Orientation to Coaching

The Orientation to Coaching course is aimed at anyone taking up coaching for the first time and provides an introduction to the fundamentals of coaching children and contributing to skill development. The course takes about three hours.

The aim of the course is to equip adults with the basic skills and information to enable them to be confident in assisting with early-development cricket programs.

Level One Coaching

The Level One Coaching course is directed towards coaches at under-age and community cricket level. The course is for people who are relatively new to coaching and wish to broaden their knowledge of the technical skills of the game, who understand appropriate and effective ways to conduct sessions and who wish to gain an awareness of the factors that motivate young people to play and enjoy cricket.

The course is conducted over a total of between 13 and 15 hours and includes a series of presentations followed by practical sessions on the skills of the game. Instruction is offered in principles of coaching, principles of teaching, communication skills and group management, and physical training, as well as the techniques of coaching cricket.

To find out more about becoming a coach, contact Cricket Australia or your state or territory association. All the contact details are listed in Chapter 13.

The best way to help a young player improve their cricket skills is to offer encouragement so that the child develops the confidence to perform. Threats of punishment can increase the amount of pressure on a young person, often leading to a mistake as a result of the fear of making an error. Praising their efforts is much more productive than criticising their faults. Working to improve their faults, a little at a time as the child grows into and begins to understand the game, is the best way to help the child.

Keeping children safe

Cricket Australia recommends that all junior coaches are police and reference checked. In some states, these checks are required by law.

The checks are undertaken because the safety and wellbeing of players, particularly young players, must be the number one consideration of all clubs and associations.

As well, all coaches of junior cricket sides are expected to be accredited and to continue their education to ensure they can implement the most appropriate and up-to-date knowledge and coaching techniques.

For more information on accreditation and screening of coaches, contact Cricket Australia or your state or territory cricket association. Contact details are listed in Chapter 13.

Defining the Spirit of Cricket

Cricket has always prided itself not only on its great skills and combative nature, but on the way the game has been played as a sport. An expectation exists within and outside the game that cricket is to be played in the right spirit.

No matter how successful the Australian team has been over the past decade, if a player steps beyond the bounds of acceptable behaviour, a public outcry usually follows. Australian cricket supporters rejoice in the success of their national side but can feel embarrassed or ashamed if a particular player behaves poorly.

The reason for this attitude by cricket fans is that cricket is owned and shared by everyone in the cricket community. The national players are seen as the representatives or custodians of the game on behalf of all Australians. The players have the responsibility to uphold the values and traditions of cricket, which have been shaped over more than two centuries of playing the game in Australia. (See Chapter 16 for Australia's first cricket game.)

But not just the national team has this responsibility. Everyone involved in cricket must play their part to preserve the integrity of the game, be they players, umpires, administrators or coaches.

Unfortunately, some people fail to live up to the traditional values and spirit of cricket. Poor behaviour by anyone involved in cricket at a national or senior level can adversely affect the attitudes of children who look up to and want to copy the standards set by their heroes.

Understanding the right way to play

Cricket Australia has developed key elements to help men and women involved in cricket to apply the spirit of the game. Cricket Australia's guide aims to foster a healthy and effective playing environment.

Fair play

According to the laws of cricket, the umpires are the sole judges of fair and unfair play. The umpires may intervene at any time and the captain and coach have the responsibility to take action against players when required.

- **Captains and coaches:** The captain or coach is responsible at all times for ensuring that play is conducted within the spirit of the game and within the laws.
- **Players and others:** Captains, coaches and umpires together set the tone for the conduct of a cricket match. Every player is expected to make an important contribution to play the game in good spirit and fairness.

Attitude to the game

Respect is the one word that sums up the spirit of the game of cricket, wherever the game is played, and at any level.

Respect for the game

The spirit of the game demands respect for:

- Your opponents
- Your captain, coach and team
- The role of the umpires
- The traditional values of cricket.

Against the spirit

The following actions are against the spirit of the game:

- To dispute an umpire's decision by word or action.
- To direct abusive language towards an opponent or umpire.
- To indulge in cheating, which includes the following: Appealing when knowing the batsman is not out; advancing towards an umpire in an aggressive manner when appealing; and attempting to distract an opponent, either verbally or by harassment with persistent clapping or unnecessary noise, under the guise of enthusiasm and motivation of your side.

Discovering cricket etiquette

In the spirit of cricket, certain unwritten laws or practices exist that should be followed to show respect for the game, your opponents and your team.

Being up on cricket etiquette is easy if you follow some very simple procedures:

Tossing the coin

Being prepared for the toss of the coin at the start of a match is very important. Here's how it happens:

- The home team captain is to always bring a coin for the toss.
- The home team captain tosses the coin; the opposition captain calls heads or tails.
- The toss of the coin is to take place on the pitch.
- Captains should always shake hands prior to and after the toss.

Entering the field to begin play

Take the trouble to learn the traditions that go with entering the field of play:

- Umpires are always the first to enter the playing field.
- The fielding side then takes the field, led by its captain.
- The two batsmen enter after the fielding team.

During play

Two unofficial but important rules apply during play:

- The batting team is to sit together on the sidelines, except where players may be warming up in preparation for batting.
- The home side, or sometimes the batting side, normally takes responsibility to keep any scoreboard up to date.

Leaving the field

The order of leaving the field is as important as entering:

- The batsmen are always first to leave the playing field.
- The fielding team follows the batsmen.

Acknowledging milestones

The art of paying respect to the opposition is of utmost importance in cricket:

- Fielding teams should always acknowledge 50 runs (a half century) and 100 runs (a century) by opposition batsmen.
- Players should acknowledge bowling achievements, such as five wickets in an innings and hat-tricks (three wickets in three balls).
- After the game, players should acknowledge the opposition by shaking hands.
- Captains should always shake hands after the match.

Supporting the game

Cricket etiquette isn't just for players. Everybody at a cricket match has a role to play:

- Coaches, parents, teachers and spectators are to respect the nature of the game, and accept that umpires and the team captains have a responsibility to conduct a match in the appropriate manner. Any noise from the sidelines (other than appropriate recognition of good performance or effort), or any signals or form of communication to players, are not in the best interests of the game.
- Coaches should communicate during drinks breaks, or during breaks in play when teams leave the field.
- Yelling from the sidelines is not condoned.
- Coaches are not to enter the field of play unless delivering drinks at the appropriate times.

Taking a greater role in assisting captains in matches involving children under 12 years of age may be appropriate for coaches.

Knowing the coaches' code of behaviour

The Australian Sports Commission developed codes of behaviour to reflect the principles and spirit of cricket in Australia.

The codes ensure that young players develop admirable sporting behaviour, leading to a positive cricket experience that encourages them to remain involved throughout their lives.

Cricket coaches have codes of conduct developed specifically for them:

- Be aware that young people participate for pleasure and winning is only part of the fun.
- Be reasonable in your demands on players' time, energy and enthusiasm.

- Display control and respect to everybody involved in cricket, including opponents, coaches, umpires, administrators, parents and spectators. Encourage your players to do the same.
- Ensure that any physical contact with a young person is appropriate to the situation and necessary for the player's skill development.
- Ensure that equipment and facilities meet safety standards and are appropriate to the age and ability of all players.
- Ensure that the time players spend with you is a positive experience.
- Never ridicule or yell at a young player for making a mistake or not coming first.
- Obtain appropriate qualifications and keep up to date with the latest cricket coaching practices and principles of growth and development of young people.
- Operate within the rules and spirit of cricket and teach your players to do the same.
- Resist overplaying the talented players. All young players need and deserve equal time, attention and opportunities.
- Respect the rights, dignity and worth of every young person, regardless of gender, ability, cultural background or religion.
- Show concern and caution towards sick and injured players. Follow the advice of a doctor when determining whether an injured player is ready to recommence training or competition and, above all, use commonsense. The wellbeing of the child is paramount.

Nurturing Young Cricketers

Administrators, teachers, coaches and parents need to understand the various stages of skill and social development that children experience, particularly between the ages of 5 and 12.

Recognising these general stages of development assists volunteers to prepare appropriate games and activities for children participating in cricket.

Developing a child's cricket abilities

The following guidelines focus on specific stages of a child's development, providing strategies on how to effectively manage children and how to nurture a skill-development pathway.

The early years

Children aged from five to seven can play modified games, such as Have-A-Go cricket. At these ages, children can:

- Build sequences of two or more skills.
- Build skills with simple sequences and lots of practice.
- Master basic movement skills, such as throwing, hitting, catching and running.
- Play an ideal format, such as Have-A-Go cricket, or take part in a simple training format.
- Practise skills individually, in pairs and in small groups, incorporated into games where possible.
- Respond to emphasis on one major skill per session.
- Respond to positive reinforcement that emphasises a key point or points of a session.
- Respond to simple instructions that have one or two quality 'cues' or themes per session.
- Respond well to positive general feedback.
- Take part in fun cardiovascular warm-ups.
- Take part in one training session per week of 20 to 30 minutes.
- Take part in warm-downs after skill-related games or activity.
- Understand that effort is more important than outcome.
- Undertake simple relays and short games.

The middle-primary years

Children aged from eight to ten years play modified games, such as Have-A-Go cricket, with an increased emphasis on skill. At these ages, children can:

- Develop a sense of team.
- Develop a strong sense of belonging.
- Enjoy a modified game that emphasises skills.
- Enjoy seeing parents develop partnerships with other parents to manage teams.
- Manage training sessions lasting 40 to 70 minutes.
- Master two to three skills rotating into modified games.
- Respond to emphasis on fun, equality and inclusion.

- Respond to the introduction of sports-specific skills, such as bowling, batting and wicketkeeping with appropriately modified rules and safety equipment.
- Respond to prompts to practise at home and with friends.
- Respond well to constructive and positive feedback.
- Take part in a session wrap-up with key points to practise.
- Take part in fun cardiovascular warm-ups, including some skill practices.
- Work well in pairs, small groups and teams.

The ideal format for children aged eight to ten is Have-A-Go cricket or one training session plus a modified game.

Early adolescence

Children aged between 11 and 14 are usually ready to begin playing in organised junior competitions. At this age, children can:

- Be attracted to fun, belonging, competition and social opportunities.
- Be disadvantaged by the introduction too early of specialised skills. Teenagers should be encouraged to work on all their skills.
- Be inclined to take criticism personally. Encourage them, don't criticise.
- Become bored with long-distance running.
- Compare themselves with others. Peer acceptance is important.
- Lack commitment to practice and patience.
- Refine skills and understand game strategies. Modified rules and safety remain important.
- Rely on family support as pivotal to their enjoyment of the game.
- Require flexible opportunities, especially for older beginners or players with special needs.
- Respond to increased intensity and complexity of challenges.
- Respond to quality instructions, which are always important.
- See sport as an opportunity for advanced freedom and independence.
- Take part in individual and group skill practices, rotating activities.

- Take part in game-related warm-ups.
- Take part in skill-related warm-ups, including core stability exercises.
- Take part in training sessions of approximately 50 to 80 minutes.
- Understand the basic underlying concepts of how sport is played.

Children aged between 11 and 14 should have one training session plus a modified game per week.

Teenage

With a solid base in juniors, teenagers of 15 and 16 years are usually ready to play lower grades of senior cricket. These teenagers can:

- Appreciate special opportunities available for talented youth.
- Carry unrealistic and media-highlighted expectations of sporting successes.
- Develop increased muscle mass for strength and explosive power, especially in males as puberty ends.
- Develop specialised skills.
- Evaluate strengths and weaknesses of their own play.
- Enjoy the fact that cricket offers players lots of ways to belong to a team and be accepted.
- Help set realistic individual sporting goals.
- Participate for social status.
- Require coach feedback, which remains important.
- Show improved ability to understand the consequences of their actions.
- Take part in game-related warm-ups.
- Take part in individual and group skill practices, rotating activities.
- Take part in skill-related warm-ups, including core stability exercises.
- Take part in training sessions from 60 to 90 minutes.
- Undertake strategy and game-sense activities to develop game awareness.

Teenagers aged 15 and 16 years can manage one training session plus one game per week.

Late teenage

Teenagers, aged 17 and 18 years, are usually playing senior cricket. The grade these teenagers play depends on their skill levels and stages of development. Teenagers in these years can:

- Continue to increase their speed, strength and size.
- Continue to specialise and refine their skills.
- Cope, generally, with pressure from parents, coaches and others.
- Develop a sophisticated awareness of how their bodies move in skill execution.
- Develop good abstract-thinking skills.
- Develop, hopefully, more security about body image.
- Develop more realistic goals about sporting abilities in the broader context of their life.
- Meet increasing demands in performance.
- Show slower rates of improvement in strength and endurance than they showed during puberty.

Avoiding early specialisation

The unique advantage of cricket over many other sports is that the game can offer children a chance to specialise in various components of the sport.

After age 12, players can benefit from understanding and experiencing all aspects of the game.

Children up until about the age of 12 are recommended to experience *all* parts of the game so a coach should rotate batting orders, bowlers, wicketkeepers and fielding positions. The risks of early specialisation include overuse injuries, overtraining, musculoskeletal injuries and depression.

Making lifestyle decisions

The sporting choices of many Australians have changed dramatically in recent years. Some cricket associations have recognised this change and have developed varying forms of cricket to cater for these needs. Social and recreational cricket is becoming a popular option, attracting new players who may never have participated in the more traditional form of the game. Midweek twilight competitions and eight- and six-a-side games are forms of cricket where players may experience a fun cricket match in a short time frame.

Clubs, schools and associations experiencing a decreasing participation of teenagers should consider offering a quicker, social form of the game. Such a game may retain current players and also attract new team members.

Expanding the juniors

Cricket does not have to be one size fits all. Offering alternatives to young players, who could be involved in the game for a whole variety of reasons, is important for officials to consider.

Junior cricket associations should look at developing different types of game and playing conditions, with appropriate progression for players from one age group to the next.

To ensure that young players are able to participate as freely and easily as possible, all junior clubs should:

- Allow a free interchange of players. If a player can only play one day of a two-day match, a replacement can be used with no restrictions.
- Consider the most appropriate scheduling for a particular format of cricket and a particular group of people. Should it be a weekend game or a weekday twilight match? Should it be for the whole season, or a limited number of weeks? Avoiding school holidays is usually best because many children are away.
- Ensure both teams bat and bowl on the same day.
- Ensure maximum participation by rotating batting orders, limiting the number of overs per bowler and changing the wicketkeeper each week.
- Ensure players have a good opportunity to experience all aspects of the game.
- Make smaller boundary sizes to allow more boundaries. Nothing makes a budding batsman feel better than hitting a four or a six.
- Provide junior cricketers with two varying competitive game formats where possible. This could be a shorter-duration, higher-participation format for the 'recreational' player and a longer version for specialist skill development, leading more directly into senior 'traditional' cricket involvement.
- Put in place fielding restrictions, or reduce the number of fielders, to allow more gaps in the field.
- Rotate fielders through all fielding positions, particularly at the lower age-group levels.
- Work to ensure all game formats comply with the recommendations of Cricket Australia's junior policy, available on its Web site (`www.cricket.com.au`).

Playing Safe

Although safety risks are present in all sports, cricket is generally a safe game when training and playing are undertaken properly.

Cricket is certainly safer than many of the football codes, but the use of a hard ball, usually by players from about the age of 11 onwards, means that the appropriate protective equipment must be worn.

Developing the correct techniques for batting, bowling, fielding and wicketkeeping is important. (For more on these techniques, refer to the chapters in Part II.)

Cricket Australia has developed guidelines to promote a safe approach to cricket at all levels.

Preventing injury

When and where do cricket injuries occur? Here are the facts:

- One third of cricket injuries to children occur during school hours.
- Almost 20 per cent of injuries occur during training or practice.

Common cricket injuries

The most common cricket injuries are:

- A direct blow from the ball, mostly to the face, fingers or hand, while batting or fielding — the most frequent cause of injury.
- A sprain, fractures and bruising.
- Overuse injuries, often associated with back injuries to fast bowlers, particularly at the elite level, and in young cricketers, are also common. (Refer to Chapter 7 for guidelines relating to the playing and training of young fast bowlers.)

Safety tips for cricket

Cricketers can avoid injuries by taking sensible precautions. With the help of coaches, players should be encouraged to:

- Play, in the case of juniors, modified cricket programs as a means of developing good technique.

- Practise good technique and attend practice sessions to help prevent injury.
- Prepare themselves for each game. Preparation is very important.
- Restrict the number of overs bowled in any one session. The actual number should take into account the bowler's physical maturity, a safeguard that is particularly important for young cricketers. (A comprehensive guide of training and playing workloads for young bowlers is detailed in Chapter 7.)
- Seek professional advice on appropriate cricket shoes.
- Study Cricket Australia's program that advocates the screening of young bowlers for risk factors, including postural stature, physical preparation, avoidance of over bowling and use of correct bowling techniques. (Refer to Chapter 13 for contact details of Cricket Australia and your state or territory association.)
- Warm up and stretch before the day's cricket begins. Bowlers, particularly fast bowlers, should warm up immediately before their bowling spell.
- Wear a suitable cricket helmet when batting, wicketkeeping up to the stumps or fielding in close. In the lower levels of junior competitions, helmets are compulsory for wicketkeepers, and players are not allowed to field close to the pitch.
- Wear appropriate safety equipment, as detailed in Chapter 4.
- Wear protective gear during training as well as in competition.
- Work with coaches, who should undergo regular accreditation and education updates to ensure they have the latest information about playing techniques.

Dealing with injuries

Clubs and schools need to appoint a safety officer and develop a procedure to deal with injuries if they occur during training or in a match. The wellbeing of the player is paramount. Coaches are to ensure that injured cricketers receive adequate treatment and full rehabilitation before they resume playing.

For help dealing with the issues that may evolve as the result of a serious injury occurring in junior cricket, contact Cricket Australia's Community Cricket department. (Refer to Chapter 13 for contact details.)

Protecting players and coaches

Children have a fundamental right to be safe from any form of abuse while involved in cricket. Protecting the rights of children is a legal requirement as well as a moral obligation. Child protection requires a commitment from all levels of cricket to ensure the environment is safe for all children. This safety standard includes an awareness of the requirements and risks, a commitment to practices that minimise the risks, and the ability to appropriately respond to incidents of child abuse.

Member protection is a term used to describe the practices and procedures that protect an organisation's members — both individual members, such as players, coaches and officials, and the member organisations, such as clubs, state associations, other affiliated associations and the national body.

Member protection involves:

- Adopting appropriate measures to ensure the right people are involved in an organisation, particularly in relation to those involved with juniors
- Promoting and providing models of positive behaviour
- Protecting members from harassment, abuse, discrimination and other forms of inappropriate behaviour
- Providing relevant education programs.

Cricket Australia and the state and territory associations each has a Member Protection Policy as part of their ongoing commitment to the health, safety and wellbeing of staff, players, coaches and officials. (See Chapter 13 for contact details.)

Field placements

Few young cricketers have the necessary judgment, concentration or reflexes to safely field close to the batsman. With the exception of the wicketkeeper and slips fielders, no player aged 14 or under should be positioned within ten metres of the batsman's stumps.

No player under 14 may enter the 'restricted zone' until after the ball:

- Is hit by the batsman
- Strikes the body or equipment of the batsman
- Passes through to the wicketkeeper.

Ground and weather conditions

Ground and weather conditions can have a significant impact on the safety and enjoyment of cricket at both junior and senior levels. Take appropriate care to avoid injuries related to poor weather. Umpires, coaches and teachers are advised to be cautious about continuing play in the rain, especially where lightning is present or where the field conditions have reached a point where they pose a danger to players.

Fostering good working relationships with local government authorities, to encourage a proactive approach to the maintenance and improvement of cricket facilities, is an important task for a cricket club. Local government authorities should be kept informed in writing of any deterioration in cricketing facilities — don't forget to thank them when upgrades and repairs have been completed.

National Club Insurance Program

The National Club Insurance Program is a joint initiative of Cricket Australia and its state and territory associations. The program has seen a number of benefits provided to cricket clubs throughout the country. Every club should now have access to insurance at an affordable and consistent price. The program's goal is to provide sustainable, long-term insurance and peace of mind.

Clubs can register for insurance with the National Club Insurance Program at `www.cricket.com.au`. Complete the online risk management module and print the certificate of currency.

For more information, contact JLT Sport for assistance. Club administrators can telephone 1300 655 684 (in the Australian Capital Territory, New South Wales, Queensland and Victoria) or 1800 882 079 (in the Northern Territory, South Australia, Tasmania and Western Australia) or visit the Cricket Australia Web site at `www.cricket.com.au`.

Facilities and equipment

The development of quality cricket facilities for training and playing is an important part in the overall enjoyment of the game for players and spectators. Go to `www.cricket.com.au` to find all the information you need to guide your club should you be considering building or upgrading your facilities.

Risk management

Identify risks and eliminate or reduce them — don't wait for something to go wrong! Ensure that your cricket ground, practice facilities and club or change rooms are of a safe and acceptable standard. If concerns exist, discuss them as a club and make a united approach to fix the problems with the ground authority, which is usually the local council. The club can often solve simple problems. Make sure facilities are checked regularly, particularly the playing field on match days to ensure no broken glass or other dangerous items have been discarded there.

Heat

Climatic conditions are different across Australia and players' tolerance of heat and humidity varies significantly. Apply commonsense guidelines.

Always consider players' health in the scheduling of matches. Sports Medicine Australia recommends that children's and adolescents' activities be postponed or cancelled if the temperature reaches 34 degrees Celsius.

Cricket Australia recommends that associations contact the Sports Medicine Australia office in their state or territory to discuss appropriate guidelines for their particular situation. More information is available on the Sports Medicine Australia Web site — `www.sma.org.au`.

Hydration

No single recommendation exists on the appropriate volume of fluid consumption due to the vast range of body types, fitness and states of acclimatisation in children and adolescents.

Young people appear to consume more fluid when the drinks offered are perceived as palatable, such as cordials instead of water. Regular and effective drinking practices should become habitual to young athletes before, during, and after activity.

Following expert advice, Cricket Australia has set the following guidelines for fluid replacement:

- Drink breaks occur every 30 to 60 minutes in all matches (every 30 minutes in conditions of extreme temperature).
- Make drinks available for individual players between drinks breaks. Advise umpires that additional drinks are sought and make every effort to ensure players waste no time.

- Encourage players to have their own drink bottles. This ensures that each player has access to an adequate level of replacement fluids and reduces the risk of spreading viruses.
- Water is the most appropriate drink for re-hydration. However, diluted cordials or sports drinks may be supplied. Flavoured drinks may be particularly palatable to children who have consistently poor drinking habits during exercise.
- Do not dip cups into large drink containers. Wash or dispose of used cups after.

Sun protection

Appropriate clothing is important for all cricketers. Light-coloured, loose-fitting clothes of natural fibres, or composite fabrics with high absorption properties are the most appropriate clothing in mild and hot conditions for practice sessions and for youngsters playing modified games before they progress to wearing whites in junior competitions.

Cricket Australia recommends that players:

- Rest in shaded areas when not on the field. If no stands or trees are available at the ground, then use artificial shades, such as umbrellas.
- Be supplied with sunscreen with a 30-plus rating and reapply it frequently.
- Wear a broad-brimmed hat.
- Wear a long-sleeved shirt.

Chapter 15

Climbing Cricket's Pyramid

In This Chapter

- Finding your level in Australian cricket
- Rising to the top
- Developing indigenous cricket
- Finding out about umpiring

Somewhere, not too far away, a cricket team is out there waiting for you. Even though you may never have picked up a bat, never spent your childhood bowling out your friends in the backyard, or fielded for your team in the juniors, a club is waiting to welcome you onto the field.

From duffer to destroyer, few other sports offer as broad a range of local teams as cricket does, which allows you to settle into a club and feel comfortable in your team. Twelve-year-old boys and 70-year-old grandfathers can play in the same side to win H-grade premierships. Some of those boys, in time, become A-grade players in the same club and move on to play in major competitions.

Every player now representing Australia in front of the roaring crowds at the big grounds, and before TV viewers at home, began their cricket career in a local junior side and progressed through a club cricket competition.

Whether you want to have a weekend hit with some mates in the local park or rise to the very top at state and national level, your talent, hard work and persistence can combine to take you on a journey through the ranks to your natural level. As those champion cricketers standing atop the pyramid today can tell you, the sky truly is the limit.

Putting the Building Blocks in Place

Every time a junior walks out to play their first game of cricket, looking like a mini sports clothes ad in their new cricket whites, that junior becomes part of the foundation stone of Australian cricket.

These youngsters are the future of a game that can take them to fame and fortune if they prove talented enough, such is the defined and refined pathway to the top that now exists in the game across this country.

Although some people don't take much notice of the game below international and first-class level — except for the success of the team they may be playing in — what happens in the lesser competitions is vital to the success of the champion Australian team.

This solid base of talent, pushing up from below, is the reason cricket in this country is so strong. The dedication of more than half a million cricketers and the many volunteers who ensure cricket prospers at the grass-roots level is what creates the platform for the national team.

Looking from the top down

Many of the players who proudly wear Australia's baggy green cap as the best of the best have often been identified, at a relatively young age, as a player of real promise, and then pushed through the cricket system. Others have been forced to fight at every stage — through local club cricket to major club competition and then on to state and national representation — to secure their place at the elite level (see Figure 15-1).

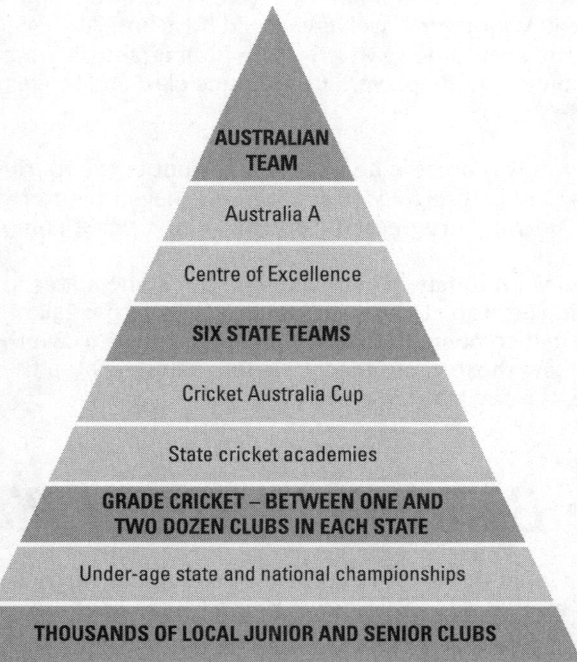

Figure 15-1: Cricket's pyramid: Most of today's cricket champions worked their way up from local competitions.

Regardless of how quickly a player makes the journey to the top, each player has taken similar steps along the pathway.

Playing for Australia

The only way anyone can be chosen to play for Australia is to represent one of the six state sides, which make up the Pura Cup first-class competition and an elite state-versus-state one-day competition.

Exceptions in the past have seen players chosen for Test cricket without playing in the Pura Cup, or Sheffield Shield, as it was known until Cricket Australia sold the naming rights in 1999. One such player was Australian Rules footballer and fast bowler, Laurie Nash, who played for Australia in the 1930s without having first played in a Sheffield Shield side (see Figure 15-2 and the sidebar, 'Aussie Rules' Nash bowls straight to the top').

Intense competition exists for places in the Australian side as well as the Pura Cup, which carries an elite standard compared to the club competitions below it. Therefore, the jump to reach these levels is now simply too great for international cricketers to qualify without some sort of first-class cricket experience. (See Chapter 19 for more on the Sheffield Shield, and refer to Chapter 3 for more on first-class cricket.)

First-class cricket is of a standard just below Test cricket. Matches must be played over at least three days to be considered first class. In the case of the Pura Cup, all matches are scheduled for four days, except the final between the two top sides at the end of the season in late March, which is played over five days. All Test matches, which are scheduled for five days, are considered first class. One-day competitions, whether played at international or state level, cannot be considered first class.

Figure 15-2: Aussie Rules' Laurie Nash represented Australia at cricket without ever playing Sheffield Shield.

Aussie Rules' Nash bowls straight to the top

A robust showman with no shortage of ability or self belief, Laurie Nash is a rare and famous example of a player who was chosen to represent Australia without ever having played in the Sheffield Shield competition.

Nash was a lively fast bowler and hard-hitting lower order batsman who also excelled as an Australian Rules footballer.

If self-confidence is the primary fuel on which most sporting champions run, then Nash's many accomplishments are easy to explain. When asked who was the greatest footballer he had ever seen, Nash famously replied: 'I see him in the mirror every morning when I shave.'

Many of Nash's football opponents would be inclined to agree with this assessment. Despite being a mere 175 centimetres in height, Nash rates as one of the best key forwards to play Aussie Rules.

Cricket was his second sport but here, too, he was exceptional.

Playing a first-class match for Tasmania long before the island state was admitted into the Sheffield Shield competition in 1977, Nash dominated against the touring South African team in Hobart during the 1931–32 season. He took 7–50 (dismissing seven South African batsmen, while conceding 50 runs), and he was promptly chosen to play the fifth Test in Melbourne a short time later, claiming 4–18 as the South Africans were dismissed for just 36.

Moving to Victoria to pursue his football career, Nash played just one further Test, years later. He played for Victoria four times as a footballer but appeared only once for his adopted state as a cricketer, against a touring England side in 1936–37, claiming 4–37, and was selected for his second and last Test in Melbourne on the strength of that performance.

To bridge the gap between state and international cricket, the Australia A team has become more and more important. The most promising state cricketers, identified as potential players for Australia, make up the Australia A team. A teams often include cricketers who may actually play the occasional Test or one-day match for Australia, but are yet to establish themselves as permanent members of the team. In June and July 2006, Australia staged a major A team tournament in Darwin and Cairns — also including A teams from India, New Zealand and Pakistan. The teams played a series of four-day, one-day and Twenty20 matches. (Refer to Chapter 3 for more on these different match formats.)

Representing your state

Representing your state is where cricket's pyramid begins to expand rapidly. Each state cricket association administers a major competition of between a dozen and two dozen clubs. Usually called grade cricket, this is the elite club competition in each state.

The best players from this level are chosen to represent their state.

To aid the development of young players moving from weekend district or grade cricket to four-day first-class cricket in the Pura Cup, Cricket Australia has a state second XI competition called the Cricket Australia Cup. This competition allows promising young players to experience the demands of interstate travel and perform over four consecutive days without the pressure of the Pura Cup. Learning to concentrate for long periods is important for promising batsmen; and experiencing the physical and mental challenge of returning to bowl for a second consecutive day is important for promising bowlers.

Quality all-rounders are cricket's most valuable players. These talented cricketers can perform more than one skill to a high level. Usually, batting and bowling are their double skills — for example, England's Andrew Flintoff. However, a wicketkeeper who can bat well — for example, Australia's Adam Gilchrist — is also considered an all-rounder.

Australia's Brad Hogg, who is dedicated to working on all his skills, not just his bowling, maintains his place in the Australian one-day team, despite being dropped from the Western Australian Pura Cup side. Hogg's dedication to polishing his bowling, batting and fielding skills is a great lesson to young players. The reward is that players who excel at more than one aspect of the game are more likely to gain selection and promotion.

Becoming an excellent fieldsman to complement your batting or bowling skills is a great way to enhance your chances of progressing to a higher level.

Advancing through the grades

Grade cricket, which is sometimes called district or premier cricket, is the first stepping stone for a talented young cricketer. The common name of *grade cricket* for this important tier in Australia's well structured cricket system becomes obvious — players work their way up grade by grade.

Competitions vary from state to state but each contains between one and two dozen clubs and each club has four grades — firsts, seconds, thirds and fourths — with the firsts the pinnacle. Although grade cricket receives almost no publicity, the standard is high. Anyone who is a regular first-grade player is a very good cricketer who, with sustained performances and a little flair, could easily find themselves representing their state.

Third and fourth grade are often no more advanced than other strong senior competitions dotted around the capital cities. These lower-grade teams are used as a nursery to develop young players. Often one or two older senior players, who have been strong performers in the firsts or seconds over many years, drop back to help guide the younger players.

Brad Hogg combines all the skills

Veteran spinner Brad Hogg has managed the remarkable achievement of maintaining his place in the Australian one-day team despite being dropped from the Western Australian Pura Cup side.

Hogg has been such an important member of the national limited-overs side, since the retirement of champion spinner Shane Warne from one-day cricket in early 2003, that the national selectors, who pick the Australian team, have continued to choose him.

First-class and one-day matches are very different forms of the game. Although bowlers are expected to take wickets in both the long and short versions of the game, a much greater emphasis on saving runs exists in the one-day game and batsmen have less time to bat so they take greater risks, offering more opportunity for bowlers to take wickets.

Hogg, a youthful and energetic 35 years of age heading into the 2006–07 season, is more than just a useful left-arm wrist spin bowler (refer to Chapter 8 for more on wrist spin bowling). He is also a livewire in the field; Hogg's speed enables him to gather up many balls that would otherwise have gone over the boundary. Add to this Hogg's ability as a useful lower-order batsman, and you have a very valuable one-day player.

Hogg has managed just four Tests in eight years, from 1996 to 2003, but he had played 85 one-day international matches, heading into the 2006–07 season, with almost all of them coming in the past four years. Hogg has claimed 107 one-day wickets, more than any other Australian spinner behind Warne's 291.

Unlike playing for your state or country, no hard and fast rules govern selection in a grade side. If you're a player with talent and ambition, then you can simply turn up to train one night with any grade club.

But be warned, this is no social romp in the park. These players take their cricket deadly seriously. Good levels of fitness are expected, with strong expectations that all players will complete sometimes lengthy training sessions twice a week, focusing on all cricket's skills. After all, these players are striving hard to improve themselves so they can work their way up the grades and maybe even be picked to play for their state. (Refer to Chapter 12 for more on training.)

Unlike state and national players, grade cricketers are almost all strictly amateur and most of them work or study full time; therefore, their cricket must fit in around other commitments. They train in the late afternoons twice a week and play on weekends, just like club cricketers at all levels right around the country.

Australia versus England on the pay scale

Australia and England may be cricket's two founding Test nations but their respective cricket systems are very different. Although Australia's leading cricketers are very well paid and state players now earn a reasonable living, a seamless transition for players moving between amateur grade clubs and state teams still takes place. This is not the case in England, where a clear divide exists between amateur and professional players. Each county club (the equivalent of an Australian state team) has a full professional list to choose from, with no cross-over into amateur ranks.

Playing in the lower tiers

Below their major elite competition, most states have one or more second-tier competitions, which are still of a high standard. In Victoria, for example, Sub-District cricket and the Victorian Junior Cricket Association both have some fine players.

Often players who have tried out at grade cricket but are unable or unwilling to make the extra commitment to continue playing at that level, drop back and continue to play in a lesser competition that still offers a good standard of the game. Sometimes these players are paid to captain or coach the team although big money is not available at this level.

Finding a club and a standard of play that is right for you is what is most important. Whether you want to play serious cricket in a tough competition or play with a few mates in a more social environment, a club and a level exists for you.

If you're just starting off and you want to find a local club, refer to Chapter 13.

Helping the Cream Rise to the Top

All the way up the Australian cricket pyramid, promising young players are given a helping hand to reach their potential. The best young talent is identified early — sometimes even before players leave primary school — with under-age representative sides chosen to bring the best players together in special tournaments.

Time to train new young talent

The academy system began as a result of Australia's least successful cricketing period, during the mid 1980s. Weakened by the almost simultaneous retirement of three great players, captain Greg Chappell, wicketkeeper Rod Marsh and fast bowler Dennis Lillee, Australia was further gutted when other experienced players were banned for defecting to a rebel tour of South Africa. South Africa was excluded from international cricket between 1970 and 1991 because of the country's racist apartheid policy. However, cricket authorities in that country, desperate for top-level competition, handsomely paid players from a number of Test countries to tour. See Chapter 23 for more on rebel tours.

Talented younger juniors are often encouraged by their clubs to try out in these tournaments. Parents, or the players themselves, can also contact any grade clubs in their area to find out if they have elite junior squads. In Victoria, for example, where grade clubs are called premier clubs, an annual carnival called the Dowling Shield takes place. Premier clubs hold trials before selecting a side to play in an under-16 carnival. Simply get in touch with your state or territory association to find the grade club closest to you. All the contact details you need can be found in Chapter 13.

Climbing the junior pyramid

The Primary School Exchange pathway — conducted by School Sport Australia — sees competitions run for under-13 players, both boys and girls, while the organisation also stages an under-15 competition for boys. Cricket Australia currently hosts an under-15 tournament for girls.

Competitions for Australia's elite young cricketers — male and female — include the Cricket Australia Cup and under-age championships for under-17 and under-19 levels.

These championships aim to bridge the gap between grade and first-class cricket, and give players the opportunity to experience competition at a national level.

The Cricket Australia Cup for men is the national Second XI competition and the playing conditions mirror those of the Pura Cup competition, with some exceptions.

The Cricket Australia Cup for women is generally staged as a week-long tournament involving most states and territories. As women's cricket continues to grow across the country, more states and territories are expected to become involved in the tournament.

The under-age championships are held annually, usually over one to two weeks, and usually include teams from each state and territory.

From the under-19 state championships, the Australian under-19 team is picked, bringing Australia's best young players into focus. Although making this elite squad is no guarantee that you're going to play for your state or country, making the team is an important stepping stone. Most of the players in the Australian team progressed from the national under-19 side.

Training at the academies

Talent identification and development has now reached such a stage in Australia that each state has its own cricket academy, where the best young talent in the state is identified and developed. Academies are like finishing schools in that they better prepare young players for the great leap from grade cricket to state cricket.

So weak was the Australian team in the mid 1980s, that Australia won just 3 of 32 Test matches from March 1984 to December 1986. During this desperate time, Australia's leading cricket administrators vowed that such a proud cricket nation would never go through such lean times again.

The junior development system was streamlined and enhanced to ensure the best talent was identified and the National Cricket Academy was set up in Adelaide to help nurture potential young stars. Early teething problems caused some setbacks and critics argued that the academy was a waste of money because the best young talent would automatically rise to play for the state and national teams anyway.

But as the talent began to filter through into the state and national sides and as the Australian team continued to improve, the wisdom of the decision to set up an academy began to show. As Australia again dominated the world of cricket from the mid 1990s, other countries began to follow Australia's lead. England followed Australia's lead to such an extent that it poached Australia's second and longest-serving academy coach, Rod Marsh, the former wicketkeeping great, to head the English academy.

The concept has now evolved a step further in Australia. Following the success of the state academies in developing elite young players from under-aged competitions, the national academy has become the finishing school for the most promising state cricketers. Even some who have played for Australia are selected for specialised training and tuition.

In 2005, the National Cricket Academy was renamed the Centre of Excellence and moved from Adelaide to Brisbane, where it shares outstanding facilities with Queensland Cricket at Allan Border Field. The Centre of Excellence can offer outdoor training almost all the year round because of the warm Queensland weather.

The fact that all manner of under-aged teams, tournaments, competitions and academies have been developed for elite young players doesn't mean for a minute that these promising cricketers have an automatic path to state and national teams. They do not! Although their training creates obvious advantages during their journey towards the top, the young players must continue to perform on the cricket field. In the end, the only way a player is selected to play at a higher level is by outstanding performances. Indeed, batsmen must score runs — Matthew Hayden is a good example — to maintain their place in any team (see sidebar, 'Matthew Hayden's strong stand'). Bowlers, on the other hand, need to consistently take wickets if they want to stay in their team.

Matthew Hayden's strong stand

Australian opening batsman, Matthew Hayden, is a great example of a player climbing the pyramid, despite being overlooked for junior development teams and squads earlier in his career. Big and powerful, Hayden pushed his way through the system because of the sheer weight of runs at every level of cricket.

The left hander was considered technically poor, despite good performances at lower levels, so he was not chosen for Australian under-age teams or the National Cricket Academy, as it was called then. However, Hayden was so prolific at grade level that he forced his way into the Queensland side as a teenager. He then scored so many runs for Queensland that the national selectors were forced to keep considering him, even though Hayden took seven years to establish himself as an Australian player.

Hayden's national career finally took off with a bang on the 2001 tour of India when Hayden scored 549 runs in the three Test series at the amazing average of 109.8 (see Chapter 20 for more on averages). Hayden scored more runs than any other Australian player has scored in a three Test series. Since then, Hayden's career has charged into the stratosphere. Despite a lean tour of England in 2005, Hayden will now be forever remembered as one of Australia's all-time greats. Of the 397 players who have represented Australia in Test cricket over 130 years, Hayden was eighth on the list of all-time run scores heading into the 2006–07 season and within easy reach of the top five.

This success is the reward for a young man with a positive attitude and a great work ethic, who persisted despite being overlooked many times.

Expanding Indigenous Cricket

Indigenous cricket has a long and proud history in Australia. So long, in fact, that the first team to represent Australia in England was made up entirely of Aboriginal players (see Figure 15-3).

Although the 1880 clash at The Oval in London is listed as the first Test on English soil, played between the two founding Test nations, England and Australia, the indigenous touring team pre-dates this landmark match by 12 years.

Australia's first indigenous team played a taxing 47 matches between May and October 1868, winning 14 games, losing 14 and drawing 19. Yet, despite this fantastic achievement from such inexperienced cricketers, the tour was not officially recognised until just a few years ago.

Figure 15-3: Australia's first indigenous team touring England in 1868.

Introducing the game

The involvement of indigenous people in Australian cricket dates back to the mid-19th century. The game was introduced by pastoralists to the members of isolated communities, outposts and missions.

Alec Henry later became the first indigenous Australian to appear in first-class cricket when he represented Queensland in 1901.

Fast bowler, Eddie Gilbert, also made an indelible impression on the national stage when he bowled Sir Donald Bradman for a rare duck in 1931. Even so, the entry of Aboriginal players to the first-class cricket arena generally remains few and far between.

Interest in the background of indigenous cricket in Australia was subsequently revived when a representative team was selected to tour England during Australia's bicentennial year, 1988, as a means of commemorating the original tour more than a century earlier.

Developing the Imparja Cup

Indigenous cricket is building its own pyramid with the rapidly expanding Imparja Cup tournament held in Alice Springs each year. From humble beginnings little more than a decade ago, the Imparja Cup has become a five-division carnival hosting close to 30 teams. The top or premier division is now a national championship with teams from every state. An increasing number of women's teams are playing in the lower divisions.

Australia's first Aboriginal team plays at the MCG in 1866

Arguably the most successful attempt at encouraging early indigenous participation in the sport was made in western Victoria. So skilful were the Aboriginal players of the region that a local indigenous team was chosen to play a match against the Melbourne Cricket Club at the MCG on Boxing Day 1866. This was 73 years before the first official Boxing Day Test at the MCG and more than a century ahead of the Boxing Day Test becoming a tradition, which now makes it the biggest event on the Australian cricketing calendar each summer.

Played before approximately 10,000 spectators, the game in 1866 was considered such a great success that eventually a squad was selected for that historic England tour almost two years later.

Commemorating the past

On 13 May 2006, Cricket Australia (CA) and most state and territory associations flew the Aboriginal flag at their offices or grounds to honour the 1868 indigenous touring team. The team had arrived in England on that day, 138 years earlier.

CA chief executive James Sutherland said the date, that would become an annual recognition date, was another way Australian cricket could pay tribute to the courage of Australia's first touring team.

'The pioneering achievements of the 1868 team have, in recent years, started to become more widely acknowledged and celebrated, and we want that history and recognition to be ongoing,' Sutherland announced.

In 2002, Australian cricket was successful in having the 1868 team inducted into the Sport Australia Hall of Fame and, in 2004, special player numbers were allocated to each member of the touring party as formal recognition of their place in Australian cricket history.

The first Imparja Cup match, held on Australia Day in 1994, took place thanks to the initiative of indigenous cricketers, Shane and Mervyn Franey, from Alice Springs, and Ross Williams from Tennant Creek. The trio wanted to host an annual match between Alice Springs and Tennant Creek to promote indigenous cricket in the Northern Territory and to enjoy a cricket match with family and friends.

Four years later, Shane Franey and Ross Williams approached Northern Territory Cricket to help organise the game and, shortly after, Cricket Australia also provided assistance to the Imparja Cup, officially recognising the event as a national competition.

Support at the territory and national level has promoted a huge growth in the Imparja Cup tournament, from just five teams in 2001 to a 28-team, five-division event in 2004.

Imparja Television, the Northern Territory indigenous TV network, has supported the carnival since its inception. The extent of this support has grown significantly over the years from a $200-petrol voucher and meat trays to a three-year corporate partnership valued at $42,000.

The event now has a budget approaching $260,000 and brings 300 cricketers to central Australia for a five-day period. Such is the popularity of the Imparja Cup tournament that Alice Springs is now struggling to find adequate venues for the games.

The greater emphasis and increased resources put into indigenous cricket by Cricket Australia and the state and territory associations in recent years have promoted modified children's games, such as Have-A-Go cricket, which is proving very popular in some of Australia's remote communities.

To become involved with indigenous cricket, you just need to contact your local state or territory cricket association (refer to Chapter 13 for all the contact details).

Taking Control as an Umpire

The star players may receive all the publicity and adulation but in many ways the umpires are the most important people on a cricket field. The cricket match would not happen without them.

Umpiring gives former players the opportunity to remain active in the game and allows those people who love cricket and want to participate without playing to be very much a part of the action. Indeed, umpiring provides the best 'seat in the house' for those who take it on.

And unlike the half a million or more club cricketers across the country, most accredited umpires appointed to stand in matches, even at a local level, are paid for their efforts!

To find out all about the basics of umpiring, refer to Chapter 2.

Becoming involved

Cricket Australia is pouring more and more resources into encouraging the development of umpires. As a first step in assisting new umpires, or those mums and dads who stand as umpires in junior games, Cricket Australia has produced an outstanding umpiring guide on CD–ROM. This is ideal for novice umpires, who can very quickly learn the basics through this easy-to-use CD. To try the CD, contact Cricket Australia (for contact details, refer to Chapter 13). Cricket Australia has also developed a standard accreditation course for everyone who wishes to become an umpire, from beginners to former Test players. This latter option was highlighted in recent years when Paul Reiffel, a former Australian fast bowler and Victorian captain, became an umpire after retiring as a player.

Opportunities exist for umpires to progress along a structured career program from local and grade level, to state panels and Cricket Australia contracts. If you wish to become an umpire, or want more information, contact Cricket Australia or your local state association (for contact details, refer to Chapter 13).

Australia is well represented on the international panel of umpires who officiate in Test and one-day international matches around the world.

In March 2002, the International Cricket Council (ICC) announced that it would appoint a select panel of umpires — the Elite Panel — to take charge of matches at international level.

The introduction of the Elite Panel aimed:

- To allow the best and most respected umpires to stand in the sport's biggest games
- To improve the overall standard of umpiring at international level
- To establish a benchmark to which future umpires could aspire.

Two umpires from the Elite Panel now stand in all Test matches and at least one member of the Elite Panel officiates in each one-day international.

Australia has three umpires on the ICC Elite Panel — Daryl Harper, Darrell Hair and Simon Taufel. The ICC has twice named Taufel as International Umpire of the Year (see Figure 15-4).

Figure 15-4: Simon Taufel, twice named International Umpire of the Year.

Umpiring to a code of behaviour

Like players and coaches, umpires are expected to abide by a code of behaviour that respects the game and all those involved in it. Above all, umpires should attempt to ensure the smooth running of a match. They are not to become too involved or dictatorial; their role is to allow the players to enjoy their game of cricket and to maintain control with a liberal measure of commonsense.

Cricket Australia developed the following code of behaviour specifically for umpires:

- Be a good sport yourself — actions speak louder than words.
- Be consistent, objective and courteous when making decisions.
- Compliment and encourage all participants.
- Condemn unsporting behaviour and promote respect for all opponents.
- Emphasise the spirit of the game rather than the errors.
- Give all young people a 'fair go' regardless of gender, ability, cultural background or religion.
- Modify rules and regulations to match the skill levels and needs of young people, in accordance with CA guidelines.
- Keep up to date with the latest available resources for umpiring and the principles of growth and development of young people.
- Place the safety and welfare of participants above all else.
- Remember, you set an example. Your behaviour and comments should be positive and supportive.

Part IV
Planet Cricket

'. . . and it is with these, your Majesty, that we plan to conquer the new world.'

In this part . . .

Cricket is played around the globe — even in the USA, where they call baseball the king bat 'n' ball game, they still have a reputable cricket competition.

From England where the game started, you can follow cricket across the oceans in the wake of the old British Empire. And the colonials — from the West Indies to India and Australia to Pakistan — have had their revenge on Mother England, as each of these at some time has led the world.

This part too looks at the wonders of women's cricket — at the influence of women who started overarm bowling, created the ashes for the Ashes series, and today see Australia as the dominant force in the female game worldwide.

And finally, this part teaches you how to be a cricket fan — how to get tickets, what to take to the game and what to do.

Chapter 16

Global Test Cricket Rivalries

In This Chapter

- Exploring the great moments of the game
- Checking out the Test playing nations
- Ranking the rankings systems
- Playing the second division
- Gazing in awe at the world's great cricket grounds
- Examining current controversies
- Rejoicing in the Ashes renaissance

Cricket may not have the worldwide appeal of soccer, but it can still lay claim to being a major world sport. Not only is cricket the national summer sport of Australia and England, but it also has huge appeal throughout the Indian sub-continent. Virtually every week of the year a Test match is going on somewhere around the globe. From Mumbai in India to Manchester in England — someone, somewhere, is donning white clothing and strapping on the batting pads even as you read this. And with the advent of pay television, fans have the possibility of watching cricket 24 hours a day, seven days a week — as many millions do in India!

This chapter examines some of the great players who, over the years, spread the game's popularity far and wide.

In addition, the ten Test playing nations come under the microscope to find out what makes each one of them unique. And to top off the chapter, the great cricket grounds of the world are brought up close to find just what makes each of them so special.

If you want the low-down on what makes Test cricket the magnificent sport it is, this chapter is for you.

Cricket through the Ages

Cricket has more traditions than you can shake a stick at, as the old saying goes. Thousands of books have been written about every aspect of the game, many of them chock full of statistics. And you can spend the rest of your life reading up on them. But what's really important are the landmark events that have taken place in the game, as discussed in the following sections.

From earliest times to Test cricket

Pinpointing when cricket was first played is difficult. No cave drawings of prehistoric men playing an impromptu game of cricket to celebrate a particularly noble kill exist, nor have hieroglyphics of Egyptian pharaohs donning cricket whites and carrying a bat been discovered.

While a certain amount of supposition surrounds the earliest findings, it took a coroner of all people to record that the game was alive and well in Guildford in England by the 16th century. In a report dated 16 January 1598, regarding a disputed piece of land, Surrey coroner, John Derrick, wrote: 'He and several of his fellowes did runne and play there at crickett'.

Not until the 18th century did regular mentions of cricket start to crop up. In 1709, Kent played London (the forerunner of the Surrey county side, which has its headquarters at The Oval). The game is widely regarded as the first between two English county sides. In 1744, the first set of laws of the game were drawn up in — surprise, surprise — a pub!

For the next century or so, cricket was mostly played by club sides and in public schools. The sport spread along with the British Empire to cover huge swathes of the globe, with the first cricket grounds being built in England and Australia.

Creaget is the game in 1300

The very English game of cricket drifts back into the mists of time. Cricket historians believe they have traced the game all the way back to the reign of King Edward I, who was crowned in 1272. The royal accounts for 1300, when Edward I was absent on a crusade, mention the payment of 100 shillings, almost a king's ransom, for his son, Prince Edward, 'playing at Creag' and other sports'. Given that the apostrophe that ends creag' was a common substitute for 'et' at the time, the sport was, in fact, called creaget.

The first recorded cricket match, indeed, European sporting event, in Australia took place in Sydney during 1803 between the military and civilians, when Governor Lachlan Macquarie ordered the manufacture of bats and balls in government workshops. However, cricket in some form probably began with the arrival of the First Fleet, which had established Australia as a British penal colony 15 years earlier.

Eventually, the game expanded to global rivalries with the first Test match played in 1877 between England and Australia at the Melbourne Cricket Ground.

The golden age

Cricket buffs often talk about the golden age — the period from around the end of the 19th century up to the outbreak of World War I — when two of cricket's most famous names were the superstars of their day: In England, the famous W.G. Grace and in Australia, the indomitable Victor Trumper.

While the colonials were pretty formal about their cricket, the golden age saw international and English county matches in the Old Dart dominated by larger-than-life characters, members of the aristocracy and even the odd Indian prince. Back then, there were more titles in an English cricket team than on the shelves of a library. During the golden age, when the sun always seemed to shine, legend has it that batsmen played with bravado and daring, hitting the bowling to all parts of the field.

The Bradman years

That Australian batsman Don Bradman gets a whole age of cricket named after him is a fitting tribute to his genius. But credit where credit is due. Bradman dominated Test cricket from the late 1920s to the outbreak of World War II, scoring centuries galore. His effectiveness caused England to adopt the very controversial bodyline tactics when touring Australia in 1932–33 (see Chapter 23 for more on cricket's great controversies). What's more, after the war, Bradman carried on the way he had before, putting bowling to the sword. In 1948, he led a team to England on what was his farewell tour and did not lose a single match. Not surprisingly, that team of players became known as The Invincibles and they remain Australia's most famous sporting team. From that side emerged greats, such as dashing batsman, Neil Harvey; fluent fast bowler, Ray Lindwall; and cavalier all-rounder, Keith Miller. (See Chapter 21 for more on Bradman and some of the game's other great players.)

The good doctor and the genius

If two figures encapsulate the golden age of cricket, they are England's Dr W.G. Grace and Australia's Victor Trumper.

Dr William Gilbert Grace was the most famous cricketer of his time. He was instantly recognisable with a big, bushy, long black beard and in later years a hefty paunch. However, in his younger days, he was a superb athlete. When just 18 years old, Grace scored a huge 224 not out for All England against the county of Surrey and if that wasn't enough, during the match he slipped off to win a 440-yard hurdles championship at Crystal Palace.

In a career spanning 43 years, Grace set cricketing records galore. He was the first player to score 100 centuries and to take 2,000 wickets in first-class cricket. He scored the first Test century by an Englishman in Test cricket.

Stories about Grace are legion. Probably the most legendary tale relates to a match at The Oval. In front of a packed crowd, Grace was bowled by a delivery. The crowd went silent but Grace simply picked up the bails, put them back on top of the stumps and told the bowler that the crowd 'had come here to watch me bat, not you bowl'. Such was the esteem that the good doctor was held in that he apparently got away with it!

Victor Trumper was everything that Grace was not — modest, unassuming and increasingly frail of body. Trumper was a strict teetotaller and non-smoker who held Grace up as one of his most admired players, as much for Grace's disdain for smoking as his natural ability and vast achievements. It may have surprised Trumper, a strong advocate of 'leading a good and healthy life', to find that Grace came to enjoy a little brandy and quail shooting before breakfast.

While Grace was robust and athletic, Trumper was all poise and style. He was regarded as the game's finest batsman until the arrival of the incomparable Don Bradman in 1928.

Trumper played 48 Tests from 1899 to 1912, averaging 39, which would be considered nothing special in today's game. But more than a century ago, turf pitches were often rough, sodden and sometimes virtually impossible to bat on. With his nimble footwork, perfect balance and wonderful eye, Trumper was regarded as a genius in such difficult conditions. Following a brilliant tour of England in 1902, Trumper was greeted by 5,000 people at a reception in Sydney on his return, such was the regard he was held in by the public.

While Grace played in five different decades, sadly Trumper lived less than four, dying in 1917 at the age of 37 after increasing ill health. Newspaper placards throughout Sydney announced his death, ahead of that day's reporting of World War I.

Steady as she goes

The 1950s and 1960s were considered a largely boring time for cricket, with slow scoring rates leading to often conservative Australian and English teams drawing matches *ad nauseam*. The spark was provided by the West Indies, a team that had some wonderful players who played cricket with a free calypso spirit. The West Indies' team's energy on the field led to the wonderful Test series, which produced a tied Test, in 1960–61 between Richie Benaud's Australians and Frank Worrell's West Indians, a side that included the brilliant all-rounder, Garfield Sobers, and imposing fast bowler, Wes Hall.

Other nations that had only recently joined Test cricket, such as New Zealand, India and Pakistan, were yet to find their feet against the big two, Australia and England. If any team could be said to be the world champs at this time, it was probably the Australians by a whisker. Through the inspired leadership of Benaud, a wonderful leg spinner, and the fast bowling skills of Graham McKenzie and Alan Davidson, Australia managed to keep ahead of the pack.

The Packer revolution

In 1977, the staid world of cricket was rocked to its very foundations when Australian media mogul Kerry Packer signed up the world's best cricketers to play in a privately run competition, World Series Cricket, which was televised on his Nine Network throughout Australia. Great players from Australia, the West Indies, England and most other Test countries turned their backs on Test matches to play World Series Cricket in return for extra money. Previously, Test players had been paid a pittance. Packer promised proper financial reward for player talent.

Packer's revolution changed the face of the game across the globe, popularising it with the one-day game and taking cricket to a whole new audience. For the first time, matches were played under floodlights with white balls and coloured clothing, and the crowds flocked in.

Crusty administrators, who did not share Packer's vision and refused him the right to telecast cricket exclusively on his network, were forced to embrace the concept two years later as traditional Test matches, minus most of the stars, continued to lose money.

As a result of this revolution, cricket has never been more popular.

Calypso cricket at its brutal best

The West Indies carried all before them in the 1980s and early 1990s, thanks to a seemingly endless battery of imposing fast bowlers. Opposition teams just couldn't cope with the accuracy and pace of the bowling. And the West Indies had great batsmen like Clive Lloyd, Vivian Richards and Gordon Greenidge to dominate the opposition bowlers.

However, the West Indian tactics weren't welcomed by everyone. Because bowling quickly requires a long run-up, the West Indies took forever to complete an over. Consequentially, the average number of runs scored in a day fell sharply and crowds became increasingly disenchanted. Laws were introduced to speed up over rates and offer greater protection to batsmen who found the ball was being bowled at them more than the stumps. See the section, 'West Indies', later in this chapter for more on the ups and recent downs of West Indian cricket.

The new golden age

Since the mid 1990s, the Australians have been at the top of the cricketing tree again and they have done this by playing wonderfully aggressive cricket. Australian batsmen have consciously gone after the bowling, looking to score as fast as possible to leave themselves enough time in the game to bowl the opposition out twice and claim victory.

Other countries, particularly England and India, decided 'if you can't beat them, join them' and started to play aggressively too. As a result, very few boring draws take place in Test cricket anymore, with most teams going at it — hell for the leather.

The past five years have provided some of the best and most attacking batting ever, along with a welcome resurgence of spin bowling, with great spinners like Australia's Shane Warne, India's Anil Kumble and Sri Lanka's Muttiah Muralitharan.

In many respects, the time has never been better for cricket fans!

Although the basics of cricket have not changed during its history, the laws of the game have evolved. The lawmakers are not afraid to tinker with the game to improve it. A few years back, umpires were given the right to call for video replays of disputed catches, stumpings and run outs. Cricket once had a staid image but over the past decade the game has proved surprisingly innovative and able to adapt to changing tastes and technology.

Looking at the Test Playing Nations

England gave cricket to the nations of its empire, and Australia has spent more than a century thanking its old colonial master by handing out regular floggings. Indeed, Australia has won more Tests than any other country, despite playing significantly fewer Tests than England.

Ten nations have full Test status. This means that only matches between these ten countries are deemed to be Test matches. Under new playing conditions recently devised by the game's governing body, the International Cricket Council (the ICC), these teams must play each other home and away at least once every six years. Major cricketing powers such as Australia, England and India are more likely to play each other at home and away every four years.

The ICC is made up of full members and associate members. Full members are Test playing nations — ten in total — and associate members are countries that aren't quite up to playing Test cricket.

Australia

So important is cricket as part of Australia's psyche that this country had a national cricket team long before it became a nation. In this large and diverse land, which spent its first century or so of European settlement as a loose collection of colonies, even the rail gauges and winter football codes were formed differently. Cricket was the one unifying force.

In this context, from the very outset, Australia punched above its weight on the cricket field, as it has done in many sports over the past 100 years. With a fraction of England's population, and facilities that were modest by comparison, Australia won the inaugural Test, beating England by 45 runs at the Melbourne Cricket Ground (MCG) in 1877.

Almost from the outset, Australia established its great tradition of fast bowling, with the imposing paceman Fred Spofforth playing just the second Test between the two countries in March 1877, only a fortnight after Test cricket began (see Figure 16-1). It was Spofforth who established the legend of the Ashes by routing England in 1882 to give Australia its first victory on English soil. (See Chapter 17 for more on the mystique of the tiny Ashes urn.)

Figure 16-1: Paceman Fred Spofforth takes Australia to its first Ashes victory.

'The Demon' Spofforth

Fred Spofforth was the greatest figure in early Australian Test cricket. The potent fast bowler became the man who finally humbled the finest cricketer of his generation, England's W.G. Grace. An imposing figure, Spofforth was tall and lean with a large, manicured moustache and hair parted down the middle. A fine athlete, he could run 100 yards in under 11 seconds. He learnt his cricket from watching other fine fast bowlers of the time, developing movement in the air and off the pitch (refer to Chapter 7 and Chapter 8 for more on bowling). Spofforth mixed his lively pace and built his game on devilish accuracy. Unlike many of his contemporaries, Spofforth studied the strengths and weaknesses of his opposing batsmen. Legend has it that in 1881, Spofforth once rode 650 km to play in a minor match and then took all 20 wickets — clean bowled!

In the same year that Spofforth finished Test cricket, Charlie 'Terror' Turner began his international career, continuing to rout the English, although by then, Australia was often the losing side. Not long into the new century, Albert 'Tibby' Cotter arrived with a slinging action that made him one of the fastest bowlers ever to represent Australia. Hurling the ball as if it were a javelin, Cotter could be as erratic as he was quick, and sadly became the only Australian Test cricketer killed in World War I.

So while Australia has produced some of the very finest batsmen ever to grace a cricket field, topped by Bradman and including current captain, Ricky Ponting, fast bowling through the ages is what has often set Australia apart. One hundred years after the first Test, this country's most charismatic fast bowler, Dennis Lillee, won an outstanding award for his fast bowling. After dominating the Centenary Test in Melbourne in 1977, to commemorate the first Test between England and Australia, Lillee was given a replica of the original medal for the best colonial bowler.

The fast bowling tradition continues today with the mellowing Glenn McGrath now the most successful fast bowler of all time. McGrath and Jason Gillespie, Australia's two leading pacemen of the past decade, are the most successful opening bowling combination ever to play for Australia, surpassing the famous pairings of Lillee and a ferocious Jeff Thomson in the 1970s, and Ray Lindwall and Keith Miller, who came to prominence during Bradman's 1948 Invincibles tour of England (see section, 'The Bradman years', earlier in the chapter).

Australia has faced two great slumps in the modern game and both revolved around two of the greatest crises to face post-war cricket in this country. The first slump came in the late 1970s when cricket was gutted by the defection of its stars to World Series Cricket. The second slump was in the mid 1980s following another defection, this time to a rebel tour of South Africa, the country banned from Test cricket from 1970 to 1991 because of its government's apartheid policy. See more on South Africa in the section, 'South Africa', later in this chapter, and Chapter 23 for more on rebel tours.

The rise and rise of Australia following its darkest cricketing period, the mid 1980s, coincided with the establishment of a cricket academy for the best young players in the country. The concept of a cricket academy has since been copied around the world and is credited as a major factor in England's return as a powerful cricketing nation. So dominant has Australia been that its two most recent captains, Steve Waugh and Ricky Ponting, have the most successful records of anyone who has ever led their country in more than ten Tests.

England

As the cradle of cricket, England rightly held the view that it was the bastion of the game. Indeed, the Marylebone Cricket Club at Lord's, the world's most famous and stuffiest cricket club, still owns the laws of cricket! For a time the MCC, established a year before the First Fleet sailed into Botany Bay in 1788 to begin European settlement in Australia, believed it owned the game. That belief wasn't unreasonable given that, until the 1970s, England toured as the MCC and the game's governing body, the International Cricket Council, was administered in paternal fashion by the hierarchy at Lord's.

Befitting its softer climate and conditions and its domination by the upper classes, cricket was always a much gentler game in England than the sport that grew up in the rough and tumble of the British colonies. Yet Englishmen of great character and skill played the game.

England had much the better of the first 25 years of Test cricket, up to the start of World War I, thanks to a host of great players, such as W.G. Grace and Wilfred Rhodes.

Between the the two world wars, Australia dominated, thanks in large part to the emergence of the exceptionally talented batsman, Don Bradman (see Chapter 21 for the ten all-time great cricketers).

After the war, the balance of power swung to and fro with England boasting master batsmen, such as Len Hutton, Peter May and Dennis Compton.

Up until the World Series split of 1977, England had played and won more Tests and been beaten less in percentage terms than any other country. Yet when World Series Cricket revolutionised the game, bringing it to a whole new audience with the mass appeal of day–night one-day matches, England's stuffy and conservative administrators refused to join in this world phenomenon. The game in England was left behind.

Despite some strong performances against weak Australian sides in the 1980s, English cricket was on the slide and it crashed in 1989 when an unheralded Australian team reclaimed the Ashes on English soil for the first time since 1934.

Ian Botham, the great England all-rounder, who was central to England's 1980s success, pointed the finger at Prime Minister Margaret Thatcher among others for selling playing fields and funding state schools so poorly that most children in England no longer played cricket.

An enormous amount of investment has taken place in English cricket in development programs and international expertise, led by former Australian wicketkeeper and academy coach, Rod Marsh, and former Zimbabwe captain, Duncan Fletcher, now the England coach. England's aim is to rebuild a sport that threatened to become a curiosity alongside the overwhelming domination of soccer.

England's surprise 2005 series victory over Australia has lifted interest in cricket in both countries to unprecedented levels, renewing the depth and significance of the game's greatest sporting rivalry. This rivalry is explored in greater detail in Chapter 17.

South Africa

South Africa was invited into the Test playing club in 1889 when England and Australia realised that they needed somebody else to play apart from each other. The Springboks, as the South African team was known in the days before racial reconciliation, proved to be tough nuts to crack, particularly on their own turf. Great Springbok players, such as all-rounder, Trevor Goddard, and batsman, Jackie McGlew, were always tough competitors against their Australian and English counterparts.

Away from home, though, the South Africans would regularly be beaten by England and Australia.

At the time, white South African society was racist, with its controversial apartheid policy splitting opinion in the cricket world. The refusal of South Africa to allow former South African 'Cape coloured' Basil d'Oliveira to tour as an English player in 1968, because he wasn't white, provoked an outcry. In 1970, the International Cricket Council banned South Africa from international cricket.

The exclusion occurred just when South African cricket was at an all-time high. The team was chock full of star players, such as Barry Richards, Graeme and Peter Pollock and Mike Procter, and had just hammered a champion Australian team 4–0.

South Africa remained banned for more than 20 years before re-admission when the winds of change saw Nelson Mandela released from jail and the political system began to change radically.

The South Africans took part in the 1992 cricket World Cup, reaching the semi finals. This set down a marker that the Proteas, as the South Africans are now called, were back as an immediate force. Their strength has been powerful pace attacks built around Allan Donald, Shaun Pollock, son of Peter, and now Makhaya Ntini, the first black African to succeed for South Africa at international level.

Gary Kirsten was a fine opening batsman and, more recently, class all-rounder Jacques Kallis was rated for a time as the best batsman in the world.

The new South Africa even managed to reach number two in the world Test cricket rankings at the turn of the millennium (see section, 'Test Cricket World Championship', later in this chapter for more on the rankings system). However, the foundations of the new South African game were seriously shaken when captain Hansie Cronje was embroiled in a match-fixing scandal (see Chapter 23 for more on this).

India and Pakistan

Such are the vagaries of cricket and politics that India and Pakistan were the same nation and therefore the same cricket team when India played its first Test in 1932. Like most new Test nations, India struggled, taking almost 20 years to win its first Test.

By then, Pakistan was a separate country, just months away from playing its own first Test. Ironically, that Test was played against India — in India.

Unlike India, Pakistan achieved a victory in Test cricket almost immediately, winning the second Test of the series.

Even so, both countries had only limited success and away from home they were often dreadful. In fact, not until 1972 did India manage to win a Test match in England.

Gradually performances by both countries improved, with India triumphing in the cricket World Cup of 1983, thanks in large part to the inspirational batting and bowling of brilliant all-rounder, Kapil Dev.

Pakistan followed India's lead by winning the World Cup in Australia in 1992. Pakistan had built an imposing side under statuesque all-rounder, Imran Khan. Imran had two of the game's fastest and most successful pacemen, Wasim Akram and Waqar Younis, although Waqar was injured for the World Cup. With batting led by the cheeky and belligerent Javed Miandad, Pakistan had become a top cricketing nation.

For much of their history, India and Pakistan have been poor teams away but often unstoppable at home because pitch conditions in both countries tended to favour spin. In Australia, the harder pitches tend to favour fast bowlers while in England, pitch conditions strongly favour seam and swing bowlers. (Refer to Chapter 8 for more on pitches.) Great spin bowlers from India's past include Bishen Bedi and, more recently, Anil Kumble.

Likewise, Pakistan has had its share of great spin bowlers, such as Abdul Qadir, and Saqlain Mushtaq, before pace took over. That pace tradition is being continued by the terrifying but temperamental Shoaib Akhtar, who at his best is regarded as the fastest bowler in the world today and possibly the fastest of all time.

India calls the World Cup to the sub-continent

While India is still building as a force on the field and is now considered one of the leading nations in Test cricket — along with England and Australia — India has become the new epicentre of world cricket. In a fanatically cricket-crazy country, which has more than a billion people, Indian dominance was inevitable. With a rapidly rising middle class, India is now said to generate as much as 70 per cent of the game's wealth. That clout means that India now virtually runs the game. Few countries dare to challenge this because they want regular tours from India for the massive television rights that are generated when cricket coverage is sold to Indian networks. As a result of this power, India demanded that the sub-continent — India, Pakistan, Sri Lanka and Bangladesh — be granted every third World Cup, cricket's major one-day cricket championship, held every four years. So in 2011, the sub-continent hosts the World Cup for the third time. England has hosted four, including the first three from 1975, with Australia and South Africa hosting one each, along with the West Indies in 2007.

To say that political relations between India and Pakistan have been a touch unfriendly over the years is something of an understatement. As recently as 2000, these two great cricket nations came close to war. However, the shared love of cricket has gone a considerable way to easing the troubles. In recent times, conflict between the two nations has been consigned to the cricket field (see Chapter 17 for more on this rivalry).

West Indies

The West Indies first played Test cricket in 1928 and, from the start, world cricket reverberated to the calypso beat. In the early years, great players such as Learie Constantine and George Headley meant that the West Indies were instantly competitive with England, although Australia triumphed easily.

But Caribbean cricket really came of age in the 1950s. Under the captaincy of John Goddard, a side brim full of talent, including a trio of great batsmen known as the three Ws — Frank Worrell, Everton Weekes and Clyde Walcott — and spinners, Alf Valentine and Sonny Ramadhin, beat England in England.

As the 1950s became the 1960s, the great all-rounder, Gary Sobers (see Chapter 21 for the Ten Greatest Cricketers) produced outstanding performances to beat England and Australia.

But, in the 1970s and 1980s, under the captaincy of first Clive Lloyd and then Vivian Richards, the West Indies became dominant, their success based on the policy of having four fast bowlers. Bowlers, such as Andy Roberts, Michael Holding, Joel Garner, Malcolm Marshall and then Curtly Ambrose and Courtney Walsh, terrified batsmen with their speed and accuracy of delivery. Thanks to this tactic, the West Indies was virtually unbeatable for the best part of two decades.

If you were reading this book a decade ago, then the story of West Indian Test cricket would have been almost totally upbeat. However, such has been the decline in cricket standards in the Caribbean over the past ten years that fears exist for the future of the game in the West Indies.

The Test side has gone from world champions to chumps in a decade, losing heavily home and away to most Test playing nations, apart from minnows Zimbabwe and Bangladesh. This slide culminated in a humiliating Test series whitewash in 2004 to England and in 2005 to Australia. Few silver linings are evident, with no great players emerging since Brian Lara, who began playing more than a decade ago. The youth of the West Indies seem keener on playing soccer than cricket.

A deep love of the game is being replaced by injured pride and indifference. The cricket authorities are hopeful that the World Cup, to be played in the West Indies in 2007, will help to reignite interest in the game.

New Zealand

The New Zealand cricket team, or Kiwis as they were known before changing their monicker to the Black Caps, began playing Test cricket in 1929, but only started to make their mark in the 1970s and 1980s. In fact, until 1973, Australia had played just one Test against New Zealand on the grounds that the Kiwis were so awful.

Then the emergence of a crop of great players, such as Glenn Turner, Martin Crowe and, in particular, all-rounder, Richard Hadlee, turned New Zealand's fortunes around. In fact, during the 1980s, the Kiwis had a strong case to be considered the second-best team in the world, behind the West Indies.

Although never quite reaching such heights again, the current Kiwi side is a good team thanks, in part, to the astute leadership of captain, Stephen Fleming. New Zealand toured Australia in 2001 under Fleming as rank underdogs but shocked the highly fancied hosts by forcing three aggressive draws and were outside chances of winning the first and third Tests.

Sri Lanka

Sri Lanka played its first Test match in 1982 and, like India and Pakistan, has relied on high quality batsmen and spin bowling for success. After initially finding the cut and thrust of Test cricket difficult, slowly but surely Sri Lanka has become a force in world cricket.

Sri Lanka's greatest triumph was winning the 1996 World Cup, helped by the exhilarating batting of Sanath Jayasuriya. More recently, the team's victories in Test cricket have been almost exclusively at home, thanks in the main to the off spin bowling of Muttiah Muralitharan.

Zimbabwe

The cricket world had high hopes when Zimbabwe was granted full Test playing status in 1992. Previous Zimbabwe teams had competed well in one-day international cricket tournaments. However, after a run of good early results, including Test victories over India and Pakistan and a 0–0 drawn series against England, Zimbabwean cricket has been dogged by infighting and player strikes. See the section, 'Understanding the Zimbabwe controversy', later in this chapter for more on the troubles in Zimbabwe.

Bangladesh

Bangladesh, the newest Test nation, was granted Test status off the back of good performances in the 1999 World Cup and on the insistence of the all-powerful Indian lobby at the International Cricket Council (ICC).

Bangladesh's performances have been, in the main, woeful, with a single Test victory over a gutted Zimbabwe and a stunning one-day international triumph over Australia the only bright spots, although the minnows pushed a tired Australia in the first Test of the 2006 series.

Teams don't just meet to play one Test match. Test nations compete in a series of Test matches — between two and five in a series. The team winning the most Test matches in the series is deemed to have won. All the scheduled matches are completed even if one side takes an unassailable lead in the series.

Australia once played six Test series against England and five Test series against a number of other countries. However, following the rise of the one-day game, adding significantly to the modern program, and an increase in the number of Test nations, almost all of Australia's series are confined to three Tests. Five Test series are still played against the most traditional rivals, England.

Test Cricket World Championship

To add further interest to Test cricket, the ICC has established a league table ranking the Test nations from best to worst based on recent performances. How points are scored is fiendishly complex. More points can be won for winning Test series against teams higher in the table. Some teams play more Tests than others so the ICC averages the points scored per Test and that constitutes the ranking and dictates where the team stands in the championship. Not surprisingly, Australia has been a clear leader since the table's inception in 2001.

A table for one-day cricket was introduced in 2002 and Australia is on top of that too!

Not only are teams ranked but players are ranked as well in Tests and one-day cricket — batsmen, bowlers and all-rounders — so you can check on exactly where your favourite players stand. Given Australia's recent success in Test and one-day cricket, lots of Australians tend to hover near the top of the player rankings.

Rankings are constantly updated so the best way to check them is on the ICC Web site (`www.icc-cricket.com`).

Because Australia was the champion side in 2005, the ICC organised a six-day Test and three one-day matches between Australia and a World XI side made up of the best players from the other Test playing nations. Australia won all the matches with such ease that the rest of the world team was criticised for lacking passion. Originally conceived to be a four-yearly clash between the champions' side and the rest of the world, the match was such a one-sided flop that it has been scrapped by the ICC. Instead a Twenty20 tournament between all the Test countries will be held in its place every four years. The first Twenty20 tournament is in South Africa in September 2007. (Refer to Chapter 3 for more on Twenty20 and one-day cricket.)

Cricket's Second Division

Cricket isn't just played in the ten Test playing nations. A host of countries field national teams.

These countries don't get to play Test cricket, which wouldn't be fair as they're not up to the standard of an Australia or England. However, the non-Test playing nations do get to compete with each other for the chance to field a team in the World Cup.

As well as the ten Test nations, including inadequate minnows, Zimbabwe and Bangladesh, the 2007 World Cup in the West Indies includes another six teams — Kenya, which has special one-day international status, Scotland, The Netherlands, Bermuda, Canada and Ireland.

These largely unheralded cricketing nations beat teams from countries including Namibia, the United Arab Emirates and the United States of America for a chance to play in the big league.

Very occasionally, when one of the second-division sides gets to play a major country in a one-day match, the second-division players will pull off a shock win. Back in 1996, Kenya beat the West Indies and, in the 2003 World Cup, the Kenyans actually made the semi finals after beating Sri Lanka. The biggest shock came in the 1983 World Cup when Zimbabwe, which was then not a Test nation, beat Australia. However, the minnows are almost always rolled over by the Test playing nations.

The smaller second-division nations are called associate members by the ICC, while Test playing countries are referred to as full members.

Stop press . . . Cricket more popular than baseball in the USA!

Our American cousins, generally, don't *get* cricket. How is it, they ask, that two teams can play a game for five days and no one wins? However, this wasn't always the case.

For a chunk of the 19th century, cricket was a big sport Stateside; some even argue that it was more popular than baseball! Lots of clubs were established in the USA, and even a national team, which played the world's first international match with Canada in 1844. In fact, the first Test match could well have been played between England and America instead of Australia — the first cricket tour by an English team to any country was to the United States of America in 1859. As late as 1932, Don Bradman was part of a private Australian team that toured the USA and Canada. But, by then, baseball had captured the hearts of Americans and cricket became a minority sport, although an estimated 10,000 cricketers still play throughout the country in local competitions. The United States cricket team has competed in major one-day tournaments. However, the game in the USA is beset by administrative problems and poor organisation. Most of the players in Team USA are drawn from ex-pat West Indian and sub-continental cricketers.

Taking in the Cathedrals of Cricket

Cricket fans are a lucky lot. They get to experience some of the most historic stadiums in the world. 'Historic' isn't code for 'dilapidated'. Many Test grounds have been redeveloped in recent years and now offer modern spectator comforts while managing to retain their own unique sense of tradition. Australians are particularly fortunate that this country has some of the largest and most modern grounds in the cricket kingdom. Most are of such a comfortable size that getting a seat is usually easy so you can watch the best players in the game doing battle in front of you. The following are Australia's current international cricket grounds, followed by some of the great stadiums on offer overseas. Go to any one of these and you are set for a unique experience.

Playing in Australia

Australia has a Test ground for every state and some more on the rise. Whether you live in one of the capital cities, or you're a country dweller who visits the city sometimes, you should take the opportunity to get along to your state's top cricket ground.

Melbourne Cricket Ground

The Melbourne Cricket Ground, the MCG, or just 'the G' as it is affectionately known, is the birthplace of Test cricket. Once described as the paddock that grew, the MCG hosted the inaugural Test back in 1877 — against England — and is now one of the largest and most imposing sporting venues on the planet.

Developed as a cricket ground in 1853, the MCG is steeped in history, yet not a brick or bolt in the new stands is older than 1992, following a massive redevelopment of the ground for the 2006 Commonwealth Games.

Also the main stadium for the 1956 Melbourne Olympic Games, the MCG has crammed in crowds of more than 121,000 to watch Australian football grand finals. Changes over the past two decades now allow the ground to hold almost 100,000 spectators in ever-increasing comfort.

Not surprisingly, the world-record crowd for a Test match day — 90,800 — is held by the MCG. Spectators packed the ground in February 1961 to watch a cavalier West Indian side at the end of the famous Test series that included a tied match (see Chapter 22 for more on cricket's first tied Test).

That crowd record is under threat after an unprecedented sellout of the first day of the now traditional MCG Boxing Day Test for the 2006–07 Ashes series against England. See Chapter 17 for more on the Ashes.

Sydney Cricket Ground

The Sydney Cricket Ground, or SCG, is another 19th-century ground with a rich history. Home over more than a century to many of Australia's finest cricketers, the SCG has hosted Test cricket since 1882, when Australia beat England — again!

Unlike Melbourne's big flash new stadium, Sydney has managed to mix the old and the new, preserving the wonderful architecture of the Members' Stand and the quaintly named Ladies' Stand.

The SCG has a smaller playing field than the MCG, offering a more intimate setting, and players often claim that the 42,000-seat arena generates the best atmosphere in the country.

Locked into a now traditional 2 January start for its main and usually only Test each year, SCG seats for the first few days often sell out so fans need to be quick to buy tickets. Unprecedented demand for the 2006–07 Ashes series saw the Test sell out less than two hours after tickets became available.

Adelaide Oval

Rightly regarded as perhaps the most picturesque Test venue in the world, Adelaide Oval has sweeping grass banks, a traditional manual scoreboard, an old members' stand and tastefully added Bradman and Chappell stands. Just walking into the ground is a joy.

Large Moreton Bay Figs offer welcome shade to those stretched out on the grass mound at the northern end, and the stunning spires of nearby St Peter's Cathedral form a wonderful backdrop. Adjacent tennis courts, playing fields, gardens and surrounding parkland enhance the sporting ambience.

And then comes the cricket, usually played on a good batting wicket and carpet-like outfield, tempting batsmen to attack the short off and leg side boundaries of this unusual, cigar-shaped arena. History and nature combine to make the Adelaide Test a delightful experience.

The Gabba, Brisbane

Named after the suburb of Woolloongabba just minutes from the city centre, the Gabba, like Brisbane, has grown up in recent years. Two decades ago, Queensland's capital city was regarded as a backwater and Queensland's major cricket ground was a motley collection of small stands with a greyhound track running around the inside of the ground. Now the Gabba, like the MCG, has plenty of history but not a stand dating back before the 1990s.

Brisbane is now a lively cosmopolitan city and the Gabba an outstanding, world-class sporting venue, which holds more than 40,000 spectators. The Gabba attracts unprecedented crowds who sit in previously unknown comfort, watching entertaining cricket played on the best pitch in the country. Once, cricket fans couldn't be bothered with Brisbane or the Gabba Test. Now both are worth a look.

The Gabba has claimed the first Test of each summer as its own. For all the players who come from long, cold winters in the southern states, nothing warms and motivates like the sun on their backs during bright November days. Players have a spring in the step as they run across the lush, warm grass. The excitement of the first Test permeates the whole crowd.

WACA Ground, Perth

The youngest of Australia's regular Test venues, Perth's WACA Ground did not host its first Test until 1970. Famed until recently for its hard, fast pitch, the Western Australian Cricket Association Ground (the WACA) was made famous by Australia's most charismatic fast bowler, Dennis Lillee. Operating from the Swan River end with the prevailing 'Fremantle Doctor', the city's famous south-westerly wind, coming over his left shoulder, Lillee terrified and tormented many batsmen while bowling for Western Australia and Australia.

Beset by decades of maladministration and wasteful redevelopments costing millions of dollars, the WACA Ground's long-term future is in doubt. Lillee and a number of other former players became so concerned about the direction of cricket in Western Australia that they led an administrative coup. Once the Wild Colonial Boy, Lillee is now, quite remarkably, president of the WACA.

The WACA is regarded by many batsmen as one of the best 'seeing' grounds in the world. That means the WACA has the best light for batting. So bright is the glare that fieldsmen usually wear sunglasses, which have become a bit of a fashion statement in the modern game.

Bellerive Oval, Hobart

With a name that is French for 'beautiful river', Bellerive Oval has the most wonderful geographical location of any major cricket ground in the country. Nestled alongside the wide and inviting, shiny-blue Derwent River, Bellerive Oval allows fans who sit high in the newly developed northern stand not only to see the cricket, but also to take in the outstanding view down the river. But be warned, sometimes even the most cloudless days in Hobart can be deceptive because the southerlies push off Antarctica and come straight up the river.

A Test ground since just 1989, Bellerive Oval has been developed into an outstanding stadium in recent years that deserves better than the occasional Test, although it hosts at least one one-day international each season. Bellerive Oval has hosted just seven Tests in 18 years but a more congested program means it is likely to be allocated a Test three out of every four years.

Darwin and Cairns

The country's two new Test venues, set amongst the unique treasures of northern Australia, have allowed international cricket to be played during the southern winter, when the traditional venues are unavailable.

The cities of Darwin and Cairns hosted the first Bangladesh tour in 2003 and Sri Lanka in 2004, proving an outstanding success and opening up the game to a whole new audience. Although problems emerged with the temporary pitch installed at Darwin's excellent Marrara Oval, the experiment as a whole was the way of the future. Rarely could you have a better holiday package than the combination of cricket and a visit to Australia's Top End.

Leading overseas grounds

England's cricket grounds are tiny when compared to most Australian venues, both in terms of the size of the playing fields and the number of spectators the grounds hold. Lord's in London is by far the largest ground, holding about 30,000. Indeed, the combined capacity of all five grounds used during Australia's 2005 tour of England add up to about the same number of spectators who can fit into the MCG — about 95,000.

Lord's, England

The world's most famous cricket ground is often referred to as 'the home of cricket'. Laid out by Thomas Lord — hence the name — in 1814, Lord's cricket ground is in a prime St John's Wood location within strolling distance of central London. Lord's is owned by the Marylebone Cricket Club (MCC). The ground was originally used by the MCC for its matches and for set piece occasions such as the annual game between Eton and Harrow schools. Lord's has hosted Test matches since 1884 and traditionally every Test playing team to tour England gets to play the host country at Lord's.

The appeal of Lord's is aesthetic as well as historic. The ground's architecture manages the rare feat of marrying up the traditional with the new. At one end of the ground stands the 19th-century pavilion with its famous Long Room. Opposite is the media centre, which looks like something out of the TV series, *Star Trek*. Somehow, it all works.

The Oval, England

The Oval is London's second cricket ground but in many respects this ground has a claim to more history even than Lord's. Australia triumphed over England in a Test match at The Oval in 1882 and the Ashes conflict was born. The Oval was also where Australia's Don Bradman made his last Test appearance in 1948. For once the great Bradman failed, bowled without scoring and thereby missed out on a career Test batting average of 100 — Bradman's Test batting average sits at 99.94.

Traditionally, the last Test match of the English summer is played at The Oval and over the years this tradition has lent a sense of drama to the Tests played there. England reclaimed the Ashes at The Oval in 1953 after nearly two decades of Australian dominance. The home side repeated the feat in 2005.

Newlands, South Africa

Newlands has plenty of history. The first Test match played at Newlands was way back in 1889.

But if awards were handed out for stunning backdrops, then Newlands cricket ground would win top billing.

Newlands is nestled in the shadow of Table Mountain in Cape Town. Nothing is quite like relaxing with a cold beer watching a game of cricket at Newlands. The experience is especially fine if you're at a floodlit one-day match, when you can see the African sun setting behind Table Mountain.

Kensington Oval, Barbados

The site of the first Test played in the West Indies in 1930, Kensington had a long and rich cricket history before the Caribbean became a major player on the international stage. Originally home of the wonderfully named Pickwick Cricket Club, Kensington Oval is regarded as the epicentre of West Indian cricket and was quite rightly awarded the final of the 2007 World Cup.

Barbados has produced many of the West Indies' finest players and along with Antigua is the most popular venue for overseas fans. Not only are these the most attractive of the major centres in the Caribbean, these grounds are also the safest. However, because of their popularity, the cost of a day at the cricket is expensive.

Eden Gardens, Calcutta

Virtually a replica of the old Melbourne Cricket Ground (MCG) before major redevelopment was carried out on the MCG in the early 1990s, this huge, round stadium is regarded by former Australian captain Steve Waugh as one of the world's great arenas. At times, Eden Gardens has probably held more than the official world record of 90,800 claimed by the MCG, only no one has bothered to count.

Estimates show that 70,000 people a day watched the amazing Test between Australia and India in 2001, when India was forced to follow-on and won. (Refer to Chapter 11 for more about the follow-on.) Needless to say, the atmosphere was electric and the noise explosive.

India can be a difficult and confronting place and Calcutta even more so. If you don't have tickets to a match at Eden Gardens through a tour group, give yourself plenty of time and patience and try to get them well before the game. Being forced into corrals by the unforgiving Calcutta police in order to buy tickets and enter the ground on match days can be a long and unpleasant experience. (See Chapter 20 for more on being a cricket fan at home and abroad.)

India, because of its large population and size, tends to use more grounds for Test cricket than any other country. Often this scenario has more to do with local cricket politics than any sort of logic. However, watching cricket in India can be a tremendous experience. The local fans are something to behold. Passionate and knowledgeable, the Indians often welcome fans from abroad into their midst. Just be sure you've got good tickets.

Troubling Times for Test Cricket

Test cricket is well over a century old and has seen plenty of ups and downs. With ten Test playing nations spanning the globe through different regions and cultures, friction is inevitable. At present, two major problems face administrators.

Understanding the Zimbabwe controversy

Zimbabwe is a country on the slide. Claims by international human rights groups against the ruling Zanu PF party, headed by President Robert Mugabe, allege vote rigging and human rights abuse. If that wasn't bad enough, the economy is in free fall and the spectre of famine hangs over large parts of the country.

Chaos has also infected Zimbabwe's cricket establishment. The nation, elected to Test match status in 1992, has suffered from a succession of controversies. First, some players have alleged that selection has been racist, with blacks favoured over whites. Second, allegations of corruption have been made against the country's cricket governing body. Both issues have led to player boycotts and a haemorrhaging of cricketing talent. In short, cricket in Zimbabwe is a mess and is showing signs of getting worse. Since 2004, the game's governing body, the International Cricket Council, has twice pressured Zimbabwe to withdraw from Test cricket for significant periods because its poor performances were harming the integrity of the game. At the time of writing this, Zimbabwe was still not back in the Test arena.

Struggling in Bangladesh

As mentioned earlier in this chapter, Bangladesh has performed very poorly since being granted Test status in 2000. The ICC has admitted that, with hindsight, the invitation to join the big league was offered too soon. Many prominent current and former Test players around the globe, including Australian captain Ricky Ponting, have suggested that Bangladesh is so bad that the team is devaluing Test cricket.

Who runs world cricket

For a large part of cricket history, the bigwigs at the Marylebone Cricket Club ran the game. They were the self-appointed 'guardians of the spirit and laws of cricket' — sounds very pompous!

The Imperial Cricket Conference was formed in 1909 with England, South Africa and Australia running the show.

The Imperial Cricket Conference eventually morphed into the International Cricket Council (ICC) by 1965. The ICC gave all the Test playing nations a say but England and Australia basically ran the game.

Today the balance of power has well and truly shifted away from Lord's and England. The ICC has moved from Lord's to Dubai. While in the corridors of power, India — with its billion-plus consumers, growing wealth and intense love of the game — is now the dominant power.

However, Bangladesh almost beat Australia in the first Test of the 2006 series, a promising sign of improvement. With a population of 120 million in a country where cricket sits alongside soccer as the major sport, hope prevails that, given time, Bangladesh can develop into a legitimate international opponent. However, the process is proving to be slow.

Breaking the Hoodoo: England's Cricket Renaissance

One of the striking aspects of international cricket in recent years has been the return to prominence of the England cricket team.

In 1999, after a 2–1 home Test series defeat to New Zealand, England was ranked the worst Test playing nation by the ICC (this was just prior to Bangladesh's admittance to the Test playing club).

English cricket had become a global joke.

But slowly at first and then more rapidly, English cricket began its rebirth on the world stage.

The old approach of chopping and changing players was ditched. Instead, the concept of Team England was born. The idea behind Team England was that the best players in the country would be identified and then developed as a team largely outside the cut and thrust of the domestic county championship (see Chapter 19 for more on domestic competitions). Top coaches, specialising in batting, bowling, fitness and fielding, were brought in to work with Team England.

Cricketing academies

Following England's 1999 defeat by New Zealand, the most promising youngsters received intense coaching at a new cricket academy built on the long-running Australian model. Indeed, the first intake for the new English academy, which included the potent all-rounder Andrew Flintoff, was actually schooled at Australia's old academy in Adelaide because the facilities in England were still being built. What's more, Australia's longstanding academy coach, former wicketkeeping great, Rod Marsh, was poached by England to coordinate the development of its cricket. (Australia's academy, now called the Centre of Excellence, is based in Brisbane, with better weather allowing outdoor playing and training most of the year.)

In short, English cricket got its act together and made the most of the player talent available.

Reviving the Ashes

England's 2–1 victory in the 2005 Ashes series was the culmination of all that hard work and has created unprecedented levels of interest in the traditional rivalry between the two countries.

Demand for tickets for the return bout in Australia in 2006–07 was overwhelming. Cricket Australia, which runs the game in this country, was forced to set up a special registry for local fans called the Australian Cricket Family. This was an attempt to stop eager English fans snapping up many of the tickets.

Tickets went on sale to members of the Australian Cricket Family on 1 June 2006 but, with more than 128,000 people registered, the system went into meltdown. Public tickets, released for the opening four days of the Sydney Test, sold out in less than two hours and by the end of the following day, the same had happened for Tests in Adelaide, Brisbane and Perth. Even Melbourne's cavernous MCG sold more than 85,000 for the first four days, with half going for the opening day, Boxing Day. In total, more than 300,000 tickets were sold in two days. Talk about rivalry! Read more about the mystique of the Ashes in Chapter 17.

Chapter 17

Taking In the Big Clashes

In This Chapter

- Exploring the magic of the Ashes
- Applauding Australia's success
- Meeting the Ashes heroes
- Fighting it out around the globe
- Putting on a big show: Cricket's World Cup
- Looking at one-day international play
- Gazing at cricket's superstars

Cricket fans are spoilt. Ten Test playing nations lock horns in Test and one-day international cricket, day in and day out around the globe. The top cricket countries compete for trophies as well as pride and money!

This chapter looks at the main international cricket clashes that have developed into intense rivalries over the years. Some great players from history are introduced as well as the superstars lighting up today's cricket firmament.

If you want to familiarise yourself with the landscape of the cricket world, this chapter is for you!

Raking over the Ashes

The *Ashes* is cricket's longest-running and most historic competition, a contest that involves only two countries, England and Australia. Every couple of years, these two countries play five Test matches to decide which team is better. Each country takes its turn to host an Ashes series and such is the aura surrounding the competition that it draws bigger crowds in Australia than any other cricket contest. Indeed, the rush for tickets approaching the 2006–07 series in Australia was unprecedented, with four of the five Tests virtually selling out within two days of the tickets becoming available!

The team that wins the most Tests in the series claims the Ashes. If the series is drawn, the team that won the previous series gets to keep the Ashes (see the next section, 'What Is the Ashes?').

Australia next tours England for an Ashes series in 2009.

What Is the Ashes?

'The Ashes' is an old English joke. The day after England was beaten by Australia in a Test match at The Oval in London during 1882, Australia's first Test victory on English soil, the English newspaper, *The Sporting Times*, published the following mock obituary:

> *'In affectionate remembrance of English cricket, which died at the Oval, 29th August 1882, deeply lamented by a large circle of sorrowing friends and acquaintances. RIP. N.B. The body will be cremated and taken to Australia.'*

The following summer, England managed to beat Australia in Melbourne and two women are said to have burnt a *cricket bail* (one of two small pieces of wood that rest on top of the stumps). The women put them into a tiny urn and, after England won in Sydney, presented the urn to the captain of the England cricket team, the wonderfully named . . . the Honourable Ivo Bligh (in those days, the poshest toff in the England team was usually made captain. Even if they couldn't play, they knew how to pass the port correctly!). See Chapter 18 for more on the contribution women made to the Ashes.

Where is the urn?

The original urn is very fragile and has been stuck in the cricket museum at Lord's in London for 80 years — where the curators charge people to see it (see Figure 17-1). In fact, despite Australia technically holding this revered trophy for large chunks of the past century, the urn has only been allowed to visit Australia twice — once in 1988 for a special Test played in Sydney to mark the bicentenary of European settlement in Australia, and again for the highly anticipated 2006–07 season.

When victorious captains are shown holding and kissing the tiny urn, which fits comfortably between the thumb and index finger, what you see is only a replica. Cricket Australia, at its headquarters in Melbourne, has a replica in a clear perspex box, which is trotted out for photo opportunities.

Figure 17-1: The fragile urn that holds the Ashes, which Australia wins but rarely brings home.

What makes the Ashes unique?

For most of the first hundred years of Test cricket, the Ashes contest was the only clash that mattered. England and Australia were the best two cricket nations on the planet — not that hard, as up until the 1920s only three countries played Test cricket. Therefore, games between these two countries were considered the pinnacle of the sport.

Several factors have helped fan the flames of Ashes competition:

- **The colonial issue:** Australians love beating the English and vice versa. For a long time, more rabid Australians saw the English as stuck up and condescending. On the flipside, some of the English played up to this stereotype by regarding the Australians as uncultured. As recently as the 1992 World Cup in Australia, the great English all-rounder, Ian Botham, joked that nothing would be better than England beating Australia in front of 100,000 convicts, a reference to Australia's European beginnings as a penal colony. However, despite occasional name-calling, deep down a great respect exists between the teams.
- **Infrequency of Test cricket:** Fewer Test matches were played in the first half of the 20th century with cricket fans on both sides feasting on the deeds of the great players in Ashes battles. When the matches were played at home, fans would cram into the grounds; when played away, fans would have to wait for newspaper reports and newsreels in the cinemas. During the early decades of Test cricket, the crowds, sometimes numbering in their thousands, would gather outside newspaper offices in Australia's capital cities for the latest word on Australia's matches played in other states or in England.
- **Almost always competitive:** For most of its history, Ashes Test matches have been extremely hard-fought contests. No one side could ever relax because they knew the other was always up for the fight. This competitiveness made most Ashes series compulsive viewing for spectators.

Ashes contests have not been without their controversy. The grand-daddy of them all was the infamous 'bodyline' tour of 1932–33, when England's fast bowlers aimed their deliveries at the bodies of the Australian batsmen with the hope that they would hit the ball in the air to fielders placed on the leg side. The tactics of the England team caused a furore in Australia and damaged diplomatic relations between the countries. (See Chapter 23 for more on this episode.)

In recent years, some commentators suggested that the Ashes contests were losing their appeal. The reason — Australia was so much better than England after 16 years of one-sided domination that it wasn't a proper contest anymore. These commentators had a point. However, England's triumph in the 2005 Ashes series and the way that cricket caught the popular imagination has shown that plenty of life still exists in the clashes between these two great cricketing nations.

In many respects, much of the chronicle of cricket is tied up in the Ashes. (Refer to Chapter 16 for more on the story of how cricket grew from a game played in the south-east of England to a major global sport.)

Unlocking the Secrets of Australian Success

For the majority of cricket Tests, Australia has dominated the cricketing world, which, until 30 years ago, basically meant England. Theories abound as to why Australia is so successful. Here are some of the most plausible:

- **Warm climate:** The Australian climate is warm and sunny, helping to breed an outdoors culture.
- **Competitive culture:** Cricket in Australia is often played in a tougher environment than in England, even at the local park.
- **Better organised structure:** Australian cricket has a clear path from the smallest juniors right through to the national team. Anyone who shines at local club level can join the major club competition in their capital city, usually called grade, district or premier cricket. State sides are selected from these major club competitions and from state sides the national team. (Refer to Chapter 15 for more on climbing the pyramid.)
- **Greater emphasis on junior development:** When Australian cricket collapsed to a rare low point in the mid 1980s, the country's administrators vowed this would never be allowed to happen again. An academy to develop the best young talent in the country was established in Adelaide and elite under-aged champions were streamlined to ensure the cream of the young cricketers rose to the top. Australia has not looked back, with most of the cricketing world following Australia's lead. England's recent success is based around developing and improving the Australian model, including pinching Australian coaches.

- **Strong domestic competition:** Just six states competing in Australia's major domestic competition ensures a far greater concentration of talent, making it a significantly tougher contest than England's domestic county championship, which has 18 teams.
- **Success breeds success:** Heroes inspire the next generation of sportsmen and Australia has had heroes a-plenty on the cricket field from the time the great fast bowler Fred Spofforth stepped onto the field in 1877 for the second Test between Australia and England. And nothing is quite like playing for your country. In Australia, this overwhelmingly means one team, the Australian cricket team. While Australia's Wallabies have a strong following in rugby union, the sport is largely confined to two states — New South Wales and Queensland. The Australian cricket team is all encompassing. This contrasts with England, where most youngsters want to be David Beckham and captain their country in football.

Gazing at Ashes Heroes

Australia may have had the best of its Ashes battles with England, but over the years both sides have produced their fair share of Ashes heroes.

In this section, you meet a number of these heroes, some past and some more recent.

Australia's Ashes heroes

Many legendary cricketers have contributed to Australia's record of Ashes wins but a few stand out for their style, charisma and exceptional feats.

Donald Bradman

The biggest battle in Test cricket is for the Ashes and the biggest name in cricket is Bradman. For two decades either side of World War II, Don Bradman put bowlers to the sword like no other batsman before or since. The Don, as he was nicknamed, was unquestionably the greatest batsman of all time and helped Australia dominate for most of his era. His achievements are looked at in greater detail in Chapter 21.

Dennis Lillee

Lillee was a thoroughbred among fast bowlers. He could bowl at lightning pace yet rarely lost accuracy, thanks in large part to his well honed and rhythmical bowling action. Lillee terrified batsmen around the globe throughout the 1970s and early 1980s, taking 355 Test wickets. When Lillee retired in 1984, this number of Test wickets was the most by any bowler.

Allan Border, Mark Taylor and Steve Waugh

These three players were successive captains of Australia and they managed to win every Ashes series from 1989 to 2003. All three led by example, scoring lots of runs. Under the astute leadership of Border, Taylor and Waugh, Australia became and has stayed the world's best cricket team.

Shane Warne

In 1993 at Old Trafford cricket ground, Manchester, Shane Warne became an instant legend with his first ball in an Ashes Test. The leg spinner spun the ball a huge distance, bowling England's best player of spin, Mike Gatting. This was dubbed 'the ball of the century', by the press. Ever since, Warne has been tormenting England's batsmen. See the section, 'Shane Warne', later in this chapter for more on the Warne phenomenon.

England's Ashes heroes

England may not be able to claim Bradman and Warne among its ranks but some very fine cricketers have represented the Old Dart. A handful of the best are listed below.

Jack Hobbs

Before the arrival of Don Bradman, Jack Hobbs was the genius batsman that every Englishman tried to emulate. In a long and glorious career, Hobbs scored an incredible world record 197 centuries in first-class cricket matches. In Tests, his run scoring prowess — particularly against Australia — was no less impressive and for this reason Hobbs is the only Englishman to make it into the *Cricket For Dummies* 'Ten Greatest Cricketers' (see Chapter 21).

Len Hutton

The finest opening batsman of his generation, Len Hutton, at the age of just 23, broke the record for the highest individual score in a Test match playing against Australia. His 364 runs helped England to a rare triumph over the Australians — although Bradman was out of the team injured at the time. Hutton's career was curtailed by the start of World War II but, after the war, he became one of England's best captains — taking his team to Australia and beating the home team in a Test series.

Ian Botham

Botham is one of the great all-rounders in cricket history and was the scourge of Australia during three Ashes series in 1985, 1987 and, most particularly, 1981. Sacked as captain after the second Test of the 1981 Ashes series, Botham went berserk with bat and ball, scoring centuries and taking wickets galore. Almost single-handedly, the incredibly powerful Botham won the Ashes, capturing the imagination of the entire country.

Developing International Rivalries

England and Australia don't have a monopoly on cricket rivalry. With ten Test playing nations, other major contests can also draw in the crowds.

The ten Test nations playing each other are Australia, England, South Africa, West Indies, New Zealand, India, Pakistan, Sri Lanka, Zimbabwe and Bangladesh.

Nowadays the international cricket schedule is very crowded. Barely a day goes by without two of the ten Test playing nations squaring off against one another in a Test or one-day international. In previous eras, entire years passed when no Test matches were played.

Pakistan versus India: The sub-continent's 'Ashes'

The Ashes may be the oldest and most historic Test series, but the contests between India and Pakistan have a claim to be the most exciting and colourful in world cricket.

Whenever Pakistan and India meet — whether in a one-day international or Test match — more than just the result of a cricket match is at stake. If one side beats the other, the losing country's national pride takes a real hit. Fans have even been known to riot following their team's defeat.

The reason for passions running so high isn't difficult to fathom. Pakistan was once part of India but, since partition in 1947, these countries have been political and military rivals. This rivalry has been fuelled by the fact that Pakistan is a Muslim country while India is mostly Hindu. When these two countries meet, the media interest is intense. Upwards of 500 journalists accompanied the 2006 visit of the Indian cricket team to Pakistan.

But don't go thinking that India versus Pakistan cricket matches are simply a war. The cricket is usually of the very highest quality with talented batsmen and bowlers on both sides.

In England and Australia, cricket has to vie with other sports for popular attention. But in India and Pakistan, cricket is the number-one sport — a bit like soccer in Brazil.

The clash of the titans: Australia versus West Indies

The West Indies were the best team in the world during the late 1970s and 1980s but eventually their crown was snatched by the Australian team. Throughout the 1990s, a riveting battle for top spot took place between these two cricketing powers for the Frank Worrell trophy. The West Indies had two great fast bowlers — Curtly Ambrose and Courtney Walsh — as well as the batting brilliance of Brian Lara, while the Australians had Shane Warne, Glenn McGrath and Steve Waugh. These contests took on epic proportions. In 1995, Australia beat the West Indies in the West Indies to end more than 15 years of Caribbean world domination and claim what was then the unofficial title of the best Test team in the world. Australia has retained the title ever since as West Indian cricket continues to slide.

Renewing hostilities: South Africa versus Australia

When South Africa was suspended from international cricket in 1970 — as a protest against the country's racist apartheid policy — the Springboks, as they were then known, had just become the best team in the world by thrashing Australia. After 21 years in the wilderness, South Africa was re-admitted to international cricket in 1991 and proved instantly competitive. Every time South Africa has played Australia since, a strong sporting hostility in both nations' newspapers precedes the real thing on the field. Although the matches between these two countries have always been hard fought, the Australians have usually continued to come out on top — much to the annoyance of the Proteas, as the South Africans are now known.

Chappell calls the ultimate 'Ashes'

Former great Australian batsman and captain, Greg Chappell, who is now coach of India, describes India–Pakistan clashes as being 'like the Ashes multiplied by 1000'. Speaking during the 2006 Indian tour of Pakistan, Chappell claimed that in 40 years of cricket he had never come across anything that matched the hysteria generated when these two nations clash. 'Unless you've experienced it, you've simply got no idea how big this is,' Chappell said.

Crossing the final frontier: Australia versus India

During the late 1990s and across the turn of the millennium, the Australians were beating every cricket team around the world — with one very big exception. No matter how hard Australia tried, the team couldn't beat India in India. Steve Waugh, the former Australian captain, described winning a Test series in India as the final frontier — very *Star Trek*. In 2001, the two teams played a three-match Test series, which Australia, under the captaincy of Steve Waugh, looked set to win. However, an amazing fight-back by India snatched victory from the Australians (see Chapter 22).

In 2004, Australia finally managed to cross the last frontier and beat India in a Test series on the sub-continent. But, by then, Steve Waugh had retired. Adam Gilchrist, deputising for an injured Ricky Ponting, was the triumphant skipper.

Australia and India compete for the Border–Gavaskar trophy, named after two former great players — Allan Border from Australia and Sunil Gavaskar from India.

Great individual performances and Test matches help build the mystique around the contests between Test nations.

Each April, the *Wisden Cricketers' Almanack* is published. Among other facts, the *Almanack* contains details on all the Test and one-day international matches played around the world in the previous year. The *Almanack* is often referred to as cricket's bible, with editions running to nearly 1,800 pages. That's a lot of cricketing trivia to take in!

Taking a Look at the World Cup

Every four years, cricket teams from all the Test playing nations and other selected countries compete in the World Cup.

During the World Cup, the teams play each other in one-day internationals. Eventually, after what has become almost two months of matches, two teams play in a final and the winner is crowned world champion.

In one-day international matches, each side has one innings limited to 50 overs. An *over* is made up of six deliveries, therefore during an innings lasting 50 overs, 300 deliveries are bowled. (Refer to Chapter 3 for more on how one-day cricket matches work.)

In one-day cricket, bowlers are limited to bowling one fifth of the total number of overs in an innings — ten overs. As a result, at least five players have to bowl in an innings. The fielding captain decides which players bowl.

In one-day international cricket, the fielding captain is forced to keep most fielders within 30 metres of the batsman during at least the first ten overs of the innings. This gives batsmen the incentive to play aggressive shots as fewer fielders are stationed near the boundary to catch the ball. As a result many teams now employ a *pinch-hitter* — a batsman who is famed for being able to play aggressive shots to take advantage of the fielding restrictions. (Refer to Chapter 11 for more on one-day tactics.)

Grabbing instant headlines

The first three World Cups, in 1975, 1979 and 1983, were held in England. For the first time, non-Test playing nations, such as Sri Lanka (first Test 1982), Zimbabwe (first Test 1992) and Canada were able to compete in a major event alongside the leading cricket countries. The first World Cup even included a side called East Africa, made up mainly of players from Kenya and Tanzania, many of Indian decent. Kenya has subsequently been granted full one-day international status, although dreadful administration and lack of finance has held back Kenya's development as a cricketing nation.

In 1975, the one-day international cricket format was in its infancy and many teams still hadn't cottoned on to the fact that special tactics were needed to win. Teams tended to play the same players that they selected for Test cricket and then hope for the best. The tournament was set alight by a magnificent final between the West Indies and Australia, which went long into the lingering English twilight before the West Indies finally triumphed amid pandemonium from excited West Indian fans. (See Chapter 22 for more on this wonderful match.)

The West Indies also won the second tournament, beating England in the final, and by that stage, the West Indies was clearly the best team in the world. In 1983, India caused a major upset by beating the West Indies in the final, thanks in part to the brilliance of all-rounder, Kapil Dev.

The 1987 tournament in India and Pakistan was the first to be held outside England. Teams started to select players who were adept at playing the one-day format rather than relying on the talent of Test cricketers. Rank outsiders at the start of the tournament after several years in the doldrums, Australia was the surprise winner, beating England in a tense final.

Stumbling in Australia

Australia has been a major force in World Cups, which makes the home team's poor performance during the only time this country hosted the event, in 1992, all the more disappointing. As reigning title holder, Australia failed to make the semi finals. All eight Test playing nations took part, as well as Zimbabwe. All nine sides played each other once, in a round-robin format. Ultimately, the four teams that won the most matches made it through to the semi finals. Pakistan won the cup after beating England in yet another close final — England's third World Cup final loss in four tournaments.

The 1996 tournament, played at grounds in India, Pakistan and Sri Lanka, was noted for its tactical innovation. Captains and coaches had at last worked out different tactics for one-day cricket. Eventually Sri Lanka beat Australia in the final, due in large part to their use of a pinch-hitter at the top of the order. This impressive performance signalled Sri Lanka's coming of age as a cricketing nation.

Dominating in England and Africa

The last two tournaments in 1999 and 2003, hosted by England and South Africa respectively, have seen Australia claim an unrivalled place in World Cup history by winning both tournaments in vastly different circumstances.

In 1999, Australia played poorly in the early matches and pressure mounted on Steve Waugh, who was in danger of losing the captaincy of the one-day team if Australia failed in the tournament. A magnificent back-to-the-wall century by Waugh against South Africa, when all looked lost, turned the team's fortunes around and set up an amazing semi final against South Africa later in the tournament. Australia stole a stunning tie amid mass hysteria; a tie was enough to claim a place in the final, where Australia easily beat Pakistan. (See Chapter 22 and 24 for more on these matches.)

The story was completely different in 2003 but with the same result. Ricky Ponting led the team to an unprecedented ten successive victories before blazing a whirlwind century against India in the final to easily triumph without losing a single match (see Figure 17-2).

But the 2003 tournament in Africa was dogged with controversy. Zimbabwe players Andy Flower and Henry Olonga, at great personal risk, donned black arm bands to protest the death of democracy in Zimbabwe. England refused to play a game in Zimbabwe because of safety fears, and New Zealand took the same attitude towards playing Kenya in Nairobi. With this win by default and then a stunning upset win over Sri Lanka, Kenya made the semi finals, but this was more a reflection on the muddled tournament than Kenya's modest place in the cricketing world.

Figure 17-2: Victory: Australian captain Ricky Ponting with the 2003 World Cup.

Criticism surrounded the expansion of the World Cup from 12 to 14 teams, with the addition of more cricketing minnows, such as The Netherlands and Namibia. The major problem was not the number of teams but the format. Divided into two groups of seven, each nation played the other six in their group, making for many meaningless, lopsided games.

The tournament has now been expanded to 16 teams for the 2007 World Cup in the West Indies but thankfully the format has changed again. Four groups of four have replaced two groups of seven, allowing only three matches in each group, with the top two teams from each group going through to a final eight, when the real competition starts. The ten Test nations plus Kenya, which has one-day international status, are automatic selections. However, the remaining five second-tier countries, known as associates, must qualify in an associates tournament. The five associate countries that qualified for the 2007 World Cup are Scotland, The Netherlands, Bermuda, Canada and Ireland.

Examining How the World Cup Works

The 16 teams that start the World Cup are narrowed down to eight, then four, two and finally a champion side emerges.

To win the cricket World Cup, a team needs to negotiate each of these three barriers:

- Qualify from the round-robin pool
- Finish as one of the top four teams in the Super Eight round
- Win the semi final and final matches.

Qualifying from the pool

The 16 teams taking part in the World Cup are divided into four groups of four. The teams in these groups play each other, and the teams finishing first and second go through to the Super Eight.

Setting up the Super Eight

The four group winners and runners-up make it through to the Super Eight. Here, the tournament mathematics start to become very, very complex.

Teams qualifying for the Super Eight take the points they score, against their fellow qualifiers for the Super Eight, into the new round of matches. What is more, teams that play each other in the group stage, don't play again in the Super Eight.

Here's how it can work in practice: Team A and team B play in the same group and both qualify for the Super Eight. In the group stage, team A beats team B so, therefore, in the Super Eight stage of the competition, team A starts with 2 points and team B with none. Team A and team B then play the other teams to qualify in the Super Eight, but they don't play each other.

Once the round of Super Eight matches is complete, the four placed at the top of the Super Eight table qualify for the semi finals.

Going for the trophy

The tournament now becomes simple again. Thank goodness! The team finishing the Super Eight with the most points plays the team finishing fourth, while the second- and third-placed teams play one another. Two winners emerge from the semi final matches to go on and compete in the World Cup final match but only one team will get the glory.

Looking at One-Day International Tournaments

One-day cricket usually has a far wider appeal than Test cricket. In Australia, matches involving Australia over the summer usually sell out in all the capital cities except Melbourne, where the 95,000-capacity Melbourne Cricket Ground has plenty of seats. One-day cricket is huge on the sub-continent, therefore lots of tournaments have sprung up around the globe looking to cash in.

The Asia Cup

Every couple of years, teams from India, Sri Lanka, Pakistan, Bangladesh, Hong Kong and the United Arab Emirates compete in a one-day international tournament. The teams compete in two groups of three, with the two top teams in each group going through to a semi final and then the final. The winner of the Asia Cup is usually one of the big three — India, Pakistan or Sri Lanka — and gets the continent's bragging rights.

The Australian triangular series

Marketing people in Australia cottoned onto the money-making potential of one-day international cricket long before their English counterparts. Since the late 1970s, Australia has played two other Test playing nations each summer in a round-robin tournament. Teams play each other up to eight times before a 'best of three' finals series.

England's NatWest series

This series is the belated English equivalent of the Australian one-day series. Each summer, since 2000, two Test playing nations have come to England to compete with the hosts. Each team plays the other two six times, and at the end of this round robin, the top two teams make it through to the final, which is played at Lord's. Sadly, England isn't that good at one-day cricket and often fail to make the final of the NatWest series.

Virtually all one-day international cricket is now televised. Interestingly, the administrators running cricket can expect to gain far more cash from selling the rights to broadcast cricket than they can from charging spectators at the ground.

No Test match equivalent to the Australia and England triangular series exists. Test matches take up to five days, making it impractical to run a series of round-robin matches. However, a world Test championship table, based on how Test teams perform home and away against each other, over a period of four years, ranks all the nations from best to worst. (Refer to Chapter 16 for more on this.)

The Champions Trophy

In 1998, the International Cricket Council (ICC), the body that runs world cricket, decided that another major one-day tournament was needed to raise money for developing the game in countries where cricket is a relatively minor sport. As a result, the Champions Trophy was born and is held every second year. Formats have changed regularly and, in 2006, the competition was reduced to include only eight of the ten Test nations.

The new format sees eight teams split into two groups of four with the top two teams from each group qualifying for the semi finals and final. Of the eight teams, the top six sides on the ICC's one-day championship table (refer to Chapter 16 and the ICC's Web site, `www.cricket-icc.com`, for more) are automatic starters. The remaining four Test nations, ranked seven to ten on the ICC's one-day championship table, have a round-robin play-off before the tournament to fill the last two places in the Champions Trophy.

Looking at the World's Leading Cricketers

The world's great tournaments — from the Ashes to the World Cup — are a showcase for the leading cricketers.

So that you can easily familiarise yourself with the movers and shakers in world cricket, the following sections give you the low-down on some of the game's current superstars.

The finest batsmen

In a tradition created by greats, such as Victor Trumper and the incomparable Don Bradman, Australia continues to boast supreme batsmen.

Ricky Ponting (Australia)

The Australian captain is on course to smash all sorts of career records and become the most productive batsman of all time. Aged only 31 leading into the much anticipated 2006–07 Ashes series, Ricky Ponting was already eighth on the list of leading Test run-scorers and ninth in one-day games, with his rapid progress up both tables likely to continue.

What's more, Ponting was listed as the best Test batsman in the world at that stage by the official ICC rankings and was third on the one-day table.

At his best, Ponting dominates the bowlers, hitting powerful, perfectly timed shots to all parts of the ground. He is a player who, when he runs into form, can absolutely destroy bowling. His match-saving 156 at Old Trafford, Manchester, in the 2005 Ashes series is rated by many to be one of the best individual innings played in modern Test cricket.

Matthew Hayden (Australia)

A tall, hard-hitting opening batsman, Matthew Hayden is famed for his ability to dominate bowlers. Following a disappointing Ashes series in 2005, he came back strongly, scoring successive centuries against the West Indies and South Africa. Hayden averages well over 50 runs each time he bats and had scored a remarkable 26 centuries in Test cricket heading into the 2006–07 season.

Rahul Dravid (India)

Rahul Dravid is probably the best defensive batsman in the world. He is an outstanding judge of when to play an aggressive or defensive shot. However, this is not to say that he is a boring batsman. His execution of aggressive shots is one of the great sights in cricket. He is a superb Test batsman, averaging more than 50 runs per innings. On top of this, Dravid is a brilliant one-day international player, able to play aggressive shots when the match situation requires.

Sachin Tendulkar (India)

Along with Brian Lara (see the end of this roll call), Sachin Tendulkar is one of the great batsmen of his or any other generation. From the day of his Test debut, aged just 16, Tendulkar stood out as a special talent. Opponents fear him but marvel at the artistry of his batting. When in form, he has the rare ability, along with the select group of truly great batsmen, of hitting well directed deliveries to the boundary when most batsmen would simply defend them. He is still relatively young, meaning he could end up breaking all sorts of records, although his career was stalled by long-term injuries in 2005 and 2006.

Virender Sehwag (India)

When he first came into Test cricket, Virender Sehwag was dubbed 'little Tendulkar' because, with his stature and the way he stands at the crease, he is the spitting image of the great Indian batsman. However, Sehwag soon moved out of Tendulkar's shadow, scoring century after exhilarating century. He is the first Indian batsman to score more than 300 runs in one innings and averages more than 50 runs each time he bats in Test cricket.

Inzamam-Ul-Haq (Pakistan)

Inzamam-Ul-Haq, or 'Inzie' as he is affectionately known, doesn't look like much of a sportsman. To put it politely, he's a little on the large side and moves like a supertanker when fielding and running between the wickets. But when Inzamam is batting, his footwork is superb, belying his size. He is a wonderful striker of a cricket ball, able, with unerring regularity, to guide the ball wide of fielders to the boundary. He is also showing himself to be a clever, thoughtful captain of an improving Pakistan team.

Kevin Pietersen (England)

Although he has played in only a handful of Test matches, the South African born Kevin Pietersen has made a huge impact. His 158 at The Oval in the final Test of the 2005 series against Australia returned the Ashes to England for the first time in 16 years. Pietersen is an incredibly potent batsman, willing to back his own ability and attack the bowling. He smashed three centuries in his first 11 one-day matches, has the amazing strike rate of almost a run a ball and averages an untouchable 65 runs every time he goes out to bat in one-day cricket. He is a natural gambler; sometimes it pays off, sometimes not. Whatever the outcome, though, Pietersen is always exciting to watch.

Brian Lara (West Indies)

One of the most accomplished batsmen of his generation, Brian Lara is natural talent personified. When all goes well, Lara is able to hit good deliveries to the boundary and put together monumental innings. Remarkably, he holds the records for the highest individual scores in Test match and first-class cricket and the most number of runs in a Test career. His captaincy has been less spectacular and he has been accused of being self-absorbed, but that is so often the case with genius.

Dominating all-rounders

Usually a great player becomes famous because of one potent skill. This player either bats with supreme skill and timing, or bowls with heart and guile to triumph with the ball. Players who can dominate more than one of cricket's disciplines at international level are a rare and valuable breed. These players are the all-rounders.

Andrew Flintoff (England)

Andrew 'Freddie' Flintoff is an electrifying cricketer. A hard-hitting batsman and aggressive fast bowler, he has stamped himself as one of the most damaging and dangerous players in the game today. He had a remarkable Ashes series in 2005 and has continued with the same high-octane performances. If there was a world's strongest cricketer competition, Flintoff would win. His strength makes him capable of devastating hitting while batting, and allows him to deliver the ball at considerable speed. However, Flintoff has more to his game than brute force. He is an astute player, able to spot his opponents' weaknesses and adjust his playing to take advantage. To cap it all, he is also one of best slip fielders in the world and, in 2006, was appointed acting England captain in place of the injured Michael Vaughan. All in all, Flintoff has a shot at joining the all-time greats.

Adam Gilchrist (Australia)

Adam Gilchrist is the best wicketkeeper–batsman ever to play the game. Over the past decade, he has dominated bowlers from around the world, hitting centuries at an incredible pace. A recent poll of Test bowlers found that Gilchrist was the batsman they feared bowling to most. Gilchrist is a force of nature as a batsman and an excellent wicketkeeper. He is one of only two current players to make it into the top-ten cricketers of all time. (See Chapter 21 for more.)

Striking bowlers

Batsmen may disagree, but the most important player in any team is a really good bowler. Without imposing bowlers, a team always struggles to win matches, no matter how good their batsmen are. Here are some of the best match winners in the business.

Glenn McGrath (Australia)

The veteran Australian fast bowler could lay claim to being one of the all-time greats. In the past decade, he has taken more than 500 wickets in Test matches. Glenn McGrath is certainly the most accurate fast bowler in the world, seemingly able to land the ball anywhere he wants on the pitch at will. His bowling has often been described as metronomic, such is his unerring accuracy.

Shaun Pollock (South Africa)

The South African seam bowler is akin to Glenn McGrath's double. Like the great Australian, Shaun Pollock relies on accuracy with his bowling. Pollock doesn't blast batsmen out with raw pace; instead he frustrates them and encourages them to make mistakes. It definitely seems to work. Pollock had taken nearly 400 Test wickets leading into the 2006–07 season. And, as a batsman, Pollock is no mug either, having scored Test centuries.

Muttiah Muralitharan (Sri Lanka)

Muttiah Muralitharan's record in Test and one-day international cricket is outstanding. He has taken more than 1,000 wickets in Test and one-day international matches combined. He is an off spinner who can put extraordinary rotation on the ball at delivery, due in part to being double jointed. His bowling arm is also crooked and this has led to accusations that his bowling action is illegal. In essence, the critics claim he throws the ball rather than bowls it. However, biomechanics testing at the University of Western Australia has cleared most of his deliveries and few would dispute the quality of Muralitharan's bowling.

Brett Lee (Australia)

The blond Australian fast bowler has put his tearaway days behind him, and with greater maturity, his bowling has become more accurate of late. Lee doesn't just rely on electrifying pace to capture his wickets in Test and one-day matches; he is also capable of getting the cricket ball to swing.

Shane Warne (Australia)

Probably the greatest spin bowler of all time and one of only two players from the current crop to make it into the ten greatest cricketers (see Chapter 21). The key to Warne's success, as a leg spin bowler, is his great accuracy, enormous self belief, and ability to fool batsmen with subtle variations. (Refer to Chapter 8 for more on leg spin bowling.) Warne is also incredibly astute, often able to spot a batsman's technical weaknesses in a matter of moments. No surprise, therefore, that Warne had almost 700 Test wickets heading into the 2006–07 season and is showing no signs of stopping.

Steve Harmison (England)

Steve Harmison is the fast bowler English cricket has been waiting years for. When on song, Harmison is an impressive sight, able to make the ball bounce sharply off the pitch. In 2004, after breaking the English record for the number of wickets captured in a calendar year, he was rated the best bowler in the world. Since, however, he has been slightly off the boil and struggled with injuries, although his skills and attributes suggest he will continue to be a potent force.

Shoaib Akhtar (Pakistan)

Shoaib Akhtar vies with Brett Lee for the mantle of world's fastest bowler. He has been clocked as bowling a cricket ball at more than 160 kph. But his bowling isn't just about raw pace. He showed, in Pakistan's 2006 home Test series victory over England, great ability to swing the ball in the air. Shoaib has always had a fiery temperament and the occasional run-in with cricket authorities. However, his athletic run-up and robust action make him exciting to watch.

Anil Kumble (India)

Since his debut in 1990, Anil Kumble has quietly built a phenomenal Test career. He is a leg spin bowler like Warne, but doesn't spin the ball as much as the great Australian. Kumble relies on varying the pace of his deliveries to bamboozle the batsmen. He rarely fails to take a wicket and has managed to chalk up more than 500 Test wickets during his illustrious career.

Chapter 18

The World of Women's Cricket

In This Chapter

- Watching women play cricket
- Taking cricket to the world
- Playing one-dayers
- Enjoying women's cricket in Australia
- Meeting cricket's best
- Following women's cricket on the Net
- Playing in Australia

Many who watch cricket's intense summer struggles without seeing a single woman in the heat of battle on television, or at Australia's major cricket grounds, may hold the mistaken belief that cricket is a man's game. Nothing could be further from the truth.

Although women may not dominate the highlights or headlines, their cricketing history is almost as long and deep as that of the men. Opportunities for girls and young women to play cricket in Australia have never been so plentiful.

This chapter examines the rich story of women's cricket, reveals the important contribution women have made to cricket, introduces Belinda Clark, the former Australian women's captain, and tells of a woman's journey, Clark's journey, through the sport of cricket.

As well, Clark offers practical tips for would-be cricketers and girls and women already playing the game.

So, if you want to find out more about the fascinating impact of women's cricket on Australian sport — how you can become involved, or how you can enjoy women's cricket from the sidelines — read on.

Bowling Cricket Over

If world cricket authorities were ever looking for someone to honour with a major trophy, they should look past famous legends of the game, such as W.G. Grace and Don Bradman, to an unknown woman called Christina Willes. From Canterbury in south-east England, Miss Willes is credited with creating the foundation for the modern game 200 years ago.

Christina Willes, sister of Kent cricketer, John Willes, is believed to have been the first person to deliver a cricket ball overarm, some time in the early 1800s. Until then, underarm bowling was the only legal way to deliver a ball in cricket. Indeed, overarm bowling was not allowed by the game's law makers until 1864, when cricket was very well established in both England and Australia.

But overarm bowling was not the only important initiative invented by women's cricket. In 1973, the first women's World Cup was staged in England, with seven teams from five nations competing, including a combined international side that included women from a number of different countries. The first women's World Cup was staged two years before the first World Cup for men took place, also in England.

Christina bowls against the fashion of the day

The story goes that when bowling to her brother, John, in the garden at home, Miss Willes found herself inconvenienced by her large, lead-weighted dress, which prevented her from performing the underarm action. Elevating the arm to just above waist height, she was able to deliver the ball without interference from her attire.

John Willes immediately recognised the possibilities of this new style of bowling and began using it in major matches, creating much controversy.

So every time you watch Australian fast bowler, Brett Lee, charging in with the crowd roaring behind him, or record-breaking spinner, Shane Warne, casting his spell over another batsman, remember it was a young woman giving her brother batting practice that made it all possible.

Eleven maids a'batting

The first recorded women's match was reported in *The Reading Mercury* on 26 July 1745 and took place between the towns of Bramley and the famous old cricketing centre of Hambledon near Guildford in Surrey. The *Mercury* reported:

'The greatest cricket match that was played in this part of England was on Friday, the 26th of last month, on Gosden Common, near Guildford, between eleven maids of Bramley and eleven maids of Hambledon, all dressed in white. The Bramley maids had blue ribbons and the Hambledon maids red ribbons on their heads. The Bramley girls got 119 notches and the Hambledon girls 127. There was of bothe sexes the greatest number that ever was seen on such an occasion. The girls bowled, batted, ran and catched as well as most men could do in that game.'

Looking at the earliest days

Women have been playing cricket for more than 250 years. In those early days, matches were held between villages, or married women played against single women, and the winning prize was often either a barrel of ale or a pair of lace gloves.

English ladies pull in the crowds

The first women's cricket club was formed in 1887 at Nun Appleton in Yorkshire and named the White Heather Club. Three years later, the only record of women ever playing professionally suddenly appeared. In response to a newspaper advertisement by a Mr Matthews, two teams were formed.

Known as the Original English Lady Cricketers, the teams travelled up and down England, accompanied by a chaperone and a manager, playing in exhibition matches to large crowds on well known grounds. Their first match pulled in 15,000 spectators. No player was permitted to play under her proper name and each was given sixpence a day expense money and provided with uniforms — red for one team and blue for the other. Despite their popularity, the teams were disbanded at the end of the season.

By the beginning of the 20th century, cricket had been included in the curriculum of some of England's larger public girls' schools and, after World War I, some of these women continued to expand the game beyond the school boundary. The popularity of cricket among women had become so great by 1926 that the Women's Cricket Association was founded in England.

Starting off in Australia

Women were playing cricket in the colonies a quarter of a century before Australia became a federation in 1901. This early start is due in no small part to one of Australia's most productive cricket families.

Edward Gregory, a Sydney orphan who later became an apprentice shoemaker and then a school master, had 13 children who made an unparalleled contribution to Australian sport. Of his seven sons, five went on to play cricket for New South Wales, with Dave Gregory becoming Australia's first Test captain. And a generation later, 20 of Edward Gregory's grandchildren represented their state at cricket, football, athletics or sailing.

Unveiling the role of women and the Ashes

The enormous contribution women have made in the development of cricket may be even greater than suspected if a story regarding the Ashes is true. Not only did a woman define the modern game by developing overarm bowling two centuries ago (refer to the section, 'Bowling Cricket Over'), and not only did a woman enhance the Ashes legend by the presentation of a tiny urn (refer to Chapter 17), but this story tells how the world's two oldest cricketing nations, England and Australia, may, in fact, be competing for a woman's veil.

It was Florence Rose Murphy who presented the England captain, the Honourable Ivo Bligh, with an urn supposedly containing the ashes of a cricket bail after his team defeated Australia at Sydney in January 1883. Miss Murphy pursued a romantic interest in the Hon Ivo and duly she became his wife.

After Ivo's death in 1927, Florence Rose presented the miniature urn holding the Ashes to the Memorial Gallery at Lord's in London.

As the story goes, her daughter-in-law, the Dowager Countess of Darnley, later confided in friends that Miss Murphy burnt her veil, not a bail — the small piece of wood that sits on top of the stumps — as was claimed at the time.

Setting alight a flimsy piece of fabric certainly would have been easier than reducing to charcoal a solid piece of wood, but the truth may never be known.

Certainly, when the Australian players tried to burn a bail to recreate the Ashes after winning the 2001 Test series in England, they found it rather difficult. The Australian dressing room at Trent Bridge, Nottingham, filled with smoke, the fire alarms screamed, and still they failed to make much of an impression on the bail they had attempted to set alight.

Several of Dave Gregory's six sisters were the motivating force behind the first public women's cricket match played in Australia in 1874. The interest continued among some of his nieces, who were also prominent women cricketers, and Dave Gregory supported them wholeheartedly until his death in 1919.

Intercolonial matches had begun by the end of the 19th century and, with the formation of the Victorian Women's Cricket Association in 1905, a number of highly enterprising interstate matches between Victoria, New South Wales and Tasmania were played.

Bringing Women's Cricket to the World

Given that women's cricket has survived and thrived without wider support, financial or otherwise, for most of its long and continuous life, great initiative and ingenuity has been required to expand the game beyond cosy domestic borders.

International women's cricket began in such circumstances when, in 1934, with less than one pound in the bank, the Australian Women's Cricket Council invited England to tour Australia. All 16 England players paid their own 80-pound ship fares, at least the equal of any air fare for the same journey today, and supplied their own equipment for the six-month tour. The first women's Test was played in Brisbane, followed by others in Sydney and Melbourne, before England added New Zealand to this new cosmopolitan club by playing a Test in Christchurch.

In another first for women, the English standard of the six-ball over was introduced from the first Test (between Australia and England) in 1934, even though eight-ball overs continued to be used in Australia by men up until 1979. The women also used a slightly smaller and lighter ball — 142 grams (five ounces), which remains the standard for women's cricket today. Men use a slightly heavier and larger 156 gram ball.

Australia, England and New Zealand played on a semi-regular basis before and after World War II, with the Australian women showing far more respect for their Kiwi opponents than the Australian men could manage. The men's team played just one Test against New Zealand, in 1948, waiting until 1973 before regular Test series between the neighbouring rivals began.

The International Women's Cricket Council was formed in 1958 to coordinate women's cricket, which was now being played regularly in Australia, England, New Zealand, South Africa, the West Indies and, more remarkably, in Denmark and The Netherlands.

Women's fast and efficient four-day Tests

Although men's Test matches are played over five days, women's Tests were originally played over three. Four-day Tests first appeared in 1957 when Australia played New Zealand; however, they weren't played regularly until 1979. The first and only five-day women's Test Australia has played was against England in 1992. Significantly, although women play a day less than men, they can still manage the same number of overs as men do in five-day Tests. Even though men struggle to bowl 90 overs in a day, women can bowl 115 overs, mainly because shorter bowling run-ups mean less time is wasted between deliveries in six-ball overs.

Indeed, while cricket has hardly taken continental Europe by storm, the Danish and Dutch Web sites, written in their native languages, are two of nine Web sites directly linked to the women's cricket section of the world's leading international cricket Web site (`www.cricinfo.com`) along with a couple of other low-profile cricketing countries — Ireland and Scotland. The other linked sites are from Australia, England, New Zealand, Pakistan and South Africa. Globally, women's cricket is not limited to these countries, but the inclusion of only these countries is a reflection of the resources and administration available to the women's game in many countries.

Indian women may not have a Web site but the Indian women's cricket team is an awakening giant. The rapid improvement by the Indian team was highlighted when it made the last World Cup final, in 2005, before being beaten by Australia. The Indian women's team is in the unique position of generating money, which enables it to go on more tours and play more cricket than any other country in what, for women, is still a very amateur game. The Indian women play in front of significant crowds and are the only women's team in the world that generates enough interest to sell television rights. Some of the leading women cricketers are employed by major corporations, basically as ambassadors, so they can put most of their time into their cricket. What Indian women's cricket lacks in infrastructure and administration is made up for in money and sheer weight of numbers.

Playing cricket's first World Cup

Only pre-apartheid South Africa had joined the women's Test playing club of Australia, England and New Zealand before the 1973 World Cup, which heralded a new and expanded era for women's cricket. Seven teams competed: Australia, England, New Zealand, Trinidad and Tobago, Jamaica, an England development side known as 'Young England' and an International XI, which included a mix of players from different countries. England and Australia played off as the only undefeated sides, with England winning easily.

Given the rapidly changing face of global politics, the South African team was banned because of the country's racist policy, just as the South African men's team had been banned from international competition in 1970. Five South African women, who applied to join the International XI, were banned for the same reason. India was also invited but, in the finest traditions of tumultuous cricket administration in that country, applied too late.

Australia has dominated the women's World Cup, winning five of the past seven tournaments, including the most recent in South Africa during 2005. England and New Zealand won the other two. Significantly, only Australia, England and New Zealand had played in a World Cup final until the 2005 tournament, when India played off against Australia.

India and the West Indies played their first Tests in the mid 1970s but the women's game did not undergo a significant international expansion until more recently. The 1997 World Cup in India more accurately reflected the cricketing globe, with 11 teams, including Pakistan, Sri Lanka and South Africa playing for the first time.

In 2005, after the eighth women's World Cup in South Africa, the women's game took a giant leap forward when the International Women's Cricket Council was officially integrated under the umbrella of the game's major governing body, the International Cricket Council (ICC), with its massive resources and clout. An ICC Women's Cricket Committee was formed to consider all matters relating to women's cricket.

Jack Hayward — cricket and soccer hero

The first women's World Cup was only possible because of a 40,000 pound donation by former World War II fighter pilot and multi-millionaire philanthropist Jack Hayward (later Sir Jack). Not surprisingly, the cup is named the Jack Hayward Trophy. Hayward also financed English women's tours to the West Indies in 1970 and 1971, and later gave a generous donation to build indoor training nets at Lord's in London (refer to Chapter 11 for more on training nets and Chapter 15 for more on Lord's). As chairman and president of the Wolverhampton Wanderers Football Club, Hayward financed a new stadium for the soccer team, which cost up to 60 million pounds — but a strong women's cricket connection remained. The captain of the England women's team during Hayward's time of generous donations, the larger-than-life Rachael Heyhoe-Flint, who was born in Wolverhampton, was elected to the Wolves board in 1997 and became the soccer club's public relations director.

Expanding too quickly

Quite remarkably, the ICC claims that women's cricket is now played in most of the 96 countries linked to cricket's governing body. The claim is amazing given that many of those countries would struggle to muster any sort of half-decent men's team. Nevertheless, the ICC is spending large sums of money on development across the globe under its somewhat inadequate three-tiered structure. Based on the structure of the men's game, the ICC has ten Test playing countries, 32 so-called associate countries, some of which are of quite reasonable standard and play regular one-day internationals, and 54 affiliate countries, which trace some sort of vague link to the game.

Like the men's game, which has seen the unfortunate and premature promotion of Zimbabwe and Bangladesh to Test status, attempts to expand the women's game have not always gone according to plan. Japan, listed as an associate cricket country by the ICC, was invited to be part of a second-tier competition, the International Women's Cricket Council Trophy, played in The Netherlands during 2003. Japan scored 28 in its opening match against Pakistan, which included 20 *extras* (runs not scored by a batsman — refer to Chapter 2 for more on extras). Indeed, the overwhelming majority of runs scored by Japan in all its five matches were not by the country's batsmen but from mistakes by the opposition bowlers delivering *no balls* and *wides* (again, refer to Chapter 2).

When Japan played the hosts, The Netherlands scored 5–375 from their 50 overs, a remarkably high score in one-day cricket, with Japan contributing 67 wides and 30 no balls. Japan replied with 74 (29 extras) to lose by 301. Needless to say, the Japanese have not been invited to another tournament, leaving the country with 14 officially listed international players. Although the leading countries have their best batsmen scoring an average of better than 40 or even 50 runs an innings — calculated from the number of runs scored in a career divided by the number of times dismissed — Japan's highest batting average of just eight belongs to fastish bowler, Kaori Kato, who is also the country's leading wicket-taker with five. Batsmen Shizuka Kubota and Ema Kuribayashi are joint leading run-scorers with 27. Both average 5.4. Not surprisingly, Japan is the only internationally recognised cricket team among men or women not to have a single player with a double-figure batting average. Scotland has the least, with four. (See Chapter 20 for an explanation of batting averages and statistics.)

Dominating in one-day cricket

Although Australia's leading male cricketers can earn more than $1 million a year in direct cricket payments, related endorsements and media opportunities, women's cricket around the world remains strictly amateur.

Indeed, women from some countries still have to meet at least some of their costs, depending on the amount of sponsorship available to the team. For this reason, the career records of the leading modern women's players are decidedly lopsided — because they play many more one-day matches than Tests.

The most Test matches ever played by a woman is just 27 by England's Janette Brittin, from 1979 to 1998. Brittin is also the highest run-scorer in women's cricket with 1,935 runs at the outstanding average of 49.61. (See Chapter 20 for more on statistics.) The most Tests by a male cricketer is 168, by former Australian captain Steve Waugh. In a 14-year international career, recently retired Australian women's captain Belinda Clark played 118 one-day internationals, but only 15 Tests were on offer for her. (See the section later in this chapter, 'Hearing about Women's Cricket: Belinda Clark'.) By contrast, her current male counterpart, Ricky Ponting, during a ten-year career, has played 252 one-day matches and 105 Tests leading into the 2006–07 season. To that stage, Australia's women had played just 66 Tests since the inaugural match in 1934, less than one a year, but 185 one-day matches since they began with the 1973 World Cup.

Rachel hits women's cricket for six

Perhaps the best known personality in women's cricket is former England captain, Rachael Heyhoe-Flint, who was awarded an MBE (Member of the British Empire) for her services to the women's game. Born in 1939, Heyhoe-Flint was a member of the national team from 1960 to 1982, hitting the first six (when the ball clears the boundary without bouncing) in women's cricket. Heyhoe-Flint was captain for 12 of those years, leading England to victory in the inaugural World Cup in 1973. She also had the distinction of leading England in the first women's Test at Lord's, London, against Australia, in 1976 to mark the 50th anniversary of the Women's Cricket Association.

The playing of the first women's Test at Lord's was somewhat remarkable given that Lord's, widely regarded as the home of cricket, is also home to the Marylebone Cricket Club (MCC), until recently one of cricket's least progressive organisations. The MCC did not allow women to become members until 1999, so it was fitting that when these stuffy old men finally discovered the other sex, Heyhoe-Flint was one of the first ten women admitted to the club, as an honorary life member.

'I never thought it would happen,' she not surprisingly remarked at the time. In 2004, Heyhoe-Flint was the first woman elected to the full committee of the MCC.

Her sporting interests outside cricket included hockey — she played as goalkeeper for the England national team in 1964 — and her *curriculum vitae* also includes becoming the United Kingdom's first female television sports presenter, in 1973.

Doubling England's Ashes

England enjoyed two Ashes Test series triumphs in 2005. The high profile victory was secured by the men, the other by the women's team. Under the captaincy of the bright Sussex cricketer, Clare Connor, the England women's team triumphed over their Australian rivals for the first time since 1963. To celebrate the double triumph, the women's and men's teams were taken on open-top bus rides through the streets of London to a huge victory party at Trafalgar Square. England's triumph is seen as testament to a higher standard of technique and fitness among women cricketers.

Playing in Australia Today

The Australian women's cricket team is one of this country's great sporting success stories, and sits atop a thriving interstate women's competition.

Many thousands of women around the country throw themselves into the game every summer and more are rolling up to play every year. Women's cricket could be considered one of Australia's great growth industries.

Participation for girls and women, playing at school and club level, has doubled to well over 50,000 in the past decade and now represents about ten per cent of Australia's cricket-playing population.

Representing the Southern Stars

Australia's women's cricket team is known as the Southern Stars and represents the pinnacle of the women's game in this country. The national team has developed a reputation as the most potent in the world, although the continuing improvement of women's cricket around the globe is presenting ever-greater challenges.

Perhaps the best sign of just how dominant the elite women have been is their staggering success at World Cups, the leading tournament in the game held every four years, which includes all the major cricketing nations.

Since England won the inaugural tournament in 1973, Australia has won five of the next seven, including the latest one in South Africa during 2005. In the modern game, Australia has rarely been beaten by anyone, which is why it came as a great shock when the Southern Stars lost the Ashes Test series against England just months after their most recent World Cup triumph.

If you think Australia's men have been dominant in their Ashes contests recently, reigning supreme from 1989 to 2005, that is nothing compared with the success of their countrywomen.

England's victory at Worcester in late August 2005 was its first win over Australia since December 1984, and, after 42 years, that meant that England had finally regained the women's equivalent of the Ashes.

Australia was quickly back on the winner's list in the 2005–06 summer — easily beating India under new captain, Karen Rolton, the standout batsman in the Australian team, and Cathryn Fitzpatrick, the standout bowler.

Here's why former Belinda Clark thinks you should keep an eye out for these two exciting players:

- **Karen Rolton:** Widely regarded as the most potent batsman in women's cricket, Rolton holds the record for the fastest century scored by a woman — 107 from just 67 balls during the 2000 World Cup in New Zealand. Vice-captain for almost a decade before assuming the leadership when long-serving captain, Belinda Clark, retired in 2005, Rolton has been a key part of Australia's success, as underlined by her superb century, which won her the Player-of-the-Match award in the 2005 World Cup final. She also held the record for the highest score in women's Test cricket, scoring 209 not out against England in 2001. (Rolton's record has since been bettered by India's Mithali Raj in 2002 and Pakistan's Kiran Baluch in 2004.) Belinda Clark describes Rolton as a 'freak'; she says, 'Karen is very powerful, but what sets her apart is a desire to play her way. She's phenomenally confident.'
- **Cathryn Fitzpatrick:** The world's fastest female bowler, Fitzpatrick generates surprising pace from a deceptively small frame, with a solid technique echoing that of Australia's leading male fast bowler, Glenn McGrath (refer to Chapter 8 for more on fast bowling). Her pace, mixed with deadly accuracy, helped to lift Australia to World Cup victory in 1997 and again in 2005 in South Africa when she was aged 37. Fitzpatrick is the first woman to take 150 one-day wickets. Clark claims that Fitzpatrick had to overcome some misguided early advice to slow down her bowling and concentrate more on accuracy. Belinda says, 'She's got a talent that others don't possess, and she's backed herself to play with flair.'

Looking at the state scene

Australia's leading women cricketers have been playing regular annual interstate tournaments since the summer of 1930–31, when New South Wales, Victoria and Queensland banded together to form the Australian Women's Cricket Council. These three states were soon joined by South Australia and Western Australia. Tasmania and the Australian Capital Territory (ACT) also played at times.

However, when the annual carnival was ruined by rain in Brisbane during the mid 1990s, officials finally recognised that more needed to be done with women's cricket at state level than a fortnightly frolic once a year.

So with sponsorship from the Commonwealth Bank, the Women's National Cricket League — the women's domestic limited-overs competition — was formed in time for the 1996–97 season, and is played over two months instead of two weeks.

The competition features five state teams — the New South Wales Breakers, Queensland Fire, South Australian Scorpions, Victoria Spirit and Western Australia Fury.

The format of the competition includes 20 qualifying matches during the season with each state playing every other state in two limited-over matches, played across the Saturday and Sunday of the same weekend.

The team that finishes the 20-round competition at the top of the points table earns the right to host the finals series. The finals series is a best-of-three competition.

Match points are awarded as follows:

- Win, 4 points
- Tie, 2 points each
- No result, 2 points each
- Loss, 0 points
- Bonus point, one point (run rate 1.25 times that of the opposition)
- Additional bonus point, one point (run rate twice that of opposition).

Just like the domestic men's competition, the women's state league is the nursery for future Australian players but, unlike the leading male cricketers, most of the best women players compete for their state. The reason is that the women have far fewer international commitments than the men, allowing them more time to play for their states. (See Chapter 19 for more on men's domestic cricket.)

The pathway for the elite women players is streamlined at under-17 level, when each state picks under-17 and under-19 teams to play in a national championship. The most promising players are then filtered into the Australian women's youth program, which caters for players aged under 23.

Hearing about Women's Best: Belinda Clark

Belinda Clark is widely regarded and respected as the best female cricketer ever to represent Australia. Finely boned with confident, square shoulders and a serious public countenance that would not be out of place in the boardroom, Clark played for Australia from 1991 to 2005, captaining the side for the past 11 years (see Figure 18-1).

Figure 18-1: World Cup Triumph: Belinda Clark retired later in 2005 after captaining Australia for 11 years.

Setting records

Heading into the 2006–07 season, Clark had made more runs in one-day cricket than any other woman (4,844), achieved the highest score of any woman in a one-day international (229 not out) and jointly held the record for the number of one-day games played (118). Her career highlight remains leading Australia to victory in the 1997 women's World Cup in front of 90,000 cricket fans packed into Eden Gardens stadium in Calcutta. 'We've never experienced anything quite like it before,' she said.

Such has been her impact on and off the field that Clark was awarded an AM (Member of the Order of Australia) in the January 2000 Australia Day honours list for services to cricket, particularly through the Australian women's cricket team, and the promotion and development of the game for women and girls.

After combining her cricket career with working for a decade in cricket administration, including game development, Clark was appointed manager of Cricket Australia's Brisbane-based Centre of Excellence, formerly known as the National Cricket Academy in Adelaide. Every year, the most promising cricketers in the country attend this highly acclaimed finishing school for the nation's best young talent.

Far more opportunities for girls and young women to play cricket exist in Australia today than when, as a four year old, Clark began to notice the game of cricket — she has early memories of her elder brother, Colin, playing with a local junior team in Newcastle during 1974.

Once also a state-level tennis player, Clark played cricket with her brother's under-16's team before she began her rise to become Australia's most-acclaimed women's cricketer.

Clark offers the following advice to any girls or women contemplating the possibility of playing cricket:

- Cricket does not have to be a mystic game of complexities. You don't need to know the fielding positions or the rules to turn up and have some fun. Most capital cities have a type of cricket game out there to suit you.
- Women with time constraints can play a modified version of cricket that takes only a couple of hours and twilight competitions are available for those who work or go to school. Some are the cricket equivalent of touch football, where you just turn up and have a game. Everything is supplied.

The best way to find out what cricket options are available in your area is simply to contact your local state cricket association (see the section, 'Finding Women's Cricket on the Internet' later in this chapter).

Belinda Clark's rise to the top

'Have a go!' is Belinda Clark's advice to young women contemplating a playing career in women's cricket. Whether you're aiming to make it to the top, or just want to enjoy the fun of fielding on the local oval, Belinda's rise to fame is an inspiration to all women playing cricket. Here Belinda shares her journey through a cricketing life in what she once thought was a world only for men.

'I was fascinated by what my brother Colin wore on his legs to play cricket so one day I put on his pads and tried to walk down the hall in our house, but they were far too big. We were mainly a tennis family but there was always the smell of linseed oil around. My brother was so proud of his bat that he used to oil it every night.

'As a family of four kids we played cricket in the backyard all the time and I really enjoyed the contests but, until I was 12, I had no idea that girls could play cricket. Then I found out that my cousin played in a girls' team in Newcastle, but by the time I was old enough to play, the team had folded.

'It was only when I went to high school that I was able to play cricket in a team. The school had a girls' side and I joined up straight away. Then things started to happen in a hurry. After a couple of games, I found myself playing for a New South Wales combined high schools side.

'To train, I went along and practised with Colin's junior team, Eastern Suburbs, and found myself playing the season with them. The team ended up producing a number of fine players, including Anthony Stuart, the New South Wales fast bowler who once took a hat-trick (three wickets in three balls) playing one-day cricket for Australia.

'It was a bit daunting at times playing as a 14-year-old in the under 16s. My fears and uncertainties were the same as anyone else's at that stage. Like facing short-pitched bowling from bigger boys who I thought were fast at the time. Occasionally, someone from the opposition would get upset that a girl was playing, but that never worried me. It was all part of the fun. I just loved the opportunity to play, to pull on the whites every weekend. There were four kids in the family and we all played three or four sports. It was a wonderful time.'

When Clark was in her late teens, cricket started to dominate her time, taking over from tennis and hockey.

'I watched a lot of cricket on television when I was young so when we played in the backyard I always tried to emulate my heroes, such as Greg Chappell and Kim Hughes (former Australian captains). I tried to copy how they batted so I could play the same sorts of shots. I drew a set of stumps on the side of the house to bowl at, which got me into trouble, and I'd aim at the same brick, which eventually got pushed through. I got into trouble for that too.

'From the ages of 14 to 16, while I was playing indoor cricket, I was lucky to receive some good technical coaching for my batting from Martin Soper, the brother of former Australian soccer player, Marshall Soper. I also practised a lot. I spent hours and hours practising batting.

'I'd say there were two key ingredients to my development as a young cricketer. The first was that I had good technical help and I did a lot of technical work when I was still reasonably young. The second was that I never got to the point where I was overloaded with cricket. I always enjoyed it and was hungry for more, dreaming of what was coming up.'

Making progress

For those girls and women who want to go further with their cricket, weekend club competitions that run during the summer months cater for everyone from the social cricketer to those who want to take it seriously and move up through the ranks.

The junior policy of Cricket Australia, which runs the game in this country, recommends that girls can play in boys' junior competitions and can be two years older than the age group. This means that a 14-year-old girl can play in a boys' under-13s team.

Clark recommends that the earlier young girls and women become involved, the easier they find the game, but she claims starting any time is never too late! A one word mantra for success is: Practise! The more you practise, the better you become and the more you enjoy it.' (Refer to Chapter 12 for more on training.)

Finding Women's Cricket on the Internet

Women's cricket is becoming more and more accessible, whether your interest is to play the game or to watch it. The best way to find out the latest information about cricket is to search for our particular interest on the Internet.

The Web sites listed here are the best sources of news and information and are followed by contact details for each state and territory association.

- `www.cricket.com.au`: The Cricket Australia (CA) Web site has great advice on how to get started in the game. Just click 'Getting involved' and a host of information will appear before your eyes. The CA Web site also offers the latest news and information on all the players and fixtures so you can find out where and when the national and state teams are playing, and lots more.
- `www.cricinfo.com`: The world's largest and most popular cricket Web site has, not surprisingly, the greatest variety of news and information on women's cricket around the globe. So detailed is the coverage that every player who has ever played Test or one-day international cricket is listed with all their achievements.
- `www.icc-cricket.com`: The International Cricket Council (ICC) is the world-governing body of the sport. In a major boost for the women's sport, women's cricket recently came under the umbrella of the ICC, with its large resources and infrastructure. The ICC Web site has a detailed women's section, covering world news and events.

On the national scene

Here are the contact details for women's cricket at national level:

- **Cricket Australia**
  Game Development General Manager
  Cricket Australia
  60 Jolimont Street, Jolimont Vic 3002
  Phone (03) 9653 9910
  Fax (03) 9653 9911
  Email: penquiries@cricket.com.au
  www.cricket.com.au
- **Women's cricket**
  Mark Sorell
  AIS/National Women's Head Coach
  C/- Commonwealth Bank Centre of Excellence
  PO Box 122, Albion Qld 4010
  Phone: (07) 3624 8300
  Fax: (07) 3624 8310
  www.cricket.com.au
  www.ais.org.au/cricket

On the state and territory scenes

Here are the state or territory details for you to contact the association closest to you:

- **Australian Capital Territory**
  Game Development Manager
  Australian Capital Territory Cricket Association
  PO Box 3379, Manuka ACT 2603
  Phone: (02) 6239 6002
  Fax: (02) 6295 7135
  Email: adawson@cricketact.com
- **New South Wales**
  Game Development Manager
  Cricket New South Wales
  PO Box 333, Paddington NSW 2021
  Phone: (02) 9339 0999
  Fax: (02) 9331 1555
  Email: womens@cricketnsw.com.au
- **Northern Territory**
  Game Development Manager
  Northern Territory Cricket
  PO Box 40895, Casuarina NT 0811
  Phone: (08) 8981 1677
  Fax: (08) 8981 1766
  Email: ntcricket@ntcricket.com.au

- **Queensland**
  Game Development Manager
  Queensland Cricket
  PO Box 575, Albion Qld 4010
  Phone: (07) 3292 3100
  Fax: (07) 3262 9160
  Email: qldc@qldcricket.com.au
- **South Australia**
  Game Development Manager
  South Australian Cricket Association
  Adelaide Oval, North Adelaide SA 5006
  Phone (08) 8300 3800
  Fax (08) 8231 4346
  Email: admin@saca.com.au
- **Tasmania**
  Game Development Manager
  Tasmanian Cricket Association
  PO Box 495, Rosny Park Tas 7018
  Phone: (03) 6282 0400
  Fax : (03) 6244 3924
  Email: info@tascricket.com.au
- **Victoria**
  Game Development Manager
  Cricket Victoria
  86 Jolimont Street, Jolimont Vic 3002
  Phone: (03) 9653 1100
  Fax: (03) 9653 1196
  Email: vca@cricketvictoria.com.au
- **Western Australia**
  Game Development Manager
  Western Australian Cricket Association
  PO Box 6045, East Perth WA 6892
  Phone: (08) 9265 7222
  Fax: (08) 9221 1823
  Email: info@waca.com.au

Chapter 19

The Domestic Cricket Scene

In This Chapter

- Laying bare the Australian domestic cricket scene
- Playing different state formats
- Changing from Sheffield Shield to Pura Cup
- Managing cricket in Australia
- Introducing the one-day limited-overs competition
- Having fun: The Twenty20 competition
- Scoring more runs

Cricket isn't all about Test matches and one-day internationals; cricket is also about the thriving domestic scene. For more than 150 years, from October to March, cricket teams from an increasing number of states — or colonies, before Australia became a nation in 1901 — have done battle.

This chapter explains how state cricket operates in Australia, looks at the importance of the domestic game and examines the various competitions you can follow.

Dividing Cricket across Six States

Domestic cricket in Australia revolves around the country's six states. As a fan, you can favour one of three separate interstate competitions — a four-day, two-innings competition; a one-day competition; and the new and immensely popular Twenty20 matches, where each game lasts just a few hours. Or you can love the lot!

Kiwis invade Aussie states

Despite being a separate country with its own international cricket team, New Zealand played in Australia's domestic one-day competition from its inception in 1969–70 to 1974–75, winning seven of ten matches and claiming the title as the best side three times during that period. New Zealand had regularly played Test cricket against other nations since 1930. However, with one exception in 1948, Australia refused to play its rival neighbour in Test cricket until the 1973–74 season, claiming the Kiwi side was too weak.

Domestic cricket is a bit like a forum for future stars to strut their stuff. Today, the competition's most important function is to produce players to represent Australia. And usually those who excel, and excel consistently for their state — particularly the exciting, young players with plenty of flair — are promoted to the national side. The goal of every player in domestic cricket in Australia is to be chosen to represent his country.

Although cricket attracts strong interest all over Australia, the Northern Territory and the Australian Capital Territory do not have teams in the domestic competition. For three seasons from 1997–98 to 1999–00, the ACT had a team in the one-day competition, winning three matches and losing 15. Current New South Wales wicketkeeper Brad Haddin, Adam Gilchrist's understudy, first came to notice in those days, becoming the only Canberra (ACT) player to score a century. However, the ACT's dream wasn't to last! The sport's national controlling body, the Australian Cricket Board (now Cricket Australia), decided a seventh team weakened the competition and discontinued the experiment.

All Test-playing nations have their own domestic competitions. However, most interesting is the West Indies (actually a group of nations), where countries, such as Trinidad and Tobago, Barbados, and Jamaica, play each other at the 'domestic' level, then come together to form the West Indian cricket team. On the other side of the world, England has 18 county sides, and that's said to be a major reason why England's cricket has been so weak for much of the past two decades. The argument goes that the talent is spread too thinly through so many counties, reducing the strength of the overall competition. The counter argument is that 18 domestic teams gives more players an opportunity to show off their skills.

Understanding Different State Cricket Formats

Now the time has come to examine Australia's domestic competition. Cricket fans are offered three separate competitions. You should take the opportunity to watch each of them and choose which you favour because you can look forward to seasons of hearty debate on the benefits (and banes) of each. Or you can just love them all because they're cricket dressed in different guises. Here they are again:

- Four-day first-class matches (Pura Cup)
- Limited-overs matches
- Twenty20 games.

First-class cricket matches are meant to be of a standard just below Test matches. In Australia, state first-class matches are played over four days with each side having two innings. Limited-overs matches, even when played between international teams, are not granted first-class status. Refer to Chapter 3 for more on how games of cricket are divided between first class and non-first class.

When state teams play each other in four-day first-class matches, the teams are competing in the Pura Cup, which for a century was known as the Sheffield Shield (see the sidebar 'Vale the Sheffield Shield').

The domestic one-day competition is much younger, running since the 1969–70 season, while Twenty20 at state level began only in January 2005.

Vale the Sheffield Shield

A great sadness descended upon many cricket followers in Australia when, in 1999, Cricket Australia sold the naming rights of the state first-class cricket competition to a sponsor and dumped the name Sheffield Shield. The Shield had a long and proud tradition. Lord Sheffield had financed and brought an England team to Australia for the 1891–92 season. At the end of the tour, he donated 150 pounds, an enormous sum of money in those days, to encourage intercolonial cricket. The three leading colonies — New South Wales, Victoria and South Australia — used the money to make a shield, bearing the Sheffield and Australian coats of arms. The Sheffield Shield was awarded to the most successful state at the end of each season.

Explaining the Pura Cup

The Pura Cup (formerly the Sheffield Shield), with its four-day first-class matches, is widely regarded as the best domestic competition in the world. With talent spread fairly evenly across just six teams, one from each state of Australia, the competition ensures that all the country's best players are concentrated together. Australia has 66 players competing against each other at first-class level during any given round of matches, compared to 198 in England, where the players are spread across 18 counties.

Until the 1981–82 season, the team that finished on top of the table was presented with what was then the Sheffield Shield. However, from 1982–83, the top two teams have played off in a five-day final for the Pura Cup, with the leading side acting as host. If the final is drawn, the Pura Cup is awarded to the team that finished on top before the final.

With each team playing ten games, lasting up to four days at a time, as well as regular one-day and Twenty20 matches, the Pura Cup is a marathon rather than a sprint. The team that comes out on top normally needs to have a good squad of players to cover for injuries, and to provide back-up when Australia selects the team's most talented players for the national side.

Some of Australia's best cricketers rarely play state matches because the international program is so cluttered with Test and one-day games. Even when there may be a gap in Australia's national schedule, players are often told to rest instead of playing for their state. In fact, some players managed many more Tests than Pura Cup matches. Leading into the 2006–07 season, Glenn McGrath had tallied just 23 Pura Cup games for New South Wales but had played 119 Tests.

Declining attendances at Pura Cup matches

Going back to the 1920s, total crowds of 80,000 or more watched the four days of Sheffield Shield matches at some of Australia's leading venues. It was an era before television brought the celebrity players into everyone's lounge room all summer long with an almost constant glut of international cricket. Going to a match was the only way to catch a glimpse of the stars, and Test players often turned out for their states, something that rarely happens today.

Sheffield Shield cricket was big news in those days and would often dominate the sports pages of the newspapers over summer between Test matches.

How times have changed! Today, Pura Cup matches are usually watched by a few hundred spectators and rarely contain any of the leading players. Likewise, their coverage in newspapers has been significantly reduced, with the national team virtually the entire focus over summer now.

However, going to watch a Pura Cup game can be a great day out. The crowd atmosphere of the big international matches may be lacking, but you'll find plenty of room to relax in comfort. Entry is relatively cheap and the cricket is usually of high quality. Because teams are desperate to gain maximum points for a victory, Pura Cup matches are often played at a fast pace and can be great entertainment.

Still, this question is often asked: With so few spectators turning up, why bother with the Pura Cup at all? The answer is that the true purpose of the Pura Cup is to develop cricketing talent for Australia's national team.

Attendances at Pura Cup matches are so low that gate receipts wouldn't cover the wages of the players. States rely in large part on handouts from Cricket Australia to make ends meet. Cricket Australia gets its cash from selling television rights and sponsorship for the national team and from large attendances at international matches.

Looking at the states

The teams that participate in the Pura Cup are drawn from the six Australian states, and rejoice in some rather colourful names.

New South Wales (Blues)

As Australia's oldest and most populous state, the fact that New South Wales has dominated domestic cricket in Australia virtually from its inception should come as no surprise. Almost 50 years before Federation, a great rivalry developed between New South Wales and Victoria. These two states regularly played inter-colonial matches and, right up until the early 1970s, the traditional Christmas period clash was not the Melbourne Test but a New South Wales–Victoria clash.

From the beginning of the Sheffield Shield in 1892, New South Wales has won the title 44 times in 104 years and regularly provides the lion's share of national team members. The greatest among their national team members was Don Bradman, unequalled as the finest player ever to grace a cricket field. Small and unexceptional in stature, Bradman created all sorts of batting records in the 1920s and 1930s. His amazing feats are revealed in Chapter 20.

Such is the depth of New South Wales cricket that the side has, in more recent times, still managed to claim the title regularly while missing up to half a dozen players on national duty. Under the captaincy of former Test fast bowler, Geoff Lawson, in the mid 1980s, the Blues are credited with changing the relatively negative face of Sheffield Shield cricket. Lawson introduced a much more attacking philosophy, which risked losing in pursuit of victory. This philosophy helped to produce two of Australia's finest attacking captains, Mark Taylor and Steve Waugh, who led Australia into its most successful era.

Victoria (Bushrangers)

New South Wales may have produced the best cricketer of all time in Don Bradman but Victoria has the most successful bowler of all time in Shane Warne. Although rare now for the best cricketers to turn out for their state, those loyal souls who follow Victoria regularly get to see Warne playing for the Bushrangers. Since Warne has retired from one-day internationals and now only plays Test matches for Australia, half his summer is free to play for his state.

Even though New South Wales may be nicknamed the Blues, Victoria considers itself the blue blood of Australian cricket. Australia's cricket administration has always been based in Melbourne, the city that attracts the biggest international crowds at the mighty Melbourne Cricket Ground, and Victoria was the original source of the sport's strong political support. Sir Robert Menzies, a Victorian who became Australia's longest-serving prime minister following World War II, loved the game so much that he instituted the Prime Minister's XI, the one-day match against touring overseas teams that has become a longstanding annual event in Canberra.

Once second only to New South Wales as the most dominant playing state, Victoria boasted some of the finest players, including spin bowler, Clarrie Grimmett, who, managed just one game before moving on to South Australia (see Figure 19-1 and also sidebar 'Clarrie lays on the spin').

Clarrie lays on the spin

The great Australian spinner Clarrie Grimmett spent years trying to become a regular in the Victorian side during the early 1920s without success. He managed just one game in 1924 before moving to Adelaide later that year. Such was the standing of almost anonymous state players in those days that Grimmett was met by a huge, cheering crowd of well-wishers when he arrived by train in Adelaide. The learned cricket folk of South Australia obviously knew they were on a winner. Small and stringy, wizened in the face and so prematurely bald that he took the unusual step of bowling in his cap, Grimmett made his belated Test debut within months at the age of 34 and became one of Australia's finest slow bowlers. Fellow leg spinner Shane Warne will be encouraged to know that Grimmett played his last Test aged 44.

Figure 19-1: Spin bowler Clarrie Grimmett played for Victoria and South Australia, then played his first Test at age 34.

Victoria's fortunes have waned in recent decades. This decline could be linked to ever greater competition from Australian football, which has most of its teams in Melbourne, attracting much of the best young sporting talent. Victoria has had few regular representatives at international level since Dean Jones made his international debut more than 20 years ago.

South Australia (Redbacks)

A founding member of the Sheffield Shield competition with New South Wales and Victoria, South Australia is responsible for one of Australia's finest sporting dynasties — having produced three Test captains from the same family. A long-serving state captain, Vic Richardson had an imposing first-class career, which spanned two decades from 1918 to 1937. He was the grandfather of two of Australia's most famous leaders, Ian and Greg Chappell. A third brother, Trevor, also played for Australia.

However, despite such wonderful pedigree and perhaps the most beautiful ground in the cricketing world — the Adelaide Oval — South Australia has struggled for state success. Just as worryingly, the Redbacks have struggled to provide regular quality cricketers for Australia in the two decades since the Chappell era.

Clearly, population restrictions exist, compared to the much larger centres of Sydney and Melbourne, but an encouraging wave of young players is just starting to emerge from South Australia.

Bowling over tradition

South Australia's Chappell brothers are synonymous with cricket in that state. While Ian and Greg made their names as skippers of Australia's Test side, their younger brother Trevor became famous for creating a cross-Tasman stir in 1981 when Australia was playing New Zealand in the third of five matches in the World Series Cup final at the MCG.

With only the tail-enders left, New Zealand needed to achieve the almost impossible and hit a six off the last ball to tie the match. Australian skipper Greg Chappell then instructed his brother Trevor, who was bowling, to use an underarm motion to roll the ball along the ground, making it impossible for the New Zealand batsman Brian McKechnie to clear the boundary.

The two New Zealand batsmen walked off the MCG in disgust. In the following days, Kiwi fans went crazy, writing 'Chappell, your underarm stinks' across their country and around Australia. And New Zealand Prime Minister Robert Muldoon was quoted saying: 'It was an act of cowardice and I consider it appropriate that the Australian team were wearing yellow.'

The underarm bowling incident has instigated debate – sometimes good-hearted, sometimes serious – between Kiwis and Australians for more than two decades. The Chappells have moved on, and the ICC has banned underarm bowling in limited-overs cricket.

Although Adelaide can be one of the hottest places in the country to play and watch cricket — the temperature can hit a sweltering 40 degrees Celsius — Adelaide Oval is also without doubt one of the most enjoyable venues. Whether you find a seat close to the action on either side of the ground, or spread your picnic rug on the grassy banks at either end, you'll find few more relaxing ways to spend a day than watching the Redbacks at the Adelaide Oval.

Queensland (Bulls)

For almost 70 years Queensland was the laughing stock of Australian cricket. Now in many ways, Queensland leads the country. The establishment states may not like it, but Queensland's go-ahead approach has made the Bulls the most progressive state in Australian domestic cricket in the early years of this millennium.

Queensland joined the Sheffield Shield in 1926–27 and for many years the Queensland players were considered the easy beats. But even when the Bulls began to put some good sides on the park, led by Greg Chappell after he left South Australia, and spearheaded by ferocious fast bowler Jeff Thomson, Queensland was always the bridesmaid. Queensland's fate became even more pointed during the Allan Border era in the 1980s and early 1990s when not even imports, such as the brilliant English all-rounder Ian Botham, could bring the state ultimate success.

From the time the Sheffield Shield final was introduced in 1982–83, Queensland played off for the title six times in ten years and failed to win it once. The breakthrough came in 1994–95, when a Queensland side under the coaching of John Buchanan, now the highly successful Australian coach, easily beat South Australia.

The celebrations lasted for weeks and the winning team went on a special tour around Queensland displaying the Sheffield Shield. That victory opened the flood gates. Queensland has won six of the past 12 Sheffield Shield/Pura Cup titles leading into the 2006–07 season and, with New South Wales, now often provides the most players to the Australian team.

Just as importantly, the Australian National Cricket Academy, now known as the Centre of Excellence, was recently moved from Adelaide to be part of Queensland's outstanding cricket facilities at the Allan Border Field in Brisbane. The Centre of Excellence recently opened a high tech, state-of-the-art facility at the Allan Border Field to further nurture each year's most promising crop of players from around the country. A dozen or so of Australia's leading young players spend up to 18 weeks training and learning at the centre.

Western Australia (Warriors)

For a state that was not admitted into the Sheffield Shield until 1947–48 and did not become part of the full program until 1956–57, Western Australia has made an outstanding contribution to Australian cricket. Despite being in the competition almost half the length of time as South Australia, Western Australia has won more Sheffield Shield/Pura Cup titles (15 to 13) and produced a significant number of quality Australian players. The best known are great fast bowler, Dennis Lillee, and former wicketkeeper, Rod Marsh.

Although questionable management in the past has seen the Warriors struggle to keep pace with other states off the field, the quality of their players has been consistently high. At one stage, seven West Australians played in the one Test side during the 1980s.

In recent seasons, that seemingly endless supply of talent from the west appears to have dried up. Where Western Australia was once a production line for fast bowlers, over the past decade it has consistently imported them from interstate. Like Victoria, Western Australia appears to be suffering a talent drain, with many of its best young sportsmen preferring Australian football.

Tasmania (Tigers)

Cricket is often considered a microcosm of life and that certainly appears to be the case in the island state. One of the first places to experience European settlement in Australia outside Sydney, Tasmania was also part of the inaugural first-class match staged in Australia — against Victoria way back in 1851.

Yet Tasmania, with its small and relatively decentralised population, wasn't admitted into the Sheffield Shield competition until 1977–78, and even then only on a part-time basis until 1982–83.

When Tasmania first began in the competition, the team relied heavily on players from overseas and interstate to be competitive. Since then, Tasmania has produced some fine home-grown products. David Boon was one of Australia's leading batsmen through the late 1980s and early 1990s. And current national captain Ricky Ponting is on course to become the most successful batsman the game has seen. With such limited population resources, no one should be surprised that Tasmania has never won the Sheffield Shield/Pura Cup, although the Tigers have finished in second place three times.

Taking on board overseas players

Occasionally in years past, state teams would import top overseas players in an attempt to win the Sheffield Shield. Some of the greatest players the game has seen, including Gary Sobers, Viv Richards, Ian Botham and Richard Hadlee, played in Australia's domestic competition during the 1960s, 1970s and 1980s.

However, Australians have always had a much greater reluctance to use overseas players in our state competition than has been the case in English county cricket. Although a dozen or more of Australia's leading state players regularly head off to play for one of the 18 English counties during the Australian winter, imports have not been used in Australia for a decade or more.

A very strong philosophy now exists in Australian cricket: The most important aspect of the domestic competition is not to win the title, but to produce quality players for the Australian side. Hence, the policy of importing players is no longer a consideration.

Scoring points in the Sheffield Shield/ Pura Cup

As attendances steadily declined at Sheffield Shield matches through the 1960s and 1970s, administrators searched for ways to make the game more attractive. For a time, bonus points were introduced to encourage faster batting and more attacking bowling, but the crowds continued to dwindle while the changes did not help the way the game was played or the development of young players.

Now the system is simply six points for winning the game and two points for the team that is ahead on the first innings if it loses or the match is drawn. No team can take more than six points from a game. In the unlikely event of a tie, each team shares three points, and if a tie occurs on the first innings, the teams share a point each in the event of a draw. A team that loses after a first innings tie also gains one point.

When the system was introduced more than 20 years ago, too many teams cautiously played to gain two points for a first innings lead before worrying about winning the game. This often led to dull draws. However, in the mid 1980s, New South Wales changed the way Sheffield Shield/Pura Cup cricket was played by attacking from the outset in every match, even if it meant it lost. In some seasons, New South Wales lost more matches than any other team in the competition with this adventurous style, but the Blues also won more matches overall, and finished on top of the table. The top team hosts the final and is always in the box seat to win the title.

Australia also has a second XI competition, called the Cricket Australia Cup, to help young players get used to four-day cricket. To go from playing club cricket on weekends to competing over four consecutive days is a big step for up-and-coming first-class cricketers, particularly bowlers. So the second XI competition gets them used to travelling, preparing and playing at first-class level without the extra intensity.

Running the Game in Australia

Although cricket in Australia is supported from the top down, with the pinnacle of the game quite rightly being the national team, Australian cricket's administration actually comes from the bottom up. Australian cricket is built like a pyramid (refer to Chapter 15) with most of the best players in each state competing in the major club competition in their capital city. Often called grade, district or premier cricket, each of these clubs provides a delegate, and these delegates largely form the cricket associations in each state.

Each of the state associations then elects representatives who make up the national body — Cricket Australia. Because of the quirks of history, founding members New South Wales, Victoria and South Australia each have three Cricket Australia members while Queensland and Western Australia have two and Tasmania one.

For many years, the chairman could only come from New South Wales, Victoria or South Australia on a rotating basis, although this changed during the 1990s.

Introducing Domestic One-Day Cricket

The biggest change to cricket has been the one-day game, packaging a strange pastime that lasted for days into a feast that can quickly be consumed by a whole new group of fans looking for instant results.

The revolution began in England's domestic competition, county cricket, in the 1960s, with the 60 overs-a-side Gillette Cup and the 40 overs-a-side Sunday League.

The one-day concept caught on fast. In fact, the money it generated probably rescued several counties from going to the wall.

Fans loved the idea that they could see a complete game of cricket in one day and were thrilled that the batsmen may have to get a move on and try to actually score runs quickly. Domestic first-class matches could be slow tactical affairs; one-day cricket offered some welcome crash, bang and wallop.

While one-day cricket brought new life to England's domestic cricket, the game has not had the same impact in Australia. One-day cricket began here in 1969–70 in a knockout format and for the first decade involved only half a dozen matches a season. Gradually a full home-and-away competition evolved, where each state plays the other five states twice, before semi finals and a final.

Old England faces change one day at a time

Although England began the one-day revolution with a complete revamp of the domestic scene and immediately saw the benefits with far greater crowds and finances, cricket's mother country showed a strange reluctance to embrace one-dayers at international level. Despite hosting the first three World Cups, in 1975, 1979 and 1983, when all the major cricketing nations and a few minor ones played off for cricket's greatest limited-overs prize, England would build only a handful of one-day matches into its annual international program. From the very early 1980s, the rest of the world wholeheartedly embraced one-day internationals as the cash cow that attracted most of the fans and the money. However, England took almost 20 years to reflect this phenomenon in its own schedule.

Domestic one-day matches in Australia are relatively popular on Friday nights and Sundays in some states with crowds of up to 5,000, and can be a great time out. Once again, the tickets are relatively cheap and, while the atmosphere is fun, the grounds are not packed like the sell-out international matches.

The future for domestic one-day cricket is that many of the matches are going to be played on Wednesday nights as part of a new pay television deal that starts at the beginning of the 2006–07 season. This deal should deliver the best of both worlds to cricket fans. You can wander along to the ground after work and catch most of the game when it is played in your capital city, or you can watch the game telecast live at home if you're a pay television subscriber.

Injecting Instant Excitement: Twenty20

The game of Twenty20 cricket has been a phenomenal success. When this revolutionary game started in England in 2003, no one was sure how it would go. Suddenly, county clubs were shocked that they had thousands of people *wanting* to come and watch domestic cricket. Soon afterwards, Twenty20 also took off in South Africa's domestic cricket scene. (For more on Twenty20 cricket, refer to Chapter 3.)

In January 2005, Twenty20 was tentatively tried in Australia for the first time, while the Victorian team was in Perth for a Pura Cup match against Western Australia. With the great Shane Warne playing for Victoria as an added drawcard, both teams agreed to play a Twenty20 match and the response was amazing.

After more than 20,000 spectators piled into the WACA Ground, the full-house sign was hoisted and more were turned away. For the first time in living memory, a domestic match was a sell-out.

Despite the cautious approach of national administrators, who were concerned how this new-age concept would fit into the rest of their cluttered program, seven matches were scheduled among the states for the 2005–06 season, including a final, and again the crowds flocked in. As a result, even more games were scheduled for the 2006–07 summer.

The rise of Twenty20 had been so dramatic that an international tournament featuring all the major cricketing nations is listed for South Africa in September 2007.

So why has this even more abbreviated form of the game become an instant success? Cricket seems to have found a winning formula for a significantly new audience, one that has adapted to changing tastes and patterns of work.

The main objections to traditional cricket are:

- Matches take too long. Even 50 overs-a-side matches can take a whole day to complete.
- Games are often played during the week and in the daytime when most people are at work.
- Too many hold-ups in play slow the game.

The modern Twenty20 is cricket's latest and most successful answer to these objections. Here's why:

- Teams are under strict instructions to bowl their 20 overs quickly. This means fewer hold-ups and games should be done and dusted in a little over three hours.
- Matches are often played in the evenings under lights after spectators have left work, or on weekends.
- Games are held in midsummer, when the weather should be at its best and the nights warm for spectators.

When giving Twenty20 cricket a boost, a note of caution must be added. Some cricket fans aren't keen on the Twenty20 format. These fans suggest the games are too short, and are all about batsmen hitting the ball as hard as possible with little technique or scientific forethought. This approach, the fans argue, takes some of the finesse out of batting, is particularly tough on bowlers, and ultimately could lead to a decline in skill level. As a result, administrators have attempted to limit the number of Twenty20 matches at international level to a handful for each team each year.

Picking up the Pace of Scoring

A funny thing has been happening in one-day cricket in recent years. Teams have been scoring far more runs and this has been leading to more exciting matches.

When one-day matches started in the 1960s, many teams used similar tactics as they did in first-class cricket. The opening batsmen would look to defend against the new ball and the innings would wind up gradually into a crescendo of run scoring at the end of the innings. Typically, innings scores of 200 runs plus were considered reasonably good.

However, teams have become more and more aware of taking advantage of fielding restrictions. The restrictions force the fielding captain to keep most of his fielders within 30 metres — an area called the infield — of the batsman, for at least the first ten overs of the batting side's innings. The fielding restrictions mean that the batsman has less chance of being caught if he hits the ball in the air, just as long as he clears the infield. (Refer to Chapter 11 for more on one-day tactics.)

The fielding restrictions encouraged batsmen to play more aggressively at the start of the innings and they haven't looked back since. Teams now often go for their shots from the start and a total of between 280 and 300 runs in a 50-over innings is now considered par for the course.

The rate of run scoring tends to be fastest in Twenty20 cricket because teams know that with 11 batsmen, the bowling side is unlikely to dismiss all of them in just 20 overs. Normally, batsmen in Twenty20 games take a couple of balls to get themselves accustomed to how the ball is bouncing off the pitch and the pace of the bowlers' deliveries, and then they go for their shots.

In one-day cricket matches, the umpires tend to be very strict in calling deliveries wide. A *wide* is called when the umpire believes that the batsman didn't have a fair chance to hit the ball because it was directed outside his or her reach. But in one-day cricket, almost any delivery directed past the batsman's leg stump that the batsman fails to hit is called as a wide. If a wide is called, then the batting team is awarded a run and the bowler has to deliver the ball again.

How Dode-maide Twenty20 happen

Although England has been the clear leader in the Twenty20 revolution, an Australian is widely credited with helping to invent it. Tony Dodemaide, a former Victorian and Australian bowler in the 1980s, headed to England after his playing career to learn about cricket administration. He spent five years as head of cricket at the famous and influential Marylebone Cricket Club, based at Lord's, and went along as the MCC representative to the England Cricket Board's first meeting to discuss a modified cricket game.

'It was probably wise the MCC sent a youngish Australian to those early meetings, rather than some of the more crusty traditionalists,' Dodemaide said. The fact that Dodemaide is now chief executive of the Western Australian Cricket Association in Perth, the first venue to host a Twenty20 match in Australia, is no surprise.

Chapter 20

Becoming a Cricket Fan

In This Chapter

- Getting to see top-class cricket
- Following Australia abroad
- Joining a famous Australian cricket ground
- Preparing for a day at the cricket
- Bringing cricket to an armchair near you
- Having fun with statistics

In this chapter, you discover everything you need to know to become an expert cricket fan. For example, you find out about getting tickets for the really important games and what to take with you on your big day out at the cricket. What's more, you can study the benefits of membership at the famous cricket ground in your capital city, and discover how you can enjoy cricket for free down at the local park. Armchair fans are also catered for with the low-down on how best to follow cricket on the box, radio, Internet and inside the pages of the major newspapers.

And in this chapter you can take your first steps into the complex and intriguing world of cricket statistics to finally perfect the art of being a cricket fan.

Watching International Cricket at the Ground

For many Australian cricket fans, a day at a Test or one-day international match is the ultimate sporting experience. At the ground, you get to watch the best players in the world going head to head, soak up the crowd atmosphere and feel like you're part of the action. Everyone is welcome.

No matter how you want to enjoy your day at the cricket, your ground has a place for you, whether you like cheering loudly in the outer, sitting quietly while taking in the game in the stands, or enjoying a family day in the specially allocated 'dry' areas, where alcohol is banned.

Test cricket crowds are almost always good-natured, and they like to show their fairness by applauding the efforts of opponents. Cricket is a family-friendly sport, often with reduced prices for children, families, students and pensioners.

Even people who don't know all the rules of the game can still enjoy a day at the cricket.

Each summer, Australia almost always plays five or six Test matches. One or two teams from Test-playing nations tour Australia each summer. Tests in Australia often start on a Thursday or Friday, with the Melbourne Test always beginning on 26 December, Boxing Day. The major and usually only Sydney Test always starts on 2 January.

Each Test match is scheduled to last five days but sometimes one side runs away with the game and the match finishes a day or two early. This possibility means that in order to be guaranteed a full day's cricket, you should try to get tickets for one of the first three days.

Poring over the rain rules

Cricket is one of the very few major spectator sports that can be derailed by a few spots of rain or even just a batch of dark clouds overhead. The two umpires decide whether the players should play through rain or bad light or whether they should trudge off the field back to the pavilion, waiting for the sky to brighten and the wet weather to subside.

To a novice cricket fan, these disappearing cricketers may appear to be a bunch of wimps. If it's good enough for footballers to slog it out in the rain and the mud during winter, why can't cricketers make it through the odd summer shower?

The reason so much fuss is made about the weather is that the pitch can be damaged by rain and become difficult to bat on. Rain makes it dangerous for bowlers, particularly fast bowlers, who risk serious injury if they lose their footing and slip in damp conditions. A wet outfield can also put fieldsmen at risk and damage the ball, making it slippery and hard to grip for the bowlers. (For more about bowlers, refer to Chapter 7 and Chapter 8.)

Similarly, poor light can make it dangerous for the batsmen because they may have trouble seeing the dark red ball in the gloom. Fast bowlers can deliver the ball at up to — and occasionally beyond — 150kph, meaning the batsmen must have a good sight of the ball to avoid being hurt.

In the old days, umpires would take players off and stop the match, seemingly at the drop of a hat — all to the general dismay of the spectators. However, these days, it seems umpires are a little more considerate of the paying public. Often umpires allow play to continue through short, light showers of rain. They get weather forecasts during the day and can better judge whether any rain is set to hang around or pass over the ground. What's more, umpires now extend the hours of play if, at some point during the day, they have to take the players off the field due to rain or poor light.

All of Australia's major grounds, except Hobart's Bellerive Oval, have floodlights, which are also used at times to extend play in Test matches when the light is poor. However, the use of lights has become less frequent because lights have been found to have little beneficial impact with the dark red ball when natural light is poor. In addition, spectators can claim refunds for their ticket money when rain or bad light stops play for a significant part of the day.

When fewer than 25 overs are bowled at a Test or one-day international, or fewer than 15 overs in a Twenty20 game and the match is not completed, you are entitled to a full refund. Alternatively, you may be able to exchange the ticket for another day of the Test or another one-day or Twenty20 game (for more on Twenty20 cricket, refer to Chapter 3).

Can't see the light for the larrikin

Umpires now use light meters to help them judge the conditions but, for many years, batsmen were allowed to appeal against the light. Lighting was often used as a ploy if a team was going badly in the hope that enough time would be lost to stop the other side from winning and force a draw. Batsmen would sometime use gamesmanship to help their case. One famous example took place between the two World Wars with former Australian captain Vic Richardson — the grandfather of the Chappell brothers — who was leading South Australia in a state match. After South Australia lost a wicket in gloomy light, Richardson marched on to the ground to bat but headed away from the pitch. 'I can hear you but I can't see you,' he cried.

However, if rain or poor light does stop play, you won't be getting a refund for transport or other costs you may incur.

Grabbing yourself a ticket

International cricket in Australia is riding a wave of sustained popularity. The key to this popularity has been more than a decade of unprecedented success driven by many stars playing exciting Test and one-day cricket. The 2006–07 season opened with enormous spectator interest in the much-anticipated Ashes series against England.

But this good news story presents cricket fans with a problem — how to get hold of a Test match or one-day international ticket?

Tickets for Test matches go on general sale a few months before the start of the international cricket season, which usually begins in November. By far the best way to obtain a ticket is online. Traditionally, Test venues had plenty of tickets for sale on the day you want to attend if you simply turned up at the ground.

With the occasional exception of the first few days of the Sydney Test, which is often sold out, cricket fans generally have no problems getting tickets for Test matches in Australia, given the generous size of most grounds. However, the 2006–07 season proved a remarkable exception, with unprecedented demand for tickets for the Ashes series, with many thousands of fans coming from England and beyond. Tickets for almost every day of every Test except Melbourne, with its 95,000-capacity Melbourne Cricket Ground (MCG), sold out within two days of going on sale. Sydney sold out in less than two hours. Usually grounds only sell the first four days of a match because they can't guarantee that play will go to a fifth day. If it does, get to the ground early and grab yourself and your friends or family a ticket.

Not only are Ashes Test tickets hot property, but one-day matches involving Australia also usually sell out quickly in most cities, with the exception of the cavernous MCG. If you want to watch Australia in action in one-day cricket or during an Ashes series, make sure you buy your tickets as soon as they go on sale or you could miss out. All the details are available online and will be explained later in this chapter.

For all the ticketing information you need about all the big games, simply go to Cricket Australia's (CA's) Web site at `www.cricket.com.au`. If you always want to be first in the queue for tickets, you can join the Australian Cricket Family. After registering online at CA's Web site, you'll be emailed all the latest information about when and where the matches are being played, any special offers that may be available and advice on how to get tickets, which include concessions for families, children, students and pensioners.

Try to get a seat in the ground that gives you a good view of the giant video replay screen. The video replay screen can really add to the enjoyment of your day watching international cricket. If you're really lucky, a camera may pick up a shot of you during one of the breaks and beam you around the ground, around the country, and even around the world. Smile and wave at the camera so everyone at home can see you're having a good time.

Testing Australia's main match grounds

If you live in or near any of Australia's state capital cities, then you're in luck. International cricket is easily accessible to you every summer. As part of an annual pilgrimage, country people often drive for hours and stay in 'town' for all five days to watch the entire Test. All five mainland capitals host at least one Test and two one-day matches every year, while Hobart hosts at least a one-day international.

Brisbane usually hosts the first Test in November while Perth and Adelaide often hold their Tests in late November or the first half of December. Melbourne and Sydney have the Boxing Day and January 2 Tests tied up respectively.

Hobart usually has a Test in November when six Tests are played during an Australian summer, which means the Apple Isle capital may get a Test three years in every four, the way playing schedules are becoming ever more cluttered.

Melbourne and Sydney host most of the one-day matches but you can always find matches played right around the country.

The main venues for international cricket in Australia are:

- **Melbourne Cricket Ground (MCG):** The MCG is the biggest and oldest venue for Test cricket in the world.

  Street address: Jolimont St, Jolimont, Melbourne
  Postal address: PO Box 175, East Melbourne, Victoria 8002
  Phone: (03) 9657 8888 or 1300 367 622

  Tickets: Ticketmaster, phone 136 100 or online at `www.ticketmaster.com.au`.

- **Sydney Cricket Ground (SCG):** The SCG always generates a wonderful atmosphere.

  Street address: Driver Ave, Moore Park, Sydney
  Postal address: GPO Box 150, Sydney, New South Wales 2001
  Phone: (02) 9360 660

  Tickets: Ticketek, phone 132 849 or online at `www.ticketek.com.au`.

- **The Gabba, Brisbane:** The Gabba is short for Woolloongabba, the suburb where the ground is located, and has recently been developed into one of the finest sports stadiums in Australia.

  Street address: Vulture St, Woolloongabba, Brisbane
  Postal address: PO Box 1085, Coorparoo DC, Queensland 4105
  Phone: (07) 3008 6166

  Tickets: Ticketmaster, phone 136 100 or online at `www.ticketmaster.com.au`.

- **Adelaide Oval:** This ground is widely regarded as one of the most attractive grounds in the world.

  Street address: Memorial Drive, North Adelaide
  Postal address: The South Australian Cricket Association, Adelaide Oval, North Adelaide, South Australia 5006
  Phone: (08) 8300 3800

  Tickets: VenueTix, phone (08) 8225 8888 or online at `www.venuetix.com.au`.

- **WACA Ground, Perth:** The WACA was made famous by the great fast bowler, Dennis Lillee, who is now president of the Western Australian Cricket Association.

  Street address: WACA Ground, Nelson Crescent, East Perth
  Postal address: WACA Ground, PO Box 6045, East Perth, WA 6892
  Phone: (08) 9265 7222

  Tickets: Ticketmaster, phone 136 100 or online at `www.ticketmaster.com.au`.

- **Bellerive Oval, Hobart:** Bellerive Oval is Australia's youngest regular international cricket venue.

  Street address: Derwent St, Bellerive, Hobart
  Postal address: Tasmanian Cricket Association, Bellerive Oval, Derwent St, Bellerive, Tasmania 7018
  Phone: (03) 6282 0400

  Tickets: Ticketmaster, phone 136 100 or online at `www.ticketmaster.com.au`.

Heading for an Overseas Tour

Following the Australia cricket team on its travels to play cricket abroad can be a lot of fun. When the Australian cricket team plays abroad, it is said to be *on tour*.

The other Test playing countries, such as England, India, West Indies and South Africa, are interesting and often fun holiday destinations and they can be great places to watch cricket. What's more, Australia sometimes tours in the winter so if you travel to watch the national side play, you can experience some wonderfully long summers.

Travelling with a supporters' tour

For years now, companies specialising in sports tours have been offering packaged holidays for Australian cricket fans to follow the exploits of their heroes abroad. These packages are called supporters' tours.

Here are some of the advantages of going on a supporters' tour:

- The tour company arranges flights, accommodation and transfers.
- The tour package includes tickets to the cricket, which can often be difficult to get.
- Tours are sometimes hosted by former Test players, making them all the more interesting.

Different companies and groups offer overseas cricket tours, particularly to England.

- The company officially endorsed by Cricket Australia is Australian Sports Tours, 404 Sturt Street, Ballarat, Victoria, 3350. You can phone them at (03) 5332 6407 or 1800 026 668, or visit them online at `www.astsports.com.au`.
- If you're young, adventurous and into loud cheering with equally loud supporters' shirts, possibly wigs and face painting, try The Fanatics at `www.thefanatics.com`.
- If you're really serious about backpacking your way around the tour, link up with `www.wavingtheflag.com`.

If you go on a supporters' tour, try to go with a friend. Doing so can be cheaper than single rates and lots more fun.

Travelling independently

You don't always have to travel in a group. You can do things — pardon the pun — off your own bat.

Travelling independently means you can:

- Draw up your own itinerary, going where you want rather than joining the herd. You'll always find great opportunities for sightseeing wherever you go, so you can enjoy the country as well as the cricket.
- Travel for a lot less money than paying to join a supporters' tour. However, you should consider the downside — you're not guaranteed tickets so you have to source and buy these yourself.

Tickets in England are never cheap or easy to get when the Australian team is playing there. Most grounds usually sell out well in advance. The West Indian grounds often put a premium on ticket prices if demand is significant from overseas tour groups and, inevitably, this happens when Australia travels to the Caribbean.

Most of the international cricket destinations are developing countries and some can be dangerous if you don't seek the right advice. The destinations can also be quite chaotic in terms of travel, accommodation and access to cricket grounds. If you don't know much about where you're going, then do plenty of research. Travel books are always a good start. If you're heading for unfamiliar territory and you're not a seasoned traveller, don't scrimp on accommodation or you won't enjoy the experience.

Before going to the airport to catch your flight, double-check that your passport and other documents are in order. Some countries, such as South Africa, won't accept your passport if it has less than six months left before expiring. Some countries also require you to have entry visas before you leave Australia, so plan well in advance and check with the embassy or local consulate of the country well before you're due to depart. Make sure you request a visa that covers you for the whole time you'll be in that country watching cricket.

Some Test-playing nations only allocate tickets in advance to people who travel with an organised supporters' tour. If you travel independently, you may have to rely on getting your hands on a ticket when you get out there. Always attempt to book online before you leave but understand that sometimes you won't be able to.

Becoming a Member at Australia's Famous Cricket Grounds

A great way to ensure that you get in to see all the state and international cricket action in your capital city is to become a member of the ground.

However, becoming a member can be a lot more difficult than it may appear. At some venues, thousands of would-be members are waiting on long waiting lists. At the Melbourne and Sydney Cricket Grounds, becoming a member can take ten years or more — so hearing that parents sometimes submit the names of their children for membership at birth should come as no surprise. In Adelaide, the wait is three to five years, while in Brisbane, Perth and Hobart, membership is much more open and immediate.

Although becoming a member often isn't cheap, the benefits can be great, starting with superior facilities. Once you join, you're assured of entry and usually get some of the best seats in the house, offering greater comfort and a superior view. As well, the catering facilities are better; you can enjoy members' dining rooms at some venues.

Grounds often allow members to buy a limited number of guest tickets so your friends and family can also attend.

Your membership may also entitle you to entry for other sports and entertainment events. Melbourne Cricket Club membership, which gets you into the MCG, is particularly popular because members can also watch about 50 Australian Football League matches a year, including many of the finals.

The MCC and the MCC

Cricket once had a reputation as a sport for toffs, particularly in England. Is it any wonder, given the reputations of the two most famous cricket clubs in the world, the Marylebone Cricket Club, based at Lord's in London, and the Melbourne Cricket Club, based at the Melbourne Cricket Ground?

Being a part of the Marylebone Cricket Club comes with a real snob factor. Members get to sport the famous egg and bacon tie — orange and red colour — and hobnob in the famous MCC members bar at Lord's, the Long Room.

Many of the top people in Britain are members of the MCC, ranging from rock stars to cabinet ministers. But the MCC has a reputation for being stuck in the past — the MCC only started to admit women members in 1999.

Joining the MCC isn't easy or straightforward. Candidates have to be proposed by four existing members in order to go on a long, long waiting list. A candidate can expect to wait 18 years before getting through the door. Why such a long wait? Existing members have to die or leave before new ones are allowed to join!

The wait isn't quite as long at the Melbourne Cricket Club and anyone can put their name down to join. The club is still run by Melbourne's establishment and both clubs demand formal dress — men must have a jacket and tie and women must be smartly attired — if you want to wander into the inner sanctum. A shirt with a collar will suffice for most other MCC areas in Melbourne.

To inquire about joining your capital city's major cricket ground, contact:

- Melbourne Cricket Club for the Melbourne Cricket Ground at www.mcc.org.au
- Sydney Cricket Ground at www.sydneycricketground.com.au
- Brisbane Cricket Ground for the Gabba at www.thegabba.org.au
- South Australian Cricket Association for the Adelaide Oval at www.cricketsa.com.au
- Western Australian Cricket Association for the WACA Ground in Perth at www.waca.com.au
- Tasmanian Cricket Association for Bellerive Oval in Hobart at www.tascricket.com.au.

For postal addresses and phone numbers of these venues, see the section, 'Testing Australia's main match grounds', earlier in the chapter.

Enjoying Your Day at the Cricket

Now that you've bought your ticket (and maybe joined the waiting list for club membership), the time is here to understand just when you'll be watching play (and when you won't).

Understanding the times of play in a Test match

A day in a Test match is split into three *sessions of play*. In Australia, the morning session of play starts at 10, 10.30 or 11 am, depending on which city is hosting the match, and the session runs for two hours. The players then troop off for lunch, which lasts 40 minutes. The middle session of play also lasts two hours, after which players again leave the field to take tea. After a 20-minute tea break, teams emerge for the final session of play, which ideally last two hours. As well, drinks breaks are called in the middle of each two-hour session to allow players further refreshment. The day's play should finish at 5, 5.30 or 6 pm, depending on when it started, but almost always goes overtime.

Often a day's play is extended for any one of the following reasons:

- **Bad light or rain stoppages:** If the players have to leave the field for any time during the day for bad light or rain, then the umpires can extend the day's play by up to an hour. When time has been lost to rain or bad light early in the match, the umpires decree that play can start up to half an hour earlier on the following days until the lost time is made up.

- **Chance of a result:** If the captain of the fielding team reckons that they have a chance of dismissing all the opposition's batsmen in their second innings and thereby winning the match, they can ask for extra time at the end of the day to finish the job. The umpires decide whether play should be extended. The right to request extra time to finish the match doesn't apply on the final day of the Test.
- **Not enough overs bowled:** In Test matches, the fielding side is supposed to bowl 90 overs in a day's play. If they fail to do this, the day's play can be extended for up to half an hour to allow the full allocation of overs to be bowled.

When 10 out of 11 of a team's batsmen are dismissed, the innings comes to an end and the players leave the field — yet again — this time for 10 minutes. This stoppage in play is called the *change of innings*. The umpires subtract two overs from the amount allocated to be bowled by the fielding team during the day.

If the umpires take the players off the field due to rain or bad light and feel that resuming play is unlikely, then play is called off for the day. The crowd leaves the ground and may be able to claim a refund on tickets. (See the section 'Poring over the rain rules' earlier in this chapter for more details on refunds.)

If rain and bad light stop play for a large part of the day, then the umpires extend the playing time — but the extension may not be enough to compensate for the time lost out of the match.

Understanding the times of play in a one-day international

Fortunately, the rules governing hours of play in a one-day international match are far more straightforward than they are for a Test match.

One-day international matches have no lunch or tea break; instead play stops at change of innings — for anything up to an hour. If the weather is good, teams play on until all the overs in the match have been bowled and a result achieved.

If rain or bad light descend, however, the umpires may start to cut the number of overs. Therefore, games can be reduced from 50 to say 40 or 30 a side.

Thankfully, in Australia, the major cricket grounds in every state except Tasmania have floodlights, so bad light is not an issue in almost all of the one-dayers each summer.

'As Time Goes By'

Seeing why cricket was once regarded as the domain of English gentry is easy: Test matches go on for days — while most of the population is at work. Watching Test matches was a leisurely pastime, with the players frequently stopping for meal and drinks breaks. Indeed, up until World War II, many Tests were 'timeless' and were played out until their conclusion, no matter how long it took. One famous Test between England and South Africa, in Durban early in 1939, lasted 10 days without a conclusion. England eventually had to abandon the match so the players could catch the ship home. Test matches are now always scheduled for five days but often finish sooner, given the much greater pace of the modern game.

A number of one-day matches have also been played under the roof of the Docklands Stadium in Melbourne so rain wasn't an issue there either. However, most one-dayers in Victoria are still played at the Melbourne Cricket Ground.

If a match is seriously disrupted by the weather, then you may find that the *Duckworth/Lewis* system comes into play. The idea of Duckworth/Lewis is that a result can be achieved even if the number of overs that each side has to bat is different (refer to Chapter 3 for more on this fiendishly complex system).

Observing proper etiquette

The whole idea of going to the cricket is to have fun watching the best players in the game and to soak up the atmosphere that can be so exhilarating. Nothing is quite like being at the game so avoid the following cricket *faux pas* and you'll enjoy your day at the cricket and, hopefully, so will those around you.

Don't stand during the over

Only leave your seat at the end of the over, otherwise you could be obscuring the view of the action for fellow spectators. Getting out of your seat during the action is a bit like standing up in the middle of a movie at the cinema. A very unpopular move!

Never walk in front of the sight screens

The sight screens are the large screens at both ends of the ground, which are white for Test cricket and black for one-day and Twenty20 matches. The sight screens are put there so that the batsmen can more easily spot the ball leaving the bowler's hand. If you wander in front of these sight screens at any time during play, the batsman will ask the umpire to stop play until you have moved. Stopping play like this is a surefire way to make you public enemy number one.

Follow instructions of stewards

Grounds employ stewards to manage the crowd. Stewards exist to ensure that everyone has a good time, that you stay safe and that nobody interferes with play. If a steward asks you to do something, such as move seat or wait while an over is completed, just do it. If you don't follow their instructions or are rude to them, you can be ejected from the ground. You can tell who the stewards are at cricket grounds because they wear clearly marked overcoats or security badges.

Some Test match spectators like to listen to the radio coverage of the cricket. If you choose to listen to the radio commentary while watching the game at the ground, be considerate to your fellow spectators and use headphones.

Don't feel tempted to run onto the field of play during or after the match. Such a move can lead to your being thrown out of the ground. You could even be arrested! Some Australian grounds have fines of up to $6,000 for running onto the field of play.

Restrain yourself during Mexican waves

Every so often, the crowd will break into a Mexican wave. While some less caring people around you may want to throw things in the air when the wave comes around, don't be tempted. If you get caught, you can expect to be ejected.

Partying

The atmosphere generated by a big cricket crowd can be something to savour. You'll find some spectators in fancy dress, such as the two fans who travel the globe following England and who dress as Sylvester the Cat and the Pink Panther. During lunch and tea intervals, music and games of kids' cricket add to the atmosphere.

Packing the cricket bag

You're free to go as you are to the cricket but you may want to consider packing a sports bag with some or all of the following items.

Binoculars

At most grounds, you are a long way from the action. A pair of binoculars can help you view the action close up as well as spot the best fancy dress outfit in the crowd.

Packed lunch

Catering facilities at many cricket grounds tend to be limited and expensive. If fast food isn't your thing, then you can bring your own packed lunch. Do not bring any cans or glass bottles. Both are banned. Plastic bottles only!

Bags are searched on entry to cricket grounds and you won't be able to bring a metal knife into the ground, even if it is for slicing bread or dealing with a particularly hefty piece of cheese.

Liquid refreshment

Taking alcohol into Australian cricket grounds is strictly banned and many grounds do not sell full-strength beer in public areas. If you want to drink at the cricket, do it in moderation so you don't ruin your outing or the enjoyment of those around you on long, hot days. Plenty of water is always a good idea to keep up the fluids.

Reading material

A good book or a newspaper can help you pass time during the lunch and tea intervals or gaps between innings.

Sun protection

If you're stuck outside for hours at a time, the sun's ultraviolet (UV) rays may well damage your skin. Be safe, slap on a 30+ sunscreen to protect yourself, even when it's cloudy overhead. Always wear a hat and think about a light, long-sleeved shirt and trousers lest you roast in the Australian summer sun.

Dressing for the members' area

The members' areas in most grounds have reasonably strict dress codes. If you're going into the members' area, even as a guest, men should wear a shirt with a collar, long trousers and shoes to be sure of gaining entry, while women should be in neat casual clothes that display a touch of modesty. Sombreros, designer T-shirts and footy shorts may be part of summer for the more flamboyant cricket followers, but they won't get you into the members' areas.

Being an Armchair Fan

Only a small number of cricket fans actually go to games; most sit at home and watch from the comfort of their armchairs. Although they miss the atmosphere of a great day out, they don't have to fork out for tickets or travel to a venue, and the fridge at home has a ready supply of refreshments. What's more, TV coverage can offer the cricket fan a uniquely close-up view of the action.

Channel Nine has televised Test and one-day cricket played in Australia since the late Kerry Packer won a battle with the Australian Cricket Board (ACB) (now Cricket Australia) for exclusive rights. Denied this in 1977 by the ACB, which wanted ABC TV to keep telecasting the game around the country, Packer signed up almost all of Australia's best players and many from around the globe for World Series Cricket (WSC). After two years of WSC in opposition to official Tests, the ACB did a deal with Packer and Nine has been the cricket channel since the 1979–80 season. (See Chapter 23 for more on World Series Cricket.)

However, controversy continues to surround the televising of matches involving Australia on overseas tours. The major free-to-air networks don't want to show cricket series in prime time because of ratings concerns, so now almost all of Australia's overseas tours can be seen live on pay television. Pay television can be a bonus for avid fans because, with digital technology, they can find a whole range of different services on their pay TV remote controls, from replays to statistics. You can even turn down the commentary and just listen to the stump mikes, revealing how mundane some of the on-field chatter between players really is.

Once only limited coverage of cricket was shown on television in the city where the Test or one-day match was being played, unless the day's tickets were sold out. This situation is changing, particularly in Sydney and Melbourne. Always check your TV guide if the cricket circus is in town and you plan to spend the day in front of the television watching it; only a couple of hours play may be shown.

Enjoying cricket on the radio

As far as many Australian cricket fans are concerned, radio, not TV, is king. The ABC started broadcasting ball-by-ball coverage of the Test cricket on the radio more than 70 years ago, and ABC cricket commentator Alan McGilvray became synonymous with listening to the cricket coverage on the 'wireless' (see Figure 20-1).

'The game is not the same without McGilvray …'

In 1934, ABC radio developed 'synthetic' broadcasts billed as live coverage. Commentators, including a young Alan McGilvray, skilfully turned dryly worded cables from England into a ball-by-ball description of play, complete with sound effects. The thwack of bat on ball was simulated by tapping a pencil against a coconut shell while a record was used to add crowd noise. McGilvray, a former New South Wales state cricketer, went on to become the voice of Australian cricket for more than five decades. He died in 1996, aged 86.

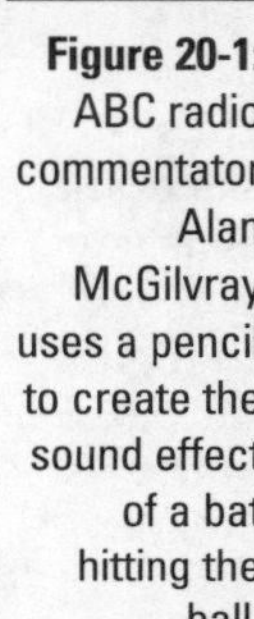

Figure 20-1: ABC radio commentator Alan McGilvray uses a pencil to create the sound effect of a bat hitting the ball.

Over the years, the coverage of cricket by the ABC radio program, *Grandstand*, as well as its signature song, *Cricket's on the Radio*, have become the soundtrack of summer for many people.

ABC's cricket coverage is free and available on ABC Local Radio and regional stations across Australia, on Radio Australia and on the Internet at `www.abc.net.au/cricket`.

Currently, the ABC has the rights to broadcast radio commentary of Australia's Test and one-day international matches at home and abroad, although not every overseas tour has ball-by-ball coverage.

Keeping up with cricket through the newspapers

Cricket swamps Australia's major metropolitan newspapers over summer. The daily newspapers in each capital city often devote a significant amount of space to cricket, and cricket is the major summer sport covered in this country's only national broadsheet, *The Australian*. Most regional and country areas are well served by the major newspapers.

Following cricket online

If you can't get to a radio or television, the best way to follow the cricket live is online. This is particularly so at work, where you can have the ball-by-ball cricket scoreboard running in the background behind whatever you might be working on. The Internet is also particularly useful for the many fans without cable television who are trying to keep up with Australia's progress overseas.

The leading Web site for cricket is www.cricinfo.com, which has teamed up with cricket's most famous publication, *Wisden Cricketers' Almanack*, to provide a comprehensive coverage of news, views and live scores of all international matches taking place around the world.

Closer to home, Cricket Australia's Web site at www.cricket.com.au offers news, views and live scores of Australia's matches. Most important, for the biggest fans, the Web site also offers a comprehensive coverage of state cricket — usually the only way to follow state cricket live.

Stump microphone, snickometer and Hawkeye

In recent years, TV coverage of cricket has been transformed through the introduction of new technology. Whiz-bang toys, deployed by the broadcasters to boost the viewing experience, include:

- **Stump microphones and cameras:** These items allow viewers to get down and dirty with the action. Viewers see the ball hurtling towards the stumps and can hear words exchanged between batsmen, bowlers, the wicketkeeper and fieldsmen close to the pitch.
- **Snickometer:** The stump microphone is also used to detect whether the batsman makes thin contact with the ball. This thin contact is called a snick and TV companies have developed technology to tell whether a sound is due to the ball making contact with the bat or just, say, a part of the batsman's anatomy, such as the forearm — a good guide, but not always decisive!
- **Hawkeye:** This device is the latest and most impressive technological toy. Originally developed by the military, allowing army tanks to aim more accurately, the Hawkeye computer tracks the ball once it leaves the bowler's hand towards the batsman. The computer then calculates the direction the ball is headed. Even if the ball strikes the batsman's pads, Hawkeye will be able to say with almost 100 per cent accuracy whether it would have hit the stumps or not. At present, umpires don't get to see Hawkeye, putting them under greater pressure out in the middle to get their decisions right, but the lucky viewer at home does.

Enjoying grass roots cricket

You don't have to pay to see a game of cricket. Literally thousands of cricket clubs and grounds exist around the country and all welcome spectators. Club matches may be a million miles away from the glitz and razzamatazz of international games but they can still offer the spectator plenty of fun and, on occasions, good quality cricket.

Getting to Grips with Statistics

Now that you're a master of the game — you're joining your local cricket ground and you know what to take and how to behave — the time has come to enjoy the cricket fan's most important skill: Understanding the stats.

An ability to interpret and, most importantly, to discuss cricket statistics can help you pass hours with your mates in the pub. Stats are the perfect subject to yarn about with the boss, stats can get you invited to the best dinner parties (well, at least those hosted by cricket buffs) and help you while away useless hours, searching out more statistics about the game of cricket.

Cricket is chock full of statistics. Nearly every action in a cricket match creates a statistic that is noted down by the *scorers*, people whose job it is to keep track of runs scored and wickets taken.

Cricket officials, players and fans use statistics to gauge how good an individual player is, compared to his or her peers and players from the past.

These statistics are called *batting averages* and *bowling averages*.

Working out a batting average

Put simply, the *batting average* is the number of career runs scored by a batsman divided by the number of times the batsman is dismissed. For example, if batsman A scores 1,000 runs in his career and is dismissed 20 times in his career, his batting average is 50.

Most averages aren't as clear cut as the preceding example but the principle is always the same.

On occasions, the batsman will be not out when the team's innings ends. The runs scored by the batsman count towards their career run total but no dismissal is recorded.

Test match and state cricket have been going for well over a century. During that time, thousands of players have represented their states or country. Statistics are a way in which an individual player's performance can be put into historical context.

Working out a bowling average

The *bowling average* is the number of runs conceded by the bowler during their career divided by the total number of batsmen the bowler dismisses. For example, bowler A has 6,000 runs scored off their bowling during their career but manages to take 200 wickets. Bowler A, therefore, has a bowling average of 30.

In one-day cricket matches, the average number of runs conceded by the bowler each over is also a key stat. This statistic is called the *economy rate*. Again, the economy rate is easy to work out — just the number of runs conceded by the bowler divided by the number of overs bowled. Therefore, if a bowler delivers 10 overs in a match and concedes 40 runs, the economy rate is 4. An economy rate around 4 or below is considered pretty good in one-day cricket matches.

Telling good from bad players using statistics

You can set a player's bowling and batting average against a series of benchmarks to ascertain whether he or she is any good.

Batting benchmarks

The following benchmarks are based on a player's batting average:

- **Less than 10:** The player is a poor batsman. In cricket jargon, these players are often referred to as *rabbits*.
- **Between 10 and 20:** The player can bat a bit but rarely makes big match-changing scores.

- **Between 20 and 30:** Every now and then the player makes a big match-changing score but doesn't do this consistently.
- **Between 30 and 40:** A good batsman who makes big scores but fails on other occasions.
- **Between 40 and 50:** Now we're cooking with gas. This is the benchmark for being a good batsman, consistently making high scores.
- **Over 50:** Batsmen who average more than 50 can have a claim to the title of great. They are world-class performers, regularly winning matches through their batting prowess.

Batting and bowling averages are often quoted in newspapers and TV coverage of cricket.

As a general rule, the higher the batsman's average the more likely he or she is to occupy a high position in the batting order. (Refer to Chapter 6 for more on batting orders.)

Bowling benchmarks

The following benchmarks are based on a player's bowling average:

- **Over 50:** Unfortunately the bowler isn't doing well, dismissing too few batsmen.
- **Between 40 and 50:** Again, the bowler isn't much good. He or she occasionally joins the party and dismisses a few batsmen but must do better.
- **Between 30 and 40:** Getting better! The bowler is capable on occasions of producing a match-winning performance.
- **Between 20 and 30:** This average is the benchmark for being a good bowler. The bowler consistently dismisses batsmen. A bowler with an average in the low 20s is likely to be considered a great player.
- **Below 20:** The bowler is an absolute star and a terror to the batsmen. Very few bowlers in cricket history average below 20 over a long period of time.

As far as batsmen are concerned, the higher the batting average the better. Bowlers, on the other hand, strive to secure as low a bowling average as possible.

Averages alter during a player's career. Some players start off with a poor average and as they improve their performance and gain experience, they get better and their average becomes more respectable. On the flip side, some players start off as bright stars only to fade away.

Matches of Twenty20 are over very quickly and often a batsman doesn't have enough time to make a really big score. Therefore, the benchmarks for deciding whether a batsman and bowler are any good have to be qualified. A batting average of over 30 and bowling average under 30 can be considered pretty handy in Twenty20 games.

Wicketkeepers are measured by the number of catches and stumpings (for more on wicketkeeping, refer to Chapter 10). Wicketkeepers are also measured in the same way as batsmen, according to their batting average. For example, in the 1970s England had two world-class wicketkeepers, Alan Knott and Bob Taylor. In terms of wicketkeeping, very little distance existed between them, with each excellent at taking catches and executing stumpings. However, when it came to batting, Knott was streets ahead. He averaged 32 runs per innings, while Taylor averaged a rather limp 18. As a result, Knott is widely recognised as the better player and he went on to star in nearly 100 Test matches.

Catching by fieldsmen is also recorded and is an important part of the game. The very best catchers usually stand next to the wicketkeeper in the *slips* (refer to Chapter 2 for fielding positions) and can average up to one and a half catches per match. Anyone who takes as many catches as they play matches is a fine catcher.

Part V
The Part of Tens

If Warney had bowled the underarm delivery . . .

In this part . . .

Now here's the fun part: Find out who are the ten greatest players of all time. This part has *Cricket For Dummies'* pick. Now see if you agree.

And how's your cricketing memory? Test it against *Cricket For Dummies*' choice of the top ten most memorable games.

Cricket's had more than its share of controversy over the years, both with players and politics. This part also lists the top ten controversies.

And best of all: This part finishes with a chapter on the ten most mind-boggling cricket feats.

Chapter 21

Ten Greatest Cricketers

In This Chapter

- Donald Bradman
- Jack Hobbs
- Sachin Tendulkar
- Gary Sobers
- Imran Khan
- Richard Hadlee
- Adam Gilchrist
- Dennis Lillee
- Malcolm Marshall
- Shane Warne

Cricket may be steeped in tradition and riddled with statistics but great players are the people who give cricket its beauty and awe. Facts and figures confirm to all how good a player is or was. However, the way the few truly great players of the game have achieved those statistics is what sets them apart from the many fine cricketers who have graced the field before them and since.

Greatness is a fluid quality in cricket and the concept of what is 'great' takes in many attributes — courage, poise, skill, artistry, determination and possibly ruthlessness. Players with long careers, who finish with a batting average above 50, or bowling average in the lows 20s, are generally accepted as 'great' by modern standards.

One way to start an argument among cricket fans is to begin talking about the very best players and then try to rank them. Almost everyone has a different order, with one exception. Don Bradman always tops the list.

But the concept of what is 'great' casts a much wider net. You can't just look down a 'great players' column on a statistics sheet. No such column exists, so picking the 'greats' is always subjective (refer to Chapter 20 for a full explanation of batting and bowling averages).

Donald Bradman, Australia

As a batsman, Don Bradman is undoubtedly head and shoulders above anyone who has ever played the game. In fact, finding anyone else who has dominated their chosen sport to the extent that Bradman dominated cricket in the 1930s and 1940s is very difficult. Perhaps Jack Nicklaus — during his stellar golf career across three decades from the 1960s — could be said to equal Bradman's achievement. Few others could match Bradman or Nicklaus.

Time and again, 'the Don' won matches and Test series for Australia literally off his own bat. His batting average is almost twice as high as any other regular batsman in the 130-year life of Test cricket. Normally a player who scores one century every four Tests is considered a legend — Bradman hit 29 centuries in 52 Test matches — better than a century every second Test. He would have played far more Tests and set even greater records if World War II hadn't taken more than eight years out of his cricket career. Bradman would have finished with the truly magical batting average of 100 if he'd made just four runs or more in his final innings in 1948. Instead, he failed to score and finished Test cricket with a batting average of 99.94.

Don Bradman (later Sir Don) was more than just a cricketer, he was a national icon. Small, with nimble feet and lightning-quick reflexes, his fame grew as this quiet and determined man became increasingly reclusive in his later years.

Bradman was the most important Australian of his time. The sporting exploits of Bradman — and Australia's greatest racehorse, Phar Lap — are said to have 'carried the spirit of a nation' through the dreadful deprivations that struck Australians during the Great Depression.

Following his retirement in 1948, Bradman had a long involvement as an administrator. Grandstands at the Sydney Cricket Ground and the Adelaide Oval are named after him. When he died in 2001, aged 92, his memorial service was broadcast on national television and a nation mourned its greatest sporting hero.

Jack Hobbs, England

Jack Hobbs is widely regarded as the finest batsman ever to play for England. Although he began his long and prosperous career a century ago, when conditions were much more difficult for batting, his impressive figures would become the envy of many modern batsmen.

A model cricketer in the widest sense, Jack Hobbs (later Sir John) became known simply as 'the Master'. He is remembered with affection, not just as a master batsman, but also as a man of the highest integrity and charm who, through years of success, remained unspoilt and unselfish. Though he appeared frail on the field, Hobbs's strength, fitness and powers of concentration were considerable.

In English domestic cricket, known as county cricket, Hobbs was in a league of his own. Of his 197 centuries, 98 were scored after he turned 40. Like Bradman, Hobbs lost potentially the best years of his career to a world war. In his case it was World War I, which cost him six years. Some say that only one finer player than Jack Hobbs existed after World War I, and that was Jack Hobbs before World War I.

Despite scoring such a huge number of runs, Hobbs was very much a team player, batting aggressively or defensively according to the needs of the team and the match situation.

Sachin Tendulkar, India

At age 16 — when many youngsters are fretting about their acne or what is the best mobile ring tone — Sachin Tendulkar was making his debut in a Test match. He was an instant hit, a master batsman while still only a boy.

In the decade that followed, Tendulkar became the biggest name in the world's biggest democracy. Such was the destructive nature of his phenomenal batting that he became known as 'The Little Master'. Short but strong, and with a determination that drives success, Tendulkar supplanted many of India's seemingly infinite gods.

Today, Tendulkar cannot go out in public for fear of being mobbed. If he goes to a restaurant or cinema with family and friends, arrangements must first be made for the location to be cleared and guarded. Tendulkar earns enormous sums of money from huge corporate contracts. However, if he wants to drive one of his expensive sports cars, he must do so at 3 am to avoid India's notorious traffic and the pandemonium created by his popularity.

For much of his career, Tendulkar has been widely regarded as the best and most dangerous batsman in the world. When Sir Donald Bradman first saw Tendulkar bat, the Don said he felt that he was watching a clone of himself.

Tendulkar raced to some of the most significant milestones in cricket. Leading into the 2006–07 season, Tendulkar had scored 35 Test centuries — more than any other player — and was one of just five players with more than 10,000 Test runs. His one-day figures are unparalleled — more than 14,000 runs and 39 centuries. However, Tendulkar's statistics have been compromised by the fact that his previous two years have been marred by injuries requiring serious elbow surgery.

Gary Sobers, West Indies

If Don Bradman stands untouchable as the game's greatest batsman, then Garfield St Aubrun Sobers — or just Gary Sobers for short — carries the mantle as the game's greatest all-rounder. Sobers was a freak because there was no job on a cricket field that he could not do.

Sobers was one of the most entertaining, devastating, powerful batsmen the game has seen, bowled both fast and spin when the occasion called for such bowling, and he was a brilliant fieldsman in any position. Relatively tall, supple, athletic and strong, Sobers played cricket with a free spirit, which infected and enthused all those fortunate enough to see him in action.

In Test matches, Sobers scored more than 8,000 runs and took 235 wickets. Any player who manages just one of these feats through an entire career is considered a very fine player. As a batsman, Sobers was capable of laying waste to the bowling. One of his most famous exploits came while playing county cricket (domestic cricket) in England. He hit 6 sixes in one over delivered by Glamorgan bowler Malcolm Nash in 1968.

Sobers, later knighted by the Queen to become Sir Garfield, was simply a genius.

Imran Khan, Pakistan

Imran Khan has a strong claim to be considered the finest all-round cricketer to emerge since Gary Sobers retired in 1974. For nearly two decades, his performances in Test matches and one-day international cricket were outstanding.

Imran Khan was a great fast bowler, taking 362 Test wickets. In fact, he may have made it into this list for his bowling alone, but he was also a fine Test batsman who scored nearly 4,000 runs, including six centuries.

Known as the 'Lion of Lahore' with his Adonis looks and flowing mane, Imran Khan was a powerful athlete who began his country's modern fast-bowling tradition.

He was a strong captain in a fractious side, making Pakistan a force outside its own country for the first time and leading the side to 1992 World Cup triumph in Melbourne.

Richard Hadlee, New Zealand

The fact that New Zealand's greatest era coincided with the rise of Richard Hadlee as one of the world's premier fast bowlers is no coincidence. The only team to beat the marauding West Indies in a Test series in the 1980s, when they dominated the world with dangerous fast bowlers and powerful batsmen, was New Zealand.

Relatively tall and wiry rather than muscular, Hadlee had a wonderful classical bowling action, which allowed him to move the ball in the air and off the pitch away from the right-handed batsman at pace. (Refer to Chapter 7 and Chapter 8 for more on fast bowling.)

Openly hostile towards batsmen, Hadlee was most damaging later in his career when he shortened his run-up and bowled 'smart' rather than attempting outright pace above all else. A fierce desire to win, combined with deadly accuracy, allowed him to become the first bowler in Test history to take more than 400 Test wickets. Hadlee was also a useful, hard-hitting batsman.

Hadlee emerged at a time when the game was blessed with great all-round cricketers — such as Pakistan's Imran Khan, England's Ian Botham and India's Kapil Dev. Although not as naturally talented as the others, Hadlee made up for it with hard work and immense determination. Hadlee retired in 1990 and was, like Gary Sobers and Donald Bradman, knighted by the Queen.

Adam Gilchrist, Australia

This brilliant wicketkeeper and batsman has been the scourge of bowlers around the globe ever since he made his belated Test debut in 1999. Many believe Adam Gilchrist hits the ball harder and further more often than nearly anyone in the long life of the game. In fact, perhaps only Gary Sobers and another great former West Indian Viv Richards have a claim to be as brutalising a batsman as Gilchrist.

Adam Gilchrist isn't just a force of nature as a batsman, he is also a world-class wicketkeeper. The fact that he is exceptionally talented at two cricketing disciplines makes him a great all-rounder. Richie Benaud, the former Australian captain and doyen of TV commentators, rates Gilchrist as one of the all-time greats. Time and again, Gilchrist has dug his team out of a hole. He bats quite low in the batting order, at number 6 or 7, and just when the opposition thinks it's doing well, Gilchrist strides to the crease and hits a century. He averages nearly 50 runs each time he bats and is well on his way to beating the record for most dismissals claimed by a wicketkeeper.

Such has been Gilchrist's devastating performances with the bat that he has redefined the modern game, making it even more imperative that wicketkeepers can also bat — although none is ever likely to hit the ball with the same brutality and consistency as Gilchrist.

He has scored runs faster than any other leading batsman in history. As a comparison, Gilchrist scores at better than 80 runs per 100 balls (this is known as a *strike rate* of better than 80). The greatest of all, Don Bradman, and Australian captain Ricky Ponting have strike rates of just under 60 runs per 100 balls.

Dennis Lillee, Australia

Just about every school boy growing up in Australia in the 1970s wanted to be Dennis Lillee. An imposing fast bowler with a drooping moustache and flowing mane, Lillee's long run-up and explosive action made every delivery a crescendo.

Frighteningly fast when he burst onto the Test scene in 1971, Lillee missed almost two years with a career-threatening back injury. Refining his classical bowling action, Lillee returned as the world's best fast bowler, combining skill and accuracy with a vicious streak that spared no batsman.

His comeback coincided with the rise of Jeff Thomson, widely regarded as the fastest bowler of all time. Together they devastated England and the West Indies in successive home summers during the mid 1970s, making Australia the undisputed world champions long before an official league table existed. (Refer to Chapter 8 for more on Jeff Thomson.)

Lillee's exceptional ability, courage, stamina and fierce desire were coupled with his theatrical love of the big stage. He was a showman! Cricket has generated few more exciting sights than watching Dennis Lillee in full flight. When he retired in 1984, Lillee was the leading wicket-taker in the world with 355 from 70 Tests and is widely regarded as the finest fast bowler ever to play the game.

Malcolm Marshall, West Indies

If Lillee has a challenger to his mantle as the greatest fast bowler of all time, Malcolm Marshall is the one. This superb athlete was the best of the most damaging cluster of fast bowlers ever assembled.

From the late 1970s to the mid 1990s, the West Indies dominated the world with a ruthless collection of fast bowlers, who redefined the game. The aggressive style of these bowlers forced administrators to make rule changes to protect batsmen and the game itself from being overrun by such brute force.

This lineage began with Andy Roberts and Michael Holding in the mid 1970s and continued with Joel Garner, Malcolm Marshall, Courtney Walsh and Curtly Ambrose as the cream of a wider crop. That these men fill six of the top eight positions among the leading wicket-takers in West Indian cricket comes as no surprise.

Best of them was Marshall, who was surprisingly short for a fast bowler but generated great pace from a lithe and whippy action, which propelled the ball at enormous speed towards the batsmen. Marshall combined this deadly ability with the subtle use of swing and seam bowling, moving the ball in the air and off the pitch to further confuse the batsmen. (Refer to Chapter 8 for more on swing and seam bowling.)

A good indication of Marshall's greatness was his *bowling average*. In Test matches a bowling average below 30 is considered good, below 25 and you're talking all-time great — Marshall's average was below 21. (Refer to Chapter 20 for information on bowling averages and the calculation of other cricket statistics.)

Marshall's story has a tragic postscript. In 1999, he died of cancer aged just 41. He may have been feared by opponents but, Marshall was also very popular. Anyone who was fortunate enough to attend the memorial cricket match in his honour at the Honourable Artillery Ground in London in 2000 can attest to the high regard in which he was held.

Shane Warne, Australia

Shane Keith Warne, the bleached blond Australian leg-spin bowler, showed himself to be a very special talent with the first ball he delivered in an Ashes Test match. Bowling to England's best player of spin, Mike Gatting, at Old Trafford, Manchester, in 1993, Warne produced what became known as the 'ball of the century'. The ball pitched outside Gatting's leg stump, spun viciously on bouncing and hit the top of Gatting's off stump. Gatting was bamboozled by a ball that must have spun a third of a metre and Warne became an instant star.

But this was only the start. Warne has been rewriting the record books ever since. Heading into the 2006–07 cricket season, Warne had taken 685 wickets, more than any other player in the life of Test cricket.

While Warne has attracted plenty of publicity for all the wrong reasons (see Chapter 23 for the Mark Waugh and Shane Warne bookie scandal, and also for Shane Warne's slimming drug ban), he has an incredibly astute cricket brain. Mike Atherton, a former England captain, believes that Warne's ability to out-think batsmen makes him the finest bowler he has played against.

The 2000 *Wisden Cricketers' Almanack* named Warne as one of the five most important cricketers of the 20th century. He literally reinvented the art of leg-spin bowling (refer to Chapter 8 for more on this type of bowling) and has been a key to Australia's success over the past decade.

Chapter 22

Cricket's Ten Best Matches

In This Chapter

- Cricket over the years — a centenary and two tied Tests
- Coming from nowhere — Australia's World Cup glory
- Batting all day — the turnaround in Calcutta
- Breaking all the records — one-day batsmen go on the rampage

Since Australia and England established the tradition of international cricket from humble beginnings back in 1877, more than 4,000 Test and one-day international matches have been played around the world. This number is being added to at a rapid rate, with one-day internationals becoming so prevalent that they can become like television's version of wallpaper — a permanent viewing fixture.

Many lopsided Test and one-day matches have come and gone over the years, to be filed in the ever-burgeoning databases of cricket statisticians. Many of those matches are long forgotten. Some of the matches have been really good games, keeping the spectators on the edges of their seats until eventually one team grabs the win. A few games, though, have been classic affairs, featuring nail-biting finishes, improbable run-scoring feats or astounding fightbacks by a team that had seemed out for the count.

This chapter examines a selection of ten classic matches. These matches may not be the greatest ever played in terms of the quality of cricket, but anyone who was in the crowd or watched the matches on television found them compulsive viewing.

Australia versus England: Centenary Test, Melbourne, 1977

The one-off match to mark 100 years of Test cricket, played between the original combatants Australia and England at the same venue, the Melbourne Cricket Ground, was special even before a ball was bowled. Many past greats from both countries were brought together at a special function on the eve of the match to celebrate this great milestone in cricketing history. Whether the cause was the enormity of the occasion, or a damp pitch that favoured the bowlers, Australia was dismissed for just 138 runs in its first innings, threatening to ruin a significant party. But, inspired by the magical fast bowler Dennis Lillee, Australia tore England apart when their turn came to bat, dismissing the shell-shocked visitors for just 95.

The crowd then witnessed some inspired batting in Australia's second innings. David Hookes, the 21-year-old blond South Australian sensation, took to the bowling of English captain Tony Greig, smashing him for five fours in one over. Then, pugnacious Rod Marsh became the first Australian wicketkeeper to score a century against England.

Australia made 419 runs in its second innings, leaving England a seemingly impossible 453 runs to win. No one gave England a hope, but a remarkable innings by the cheeky Derek Randall, who hit 174 runs, his first century in just his fifth Test, saw England come within a whisker of pulling off a famous and unlikely win. In fact, at the tea interval on the fifth and final day, England looked favourites to carry away the glory. But some fine bowling by Lillee (refer to Chapter 21 for more on this bowling legend) saw Australia home by a margin of 45 runs. Amazingly, this figure was the identical victory margin to the first Test played 100 years earlier.

Australia versus West Indies: Tied Test, Brisbane, 1960

In more than 1800 Test matches, only two tied results had been recorded coming into the 2006–07 season. A *tie* occurs when both sides have completed their two innings and the aggregate scores are level. The first tied match, at Brisbane's Gabba in 1960, was a classic encounter between two great sides. Both the West Indies and Australia had star players galore. All-time greats, such as Gary Sobers, Frank Worrell and Wes Hall, lined up for the West Indies, while the Australians could boast Richie Benaud, Alan Davidson and Neil Harvey.

Australia was in terrible trouble on the last day, before Benaud and Davidson, wonderful bowlers who also attacked with the bat, took Australia to the verge of victory with some inspired batting. Then, just as dramatically, the game turned again as Australia attempted to scramble the last few runs for victory. By then, Australia should have won the match, needing just seven runs to win with four wickets in hand. But some brilliant fielding by Joe Solomon when his throw hit the stumps to run out the last man, Ian Meckiff, in lengthening shadows during the final moments of the match, resulted in the first tie from 502 matches played over 83 years.

This match was the first Test of the 1960–61 summer and the brilliant cricket inspired a nation after the recent boring series against England. So popular were the touring West Indians that a world-record crowd of 90,800 turned up to watch a day's play during the fifth and final Test at the Melbourne Cricket Ground. After the Test, thousands turned out to cheer the West Indians during a ticker-tape parade through the streets of Melbourne before the team members were guests of honour at a civic reception.

Australia versus India: Tied Test, Madras, 1986

Drama aplenty set in long before the 1986 Tied Test between Australia and India finished amid overwhelming tension in just the second tied Test to be played in the long and glorious life of cricket.

The drama began with one of the most remarkable and courageous innings of all time by young Victorian Dean Jones. Playing just his third Test, and desperate to establish himself in a side attempting to rebuild after plunging to depths never previously experienced by Australian teams, Jones literally put his life on the line for his country.

Not out after the first day, Jones batted on to score a brilliant 210, but his eight-hour innings took a heavy toll in the heat and humidity of Madras. By the time he was dismissed, Jones had become so dehydrated that he was unable to keep down fluids and was a physical and emotional mess. So concerned were the Australians that Jones was raced to hospital by ambulance and put on a saline drip. (See Chapter 24 for more on Jones's extraordinary innings.)

Dean Jones returned to complete the match, but it appeared that all his bravery and brilliance were in serious danger of coming to nothing on the final day as India charged towards an unlikely victory. Australia had controlled the match from the outset and captain Allan Border had *declared* twice (closed each innings before all his batsmen were out). (Refer to Chapter 11 for more on declaring.)

In lengthening shadows and with Australian tempers flaring, colourful Australian spinner Greg Matthews was bowling to India's last and least-accomplished batsman, Maninder Singh, with scores level. Only one delivery remained in the match when Indian umpire V. Vikram Raju gave Maninder out leg before wicket (refer to Chapter 2 for more on dismissals).

This result was all the more remarkable given that international cricket sides that toured India often felt that the umpires favoured the home side — which certainly wasn't the case on this occasion as the shocked Australians celebrated this most unexpected result.

England versus Australia: Test Match, The Oval, London, 1882

The year 1882 saw only the ninth Test match ever played, but the year also marked the start of cricket's oldest competition — the Ashes.

The Test match between England and Australia was a very low-scoring affair, nothing unusual in those early days given that the pitch was often poorly made and difficult to bat on. Australia was dismissed for just 63 runs in its first innings and England fared little better in response, notching up a paltry 101. The Australian second innings total of 122 was relatively poor but, in the context of the match, proved crucial. England was left just 85 runs to win but somehow managed to be bowled out for 77, with the legendary W.G. Grace (refer to Chapter 16 for more on the great W.G. Grace) top scoring with 32. Australia, therefore, won an incredibly close contest by just seven runs. The hero for Australia was fast bowler Fred 'The Demon' Spofforth, who took 14 wickets for just 88 runs during the match. The English sporting fans were taken aback by England's first loss to Australia at home.

After the match, the mock obituary carried in England's *The Sporting Times* stated that the body of English cricket would be cremated and the Ashes taken to Australia. (Refer to Chapter 16 for more on Australia's first great fast bowler, Fred Spofforth, and Chapter 17 and Chapter 18 for more on the making of the Ashes legend.)

India versus Australia: Test Match, Calcutta, 2001

You can file the second Test match between India and Australia in 2001 — along with Headingley, Leeds, 1981 — under Lazarus-like comebacks. The world champion Australians were attempting to stretch their amazing Test record of successive victories to 17 and claim their first series victory in India for 32 years. The rampaging Australians had beaten every team they'd played at home and away over the previous five years and considered beating India in India as the final frontier.

The Australians comfortably won the first match in the three-match series. Halfway through the second Test at Calcutta, Australian captain Steve Waugh and his men thought that final frontier was about to be crossed. The Australians had enforced the follow-on and victory seemed only a matter of time. Then, relentless Indian batsman Rahul Dravid joined V.V.S. Laxman and a funny thing happened. The Australians just couldn't get either of these Indian batsmen out. Dravid and Laxman batted and batted and batted, from late on the third day, right through the fourth and into the last, putting the Australian bowling to the sword with a partnership of 376. When, finally, Laxman was out for 281, the match and the series had turned around. On the final day of the match, the Indian captain Sourav Ganguly declared the innings and the Australians were batting to save the match. But save it they could not, and India went on to win by a mighty 171 runs. And to rub salt into Aussie wounds, the Indians went on to win the final match of the series by two wickets and claim a 2–1 series triumph.

Sometimes after the completion of both teams' first innings, the team that has just batted has scored far fewer runs than the side that batted first. For example, team A scored 600 runs while team B managed just 200 runs. When a big enough gap exists, the fielding side is allowed to tell the batting side to bat again. This situation is called enforcing the *follow-on* (refer to Chapter 11 for more on when a follow-on can happen).

England versus Australia: Test Match, Edgbaston, Birmingham, 2005

When Australian tail-end batsman Michael Kasprowicz was dismissed by Andrew Flintoff on the fourth morning of the crucial 2005 Ashes Test match, the cricketing world was turned upside down. England had beaten their old foes by just two runs, the narrowest victory margin in more than a century of Ashes contests. The series was levelled at 1–1 and ultimately England went on to win the Ashes for the first time since 1987.

However, the result could have been so different. An hour before play, Australia's best fast bowler Glenn McGrath injured himself during fielding practice and had to withdraw, and then captain Ricky Ponting confounded the experts by electing to field anyway. During the first day, England rattled up 400 runs and took charge. England dominated the game and by the fourth morning Australia looked dead in the water, needing more than 100 runs for victory with only bowlers, Shane Warne, Brett Lee and Kasprowicz, left to bat. But with great heroics amid ever-growing drama and tension, this unlikely trio brought Australia to the brink of a remarkable triumph. That is, until England's Andrew Flintoff dismissed Kasprowicz, sending England's cricket fans into rapture. Lee, standing near Flintoff, slumped over his bat in despair at such a close failure. The endearing image of the Test and the series was Flintoff taking a compassionate moment to put a comforting arm around the heroic Lee before heading off to celebrate with his team mates.

South Africa versus Australia: World Cup Semi Final, Edgbaston, Birmingham, 1999

The Australians had employed some amazing and heroic play to reach the semi finals of the 1999 World Cup but, not for the first time, their campaign appeared doomed.

Only a brilliant, defiant century from captain Steve Waugh had enabled Australia to come back from the dead against South Africa in an earlier match, saving Australia from an embarrassing early exit — but the luck had appeared to run out.

Having dismissed Australia for a modest 213, South Africa was 0–48 in reply when brilliant leg spinner Shane Warne came into the attack as Australia's last throw of the dice. Warne claimed three wickets for only five runs, including South African captain Hansie Cronje and the game was turned on its head.

Tense from that moment on, the match came down to a drama-filled last over, bowled by Damien Fleming. South Africa needed nine runs to win but had lost nine wickets. One more wicket and victory was Australia's. One of the best players during the tournament, South African all-rounder Lance Klusener, smashed the first two deliveries of the over to the boundary for two fours. The two fours meant that the scores were level. South Africa had four deliveries left to score just one run and claim a famous win. No runs were scored off the third delivery and the tension, it turned out, became unbearable for the South Africans.

Klusener made contact with the fourth ball of the over and set off to run a single, but his batting partner Allan Donald had no intention of going for the run. A horrendous mix-up ensued, and Donald was run out as Fleming gathered the ball and carefully underarmed it to wicketkeeper Adam Gilchrist to complete the dismissal. With scores level, the match was tied. However, because Australia had achieved a miraculous victory over South Africa earlier in the tournament, the Australians went through to the final, thrashing Pakistan to claim cricket's greatest one-day cricket prize.

Australia versus West Indies: First World Cup Final, Lord's, London, 1975

Anyone who had doubts about the future of one-day cricket at international level should have had them dispelled after one amazing day at Lord's, the ground that is widely regarded as the home of cricket (refer to Chapter 3 for more on one-day cricket and Chapter 16 for more on Lord's).

Only 18 one-day international matches had been played among the leading cricket nations since the inception of one-dayers in 1971 when often reactionary administrators took the bold decision to hold a cricket World Cup. So, 45 years after the soccer World Cup began, eight international teams, including an East African XI made up of Kenyan, Tanzanian and Ugandan players, took part in the first collective one-day international cricket tournament.

The tournament proved an amazing success and reached a crescendo on 21 June 1975, when the two best teams in the game played off in a stunning final that contained amazing skill, great performances and high drama. Australia's potent pace attack, led by Dennis Lillee, saw the Australians off to a great start with early wickets. Then, imposing West Indian captain Clive Lloyd, known as the 'Big Cat' because of his unmatched power and grace, scored one of the great limited-overs centuries — 102 from just 85 deliveries — as the West Indies raced to the seemingly unassailable total of 291.

With Australia batting, a young Viv Richards brilliantly *threw down the stumps* (hit them with a direct throw) to claim three decisive run outs (refer to Chapter 2 for more on dismissals). Richards' victims included Australian captain Ian Chappell and his brother Greg Chappell, the future captain.

The crowd, made up almost entirely of expatriate West Indians, was singing, chanting, dancing and clapping to a wild and hypnotic beat as the sun began to set on the game and the Australians.

Just when all seemed lost, two men known for their ferocious bowling, not their modest batting — Dennis Lillee and Jeff Thomson — were inexplicably taking the Australians towards their victory target. The time was almost 8.30 pm in the long English midsummer twilight when Thomson sliced a catch to fieldsman Viv Richards, and the crowd, believing the game was over, charged onto the field. But Thomson had heard a call of 'no ball', which meant it was an illegal delivery (refer to Chapter 2) so the bowler could not dismiss the batsman.

A short time after order was finally restored, Thomson was run out and the West Indies won by 17 runs. This match was the beginning of the one-day phenomenon that would soon sweep the cricket world.

South Africa versus Australia: One-Day International, Johannesburg, 2006

The 2006 one-dayer between South Africa and Australia in Johannesburg rewrote nearly all the one-day international match records. The never-before-achieved one-day team total of 400 from 50 overs (300 balls) was smashed as the rampant Australians charged to an incredible 434 for the loss of just four batsmen. Australian captain Ricky Ponting led the way with a blistering 164 runs.

Just as everyone was soaking up the enormity of this incredible feat, South Africa did the unthinkable and chased down the score. Helped by a superb innings of 90 from captain Graeme Smith and Herschelle Gibbs (who hit 175), South Africa surpassed Australia's total to win the game with one delivery remaining. In total, the two teams between them had scored 872 runs in the match off just 99 overs and five deliveries in a little over six hours. This score was 179 runs more than had ever been scored in a one-day match. The cricket world was stunned as were the thousands of spectators lucky enough to have witnessed it.

One player who probably wishes he could forget this unforgettable match was Australian fast bowler Mick Lewis. Lewis bowled 10 overs in the match and conceded — you guessed it — a world record 113 runs. A very bad day at the office!

England versus Australia: Test Match, Headingley, Leeds, 1981

Bookmakers don't often get things badly wrong. And few cricket fans thought the bookies had made a mistake when the scoreboard at Headingley, Leeds, flashed up the odds during the third Test match between England and Australia in 1981.

England was in dire straits. Australia, 1–0 up in the six-match series, had managed to score 401 in its first innings. In response, England floundered to 174 all out. The only player to perform was all-rounder Ian Botham, who had resigned the captaincy after failing to score in either innings of the previous Test.

After being forced to follow on, England, at first, fared even worse, slipping headlong towards defeat with seven batsmen dismissed for 135 runs. This score meant England still needed nearly 100 runs just to make Australia bat again.

No wonder the bookmakers were offering odds of 500–1 on an England win. Even the England team had given up hope, checking out of its hotel the night before in the expectation of being beaten.

But then what became known as the 'miracle of Headingley' occurred. Ian Botham, supported by bowlers Graham Dilley, Chris Old and Bob Willis, went berserk, hitting the ball to all parts of the field and scoring runs galore. Botham hit 149 not out and England was finally dismissed for 356, leaving Australia 130 runs to win on the final day of the match.

The Australians initially went well and scored 56 runs with just one of their batsmen being dismissed when England fast bowler Bob Willis roared in to produce the best bowling of his life. Willis bowled at lightning pace and decimated the Australian batting, taking eight wickets in the innings. The Australians were dismissed for 111 and England had claimed what must remain its most famous victory.

Chapter 23

Ten Great Cricket Controversies

- Investigating match-fixing
- Defying the bookies
- Shaming South Africa
- Joining the circus
- Attacking with bodyline
- Slimming Shane Warne
- Rebelling in South Africa
- Banning d'Oliveira from home
- Forfeiting a Test
- Throwing a dud

Sadly, most of cricket's greatest controversies have had their germination off the field. That situation almost always applies — whether the problem is match-fixing and illegal betting, South Africa's apartheid years or a revolution that saw most of the world's great players desert the traditional game.

For most people, cricket is a game that is played and watched for fun. Cricket has many unique qualities and the game brings together an eclectic bunch of nations, which were once the heart of the long-faded British Empire. However, the sport, which gives so many people so much joy, has such a powerful hold in some countries that it has driven men to do strange things for dubious personal advantage. The very heart of the game is attacked when cricket is not being played and administered with the purest of intentions.

For me (co-author Malcolm Conn), it has been an extraordinary experience to report on many of these controversies as they unfolded. In this chapter, I look at the ten biggest controversies that have rocked the cricketing world.

Uncovering Match-Fixing

For the second half of the 1990s, international cricket buzzed with the unsavoury undercurrent of claims that not all players were above board. According to the claims, some of the game's biggest names, particularly on the Indian sub-continent, were being bought by illegal bookmakers to 'fix' matches by performing poorly.

The cricket world would later learn that the tentacles of this pernicious practice had touched Australia as far back as 1992 when Dean Jones, the fine Victorian batsman, was offered a biscuit tin full of US dollars by an illegal bookmaker in return for 'information' during an Australian tour of Sri Lanka. A shocked Jones rejected the payment and reported the offer to team management, but no one in the Australian camp understood the implications of what had happened.

The first public revelations came two years later when the now-disgraced Pakistan captain of the time, Salim Malik, offered spinners, Shane Warne and Tim May, and premier batsman, Mark Waugh, large sums of money to fail at various stages during Australia's 1994 tour of Pakistan. Again, the Australians rejected the advances.

These allegations were investigated by an inquiry in Pakistan but such was the toothless state of the game's governing body, the International Cricket Council, and the mistrust between cricket nations, that Warne, May and Waugh refused to return to Pakistan to testify at the hearing and nothing was ever proved.

When Australia returned to Pakistan in 1998, concerns about players throwing matches for money in that country had become so great that a judicial hearing was taking place in the Lahore High Court to try to uncover the facts behind the rumours. A string of Pakistan's leading players were dragged through the courts, with Salim Malik and Pakistan's greatest fast bowler at the time, Wasim Akram, a former captain, among those facing the most serious allegations.

So angry did the judge become with the players' lack of cooperation that he threatened to put Pakistan's Inzamam-Ul-Haq, in jail if his memory did not improve, which it duly appeared to do.

With May retired and Warne injured, Mark Waugh was the only Australian on that 1998 tour who had been approached by Malik four years earlier. Waugh was whisked away at dawn following the first Test of the series and attended a secret hearing, giving damning evidence against Malik for his approach to fix matches on the 1994 tour.

Following the hearing, the judge banned Malik for life and was so unhappy with the lack of cooperation by the Pakistani players that he fined six of them and recommended Akram never captain his country again.

Mark Waugh–Shane Warne Bookie Scandal

During continuing claims of match-fixing by illegal bookmakers during the late 1990s, fingers were always pointed towards the Indian sub-continent. While I was covering the 1998 match-fixing hearing in the Lahore High Court, a member of the Pakistan legal team attempting to uncover this corruption in cricket showed me a letter linking Mark Waugh to an illegal bookmaker.

I didn't believe the contents of the letter. Waugh was one of Australia's finest batsmen at the time and had an outstanding record on the sub-continent in one-day cricket, where most of the corruption was alleged to be taking place. Two months later, this indignation turned to disbelief in the dark corner of a Brisbane bar, part-owned by record-breaking Australian wicketkeeper, Ian Healy. Only hours after the official launch of the 1998–99 season, someone intimately involved in Australian cricket was telling me that Mark Waugh was indeed involved with an illegal bookmaker. The suggestion was not about match-fixing, but the claim was that Waugh had taken money in exchange for supplying information.

The Australian Cricket Board (now Cricket Australia), the game's governing body in this country, simply stone-walled when asked about these claims. Chief executive, Malcolm Speed, now chief executive of the International Cricket Council, offered a flat 'no comment' to any and all questions regarding the link between Mark Waugh and illegal bookmakers.

However, after a month of investigation, the fact became clear that Waugh was indeed involved and Cricket Australia was forced to reveal that not only had Waugh taken money from illegal bookmakers, but so had Shane Warne.

The worst aspect of this scandal was that the incidents had taken place in 1994 and the cricket board had covered them up. Key board officials had learnt about the incidents in early 1995, had secretly fined Warne and Waugh only the amounts they claimed to have been given by the illegal bookmaker they knew as 'John'. Warne and Waugh were then put on a plane with the rest of the Australian team to the West Indies.

The incidents were hushed up to avoid concerns that a scandal would impact on Australia's tour to the West Indies. With none of the controversy made public, this tour became a defining moment for cricket. The once mighty West Indian team was finally beaten in a Test series for the first time in 15 years and dethroned as unofficial world champions by the Australians, who have held the title since.

The Hansie Cronje Affair

While the dark clouds of match-fixing and illegal betting swirled around cricket for much of the 1990s, the extent of this underworld activity wasn't exposed until 2000. A new scandal exploded while Australia was making a short tour of South Africa. On the day the Australians were due to land in Johannesburg, Indian police in Delhi claimed to have tapped phone conversations of South African captain Hansie Cronje talking to illegal bookmakers on South Africa's recent tour to India.

Transcripts of the phone recordings were released detailing some of these alleged conversations. The whole of South Africa was outraged by the accusations. Cronje fronted a press conference with other players named in the transcripts to emphatically deny the claims.

Hansie Cronje was a national icon, embodying everything that South Africans love about their sportsmen. He was tough, uncompromising, made the most of his talent and was an inspirational captain who could get the best play out of his team mates — or this was how Hansie Cronje seemed.

Then, Cronje cracked. The South African confessed in tears to the match-fixing accusations, leaving the nation in shock. Later, in 2000, during a public hearing in Cape Town, Cronje, as the star witness, revealed illicit involvement with illegal bookmakers, the result being that he received about $200,000 in total. Cronje attempted to get a number of his team mates involved at various stages. Opening batsman Herschelle Gibbs was banned for six months and heavily fined for agreeing to fail in a match, although he never received any money and never carried out Cronje's instructions.

Cronje's involvement with illegal bookmakers dated back to 1996, when then Indian captain Mohammed Azharuddin introduced him to Mukesh Gupta, known as 'John'. The Indian government was furious that Indian cricket authorities had failed to take any action, despite persistent rumours of wrongdoing, and a police investigation was ordered. Gupta was arrested and, in a statement, alleged that he had paid money for either information or match-fixing to a number of the world's leading players at the time. The players allegedly included Australia's Mark Waugh and national captains Arjuna Ranatunga of Sri Lanka, Martin Crowe of New Zealand and Alec Stewart of England. All the players named denied these claims and, because Gupta refused to give evidence at subsequent hearings, none of the claims was proven.

The outcome was that Cronje and Azharuddin were banned from cricket for life, while three other Indian cricketers were banned for varying periods. Stung into life by the shock of these allegations, the International Cricket Council set up an anti-corruption unit and now claims to have cleaned up the game.

The whole sorry tale had a tragic ending when Cronje was killed in a plane crash in 2002. Cronje's name, although still venerated by some in South Africa, has become synonymous with all that's dark about sport and bookmaking.

Kerry Packer's Cricketing Circus

Although the greatest threat cricket has ever faced came from the cancerous inroads of match-fixing and illegal betting, the biggest upheaval was without doubt the splitting of the game in 1977. An attempt by media mogul Kerry Packer to gain exclusive broadcast rights of cricket in Australia was rejected by the Australian Cricket Board (now Cricket Australia). The board wanted to continue showing the game around Australia on ABC TV.

A furious Packer, who owned the Nine Network, stormed out of a meeting with the board, famously saying, 'It's every man for himself and may the devil take the hindmost'. What happened next was breathtaking in its audaciousness. International cricketers around the world were paid so poorly by out-of-touch and reactionary administrators that Packer simply bought almost all the good players and set up his own cricket 'circus' to run in competition with the traditional game.

For two Australian summers, 1977–78 and 1978–79, World Series Cricket (WSC), as the new competition was called, ran in competition with traditional Australian Test series. WSC players were banned by cricket authorities from even training at any facilities controlled by state cricket associations. WSC was also banned from most major cricket venues, although this move in itself caused disputes at some grounds.

Cleverly promoted with the hit song *Come on Aussie, Come on*, World Series Cricket introduced a string of innovations to the game, bringing cricket to a whole new audience.

Chief among this new age cricket's appeal was an emphasis on one-day cricket and the introduction of day-night one-day matches, played under flood lights with white balls and coloured clothes. After a slow start, the crowds poured into the one-day matches, with Packer at one stage demanding that the gates of the Sydney Cricket Ground be thrown open to let in a huge crowd queueing outside.

With the Australian Cricket Board losing $2 million in the battle, the board conceded, a truce was called, Packer won the television rights, and cricket was never the same again. Although Test cricket has increased in popularity over the past decade because of the greater pace at which the game is now played, one-day cricket remains the major source of revenue for most cricketing nations.

Bodyline: The Most Famous Controversy

Cricket claims a unique quality among all sports because the game is governed not just by laws, but also a preamble defining the spirit of cricket. This spirit of the game holds the captains ultimately responsible for not only playing fairly but for ensuring that they uphold the finest traditions of the game. Consequently, Australians greeted the now-banned tactics of England's attack on the bodies of batsmen, during the now infamous *bodyline* series more than 70 years ago, with a great sense of outrage.

When the English cricket team toured Australia in 1932–33, they had one huge problem — Donald Bradman. The diminutive Australian had put England's bowling to the sword in previous Test series and was poised to do so again. To counter Australia's ace in the pack, austere England captain Douglas Jardine adopted bodyline tactics. Bodyline involved the fastest England bowlers, led by the infamous Harold Larwood, aiming their deliveries at the batsman's body — batsmen did not wear helmets in those days — putting them in fear of being struck and injured. The idea was that, in an effort to defend their body, the batsmen would hit the ball in the air to a gaggle of fielders in a semicircle on the leg side, and the fielders would take a catch and dismiss the batsman. (Refer to Chapter 2 for an explanation of the leg side.)

From a results perspective, the tactic worked wonders. England won back the Ashes and Bradman's performances fell from the extraordinary to just very good. But bodyline was a PR disaster for England. Australian players were badly injured and the Australians became so angry that a riot threatened to break out during the Adelaide Test, when captain Billy Woodfull was struck a painful blow below the heart and wicketkeeper Bert Oldfield was hit on the head while batting. Bodyline soured Anglo–Australian relations to the point where protests were made at the highest levels of government.

The unsavoury tactic led to a rule change restricting the number of fielders a captain can place backwards of the square leg umpire to just two. Long term, bodyline didn't stop Bradman. 'The Don' went on to dominate contests between the two countries until his retirement in 1948. (Refer to Chapter 12 for more on Bradman.)

Shane Warne's Drug Bust

If ever a cricketer should have 'controversy' included as part of his name, Shane Keith Warne would be that player. The most successful bowler in the history of the game simply can't avoid scandal. Whatever may have taken place in Warne's highly publicised life, Warne has the dubious record of being the only Australian cricketer ever found guilty of taking a banned drug.

On the eve of Australia's first match in the 2003 World Cup, played in southern Africa, a tearful Warne told his stunned team mates that he had tested positive to a banned diuretic, which is used as a masking agent for steroids. What he had planned as a grand farewell to one-day cricket, after announcing he would retire from the limited-overs game at the end of the World Cup, became a disgraced departure as he left Johannesburg on the same day Australia began its World Cup campaign with a stunning victory over Pakistan.

Warne claimed that all he had taken was a slimming tablet given to him by his mother. However, later revelations emerged that anti-doping tests had picked up traces of more than one drug in his system, and an inquiry found that Warne had given a pack containing more of the tablets to the team's physiotherapist before leaving South Africa.

Dismayed team mates believed that Warne had become a victim of his own vanity rather than anything more sinister, despite Warne's rapid recovery from a serious shoulder injury earlier in the season. Angry captain Ricky Ponting branded Warne naive and stupid.

The Australian one-day captain chose the same words Warne had used to describe himself during the illegal bookie scandal that had engulfed him and Mark Waugh in 1998 (see section, 'Mark Waugh–Shane Warne Bookie Scandal' earlier in this chapter). Warne faced a two-year minimum suspension unless mitigating circumstances were found and, in the end, was lucky to be banned for only 12 months by an anti-doping hearing in Melbourne.

In his absence, Australia charged through the tournament unbeaten to win the World Cup for a third time, claiming 11 successive victories and thrashing India in the final. Reserve spinner, Brad Hogg, did a wonderful job in Warne's absence and Warne never played one-day cricket for Australia again, although he did turn out for a World XI in a tsunami-relief match at the Melbourne Cricket Ground in January 2005.

Rebel Tours to South Africa

South Africa's 21-year ban from international cricket was a running sore, sparking controversy after controversy. When South Africa was sent into the cricketing wilderness in 1970, the country's cricketing authorities didn't take it lying down. The South Africans started to recruit top international players from Sri Lanka, the West Indies, Australia and England to tour as part of quasi-national teams. Throughout the 1980s, these rebel tours, as they were dubbed, threw the cricketing world into chaos. Players were allowed to work in South Africa as individuals, coaching and playing for local club sides, but were barred from taking part in these tours. Many top players saw this as an anomaly and were happy to take the big piles of South African rand they were offered.

The cricketing authorities got tough with the rebel players, banning them from international cricket. In some cases, this ban effectively ended their international careers.

Australia was gutted by the defections of some leading players, captained by former Australian skipper Kim Hughes, during rebel tours over the summers of 1985–86 and 1986–87.

These defections came at a time when Australia was already struggling to cope with the retirement of three great players — fast bowler, Dennis Lillee; captain and master batsman, Greg Chappell; and wicketkeeper, Rod Marsh.

From the retirement of these players in early 1984, until England retained the Ashes in Melbourne during late December 1986, Australia won just 3 of 32 Tests, the worst period in the country's cricketing history.

Protests from the anti-apartheid movement in South Africa eventually helped put a stop to the rebel tours. In 1989, a team of ex-England cricketers, captained by Mike Gatting, toured South Africa and were met with huge protests so the tour was called off early. Within two years, the political winds of change had seen Nelson Mandela released from jail as the racist apartheid system crumbled. South Africa was readmitted to international cricket in 1991.

The Basil d'Oliveira Affair

Basil d'Oliveira was a fine player, a brave and hard-hitting batsman and an accurate medium pace bowler. 'Dollie', as d'Oliveira was affectionately known, hailed from Cape Town. However, because he was defined as coloured under the racist rules of apartheid South Africa, d'Oliveira was barred from representing the country of his birth. So the South African moved to England to play. After six years in his adopted country, d'Oliveira was selected for the England cricket team and put in several brilliant performances.

Yet, when the team to tour South Africa in 1968 was announced, d'Oliveira was not named, despite having scored an innings of 158 runs in the previous match. Accusations claimed that England's cricketing authorities had caved in to pressure from the South African authorities, who would be angry if Dollie toured there.

However, an injury to one of England's touring party saw Dollie drafted into the squad to tour South Africa. The South African government reacted furiously, demanding that he be withdrawn. The upshot was that the tour was cancelled. In 1970, South Africa was banned from international cricket, and the country headed into the cricketing wilderness for 21 years. Ironically, just at the moment of exile, South Africa had produced the nation's best cricket side, which had just thrashed Australia in a Test series.

Ironically, too, d'Oliveira eventually lost his place in the England side to another South African-born all-rounder, Tony Greig. Greig went on to captain England before becoming one of the first players to sign for World Series Cricket, the new cricketing revolution based in Australia.

The Day Pakistan Refused to Play

Sunday 20 August 2006 will be remembered as the day cricket lost its commonsense; a day of shame for cricket, highlighting all the worst aspects of a game played across deep cultural divides, leading to misunderstandings and mistrust.

The fourth Test between England and Pakistan at The Oval in London was building towards a gripping finale. Already 2–0 down in the four Test series, Pakistan had played well to take a commanding lead in the last Test, but England was fighting back in its second innings.

Midway through the fourth afternoon, controversial Australian umpire Darrell Hair noticed something unusual about the ball that he was not happy with and pointed to the ball in conversation with fellow umpire Billy Doctrove, of the West Indies. Hair then signalled a five-run penalty to England against Pakistan for alleged ball tampering.

Play resumed until the tea break 16 overs later, but the Pakistanis were angry that the ball-tampering charge amounted to accusations that they were cheating, which greatly upset the team. In protest, captain Inzamam-Ul-Haq did not lead his side back onto the field following the tea break.

Umpires Hair and Doctrove appeared, along with the England batsmen. After 20 minutes, Hair returned to the Pakistani rooms but still the players refused to emerge, prompting the umpires to enforce the first forfeit in 129 years of Test cricket, in front of a sell-out crowd of 23,000. Cricket spectators and fans around the world levelled their outrage at Hair for the forfeit and Pakistan for refusing to play.

Not only was Pakistan left facing the serious charge of ball tampering but Inzamam was also charged with one of the great crimes in cricket, bringing the game into disrepute. By not continuing with the match he had flouted the most important aspect of the game — the spirit of cricket.

Bowlers Throwing — Cricket's Endless Curse

For 200 years, controversy has raged in cricket about how the bowler should deliver the ball to the batsman. In the game's formative years, the ball was always bowled underarm but, in the early 1800s, that began to change.

This change is said to have been inspired when a young woman, Christina Willes, was giving batting practice to her brother John in the family garden at Canterbury, England. Miss Willes was forced to bowl roundarm to avoid becoming tangled in her elaborate dress.

John Willes, a prominent cricketer with county Kent, instantly realised the possibilities of this new style of bowling and began using it, amid much controversy. Eventually roundarm bowling, when the ball is delivered from the side below shoulder height, was allowed but it wasn't until 1864, just 13 years before the first Test match was played, that modern overarm bowling was legalised.

However, this new form of delivery created as many problems as it solved. For a delivery to be considered legal, the elbow must not flex as the bowler brings his or her arm over. If the elbow is bent, and then straightened as the ball is delivered, the action is considered a throw. If the umpire believes the elbow flexed, the umpire can call 'no ball', which means the bowler cannot dismiss the batsman, the batting team is awarded a run and the bowler must deliver the ball again.

If an umpire calls a bowler for throwing at international level, the action creates great controversy. The bowler is often branded a 'chucker' by cricket followers, which is considered a form of cheating.

The issue came to a head on Boxing Day, 1995, in a Test between Australia and Sri Lanka at the Melbourne Cricket Ground when umpire Darrell Hair 'called' young Sri Lankan spinner Muttiah Muralitharan seven times for throwing in three overs. 'Murali', as he is known, was also called seven times for throwing during a one-day match in Brisbane later in that 1995–96 season.

Despite questions about his unusual action, Murali has never been called by umpires anywhere else in the world, but he was called again in Australia during the 1998–99 season in a one-day match against England in Adelaide. This call prompted angry Sri Lankan captain, Arjuna Ranatunga, to stop the game and attempt to lead his players off the field. The game eventually resumed but the throwing controversy only grew bigger.

In recent years, a great deal of scientific work to analyse bowling actions has been undertaken, particularly by biomechanics experts at the University of Western Australia. A variety of attempts have been made to rewrite the bowling laws. Following expert advice, the latest law, introduced in 2005, allows bowlers to flex their elbows by up to 15 per cent before a delivery is considered illegal. This angle is the point at which a bowler's elbow flex is said to become obvious to the naked eye.

The controversy has become so big that umpires at international level no longer call players for throwing on the field. The umpires make a report to the match referee, usually a retired Test player, who then sends the report to the International Cricket Council, the game's governing body. The bowler is banned from bowling until he submits himself to expert analysis — which Murali has done and was cleared — and the bowler may be forced to modify the action before being allowed to bowl again. If a bowler is found to have an illegal action twice within a two-year period, the bowler is automatically banned for a year.

A number of players, usually off spinners, have been reported in recent years. The bowling action of off spinners can lead to throwing because the bowlers are turning their wrists clockwise and flicking the ball with the index finger on release in an attempt to spin the ball into the right-handed batsman. Exaggerated attempts to spin the ball can lead to a flick of the elbow, particularly if the bowler attempts to bowl a *doosra*. A doosra occurs when the off spinner turns the wrist around to the face of the batsman in an attempt to make the ball spin away from the right hander. (Refer to Chapter 8 for more on off-spin bowling and the doosra.)

Murali refused to tour Australia with Sri Lanka in 2004 because he claimed that Australian crowds gave him a hard time, constantly calling 'no ball' when he bowled. He did tour Australia during the 2005–06 season and again became frustrated by the constant heckling. Murali submitted himself to further tests at the University of Western Australia, where experts again cleared his unusual bowling action. They claimed Murali gives the optical illusion of throwing because he has a birth deformity that prevents him from straightening his arm, and he has an unusually flexible wrist.

Despite all this controvery, Murali is the second most successful Test bowler in the world behind Shane Warne. Going into the 2006–07 season, Murali had taken 635 Test wickets and more than 400 wickets in one-day matches, making him the only bowler in history to claim 1,000 international wickets.

Chapter 24

Ten Mind-Boggling Cricket Feats

In This Chapter

- Amazing batting and bowling
- Marvelling at cricketing miracles
- Looking at astounding cricket stats
- Paying respect to the best

So much cricket is played in these frantic, modern times, that these days watching the game can seem a bit like an endless video loop playing over and over again. However, players and their performances have enhanced the game over many years, creating awesome spectacles at times and building a rich tradition, which is to be heartily savoured.

In this chapter of phenomenal achievements, the 'They did what?' statistics and the big-match performances add a sense of the extra special to the game of cricket.

Deano's Death-Defying Double

In the mid 1980s, Victorian batsman Dean Jones was a precocious but unfulfilled talent, desperate to prove that he was worthy of a place in the Australian Test team. Given another chance on the 1986 tour of India, Jones, in just his third Test, not only cemented his credentials as an Australian player but created a legend with an innings so brave that the effort put his life at risk.

Batting in the heat and humidity of Madras, Jones was overjoyed when he reached his first Test century but, as he batted on, the oppressive conditions began to take a heavy toll.

'I got to about 120 then I started to shut down,' Jones recalled years later. 'Everything was just cramping and I was starting to vomit everywhere.'

Jones pressed on, flaying the Indian spinners, but when he reached 174 he told his batting partner and flint-hard captain, Allan Border, that he could not go on and wanted to retire hurt.

Not realising the seriousness of Jones's condition, Border chided Jones that he would be replaced by a 'tough' Queenslander, Border's state team mate, Greg Ritchie.

His pride stung, Jones batted on and was 202 not out at the tea break. Team physiotherapist Errol Alcott was concerned about the batsman's health as Jones was unable to keep any fluids or refreshments down. Two of his team mates held Jones under a cold shower during the 20-minute break and then dressed him again as Border ordered Jones to resume his innings.

Jones lasted just another 14 minutes before being dismissed for 210. When he returned to the dressing room, his body went into spasms as his muscles continually cramped. He was rushed by ambulance to hospital, where seven bottles of saline were administered to rehydrate the batsman.

Border admitted later that he had no idea Jones had been so ill. Told that the young batsman collapsed after returning to the dressing rooms, Border later said that his immediate reaction was to think, 'What have I done? I could have killed this bloke!'

Jones recovered and played out the match to its dramatic conclusion — becoming just the second tie in Test cricket history. (Refer to Chapter 22 for more on this famous game.)

Brian Lara's Record Scores

The English cricket team must hate the sight of Brian Lara, the great West Indian batsman. Lara has broken the record for the highest Test innings by a batsman not just once but twice. Both times, when breaking the record, Lara was playing against England. Back in 1994, at Antigua, he broke Sir Gary Sobers' 36-year-old record for the highest individual Test innings score, smashing 375 runs. Australia's Matthew Hayden claimed the record with 380 against Zimbabwe in Perth during 2003 but, less than a year later, the remarkable Lara won it back. Again, against another set of sorry English bowlers in Antigua, he became the first man to score 400 runs in a Test match innings.

As if these magnificent feats weren't enough, Lara also holds the record for the highest score in a first-class cricket match (refer to Chapter 3 for more on this match format). Just a few weeks after his first destruction of England's bowlers at Antigua in 1994, Lara bludgeoned 501 not out against Durham at Edgbaston. Sadly, few spectators were in the ground to see this stupendous cricketing achievement.

Lara leaves no doubt about his extraordinary ability with the bat. Short, like most of cricket's great batsmen through the ages, Lara plays strokes as though the bat is simply an extension of his fluid, flowing arms. For much of his career, from the early 1990s to the mid 2000s, Australia's bowlers regarded Lara as the most difficult batsman in the world to bowl a ball at. No doubt the English feel the same!

Bob Massie's Remarkable Debut

When Australia took the field for the Lord's Test against England in London during the 1972 Ashes tour (refer to Chapter 16 for more on the Ashes), little attention was paid to a young West Australian fast bowler named Bob Massie. Australia had lost the first Test at Old Trafford in Manchester and Massie was brought into the side to beef up Australia's fast bowling attack.

Playing his first Test, Massie soon grabbed the spotlight, doing amazing things with the ball as he claimed wicket after English wicket. Swinging the ball prodigiously into and away from the batsmen in humid conditions, Massie claimed eight of a possible ten English wickets in the first innings and repeated this amazing feat in the second.

Australia easily won the Test and Massie's name went into folklore as the most successful bowler on *debut* (playing his first Test). Massie's feat of 16 wickets in his first Test was later equalled by Indian spinner, Narendra Hirwani, against the West Indies in 1988.

Both these very different bowlers had one surprising experience in common: Their Test careers failed to flourish. Unable to repeat his ability to swing the ball consistently, Massie managed just five more Tests and his international career was over, seven months after it began. Hirwani played a modest 17 Tests in total, spread over eight years.

Laker's Destruction of Australia

During a few cloudy days at the Old Trafford cricket ground in Manchester during 1956, English spin bowler Jim Laker achieved cricketing immortality. Virtually single-handedly, Laker won a Test match for England against a great Australian team. He took 19 of the 20 Australian wickets to fall during the match for just 90 runs, the most successful bowling performance in any single Test in the history of cricket. And if you consider the Australian team was chock full of star players, Laker's achievements gain even greater magnitude. Some of the Australian players complained that the pitch was treacherous for batting and helped the spin bowling of Laker, but his performance was a truly mind-boggling cricketing feat. Laker's achievement is all the more amazing considering another fine English spinner, Tony Lock, managed to claim just one wicket in the match.

Although Laker began his Test career in 1948, he could not command a regular place in the England team until that remarkable summer of 1956. A Yorkshireman of few words, his approach to cricket and to life was independent, detached and cool. That Laker became a popular television commentator, following his retirement in 1964, came as something of a surprise.

Australia's Sixteen Test-Winning Streak

Between October 1999 and March 2001, Australia won 16 Test matches in a row, beating all comers to register the longest winning streak in Test history. The Australian team, captained by Steve Waugh, and containing star players, Shane Warne, Glenn McGrath and Andrew Gilchrist, didn't just beat their opponents, they hammered them. Not even poor weather could stop the Australians from carrying away the spoils and confirming their status as one of the greatest cricket teams of all time.

But this unprecedented winning streak came to an end in dramatic fashion. After beating India comfortably in the first match of a three-match series, the Australians looked set to register yet another win in the second Test at Calcutta. However, a stunning fightback from India, led by batsmen V.V.S. Laxmann and Rahul Dravid, produced an against-the-odds win for India. (Refer to Chapter 22 for more on the greatest cricket matches ever played.)

This amazing winning streak was made all the more remarkable for two reasons. First, the great West Indian teams of the 1980s, widely regarded as the best and most brutal ever to play the game because of their endless supply of fast bowlers, managed no more than 11 wins in a row.

Second, Australia's stunning run of success came after a poor start for Australia's new captain, Steve Waugh. Waugh had taken over from another very fine skipper, Mark Taylor. Now widely regarded as one of the finest and toughest Australian players and captains of all time, Waugh won just two of his first seven Tests as leader, before claiming the next 16 on the trot.

Steve Waugh's World Cup Miracle

While Australia's tied semi final against South Africa in the 1999 World Cup is regarded as one of the best matches of all time, Australia's earlier match against South Africa in that tournament was the game that added another enormous chapter to the legend of Steve Waugh.

Renowned as a fighter who had to rebuild his game to regain a place in the Test side in the early 1990s, Waugh had his tough-as-teak tenacity sorely tried as Australia made a terrible start to the 1999 World Cup. Coming straight from the West Indies, where Australia had struggled to level the Test series at two all, Waugh was under mounting pressure to retain the captaincy of the one-day side.

Imposing iron discipline, which put some senior members of the team off side, Australia lost successive matches to New Zealand and Pakistan, leaving the Australians on the verge of an embarrassingly early exit from the World Cup.

That exit seemed about to take place when South Africa scored a difficult target of 271 and the Australians lost three early wickets in the run chase. As Steve Waugh began to build his innings, attempting a recovery mission, he hit a simple catch to South Africa's best fieldsman, Herschelle Gibbs. So excited was Gibbs that he attempted to throw the ball up, even before he had caught it, and dropped it. Waugh couldn't resist telling Gibbs that he had cost his side the match.

With renewed vigour, Waugh pressed on, even though Australia ended up needing 98 from just 95 balls when Ricky Ponting was dismissed. Scoring more than a run a ball for such a sustained period appeared impossible but Waugh willed a win and slogged his way to a defiant century, achieving victory with just two balls to spare.

Australia later tied a wonderful semi final against South Africa but, because of that earlier victory over the South Africans, Australia advanced to the final, thrashing Pakistan to claim a second World Cup against the odds.

A story began to circulate that Waugh had, in fact, told Gibbs, 'You know you've just dropped the World Cup' after that fateful drop of the ball. Waugh laughed when the story was relayed to him, but denied it. 'I wished I'd thought of that,' he said.

Shane Warne: The Master Bowler

The most successful bowler the world has ever seen, Shane Warne appears indestructible. The master spinner has overcome both injury and controversy to carve an unparalleled place in Test history. His contribution to the game is so much greater than having the fabulous mantle of claiming the most Test wickets.

Going into the 2006–07 season, Warne had taken 685 Test wickets during a 15-year career. This result is an amazing achievement, given that anyone who takes 200 Test wickets is considered to have had an outstanding career. Only 12 of the 293 players who have bowled for Australia during 130 years of Test cricket have managed 200 wickets or more. Another fine leg-spinner, Stuart MacGill, was poised on 198 heading into the 2006–07 season.

Warne has managed his remarkable feat despite a dreadful start as an Australian player and serious shoulder and spinning-finger operations, which threatened his career. As well, Warne has been fined for selling information to an illegal bookmaker, and has undergone a 12-month drugs ban. (Refer to Chapter 23 for more on Warne's bookie and drug scandals.)

After his first four innings, played across three Tests, Warne had taken just one wicket at a cost of 335 runs, one of the worst starts for a bowler ever recorded in international cricket. His famous first delivery in an Ashes Test back in 1993, which spun alarmingly to bowl England veteran, Mike Gatting, was what put Warne on the path to fame and fortune.

Launched into the stratosphere by what was dubbed 'the ball of the century', Warne became one of cricket's biggest personalities. Love him or hate him, Warne brought crowds to games just to watch him bowl brilliant leg-spin, combining his great skill with drama and theatrics. (Refer to Chapter 8 for more on spin bowling.)

Warne is widely regarded as Australia's second greatest player behind the incomparable Don Bradman. Now one of the most famous players of all time, Warne has made more money out of the game than any of his countrymen.

However much money Warne may have made, he deserves every cent for revitalising the wonderful art of spin bowling, following decades of relentless and unforgiving pace bowling. Not bad for a chubby kid who couldn't get anyone out when he began. (Refer to Chapter 21 for more on Warne.)

Botham's Miracle Ashes Triumph

The 1981 Test series between England and Australia will always be known as Botham's Ashes. However, after the second match of the six-match Test series, with Australia 1–0 up and Ian Botham, the great English all-rounder, having resigned as team captain, a miracle did not look like it was going to occur.

An *all-rounder* is a player who is good at both batting and bowling.

Then, in the third Test at Headingley (refer to Chapter 22 for more on this match), Botham inspired England to probably the most incredible comeback win of all time, scoring 149 in England's second innings and taking six wickets in the match.

In the next Test match at Edgbaston, with Australia seemingly coasting to victory, Botham produced an amazing match-winning bowling performance, dismissing five Australian batsmen for just one run.

The legend of Botham's Ashes was confirmed in the fifth Test match at Old Trafford, Manchester. Again, England was in danger of losing, only for that man Botham to pull another rabbit from the hat. He hit an innings of 118, widely recognised as one of the greatest of all time for its display of sheer power and aggression. The match was eventually won by England and so were the Ashes, 3–1. Botham never quite reached the same heights again but any English cricket fan fortunate enough to witness his performances in the summer of 1981 is guaranteed to get misty-eyed over his exploits.

England and Australia compete for the Ashes, which reside in a tiny urn well over a century old. The Ashes are cricket's oldest and greatest contest (refer to Chapter 17 for more on the Ashes rivalry).

Kenya Makes the World Cup Semi Final

Kenya was supposed to be just making up the numbers at the World Cup in 2003. The country's cricket team isn't even considered good enough to play Test cricket. However, in order to encourage the development of the game in the East African nation, Kenya was given one-day international status in 1996, although the team's progress has been disappointing and the game's administration poor.

As a participating nation in the 2003 World Cup in southern Africa, Kenya hosted some matches in Nairobi. The Kenyan team was not taken seriously but, through a bizarre series of events, the Kenyans made it all the way to the semi finals.

Kenya received points for a walkover when New Zealand refused to play in Nairobi for safety reasons, and then England refused to play Zimbabwe in Zimbabwe for the same reason, so Kenya gained even more advantage. Kenya then caused a mighty upset, beating Sri Lanka in Nairobi.

The fairytale came to an end when the Kenyans were beaten by a strong Indian side. Nevertheless, Kenya's march to the semi finals remains one of cricket's greatest shocks.

Sixteen teams will compete in the 2007 cricket World Cup, ten Test playing nations and six associate countries of the International Cricket Council (ICC). The associate members have to compete in a tournament to qualify to play with the big boys in the World Cup. Matches in the World Cup are one-day internationals, which are limited to 50 overs a side. (Refer to Chapter 17 for more on how the World Cup works.)

Bradman's Colossal Batting

The performances of Australian batsman Donald Bradman are mentioned numerous times during this book. The reason is that Bradman was of a different magnitude to any player who has ever lived. During his Test match career, interrupted by World War II, 'the Don', as he was known, played in 52 Test matches, scoring nearly 7,000 runs at an average of 99.94. Just to put this achievement into context, the next highest batting average achieved by any regular batsman in Test cricket is around the 60 runs an innings mark.

From a purely statistical basis, the Don was nearly 50 per cent better than any other batsman in the long history of the game. And Bradman's average would have been even more impressive had he not, in his last innings at The Oval in 1948, been dismissed for 0 by England spin bowler, Eric Hollies. If the Don had scored just four runs in this final innings, his Test batting average would have reached the magical 100.

Bradman was also unique for the rate at which he scored centuries — 100 or more runs in an innings. The very best players in the current Australian side, such as Ricky Ponting and Matthew Hayden, two of the finest batsmen in the world, make a century every three Tests on average. Bradman made a century every one and a half Tests — that's every third time he went out to bat. To top it all off, 12 of his 29 centuries were scores of 200 or better and twice he scored more than 300.

Bradman's batting average and rate of centuries are probably the most impressive achievements in cricket. His results underly the impression of a genius sportsmen whose performances were almost superhuman. No wonder, therefore, Donald Bradman makes number one in the list of the greatest cricketers ever (refer to Chapter 21 for the ten greatest cricketers).

A batting average is worked out by dividing the number of runs scored by the batsman during his or her career by the number of times they were dismissed. Refer to Chapter 20 for more on working out batting and bowling averages and what constitutes a poor, good, great and Bradman-esque average.

Appendix
Glossary

Half the battle of being a cricket fan is to sound like one. Cricket has a language all of its own. To help you decipher the jargon of cricket, here's a glossary of frequently used words and phrases that can make the cricket world an easier place to inhabit.

arm ball: A delivery from a slow bowler that has no spin on it and so does not turn into or away from the batsman as expected. Instead, the ball continues straight on or drifts in the air a little in the opposite direction to which it would have spun.

Ashes: A tiny decorative urn containing some ashes, which has become the symbolic prize for a Test series played between England and Australia.

average: A batting average is the total number of career runs scored by a batsman, divided by the number of times dismissed. A bowling average is the total number of runs scored off a bowler, divided by the number of career wickets.

ball: The standard cricket ball weighs 156 grams and is red. For one-day games played at international or domestic level, such as state level in Australia, the ball is white. About the size of a tennis ball but very hard, a cricket ball is made of a cork and latex inner core tightly bound with string and then encased in leather. A women's cricket ball is slightly smaller at 142 grams and a junior ball is smaller again at about 135 grams. The ball has a slightly raised seam around it about the width of the thumb.

ball tampering: Illegally changing the condition of the ball by deliberately scuffing the surface, picking or lifting the seam of the ball, or applying artificial substances.

bat pad: A fielding position close to the batsman, designed to catch balls that lob off the bat, often via the batsman's pads.

beamer: A dangerous and usually accidental delivery — bowled by a fast bowler — that travels towards the batsman's head or upper body without bouncing. Such deliveries are frowned upon and a bowler can be banned for using them.

belter: A pitch that so heavily favours batsmen that lots of runs are scored.

bend your back: The act of a bowler using extra effort to try to make the ball travel faster or bounce higher off a pitch.

bodyline: A now illegal tactic used by England captain Douglas Jardine during England's 1932–33 tour of Australia. Fast bowlers attempted to hit the batsmen rather than the stumps, forcing batsmen to protect themselves by fending the ball away. This action often presented catches to close fielders. This positioning of the fieldsmen was also known as leg theory.

bouncer: A delivery from a fast bowler, bowled about halfway down the pitch, that bounces to head or upper body height. This type of delivery is usually an attempt to intimidate the batsman.

boundary: The perimeter of a cricket field, which at international level is usually marked by a rope. Boundary can also be used to describe a scoring shot that travels to the boundary, scoring four runs.

box: A piece of triangular, bowl-shaped plastic with padded edges used to protect the groin of male batsmen and wicketkeepers.

bump ball: A ball that comes off the bottom of the bat and almost instantly goes into the ground before being caught by a fielder. This type of shot can give the false appearance that the batsman has been dismissed.

bumper: See **bouncer**.

bye: Runs scored when the batsman misses the ball and the wicketkeeper fails to take it cleanly.

carried the bat: Description of an opening batsman who was not dismissed when all of his team mates were out in a particular innings.

chinaman: A delivery spun with the wrist by a left-arm slow bowler that turns into a right-handed batsman. Named after Ellis 'Puss' Achong, a West Indian cricketer of Chinese extraction who played six Tests from 1930 to 1935.

chucker: A derogatory term that describes a bowler who throws the ball instead of bowling it. A chucker's action is both illegal and controversial.

closing the face: Turning the face of the bat inwards and, in doing so, hitting the ball to the leg side.

cross bat: A shot played with a horizontal bat.

dead ball: The ball is out of play. No runs can be scored or wickets taken.

declaration: When the captain of the batting team decides to end his team's innings before all his players have been dismissed.

dolly: A simple catch.

doosra: A Hindi and Urdu word which means 'the other one'. Developed as the opposite of the off break. Instead of the ball from a right-handed bowler spinning back into a right-handed batsman, the doosra spins away from the right hander.

duck: A batsman failing to score any runs.

Duckworth/Lewis: The system used to recalculate target scores in one-day matches shortened due to rain. Named after Frank Duckworth and Tony Lewis, the two English mathematicians who devised it.

economy rate: The average number of runs a bowler concedes per over.

extras: Runs not scored by batsmen. There are four common types of extras: Byes, leg byes, wides and no balls. Also known as sundries.

finger spin: Using the index finger to flick the ball as the bowler delivers it, spinning the ball clockwise for right-handed bowlers and anti-clockwise for left-handed bowlers.

flipper: A variation of the leg spinner. The ball is flicked out of the front of the hand, not twirled out the back of the hand like a normal leg break. Difficult to bowl, a flipper hurries onto the batsman. A flipper is used sparingly as a surprise tactic.

full toss: A delivery that reaches the batsmen without bouncing. Above waist height, a full toss becomes a beamer.

good length: The ideal length that the bowler aims for, getting the batsman in two minds — whether to play forward or back.

googly: The leg spinner's variation that turns into the right-hander batsman, instead of away. Also known as a wrong 'un.

grubber: A delivery that hardly bounces. Also known as a shooter.

half volley: A delivery that lands just in front of the batsman. A half volley is considered the ideal ball to drive, the most common shot in cricket.

handled the ball: A batsman who deliberately touches the ball can be given out.

Hawkeye: Military technology that tracks the path of the ball. Hawkeye is used by television networks to plot the course of deliveries, usually when a batsman is struck on the pads and may have been given out leg before wicket (LBW).

hit the ball twice: A batsman can be dismissed for hitting the ball twice after a delivery has been bowled unless the batsman is specifically attempting to stop the ball hitting their stumps.

ICC: International Cricket Council, the cricket world's governing body.

in: Batsman who is currently batting.

infield: The region of the playing field, up to about 30 metres from the batsman on strike, which usually contains most of the fieldsmen. The infield is marked by a white circle in one-day international matches.

inner: A thin, cloth glove worn inside wicketkeeping gloves.

innings: Describes when a team or individual bats in a match. In some matches, such as Test or first-class games, each team has two innings.

inside edge: The edge of a cricket bat closest to the body of the batsman, on the leg side as the bat is held vertically. The inside edge is also used to describe a deflection when the ball comes off the inside edge after being delivered by the bowler.

inside out: Describing the hitting of a ball pitched on or outside leg stump to the off side of the field. The batsman turns the blade of the bat inside out to play the shot.

inswinger: A delivery that swings through the air from the off side to the leg side in towards the batsman.

International Cricket Council: Cricket world's governing body. See **ICC**.

king pair: Dismissed first ball in both innings of a two-innings match.

leading edge: When the batsman turns the bat towards the leg side (on side) too early and the ball hits the edge facing the bowler, sometimes resulting in a simple catch to the bowler.

leg break or leg spinner: A delivery flicked out the back of the hand by a right-arm bowler that spins away from a right-handed batsman.

leg bye: When the ball deflects off the batsman's pads or body without hitting the bat and runs are scored.

leg cutter: A delivery that lands on the seam of the ball when it hits the pitch and moves away from the batsman.

leg side: The field on the side of the pitch that is closest to the batsman's legs.

length: Where the ball lands on the pitch relative to the batsman.

line: The direction a delivery is travelling in relation to the stumps.

long hop: A delivery that pitches a long way in front of the batsman and is easy to hit for runs.

loop: Used to describe the flight of the ball bowled by a spinner if the ball drops in the air on its way towards the batsman.

maiden: An over where no runs are scored off the bowler.

MCC: Initials for the Marylebone Cricket Club, the game's most famous and influential cricket club, based at Lord's in London. Also, the initials of the Melbourne Cricket Club, based at the Melbourne Cricket Ground.

new ball: In Test and most first-class cricket, the fielding captain is allowed to replace the old ball with a new one after every 80 overs.

nick: When the ball just touches the outside edge of the bat and is usually caught by the wicketkeeper.

nightwatchman: Usually a bowler but sometimes a wicketkeeper who is promoted up the batting order towards the end of a day's play, when a wicket falls, in order to save the team's good batsmen for the next day's play.

no ball: An illegal delivery called by the umpire behind the stumps, usually when the bowler has overstepped the front crease. A one-run penalty is awarded to the batting team, the bowler cannot dismiss the batsman and the bowler must bowl the delivery again.

obstructing the field: A batsman can be out if they deliberately obstruct the fielding side catching or gathering the ball or completing a run out.

off break or off spinner: A delivery, flicked by the index finger, that spins the ball back into the right-handed batsman from off to leg.

off cutter: A delivery that lands on the seam of the ball when it hits the pitch and moves back into the right-handed batsman.

off the mark: When the batsman scores the first run of their innings.

off side: The field on the side of the pitch furthest away from the batsman's legs and closest to the outside edge of the bat.

on side: See **leg side**.

out: When a batsman is dismissed.

outside edge: The edge of the bat furthest away from the batsman's body.

outswinger: A delivery that moves away from the batsman in the air from the leg to off side.

over: Six consecutive legal deliveries from a bowler, which are delivered from one end.

pair: When a batsman fails to score in both innings of a two-innings match.

pinch-hitter: Lower-order batsman promoted to try to make quick runs.

pitch: The playing surface in the centre of the field exactly 20.12 metres (22 yards) long and up to 3.05 metres (10 feet) wide.

played on: When a delivery hits the bat then goes on to hit the stumps and bowl the batsman out.

plumb: When the batsman is obviously leg before wicket.

protector: See **box**.

pull: A horizontal bat shot played to a short delivery that bounces a long way in front of the batsman and is hit through the leg side.

retire: End a batsman's innings even though the batsman has not been dismissed. The batsman is considered out and cannot return later to continue batting.

retire hurt: Forced to leave the field because of illness or injury. The batsman is not dismissed and can return later to complete their innings.

return crease: Parallel white lines pointing down the pitch, either side of the stumps at both ends.

reverse sweep: This horizontal bat stroke is played by dropping to one knee like a conventional sweep but reversing the hands so the ball is swept in the opposite direction — behind point instead of square leg. A risky stroke that's sometimes used in one-day cricket.

reverse swing: First mastered by Pakistani fast bowlers in the 1980s and 1990s, with this delivery the bowler can make an old ball deviate in the air in the opposite direction to conventional swing with a new ball.

ring field: Expression used to explain standard field placings when most players are positioned in a circle about 25 to 30 metres from the batsman to prevent runs being scored.

roller: A roller is used on turf pitches to make the surface flat and hard. Heavy and light rollers are also used throughout a Test or first-class match between innings. The batting captain has the option of which roller to use.

rough: The area of a turf pitch that is scuffed up and loosened by the action of a bowler running through in their follow-through about a metre in front of the batting crease and usually about a third of a metre outside a right-handed batsman's leg stump. Spinners often try to land the ball in the rough when bowling later in a match to gain greater spin on the abrasive surface.

run chase: Generally the fourth innings of a first-class or Test match, and the latter stages of a one-day game, when the match situation has been reduced to a set figure for victory, in a set time or maximum number of overs.

run rate: Of particular importance in a one-day game, the run rate is the average number of runs scored per over, and is used as a guide to a team's progress.

run-up: Describes the bowler running up to the pitch to deliver the ball to the batsman. Also describes the area where the bowler runs up to the pitch.

runner: A player dressed in full batting gear used by an injured batsman who cannot run. The injured batsman bats normally but does not run. Instead the runner will do the running in their place.

seam: The ridge of stitching about as wide as a thumb that holds the two halves of a ball together, and sometimes causes deviation off the pitch when the ball lands. The seam also acts as a rudder that allows the ball to swing in the air into or away from the batsman if the conditions are right.

shooter: See **grubber**.

shoulder arms: When a batsman decides to lift the bat high in the air and let the ball pass through to the wicketkeeper rather than risk being dismissed by playing at it.

side-on: Describes the position of a batsman's body when facing a bowler and the position a bowler moves their body into as they are about to deliver the ball.

sitter: A very easy catch.

sledging: Abuse delivered by a fieldsman at the batsmen in an attempt to unsettle them. Considered against the spirit of the game and can lead to punishment in extreme cases.

slog: Used to describe a wild and ugly shot that often ends in dismissal.

slog sweep: Played on one knee like a sweep but the ball is usually hit from on or outside off stump over mid wicket instead of on or outside leg stump behind square leg.

slogger: A batsman who hits the ball hard but in an unattractive or technically incorrect fashion.

slower ball: A fast bowler delivering the ball at a significantly reduced pace with no noticeable change of action in an attempt to deceive the batsman. A slower ball is usually delivered by holding the ball further back in the hand or spreading the fingers holding the ball wide apart.

standing back and standing up: Wicketkeeper's positions for a particular bowler. Wicketkeepers usually stand back from the stumps for fast bowlers and up to the stumps for spinners.

stock ball: A bowler's regular type of delivery.

stonewall: Bat very defensively to avoid dismissal at the expense of scoring runs.

strike rate: The average number of runs a batsman scores per 100 balls and the number of deliveries on average a bowler takes to claim a wicket.

sundries: See **extras**.

swing: The act of making the ball deviate in the air into or away from the batsman.

tail-ender: Usually bowlers who come in towards the end of an innings, generally numbers 8, 9, 10 and 11, who are not noted for their batting skills.

ton: Slang term for a century (100 runs by a batsman in one innings).

tonk: Slang term for a big hit by a batsman.

twelfth (12th) man: A substitute fielder who is not allowed to bat or bowl.

walk: When a batsman leaves the field without waiting for the umpire's decision after they have been caught, usually when the ball has just touched the edge of the bat and there is some doubt. Most batsmen wait for the umpire's decision.

wicket: One of cricket's more confusing terms. Wicket is an alternative word for pitch and also describes the collective set of three stumps, topped by two bails, at each end of the pitch.

wide: A delivery the umpire deems too wide for the batsman to hit. The umpire signals this by stretching both arms out horizontally, an extra run is added to the total and the ball is bowled again

wrist spin: When a ball is spun by flicking it out the back of the hand with the wrist. A right-arm wrist spinner usually turns the ball from leg to off (leg spin) away from the right-handed batsman, while a left-arm wrist spinner turns the ball from off to leg into the right-handed batsman (see also **chinaman**).

wrong 'un: Australian term for a googly; a leg spinner's delivery that turns into the right-handed batsman going in the opposite direction to the standard leg break.

yorker: A full-pitched delivery that is aimed at the batting crease so that the ball goes under the bat and bowls the batsman.

Index

• D •

• E •

• F •

• S •

• U •

• V •

• W •

• Z •

Notes

Notes

Notes

FOR DUMMIES®

Australian Editions

Business

1-74031-109-4
$39.95

1-74031-061-6
$39.95

1-74031-004-7
$39.95

1-74031-124-8
$39.95

1-74031-166-3
$39.95

1-74031-041-1
$39.95

1-74031-067-5
$39.95

1-74031-033-0
$39.95

1-74031-125-6
$29.95

Reference

1-74031-071-3
$39.95

1-74031-030-6
$39.95

Gardening

1-74031-007-1
$39.95

FOR DUMMIES®

Australian Editions

Technology

1-74031-086-1
$39.95

1-74031-160-4
$39.95

1-7403-1159-0
$39.95

1-74031-123-X
$39.95

Cooking

1-74031-010-1
$39.95

1-74031-008-X
$39.95

1-74031-040-3
$39.95

Pets

1-74031-028-4
$39.95

Parenting

1-74031-103-5
$39.95

1-74031-042-X
$39.95

Health & Fitness

1-74031-143-4
$39.95

1-74031-140-X
$39.95

Health & Fitness Cont.

Australian Editions

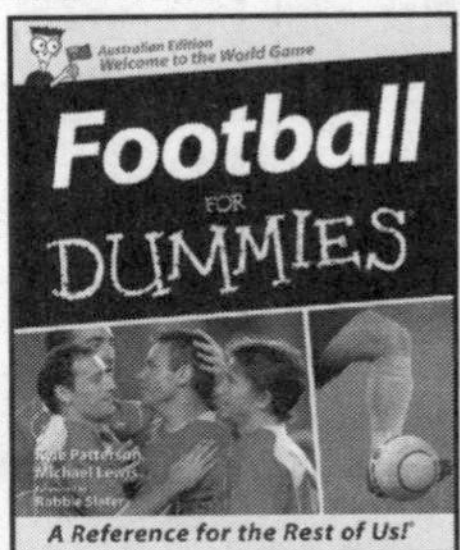

1-74031-122-1
$39.95

1-74031-135-3
$39.95

1-74031-054-3
$39.95

1-74031-009-8
$39.95

1-74031-011-X
$39.95

1-74031-044-6
$39.95

1-74031-035-7
$39.95

1-74031-006-3
$39.95

1-74031-059-4
$39.95

1-74031-074-8
$39.95

1-74031-073-X
$39.95

1-74031-094-2
$39.95